FORD
F100-350 PICKUPS
1969-1987 GAS & DIESEL
SHOP MANUAL

ALAN AHLSTRAND
Editor

CLYMER PUBLICATIONS

*World's largest publisher of books
devoted exclusively to automobiles and motorcycles*

A division of INTERTEC PUBLISHING CORPORATION
P.O. Box 12901, Overland Park, Kansas 66212

Copyright ©1987 Intertec Publishing Corp.

FIRST EDITION
First Printing December, 1979

SECOND EDITION
Revised by Alfred A. Pegal to include 1980-1981 models
First Printing April, 1981

THIRD EDITION
Revised by Kalton C. Lahue to include 1982 models
First Printing February, 1982
Second Printing August, 1982

FOURTH EDITION
Revised by Kalton C. Lahue to include 1983 models
First Printing June, 1983
Second Printing September, 1983
Third Printing March, 1984
Fourth Printing November, 1984

FIFTH EDITION
Revised by Kalton C. Lahue to include 1984 models
First Printing March, 1985
Second Printing August, 1985
Third Printing January, 1986
Fourth Printing May, 1986

SIXTH PRINTING
Revised by Kalton C. Lahue to include 1985-1986 models
First Printing September, 1986

SEVENTH EDITION
Revised by Kalton C. Lahue to include 1987 models
First Printing April, 1987
Second Printing November, 1987

Third Printing June, 1988

Printed in U.S.A.

ISBN: 0-89287-303-5

Production Coordinator, Blesilda Jacinto

COVER: Photographed by Michael Brown Photographic Productions, Los Angeles, California.

677293

CONTENTS

QUICK REFERENCE DATA

ENGINE OIL CAPACITY

Engine	Capacity*
170 cid 6-cyl.	6 qt.
232 cid V6	5 qt.
240 and 300 cid 6-cyl.	5 qt.
420 cid V8 diesel	9 qt.
All V8 gasoline engines	5 qt.

*Add 1 qt. with filter change.

ENGINE IDLE SPEED (RPM)

170 cid 6	
1969	750
1970-1971	775
1972	750
232 cid V6	See engine decal
240 cid 6	
1969	550 (auto.); 775/500* (manual)
1970	
F-250	550 (auto.); 600 (manual)
F-100	850/500* (manual); 575/500* (auto.)
1971	
F-250	550 (auto.); 600 (manual)
F-150	550/500* (auto.); 775/500* (manual)
1972	850/500* (manual); 600/500* (auto.)
1973-on	See engine decal
255 cid V8	See engine decal
300 cid 6	
1969	525 (auto.); 600 (manual)
1970-1972	550 (auto.); 600 (manual)
1973-on	See engine decal
302 cid V8	
1969	550 (auto.); 650 (manual)
1970	600 (auto.); 675 (manual)
1971	600 (auto. w/AC); 600/500* (auto.); 800/500* (manual)
1972	600/500* (auto.); 800/500* (manual)
1973-on	See engine decal
351W/351M cid V8	See engine decal
360/390 cid V8	
1969-1972	550 (auto.); 650 (manual)
1973-on	See engine decal
400 cid V8	See engine decal
420 cid V8 diesel	950/750*
460 cid V8	See engine decal

*Higher speed with solenoid energized; lower speed with solenoid off.

GENERAL ENGINE TORQUE RECOMMENDATIONS

	ft.-lb
Valve covers	
170 cid 6-cyl.	3-5
232 V6	36-61 in.-lb.
240/300 cid 6-cyl.	4-7
All V8 except 460	3-5
460 V8	5-6
Carburetor attaching nuts	12-15
Rocker arm	
stud/bolt-to-cylinder head	
170 cid 6-cyl.	30-35
240/300 cid 6-cyl., breakaway torque	4.5-15
232 V6	18.4-25.8 in 2 stages
All other V8	18-25 (press fit 255/302 V8)
Oil drain plug	15-20
Oil pan bolts	
170 cid 6-cyl.	7-9
240/300 cid 6-cyl.	10-15
232 cid V6	80-106 in.-lb.
all V8 1/4 in. bolts	7-9
5/16 in. bolts, 351M/400	11-13
All other V8 5/16 in. bolts	9-11
Intake manifold attaching bolts	
170 cid 6-cyl.	23-28
232 cid V6	18.4 in 3 stages
240/300 cid 6-cyl.	28-33
All V8	23-25
Exhaust manifold	
170 cid 6-cyl.	13-18
232 cid V6	15-22
240/300 cid 6-cyl.	23-28
All V8	18-24
Main bearing	
All inline 6-cyl.	60-170
232 cid V6	65-81
1983 460 cid V8	95-105
All other V8	18-24
Connecting rod nuts	
232 cid V6	31-36
255/302 V8 and 170 cid 6-cyl.	19-24
All others	40-45
Spark plugs	
All inline 6-cyl.	15-25
V6	17-22
All V8	10-15
Cylinder head nuts/bolts	
All inline 6-cyl.	50-55, 55-60 and 70-75 ft.-lb. in 3 stages
232 cid V6	47, 55, 63 and 74 ft.-lb. in 4 stages
255/302 V8	55, 65 and 65-72 ft.-lb. in 3 stages
351W/351M V8	85, 95 and 105-12 ft.-lb. in 3 stages
460 V8	80, 110 and 130-180 ft.-lb. in 3 stages

CYLINDER AND DISTRIBUTOR NUMBERING

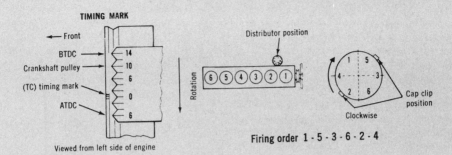

Firing order 1 - 5 - 3 - 6 - 2 - 4

INLINE 6-CYLINDER ENGINES

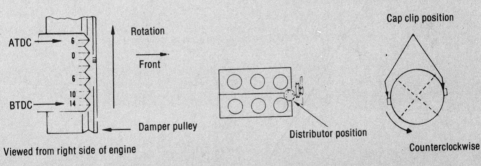

FIRING 1-4-2-5-3-6

V6 ENGINE

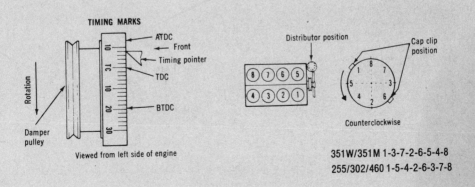

351W/351M 1-3-7-2-6-5-4-8
255/302/460 1-5-4-2-6-3-7-8

V8 ENGINES

TRANSMISSION OIL AND CAPACITY

Transmission	Oil grade	Approximate refill capacity
Ford 3-speed manual	SAE 80W transmission lubricant	3.5 pt.
SROD 4-speed manual	SAE 80W transmission lubricant	4.5 pt.
TOD 4-speed manual	SAE 80W transmission lubricant	4.5 pt.
T-19B 4-speed manual	SAE 50W engine oil	7.0 pt.
New Process 435 4-speed manual		
Without extension	SAE 80W transmission lubricant	6.5 pt.
With extension	SAE 80W transmission lubricant	7.0 pt.
C4 automatic		
300 cid engine	Type F ATF	20.0 pt.
302 cid engine	Type F ATF	17.5 pt.
351, 400 and		
460 cid engines	Type F ATF	24.5 pt
C5 automatic	Type H ATF	24 pt.
C6 automatic		
1969-1977	Type F ATF	25.5 pt.
1978-on	DEXRON II	23.5 pt.
Automatic overdrive (AOD)	Dexron II ATF	24 pt.

RECOMMENDED OIL GRADES MULTIGRADE

Consistent Temperature	Oil Grade
Multigrade oils	
Below 32°F	
−10°F to +90°F	SAE 5W-30*
Above +10°F	SAE 10W-30. SAE 10W-40
	SAE 20W-40
Monograde oils	
−10°F to 32°F	SAE 10W
10°F to 60°F	SAE 20W. SAE 20
32°F to 90°F	SAE 30
Above 60°F	SAE 40

*If the vehicle is being operated at sustained highway speeds.
the next heavier grade of oil should be used.

BATTERY CHARGE PERCENTAGE

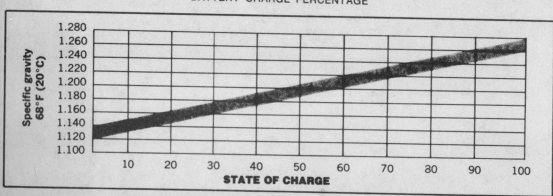

FORD
F100-350 PICKUPS
1969-1987 GAS & DIESEL
SHOP MANUAL

INTRODUCTION

This detailed, comprehensive manual covers all 1969-1987 F-series Ford pickup trucks. The expert text gives complete information on maintenance, repair and overhaul. Hundreds of photos and drawings guide you through every step. The book includes all you need to know to keep your Ford pickup running right.

Chapters One through Eleven contain general information on all models and specific information on 1969-1979 models. The supplement at the end of the book contains information on 1980 and later models which differs from earlier years.

Where repairs are practical for the owner/mechanic, complete procedures are given. Equally important, difficult jobs are pointed out. Such operations are usually more economically performed by a dealer or independent garage.

A shop manual is a reference. You want to be able to find information fast. As in all Clymer books, this one is designed with this in mind. All chapters are thumb tabbed. Important items are indexed at the rear of the book. Finally, all the most frequently used specifications and capacities are summarized on the *Quick Reference* pages at the front of the book.

Keep the book handy. Carry it in your glove box. It will help you to better understand your pickup, lower repair and maintenance costs and generally improve your satisfaction with your vehicle.

CHAPTER ONE

GENERAL INFORMATION

The troubleshooting, tune-up, maintenance, and step-by-step repair procedures in this book are written for the owner and home mechanic. The text is accompanied by useful photos and diagrams to make the job as clear and correct as possible.

Troubleshooting, tune-up, maintenance, and repair are not difficult if you know what tools and equipment to use and what to do. Anyone not afraid to get their hands dirty, of average intelligence, and with some mechanical ability can perform most of the procedures in this book.

In some cases, a repair job may require tools or skills not reasonably expected of the home mechanic. These procedures are noted in each chapter and it is recommended that you take the job to your dealer, a competent mechanic, or machine shop.

MANUAL ORGANIZATION

This chapter provides general information and safety and service hints. Also included are lists of recommended shop and emergency tools as well as a brief description of troubleshooting and tune-up equipment.

Chapter Two provides methods and suggestions for quick and accurate diagnosis and repair of problems. Troubleshooting procedures discuss typical symptoms and logical methods to pinpoint the trouble.

Chapter Three explains all periodic lubrication and routine maintenance necessary to keep your vehicle running well. Chapter Three also includes recommended tune-up procedures, eliminating the need to constantly consult chapters on the various subassemblies.

Subsequent chapters cover specific systems such as the engine, transmission, and electrical systems. Each of these chapters provides disassembly, repair, and assembly procedures in a simple step-by-step format. If a repair requires special skills or tools, or is otherwise impractical for the home mechanic, it is so indicated. In these cases it is usually faster and less expensive to have the repairs made by a dealer or competent repair shop. Necessary specifications concerning a particular system are included at the end of the appropriate chapter.

When special tools are required to perform a procedure included in this manual, the tool is illustrated either in actual use or alone. It may be possible to rent or borrow these tools. The inventive mechanic may also be able to find a suitable substitute in his tool box, or to fabricate one.

The terms NOTE, CAUTION, and WARNING have specific meanings in this manual. A NOTE provides additional or explanatory information. A CAUTION is used to emphasize areas where equipment damage could result if proper precautions are not taken. A WARNING is used to stress those areas where personal injury or death could result from negligence, in addition to possible mechanical damage.

SERVICE HINTS

Observing the following practices will save time, effort, and frustration, as well as prevent possible injury.

Throughout this manual keep in mind two conventions. ''Front'' refers to the front of the vehicle. The front of any component, such as the transmission, is that end which faces toward the front of the vehicle. The "left" and "right" sides of the vehicle refer to the orientation of a person sitting in the vehicle facing forward. For example, the steering wheel is on the left side. These rules are simple, but even experienced mechanics occasionally become disoriented.

Most of the service procedures covered are straightforward and can be performed by anyone reasonably handy with tools. It is suggested, however, that you consider your own capabilities carefully before attempting any operation involving major disassembly of the engine.

Some operations, for example, require the use of a press. It would be wiser to have these performed by a shop equipped for such work, rather than to try to do the job yourself with makeshift equipment. Other procedures require precision measurements. Unless you have the skills and equipment required, it would be better to have a qualified repair shop make the measurements for you.

Repairs go much faster and easier if the parts that will be worked on are clean before you begin. There are special cleaners for washing the engine and related parts. Brush or spray on the cleaning solution, let it stand, then rinse it away with a garden hose. Clean all oily or greasy parts with cleaning solvent as you remove them.

WARNING
Never use gasoline as a cleaning agent. It presents an extreme fire hazard. Be sure to work in a well-ventilated area when using cleaning solvent. Keep a fire extinguisher, rated for gasoline fires, handy in any case.

Much of the labor charge for repairs made by dealers is for the removal and disassembly of other parts to reach the defective unit. It is frequently possible to perform the preliminary operations yourself and then take the defective unit in to the dealer for repair, at considerable savings.

Once you have decided to tackle the job yourself, make sure you locate the appropriate section in this manual, and read it entirely. Study the illustrations and text until you have a good idea of what is involved in completing the job satisfactorily. If special tools are required, make arrangements to get them before you start. Also, purchase any known defective parts prior to starting on the procedure. It is frustrating and time-consuming to get partially into a job and then be unable to complete it.

Simple wiring checks can be easily made at home, but knowledge of electronics is almost a necessity for performing tests with complicated electronic testing gear.

During disassembly of parts keep a few general cautions in mind. Force is rarely needed to get things apart. If parts are a tight fit, like a bearing in a case, there is usually a tool designed to separate them. Never use a screwdriver to pry apart parts with machined surfaces such as cylinder head and valve cover. You will mar the surfaces and end up with leaks.

Make diagrams wherever similar-appearing parts are found. You may think you can remember where everything came from — but mistakes are costly. There is also the possibility you may get sidetracked and not return to work for days or even weeks — in which interval, carefully laid out parts may have become disturbed.

Tag all similar internal parts for location, and mark all mating parts for position. Record number and thickness of any shims as they are removed. Small parts such as bolts can be identified by placing them in plastic sandwich bags that are sealed and labeled with masking tape.

Wiring should be tagged with masking tape and marked as each wire is removed. Again, do not rely on memory alone.

When working under the vehicle, do not trust a hydraulic or mechanical jack to hold the vehicle up by itself. Always use jackstands. See **Figure 1**.

Disconnect battery ground cable before working near electrical connections and before disconnecting wires. Never run the engine with the battery disconnected; the alternator could be seriously damaged.

Protect finished surfaces from physical damage or corrosion. Keep gasoline and brake fluid off painted surfaces.

Frozen or very tight bolts and screws can often be loosened by soaking with penetrating oil like Liquid Wrench or WD-40, then sharply striking the bolt head a few times with a hammer and punch (or screwdriver for screws). Avoid heat unless absolutely necessary, since it may melt, warp, or remove the temper from many parts.

Avoid flames or sparks when working near a charging battery or flammable liquids, such as brake fluid or gasoline.

No parts, except those assembled with a press fit, require unusual force during assembly. If a part is hard to remove or install, find out why before proceeding.

Cover all openings after removing parts to keep dirt, small tools, etc., from falling in.

When assembling two parts, start all fasteners, then tighten evenly.

The clutch plate, wiring connections, brake shoes, drums, pads, and discs should be kept clean and free of grease and oil.

When assembling parts, be sure all shims and washers are replaced exactly as they came out.

Whenever a rotating part butts against a stationary part, look for a shim or washer. Use new gaskets if there is any doubt about the condition of old ones. Generally, you should apply gasket cement to one mating surface only, so the parts may be easily disassembled in the future. A thin coat of oil on gaskets helps them seal effectively.

Heavy grease can be used to hold small parts in place if they tend to fall out during assembly. However, keep grease and oil away from electrical, clutch, and brake components.

High spots may be sanded off a piston with sandpaper, but emery cloth and oil do a much more professional job.

Carburetors are best cleaned by disassembling them and soaking the parts in a commercial carburetor cleaner. Never soak gaskets and rubber parts in these cleaners. Never use wire to clean out jets and air passages; they are easily damaged. Use compressed air to blow out the carburetor, but only if the float has been removed first.

Take your time and do the job right. Do not forget that a newly rebuilt engine must be broken in the same as a new one. Refer to your owner's manual for the proper break-in procedures.

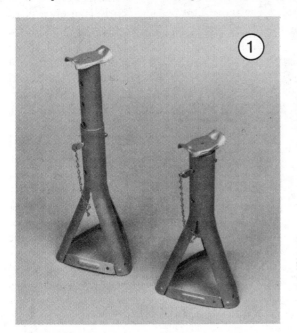

SAFETY FIRST

Professional mechanics can work for years and never sustain a serious injury. If you observe a few rules of common sense and safety, you can enjoy many safe hours servicing your vehicle. You could hurt yourself or damage the vehicle if you ignore these rules.

1. Never use gasoline as a cleaning solvent.

2. Never smoke or use a torch in the vicinity of flammable liquids such as cleaning solvent in open containers.

3. Never smoke or use a torch in an area where batteries are being charged. Highly explosive hydrogen gas is formed during the charging process.

4. Use the proper sized wrenches to avoid damage to nuts and injury to yourself.

5. When loosening a tight or stuck nut, be guided by what would happen if the wrench should slip. Protect yourself accordingly.

6. Keep your work area clean and uncluttered.

7. Wear safety goggles during all operations involving drilling, grinding, or use of a cold chisel.

8. Never use worn tools.

9. Keep a fire extinguisher handy and be sure it is rated for gasoline (Class B) and electrical (Class C) fires.

EXPENDABLE SUPPLIES

Certain expendable supplies are necessary. These include grease, oil, gasket cement, wiping rags, cleaning solvent, and distilled water. Also, special locking compounds, silicone lubricants, and engine cleaners may be useful. Cleaning solvent is available at most service stations and distilled water for the battery is available at most supermarkets.

SHOP TOOLS

For proper servicing, you will need an assortment of ordinary hand tools (**Figure 2**).

As a minimum, these include:

a. Combination wrenches
b. Sockets
c. Plastic mallet
d. Small hammer
e. Snap ring pliers
f. Gas pliers
g. Phillips screwdrivers
h. Slot (common) screwdrivers
i. Feeler gauges
j. Spark plug gauge
k. Spark plug wrench

Special tools necessary are shown in the chapters covering the particular repair in which they are used.

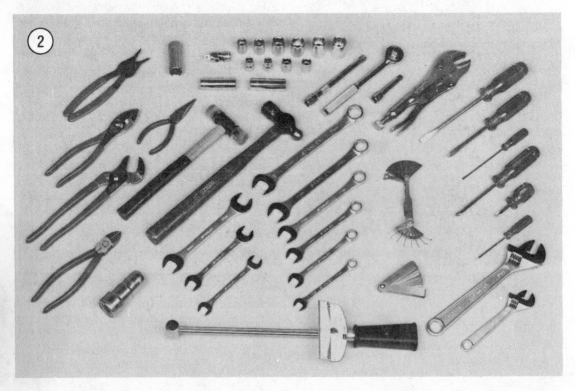

Engine tune-up and troubleshooting procedures require other special tools and equipment. These are described in detail in the following sections.

EMERGENCY TOOL KIT

A small emergency tool kit kept in the trunk is handy for road emergencies which otherwise could leave you stranded. The tools listed below and shown in **Figure 3** will let you handle most roadside repairs.

a. Combination wrenches
b. Crescent (adjustable) wrench
c. Screwdrivers — common and Phillips
d. Pliers — conventional (gas) and needle nose

e. Vise Grips
f. Hammer — plastic and metal
g. Small container of waterless hand cleaner
h. Rags for clean up
i. Silver waterproof sealing tape (duct tape)
j. Flashlight
k. Emergency road flares — at least four
l. Spare drive belts (water pump, alternator, etc.)

TROUBLESHOOTING AND TUNE-UP EQUIPMENT

Voltmeter, Ohmmeter, and Ammeter

For testing the ignition or electrical system, a good voltmeter is required. For automotive use, an instrument covering 0-20 volts is satisfac-

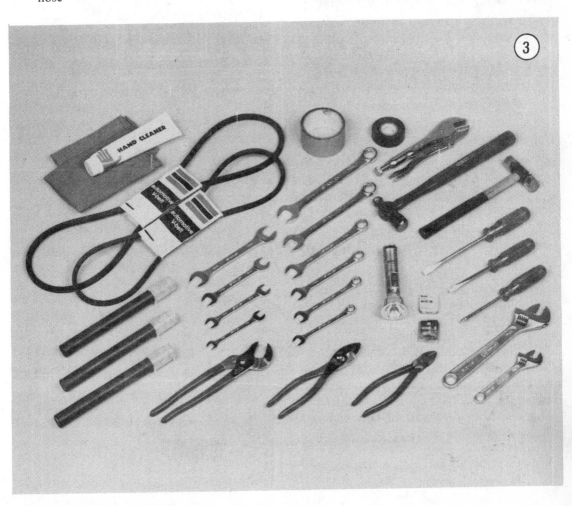

tory. One which also has a 0-2 volt scale is necessary for testing relays, points, or individual contacts where voltage drops are much smaller. Accuracy should be ± ½ volt.

An ohmmeter measures electrical resistance. This instrument is useful for checking continuity (open and short circuits), and testing fuses and lights.

The ammeter measures electrical current. Ammeters for automotive use should cover 0-50 amperes and 0-250 amperes. These are useful for checking battery charging and starting current.

Several inexpensive vom's (volt-ohm-milliammeter) combine all three instruments into one which fits easily in any tool box. See **Figure 4**. However, the ammeter ranges are usually too small for automotive work.

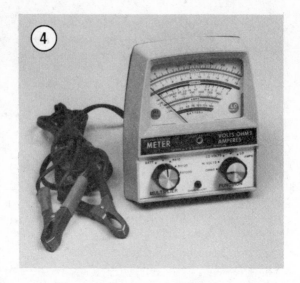

Hydrometer

The hydrometer gives a useful indication of battery condition and charge by measuring the specific gravity of the electrolyte in each cell. See **Figure 5**. Complete details on use and interpretation of readings are provided in the electrical chapter.

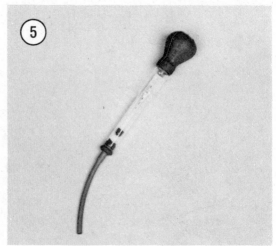

Compression Tester

The compression tester measures the compression pressure built up in each cylinder. The results, when properly interpreted, can indicate general cylinder and valve condition. See **Figure 6**.

Vacuum Gauge

The vacuum gauge (**Figure 7**) is one of the easiest instruments to use, but one of the most difficult for the inexperienced mechanic to interpret. The results, when interpreted with other findings, can provide valuable clues to possible trouble.

To use the vacuum gauge, connect it to a vacuum hose that goes to the intake manifold. Attach it either directly to the hose or to a T-fitting installed into the hose.

NOTE: *Subtract one inch from the reading for every 1,000 ft. elevation.*

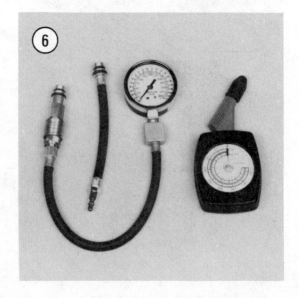

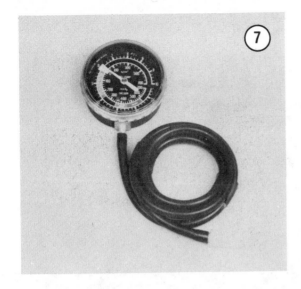

Fuel Pressure Gauge

This instrument is invaluable for evaluating fuel pump performance. Fuel system trouble-shooting procedures in this manual use a fuel pressure gauge. Usually a vacuum gauge and fuel pressure gauge are combined.

Dwell Meter (Contact Breaker Point Ignition Only)

A dwell meter measures the distance in degrees of cam rotation that the breaker points remain closed while the engine is running. Since this angle is determined by breaker point gap, dwell angle is an accurate indication of breaker point gap.

Many tachometers intended for tuning and testing incorporate a dwell meter as well. See **Figure 8**. Follow the manufacturer's instructions to measure dwell.

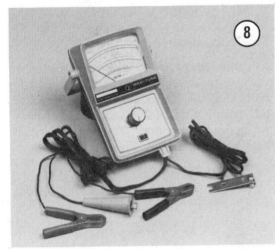

Tachometer

A tachometer is necessary for tuning. See **Figure 8**. Ignition timing and carburetor adjustments must be performed at the specified idle speed. The best instrument for this purpose is one with a low range of 0-1,000 or 0-2,000 rpm for setting idle, and a high range of 0-4,000 or more for setting ignition timing at 3,000 rpm. Extended range (0-6,000 or 0-8,000 rpm) instruments lack accuracy at lower speeds. The instrument should be capable of detecting changes of 25 rpm on the low range.

Strobe Timing Light

This instrument is necessary for tuning, as it permits very accurate ignition timing. The light flashes at precisely the same instant that No. 1 cylinder fires, at which time the timing marks on the engine should align. Refer to Chapter Three for exact location of the timing marks for your engine.

Suitable lights range from inexpensive neon bulb types ($2-3) to powerful xenon strobe lights ($20-40). See **Figure 9**. Neon timing lights are difficult to see and must be used in dimly lit areas. Xenon strobe timing lights can be used outside in bright sunlight. Both types work on this vehicle; use according to the manufacturer's instructions.

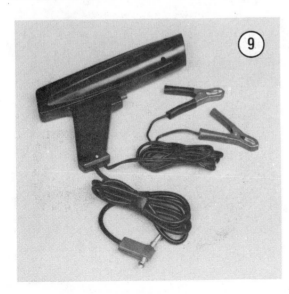

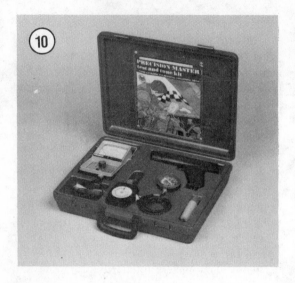

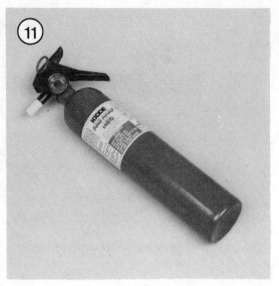

Tune-up Kits

Many manufacturer's offer kits that combine several useful instruments. Some come in a convenient carry case and are usally less expensive than purchasing one instrument at a time. **Figure 10** shows one of the kits that is available. The prices vary with the number of instruments included in the kit.

Fire Extinguisher

A fire extinguisher is a necessity when working on a vehicle. It should be rated for both *Class B* (flammable liquids—gasoline, oil, paint, etc.) and *Class C* (electrical—wiring, etc.) type fires. It should always be kept within reach. See **Figure 11**.

CHAPTER TWO

TROUBLESHOOTING

Troubleshooting can be a relatively simple matter if it is done logically. The first step in any troubleshooting procedure must be defining the symptoms as closely as possible. Subsequent steps involve testing and analyzing areas which could cause the symptoms. A haphazard approach may eventually find the trouble, but in terms of wasted time and unnecessary parts replacement, it can be very costly.

The troubleshooting procedures in this chapter analyze typical symptoms and show logical methods of isolation. These are not the only methods. There may be several approaches to a problem, but all methods must have one thing in common — a logical, systematic approach.

STARTING SYSTEM

The starting system consists of the starter motor and the starter solenoid. The ignition key controls the starter solenoid, which mechanically engages the starter with the engine flywheel, and supplies electrical current to turn the starter motor.

Starting system troubles are relatively easy to find. In most cases, the trouble is a loose or dirty electrical connection. **Figures 1 and 2** provide routines for finding the trouble.

CHARGING SYSTEM

The charging system consists of the alternator (or generator on older vehicles), voltage regulator, and battery. A drive belt driven by the engine crankshaft turns the alternator which produces electrical energy to charge the battery. As engine speed varies, the voltage from the alternator varies. A voltage regulator controls the charging current to the battery and maintains the voltage to the vehicle's electrical system at safe levels. A warning light or gauge on the instrument panel signals the driver when charging is not taking place. Refer to **Figure 3** for a typical charging system.

Complete troubleshooting of the charging system requires test equipment and skills which the average home mechanic does not possess. However, there are a few tests which can be done to pinpoint most troubles.

Charging system trouble may stem from a defective alternator (or generator), voltage regulator, battery, or drive belt. It may also be caused by something as simple as incorrect drive belt tension. The following are symptoms of typical problems you may encounter.

1. *Battery dies frequently, even though the warning lamp indicates no discharge* — This can be caused by a drive belt that is slightly too

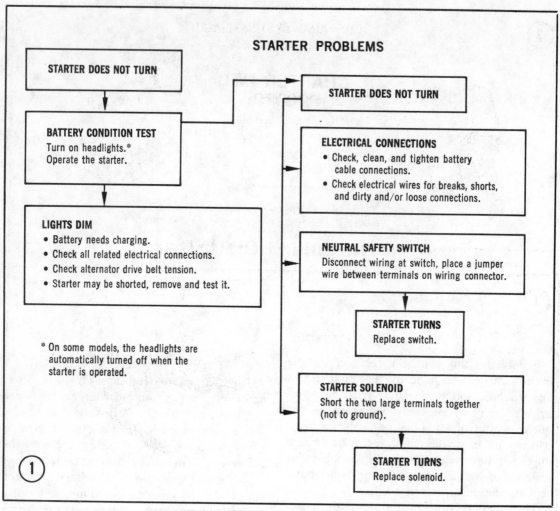

STARTER PROBLEMS

STARTER DOES NOT TURN

BATTERY CONDITION TEST
Turn on headlights.*
Operate the starter.

LIGHTS DIM
• Battery needs charging.
• Check all related electrical connections.
• Check alternator drive belt tension.
• Starter may be shorted, remove and test it.

* On some models, the headlights are
  automatically turned off when the
  starter is operated.

STARTER DOES NOT TURN

ELECTRICAL CONNECTIONS
• Check, clean, and tighten battery
  cable connections.
• Check electrical wires for breaks, shorts,
  and dirty and/or loose connections.

NEUTRAL SAFETY SWITCH
Disconnect wiring at switch, place a jumper
wire between terminals on wiring connector.

STARTER TURNS
Replace switch.

STARTER SOLENOID
Short the two large terminals together
(not to ground).

STARTER TURNS
Replace solenoid.

①

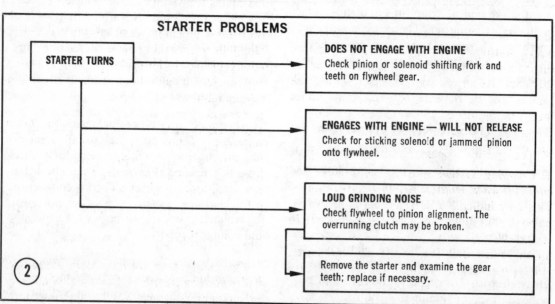

STARTER PROBLEMS

STARTER TURNS

DOES NOT ENGAGE WITH ENGINE
Check pinion or solenoid shifting fork and
teeth on flywheel gear.

ENGAGES WITH ENGINE — WILL NOT RELEASE
Check for sticking solenoid or jammed pinion
onto flywheel.

LOUD GRINDING NOISE
Check flywheel to pinion alignment. The
overrunning clutch may be broken.

Remove the starter and examine the gear
teeth; replace if necessary.

②

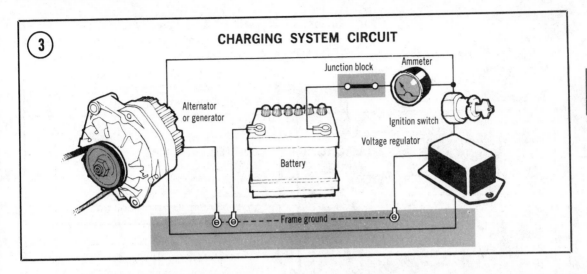

CHARGING SYSTEM CIRCUIT

③

Alternator or generator

Junction block

Ammeter

Ignition switch

Voltage regulator

Battery

Frame ground

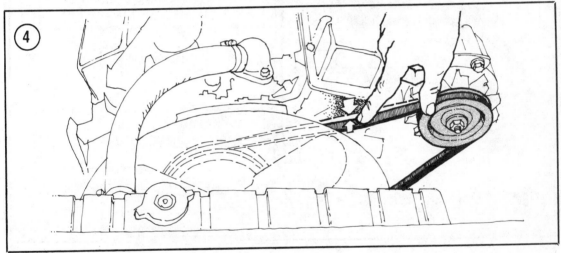

④

loose. Grasp the alternator (or generator) pulley and try to turn it. If the pulley can be turned without moving the belt, the drive belt is too loose. As a rule, keep the belt tight enough that it can be deflected about ½ in. under moderate thumb pressure between the pulleys (**Figure 4**). The battery may also be at fault; test the battery condition.

2. *Charging system warning lamp does not come on when ignition switch is turned on* — This may indicate a defective ignition switch, battery, voltage regulator, or lamp. First try to start the vehicle. If it doesn't start, check the ignition switch and battery. If the car starts, remove the warning lamp; test it for continuity with an ohmmeter or substitute a new lamp. If the lamp is good, locate the voltage regulator

and make sure it is properly grounded (try tightening the mounting screws). Also the alternator (or generator) brushes may not be making contact. Test the alternator (or generator) and voltage regulator.

3. *Alternator (or generator) warning lamp comes on and stays on* — This usually indicates that no charging is taking place. First check drive belt tension (**Figure 4**). Then check battery condition, and check all wiring connections in the charging system. If this does not locate the trouble, check the alternator (or generator) and voltage regulator.

4. *Charging system warning lamp flashes on and off intermittently* — This usually indicates the charging system is working intermittently.

Check the drive belt tension **(Figure 4)**, and check all electrical connections in the charging system. Check the alternator (or generator). *On generators only*, check the condition of the commutator.

5. *Battery requires frequent additions of water, or lamps require frequent replacement* — The alternator (or generator) is probably overcharging the battery. The voltage regulator is probably at fault.

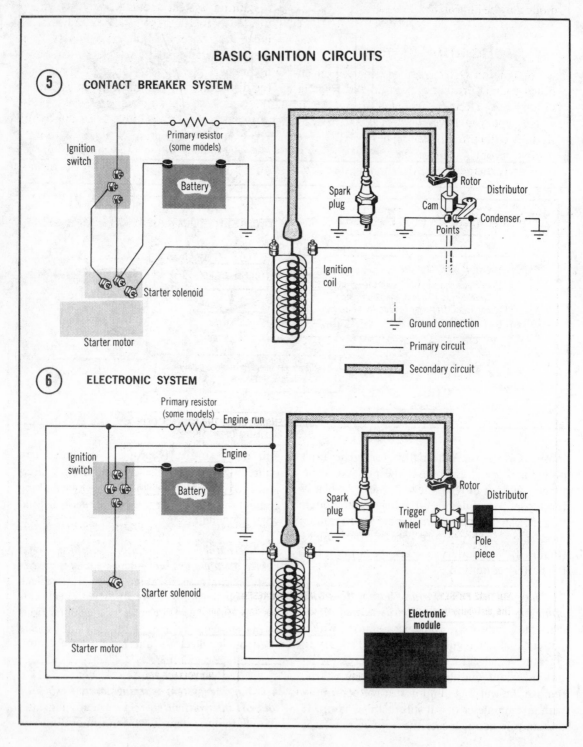

BASIC IGNITION CIRCUITS

5 **CONTACT BREAKER SYSTEM**

6 **ELECTRONIC SYSTEM**

6. *Excessive noise from the alternator (or generator)* — Check for loose mounting brackets and bolts. The problem may also be worn bearings or the need of lubrication in some cases. If an alternator whines, a shorted diode may be indicated.

IGNITION SYSTEM

The ignition system may be either a conventional contact breaker type or an electronic ignition. See electrical chapter to determine which type you have. **Figures 5 and 6** show simplified diagrams of each type.

Most problems involving failure to start, poor performance, or rough running stem from trouble in the ignition system, particularly in contact breaker systems. Many novice troubleshooters get into trouble when they assume that these symptoms point to the fuel system instead of the ignition system.

Ignition system troubles may be roughly divided between those affecting only one cylinder and those affecting all cylinders. If the trouble affects only one cylinder, it can only be in the spark plug, spark plug wire, or portion of the distributor associated with that cylinder. If the trouble affects all cylinders (weak spark or no spark), then the trouble is in the ignition coil, rotor, distributor, or associated wiring.

The troubleshooting procedures outlined in **Figure 7** (breaker point ignition) or **Figure 8**

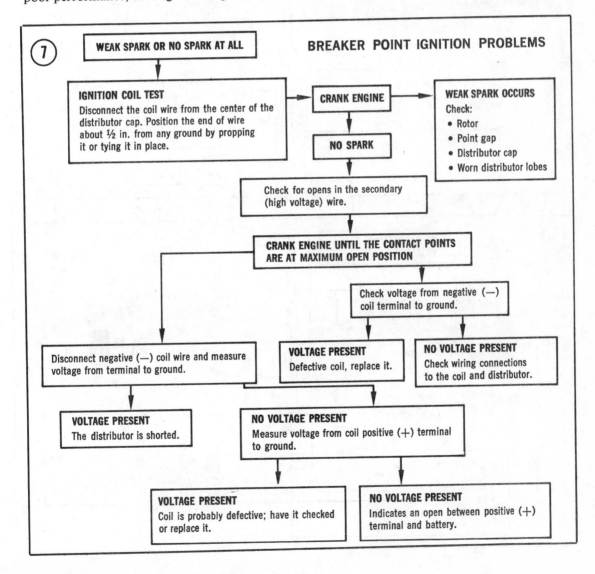

(electronic ignition) will help you isolate ignition problems fast. Of course, they assume that the battery is in good enough condition to crank the engine over at its normal rate.

ENGINE PERFORMANCE

A number of factors can make the engine difficult or impossible to start, or cause rough running, poor performance and so on. The majority of novice troubleshooters immediately suspect the carburetor or fuel injection system. In the majority of cases, though, the trouble exists in the ignition system.

The troubleshooting procedures outlined in **Figures 9 through 14** will help you solve the majority of engine starting troubles in a systematic manner.

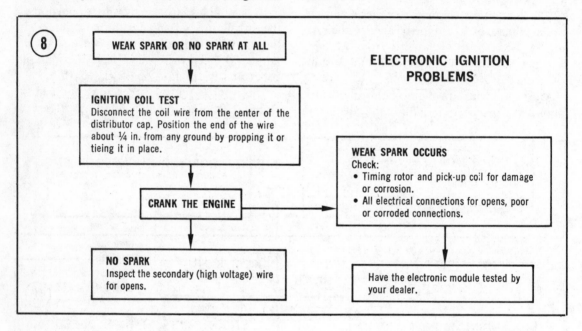

⑧ WEAK SPARK OR NO SPARK AT ALL

ELECTRONIC IGNITION PROBLEMS

IGNITION COIL TEST
Disconnect the coil wire from the center of the distributor cap. Position the end of the wire about ¼ in. from any ground by propping it or tieing it in place.

WEAK SPARK OCCURS
Check:
• Timing rotor and pick-up coil for damage or corrosion.
• All electrical connections for opens, poor or corroded connections.

CRANK THE ENGINE

NO SPARK
Inspect the secondary (high voltage) wire for opens.

Have the electronic module tested by your dealer.

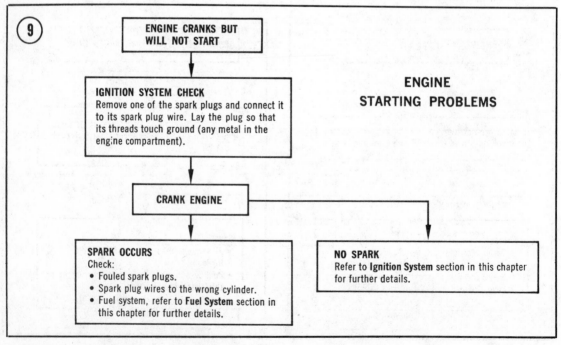

⑨ ENGINE CRANKS BUT WILL NOT START

ENGINE STARTING PROBLEMS

IGNITION SYSTEM CHECK
Remove one of the spark plugs and connect it to its spark plug wire. Lay the plug so that its threads touch ground (any metal in the engine compartment).

CRANK ENGINE

SPARK OCCURS
Check:
• Fouled spark plugs.
• Spark plug wires to the wrong cylinder.
• Fuel system, refer to **Fuel System** section in this chapter for further details.

NO SPARK
Refer to **Ignition System** section in this chapter for further details.

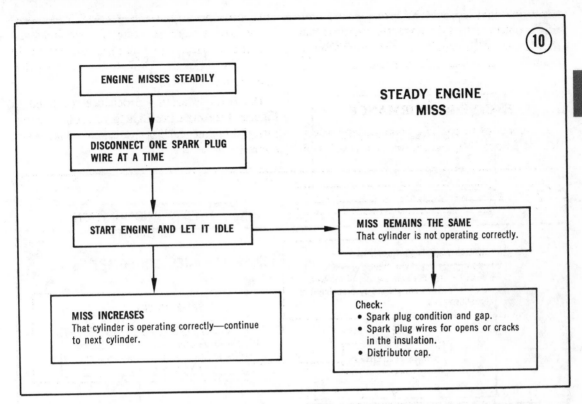

2

⑩

ENGINE MISSES STEADILY

STEADY ENGINE MISS

DISCONNECT ONE SPARK PLUG WIRE AT A TIME

START ENGINE AND LET IT IDLE

MISS REMAINS THE SAME
That cylinder is not operating correctly.

MISS INCREASES
That cylinder is operating correctly—continue to next cylinder.

Check:
• Spark plug condition and gap.
• Spark plug wires for opens or cracks in the insulation.
• Distributor cap.

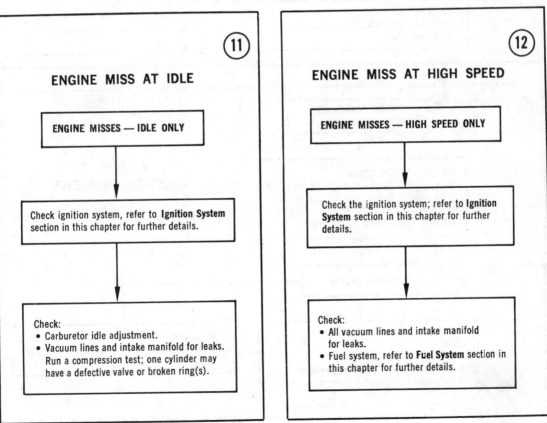

⑪

ENGINE MISS AT IDLE

ENGINE MISSES — IDLE ONLY

Check ignition system, refer to **Ignition System** section in this chapter for further details.

Check:
• Carburetor idle adjustment.
• Vacuum lines and intake manifold for leaks. Run a compression test; one cylinder may have a defective valve or broken ring(s).

⑫

ENGINE MISS AT HIGH SPEED

ENGINE MISSES — HIGH SPEED ONLY

Check the ignition system; refer to **Ignition System** section in this chapter for further details.

Check:
• All vacuum lines and intake manifold for leaks.
• Fuel system, refer to **Fuel System** section in this chapter for further details.

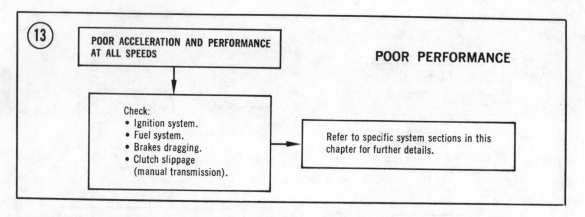

⑬ POOR ACCELERATION AND PERFORMANCE
AT ALL SPEEDS

POOR PERFORMANCE

Check:
• Ignition system.
• Fuel system.
• Brakes dragging.
• Clutch slippage
(manual transmission).

Refer to specific system sections in this
chapter for further details.

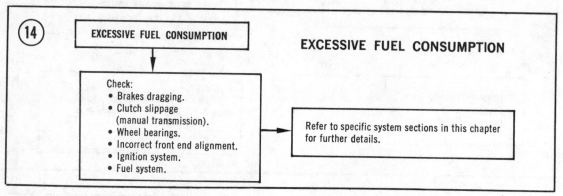

⑭ EXCESSIVE FUEL CONSUMPTION

EXCESSIVE FUEL CONSUMPTION

Check:
• Brakes dragging.
• Clutch slippage
(manual transmission).
• Wheel bearings.
• Incorrect front end alignment.
• Ignition system.
• Fuel system.

Refer to specific system sections in this chapter
for further details.

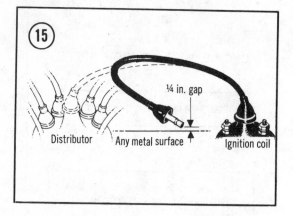

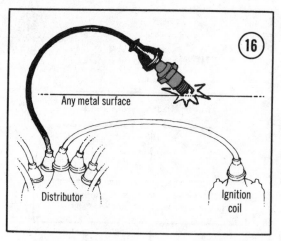

Some tests of the ignition system require running the engine with a spark plug or ignition
coil wire disconnected. The safest way to do
this is to disconnect the wire with the engine
stopped, then prop the end of the wire next to a
metal surface as shown in **Figures 15 and 16**.

WARNING
*Never disconnect a spark plug or igni-
tion coil wire while the engine is running. The high voltage in an ignition
system, particularly the newer high-*
*energy electronic ignition systems could
cause serious injury or even death.*

Spark plug condition is an important indication of engine performance. Spark plugs in a
properly operating engine will have slightly pitted electrodes, and a light tan insulator tip.
Figure 17 shows a normal plug, and a number
of others which indicate trouble in their respective cylinders.

• Appearance—Firing tip has deposits of light gray to light tan.
• Can be cleaned, regapped and reused.

• Appearance—Glazed yellow deposits with a slight brownish tint on the insulator tip and ground electrode.
• Replace with new plugs.

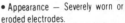

• Appearance—Dull, dry black with fluffy carbon deposits on the insulator tip, electrode and exposed shell.
• Caused by—Fuel/air mixture too rich, plug heat range too cold, weak ignition system, dirty air cleaner, faulty automatic choke or excessive idling.
• Can be cleaned, regapped and reused.

• Appearance — Brown colored hardened ash deposits on the insulator tip and ground electrode.
• Caused by—Fuel and/or oil additives.
• Replace with new plugs.

• Appearance — Severely worn or eroded electrodes.
• Caused by—Normal wear or unusual oil and/or fuel additives.
• Replace with new plugs.

• Appearance—Wet black deposits on insulator and exposed shell.
• Caused by—Excessive oil entering the combustion chamber through worn rings, pistons, valve guides or bearings.
• Replace with new plugs (use a hotter plug if engine is not repaired).

• Appearance — Melted ground electrode.
• Caused by—Overadvanced ignition timing, inoperative ignition advance mechanism, too low of a fuel octane rating, lean fuel/air mixture or carbon deposits in combustion chamber.

• Appearance — Yellow insulator deposits (may sometimes be dark gray, black or tan in color) on the insulator tip.
• Caused by—Highly leaded gasoline.
• Replace with new plugs.

• Appearance—Melted center electrode.
• Caused by—Abnormal combustion due to overadvanced ignition timing or incorrect advance, too low of a fuel octane rating, lean fuel/air mixture, or carbon deposits in combustion chamber.
• Correct engine problem and replace with new plugs.

• Appearance—Yellow glazed deposits indicating melted lead deposits due to hard acceleration.
• Caused by—Highly leaded gasoline.
• Replace with new plugs.

• Appearance—Melted center electrode and white blistered insulator tip.
• Caused by—Incorrect plug heat range selection.
• Replace with new plugs.

2

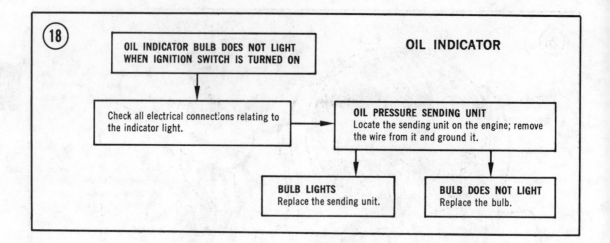

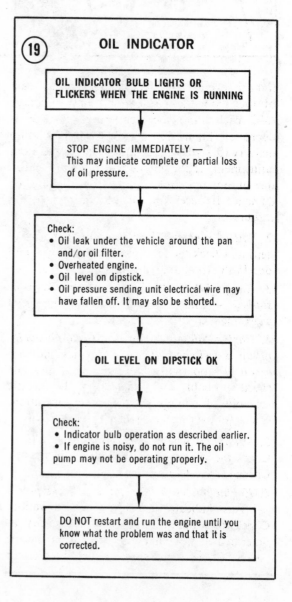

ENGINE OIL
PRESSURE LIGHT

Proper oil pressure to the engine is vital. If oil pressure is insufficient, the engine can destroy itself in a comparatively short time.

The oil pressure warning circuit monitors oil pressure constantly. If pressure drops below a predetermined level, the light comes on.

Obviously, it is vital for the warning circuit to be working to signal low oil pressure. Each time you turn on the ignition, but before you start the car, the warning light should come on. If it doesn't, there is trouble in the warning circuit, not the oil pressure system. See **Figure 18** to troubleshoot the warning circuit.

Once the engine is running, the warning light should stay off. If the warning light comes on or acts erratically while the engine is running there is trouble with the engine oil pressure system. *Stop the engine immediately*. Refer to **Figure 19** for possible causes of the problem.

FUEL SYSTEM
(CARBURETTED)

Fuel system problems must be isolated to the fuel pump (mechanical or electric), fuel lines, fuel filter, or carburetor. These procedures assume the ignition system is working properly and is correctly adjusted.

1. *Engine will not start* — First make sure that fuel is being delivered to the carburetor. Remove the air cleaner, look into the carburetor throat, and operate the accelerator

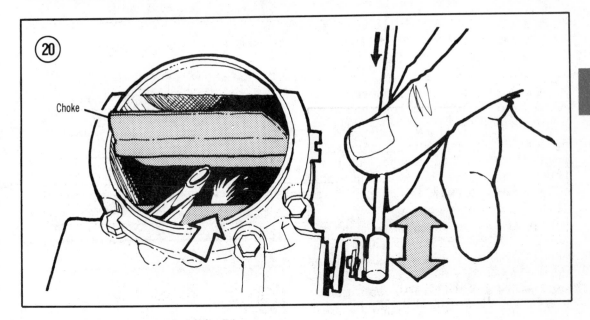

Choke

linkage several times. There should be a stream of fuel from the accelerator pump discharge tube each time the accelerator linkage is depressed (**Figure 20**). If not, check fuel pump delivery (described later), float valve, and float adjustment. If the engine will not start, check the automatic choke parts for sticking or damage. If necessary, rebuild or replace the carburetor.

2. *Engine runs at fast idle* — Check the choke setting. Check the idle speed, idle mixture, and decel valve (if equipped) adjustment.

3. *Rough idle or engine miss with frequent stalling* — Check idle mixture and idle speed adjustments.

4. *Engine "diesels" (continues to run) when ignition is switched off* — Check idle mixture (probably too rich), ignition timing, and idle speed (probably too fast). Check the throttle solenoid (if equipped) for proper operation. Check for overheated engine.

5. *Stumbling when accelerating from idle* — Check the idle speed and mixture adjustments. Check the accelerator pump.

6. *Engine misses at high speed or lacks power* — This indicates possible fuel starvation. Check fuel pump pressure and capacity as described in this chapter. Check float needle valves. Check for a clogged fuel filter or air cleaner.

7. *Black exhaust smoke* — This indicates a badly overrich mixture. Check idle mixture and idle speed adjustment. Check choke setting. Check for excessive fuel pump pressure, leaky floats, or worn needle valves.

8. *Excessive fuel consumption* — Check for overrich mixture. Make sure choke mechanism works properly. Check idle mixture and idle speed. Check for excessive fuel pump pressure, leaky floats, or worn float needle valves.

FUEL SYSTEM (FUEL INJECTED)

Troubleshooting a fuel injection system requires more thought, experience, and know-how than any other part of the vehicle. A logical approach and proper test equipment are essential in order to successfully find and fix these troubles.

It is best to leave fuel injection troubles to your dealer. In order to isolate a problem to the injection system make sure that the fuel pump is operating properly. Check its performance as described later in this section. Also make sure that fuel filter and air cleaner are not clogged.

FUEL PUMP TEST (MECHANICAL AND ELECTRIC)

1. Disconnect the fuel inlet line where it enters the carburetor or fuel injection system.

2. Fit a rubber hose over the fuel line so fuel can be directed into a graduated container with about one quart capacity. See **Figure 21**.

3. To avoid accidental starting of the engine, disconnect the secondary coil wire from the coil or disconnect and insulate the coil primary wire.

4. Crank the engine for about 30 seconds.

5. If the fuel pump supplies the specified amount (refer to the fuel chapter later in this book), the trouble may be in the carburetor or fuel injection system. The fuel injection system should be tested by your dealer.

6. If there is no fuel present or the pump cannot supply the specified amount, either the fuel pump is defective or there is an obstruction in the fuel line. Replace the fuel pump and/or inspect the fuel lines for air leaks or obstructions.

7. Also pressure test the fuel pump by installing a T-fitting in the fuel line between the fuel pump and the carburetor. Connect a fuel pressure gauge to the fitting with a short tube **(Figure 22)**.

8. Reconnect the coil wire, start the engine, and record the pressure. Refer to the fuel chapter later in this book for the correct pressure. If the pressure varies from that specified, the pump should be replaced.

9. Stop the engine. The pressure should drop off very slowly. If it drops off rapidly, the outlet valve in the pump is leaking and the pump should be replaced.

EMISSION CONTROL SYSTEMS

Major emission control systems used on nearly all U.S. models include the following:

a. Positive crankcase ventilation (PCV)

b. Thermostatic air cleaner

c. Air injection reaction (AIR)

d. Fuel evaporation control

e. Exhaust gas recirculation (EGR)

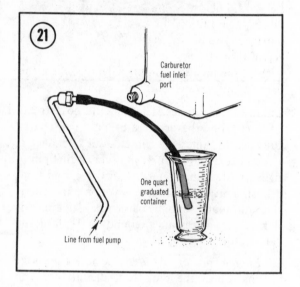

Carburetor fuel inlet port

One quart graduated container

Line from fuel pump

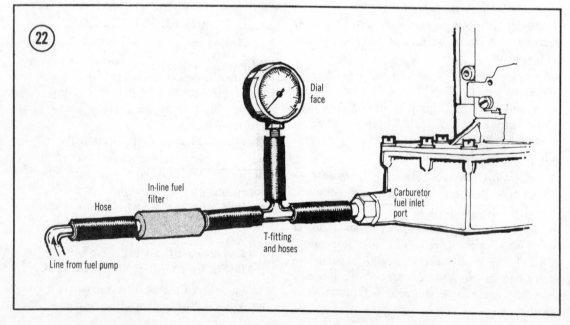

Dial face

In-line fuel filter

Hose

Carburetor fuel inlet port

T-fitting and hoses

Line from fuel pump

Emission control systems vary considerably from model to model. Individual models contain variations of the four systems described here. In addition, they may include other special systems. Use the index to find specific emission control components in other chapters.

Many of the systems and components are factory set and sealed. Without special expensive test equipment, it is impossible to adjust the systems to meet state and federal requirements.

Troubleshooting can also be difficult without special equipment. The procedures described below will help you find emission control parts which have failed, but repairs may have to be entrusted to a dealer or other properly equipped repair shop.

With the proper equipment, you can test the carbon monoxide and hydrocarbon levels.

Figure 23 provides some sources of trouble if the readings are not correct.

Positive Crankcase Ventilation

Fresh air drawn from the air cleaner housing scavenges emissions (e.g., piston blow-by) from the crankcase, then the intake manifold vacuum draws emissions into the intake manifold. They can then be reburned in the normal combustion process. **Figure 24** shows a typical system. **Figure 25** provides a testing procedure.

Thermostatic Air Cleaner

The thermostatically controlled air cleaner maintains incoming air to the engine at a predetermined level, usually about 100°F or higher. It mixes cold air with heated air from the exhaust manifold region. The air cleaner in-

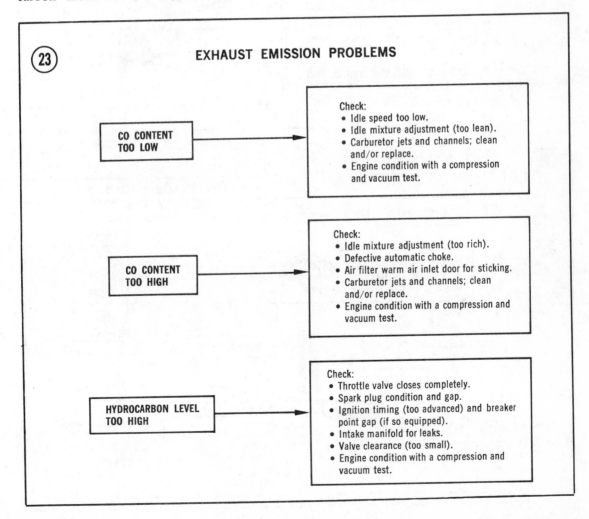

(23) EXHAUST EMISSION PROBLEMS

CO CONTENT TOO LOW

Check:
- Idle speed too low.
- Idle mixture adjustment (too lean).
- Carburetor jets and channels; clean and/or replace.
- Engine condition with a compression and vacuum test.

CO CONTENT TOO HIGH

Check:
- Idle mixture adjustment (too rich).
- Defective automatic choke.
- Air filter warm air inlet door for sticking.
- Carburetor jets and channels; clean and/or replace.
- Engine condition with a compression and vacuum test.

HYDROCARBON LEVEL TOO HIGH

Check:
- Throttle valve closes completely.
- Spark plug condition and gap.
- Ignition timing (too advanced) and breaker point gap (if so equipped).
- Intake manifold for leaks.
- Valve clearance (too small).
- Engine condition with a compression and vacuum test.

cludes a temperature sensor, vacuum motor, and a hinged door. See **Figure 26**.

The system is comparatively easy to test. See **Figure 27** for the procedure.

Air Injection Reaction System

The air injection reaction system reduces air pollution by oxidizing hydrocarbons and carbon monoxide as they leave the combustion chamber. See **Figure 28**.

The air injection pump, driven by the engine, compresses filtered air and injects it at the exhaust port of each cylinder. The fresh air mixes with the unburned gases in the exhaust and promotes further burning. A check valve prevents exhaust gases from entering and damaging the air pump if the pump becomes inoperative, e.g., from a fan belt failure.

Figure 29 explains the testing procedure for this system.

Fuel Evaporation Control

Fuel vapor from the fuel tank passes through the liquid/vapor separator to the carbon canister. See **Figure 30**. The carbon absorbs and

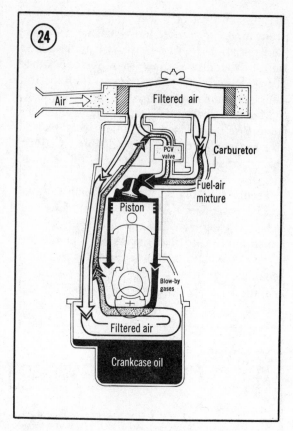

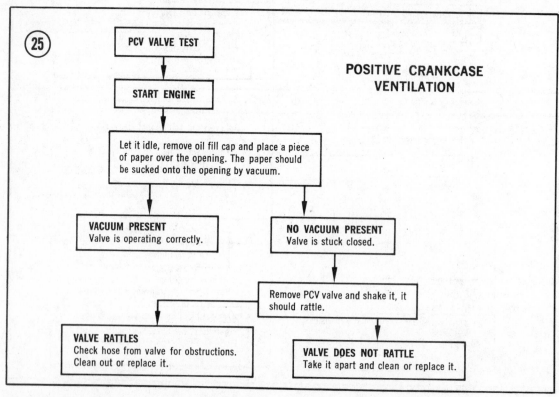

2

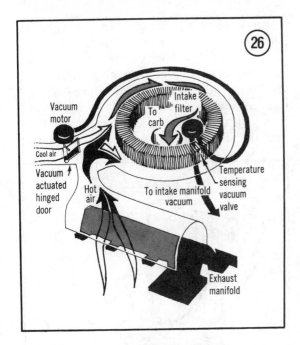

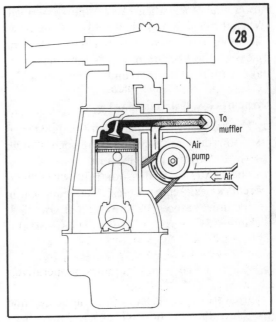

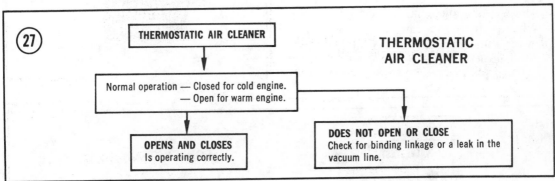

THERMOSTATIC AIR CLEANER

THERMOSTATIC AIR CLEANER

Normal operation — Closed for cold engine.
— Open for warm engine.

OPENS AND CLOSES
Is operating correctly.

DOES NOT OPEN OR CLOSE
Check for binding linkage or a leak in the vacuum line.

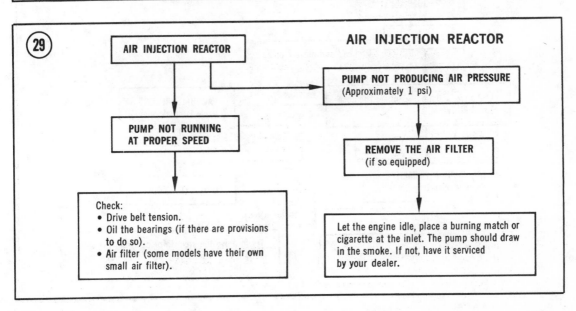

AIR INJECTION REACTOR

AIR INJECTION REACTOR

PUMP NOT PRODUCING AIR PRESSURE
(Approximately 1 psi)

PUMP NOT RUNNING AT PROPER SPEED

REMOVE THE AIR FILTER
(if so equipped)

Check:
• Drive belt tension.
• Oil the bearings (if there are provisions to do so).
• Air filter (some models have their own small air filter).

Let the engine idle, place a burning match or cigarette at the inlet. The pump should draw in the smoke. If not, have it serviced by your dealer.

stores the vapor when the engine is stopped. When the engine runs, manifold vacuum draws the vapor from the canister. Instead of being released into the atmosphere, the fuel vapor takes part in the normal combustion process.

Exhaust Gas Recirculation

The exhaust gas recirculation (EGR) system is used to reduce the emission of nitrogen oxides (NOx). Relatively inert exhaust gases are introduced into the combustion process to slightly reduce peak temperatures. This reduction in temperature reduces the formation of NOx.

Figure 31 provides a simple test of this system.

ENGINE NOISES

Often the first evidence of an internal engine trouble is a strange noise. That knocking, clicking, or tapping which you never heard before may be warning you of impending trouble.

While engine noises can indicate problems, they are sometimes difficult to interpret correctly; inexperienced mechanics can be seriously misled by them.

Professional mechanics often use a special stethoscope which looks similar to a doctor's stethoscope for isolating engine noises. You can do nearly as well with a "sounding stick" which can be an ordinary piece of doweling or a section of small hose. By placing one end in contact with the area to which you want to listen and the other end near your ear, you can hear

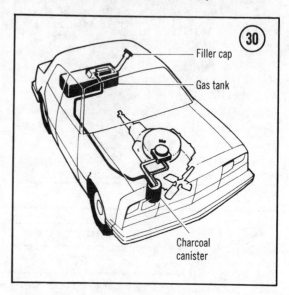

30

Filler cap

Gas tank

Charcoal canister

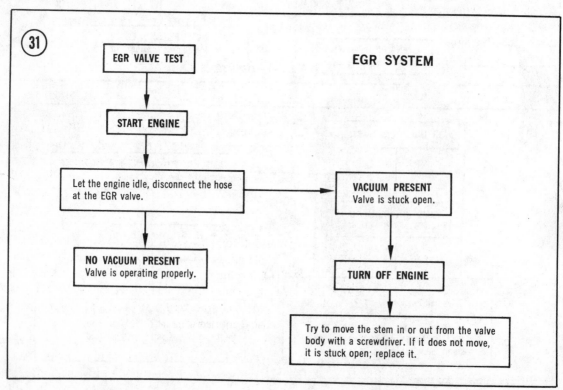

31

EGR VALVE TEST

EGR SYSTEM

START ENGINE

Let the engine idle, disconnect the hose at the EGR valve.

VACUUM PRESENT
Valve is stuck open.

NO VACUUM PRESENT
Valve is operating properly.

TURN OFF ENGINE

Try to move the stem in or out from the valve body with a screwdriver. If it does not move, it is stuck open; replace it.

sounds emanating from that area. The first time you do this, you may be horrified at the strange noises coming from even a normal engine. If you can, have an experienced friend or mechanic help you sort the noises out.

Clicking or Tapping Noises

Clicking or tapping noises usually come from the valve train, and indicate excessive valve clearance.

If your vehicle has adjustable valves, the procedure for adjusting the valve clearance is explained in Chapter Three. If your vehicle has hydraulic lifters, the clearance may not be adjustable. The noise may be coming from a collapsed lifter. These may be cleaned or replaced as described in the engine chapter.

A sticking valve may also sound like a valve with excessive clearance. In addition, excessive wear in valve train components can cause similar engine noises.

Knocking Noises

A heavy, dull knocking is usually caused by a worn main bearing. The noise is loudest when the engine is working hard, i.e., accelerating hard at low speed. You may be able to isolate the trouble to a single bearing by disconnecting

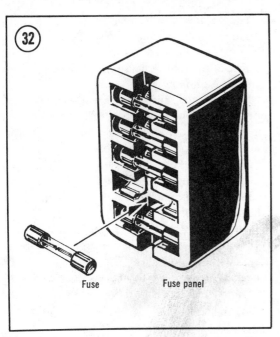

Fuse   Fuse panel

the spark plugs one at a time. When you reach the spark plug nearest the bearing, the knock will be reduced or disappear.

Worn connecting rod bearings may also produce a knock, but the sound is usually more "metallic." As with a main bearing, the noise is worse when accelerating. It may even increase further just as you go from accelerating to coasting. Disconnecting spark plugs will help isolate this knock as well.

A double knock or clicking usually indicates a worn piston pin. Disconnecting spark plugs will isolate this to a particular piston, however, the noise will *increase* when you reach the affected piston.

A loose flywheel and excessive crankshaft end play also produce knocking noises. While similar to main bearing noises, these are usually intermittent, not constant, and they do not change when spark plugs are disconnected.

Some mechanics confuse piston pin noise with piston slap. The double knock will distinguish the piston pin noise. Piston slap is identified by the fact that it is always louder when the engine is cold.

ELECTRICAL ACCESSORIES

Lights and Switches (Interior and Exterior)

1. *Bulb does not light* — Remove the bulb and check for a broken element. Also check the inside of the socket; make sure the contacts are clean and free of corrosion. If the bulb and socket are OK, check to see if a fuse has blown or a circuit breaker has tripped. The fuse panel (**Figure 32**) is usually located under the instrument panel. Replace the blown fuse or reset the circuit breaker. If the fuse blows or the breaker trips again, there is a short in that circuit. Check that circuit all the way to the battery. Look for worn wire insulation or burned wires.

If all the above are all right, check the switch controlling the bulb for continuity with an ohmmeter at the switch terminals. Check the switch contact terminals for loose or dirty electrical connections.

2. *Headlights work but will not switch from either high or low beam* — Check the beam selector switch for continuity with an ohmmeter

at the switch terminals. Check the switch contact terminals for loose or dirty electrical connections.

3. *Brake light switch inoperative* — On mechanically operated switches, usually mounted near the brake pedal arm, adjust the switch to achieve correct mechanical operation. Check the switch for continuity with an ohmmeter at the switch terminals. Check the switch contact terminals for loose or dirty electrical connections.

4. *Back-up lights do not operate* — Check light bulb as described earlier. Locate the switch, normally located near the shift lever. Adjust switch to achieve correct mechanical operation. Check the switch for continuity with an ohmmeter at the switch terminals. Bypass the switch with a jumper wire; if the lights work, replace the switch.

Directional Signals

1. *Directional signals do not operate* — If the indicator light on the instrument panel burns steadily instead of flashing, this usually indicates that one of the exterior lights is burned out. Check all lamps that normally flash. If all are all right, the flasher unit may be defective. Replace it with a good one.

2. *Directional signal indicator light on instrument panel does not light up* — Check the light bulbs as described earlier. Check all electrical connections and check the flasher unit.

3. *Directional signals will not self-cancel* — Check the self-cancelling mechanism located inside the steering column.

4. *Directional signals flash slowly* — Check the condition of the battery and the alternator (or generator) drive belt tension (**Figure 4**). Check the flasher unit and all related electrical connections.

Windshield Wipers

1. *Wipers do not operate* — Check for a blown fuse or circuit breaker that has tripped; replace or reset. Check all related terminals for loose or dirty electrical connections. Check continuity of the control switch with an ohmmeter at the switch terminals. Check the linkage and arms for loose, broken, or binding parts. Straighten out or replace where necessary.

2. *Wiper motor hums but will not operate* — The motor may be shorted out internally; check and/or replace the motor. Also check for broken or binding linkage and arms.

3. *Wiper arms will not return to the stowed position when turned off* — The motor has a special internal switch for this purpose. Have it inspected by your dealer. Do not attempt this yourself.

Interior Heater

1. *Heater fan does not operate* — Check for a blown fuse or circuit breaker that has tripped. Check the switch for continuity with an ohmmeter at the switch terminals. Check the switch contact terminals for loose or dirty electrical connections.

2. *Heat output is insufficient* — Check the heater hose/engine coolant control valve usually located in the engine compartment; make sure it is in the open position. Ensure that the heater door(s) and cable(s) are operating correctly and are in the open position. Inspect the heat ducts; make sure that they are not crimped or blocked.

COOLING SYSTEM

The temperature gauge or warning light usually signals cooling system troubles before there is any damage. As long as you stop the vehicle at the first indication of trouble, serious damage is unlikely.

In most cases, the trouble will be obvious as soon as you open the hood. If there is coolant or steam leaking, look for a defective radiator, radiator hose, or heater hose. If there is no evidence of leakage, make sure that the fan belt is in good condition. If the trouble is not obvious, refer to **Figures 33 and 34** to help isolate the trouble.

Automotive cooling systems operate under pressure to permit higher operating temperatures without boil-over. The system should be checked periodically to make sure it can withstand normal pressure. **Figure 35** shows the equipment which nearly any service station has for testing the system pressure.

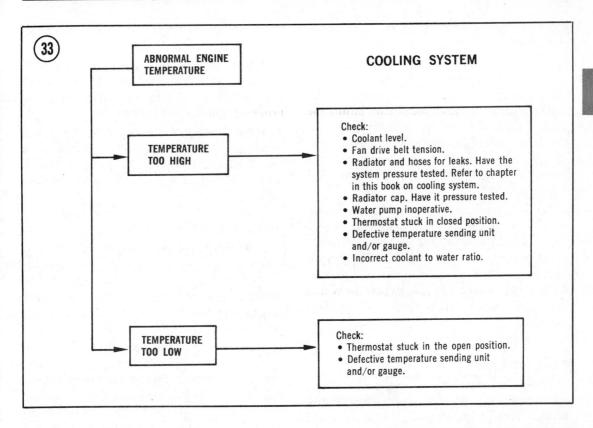

③③ ABNORMAL ENGINE TEMPERATURE — COOLING SYSTEM

TEMPERATURE TOO HIGH

Check:
- Coolant level.
- Fan drive belt tension.
- Radiator and hoses for leaks. Have the system pressure tested. Refer to chapter in this book on cooling system.
- Radiator cap. Have it pressure tested.
- Water pump inoperative.
- Thermostat stuck in closed position.
- Defective temperature sending unit and/or gauge.
- Incorrect coolant to water ratio.

TEMPERATURE TOO LOW

Check:
- Thermostat stuck in the open position.
- Defective temperature sending unit and/or gauge.

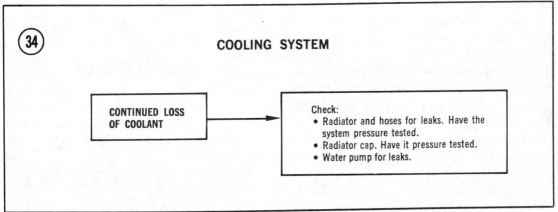

③④ COOLING SYSTEM

CONTINUED LOSS OF COOLANT

Check:
- Radiator and hoses for leaks. Have the system pressure tested.
- Radiator cap. Have it pressure tested.
- Water pump for leaks.

CLUTCH

All clutch troubles except adjustments require transmission removal to identify and cure the problem.

1. *Slippage* — This is most noticeable when accelerating in a high gear at relatively low speed. To check slippage, park the vehicle on a level surface with the handbrake set. Shift to 2nd gear and release the clutch as if driving off. If the clutch is good, the engine will slow and stall. If the clutch slips, continued engine speed will give it away.

Slippage results from insufficient clutch pedal free play, oil or grease on the clutch disc, worn pressure plate, or weak springs.

2. *Drag or failure to release* — This trouble usually causes difficult shifting and gear clash, especially when downshifting. The cause may be excessive clutch pedal free play, warped or bent pressure plate or clutch disc, broken or

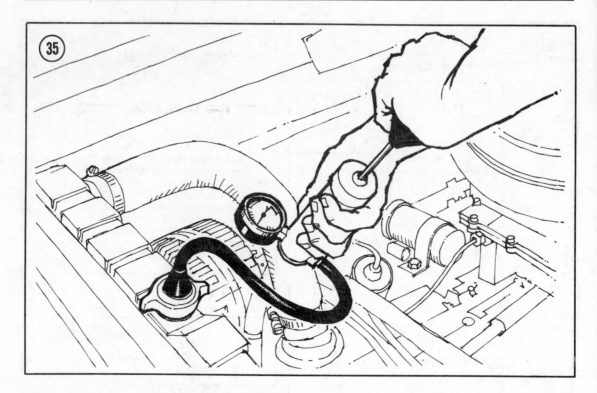

loose linings, or lack of lubrication in pilot bearing. Also check condition of transmission main shaft splines.

3. *Chatter or grabbing* — A number of things can cause this trouble. Check tightness of engine mounts and engine-to-transmission mounting bolts. Check for worn or misaligned pressure plate and misaligned release plate.

4. *Other noises* — Noise usually indicates a dry or defective release or pilot bearing. Check the bearings and replace if necessary. Also check all parts for misalignment and uneven wear.

MANUAL TRANSMISSION/TRANSAXLE

Transmission and transaxle troubles are evident when one or more of the following symptoms appear:

   a. Difficulty changing gears

   b. Gears clash when downshifting

   c. Slipping out of gear

   d. Excessive noise in NEUTRAL

   e. Excessive noise in gear

   f. Oil leaks

Transmission and transaxle repairs are not recommended unless the many special tools required are available.

Transmission and transaxle troubles are sometimes difficult to distinguish from clutch troubles. Eliminate the clutch as a source of trouble before installing a new or rebuilt transmission or transaxle.

AUTOMATIC TRANSMISSION

Most automatic transmission repairs require considerable specialized knowledge and tools. It is impractical for the home mechanic to invest in the tools, since they cost more than a properly rebuilt transmission.

Check fluid level and condition frequently to help prevent future problems. If the fluid is orange or black in color or smells like varnish, it is an indication of some type of damage or failure within the transmission. Have the transmission serviced by your dealer or competent automatic transmission service facility.

BRAKES

Good brakes are vital to the safe operation of the vehicle. Performing the maintenance speci-

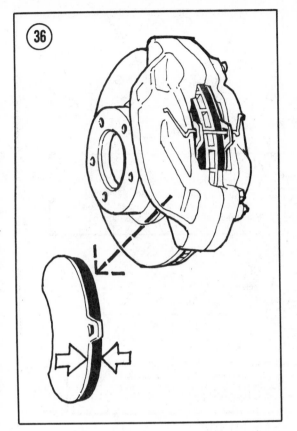

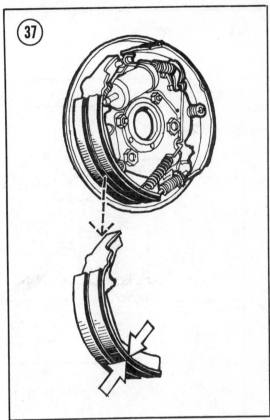

2

fied in Chapter Three will minimize problems with the brakes. Most importantly, check and maintain the level of fluid in the master cylinder, and check the thickness of the linings on the disc brake pads **(Figure 36)** or drum brake shoes **(Figure 37)**.

If trouble develops, **Figures 38 through 40** will help you locate the problem. Refer to the brake chapter for actual repair procedures.

STEERING AND SUSPENSION

Trouble in the suspension or steering is evident when the following occur:

a. Steering is hard
b. Car pulls to one side
c. Car wanders or front wheels wobble
d. Steering has excessive play
e. Tire wear is abnormal

Unusual steering, pulling, or wandering is usually caused by bent or otherwise misaligned suspension parts. This is difficult to check

without proper alignment equipment. Refer to the suspension chapter in this book for repairs that you can perform and those that must be left to a dealer or suspension specialist.

If your trouble seems to be excessive play, check wheel bearing adjustment first. This is the most frequent cause. Then check ball-joints (refer to Suspension chapter). Finally, check tie rod end ball-joints by shaking each tie rod. Also check steering gear, or rack-and-pinion assembly to see that it is securely bolted down.

TIRE WEAR ANALYSIS

Abnormal tire wear should be analyzed to determine its causes. The most common causes are the following:

a. Incorrect tire pressure
b. Improper driving
c. Overloading
d. Bad road surfaces
e. Incorrect wheel alignment

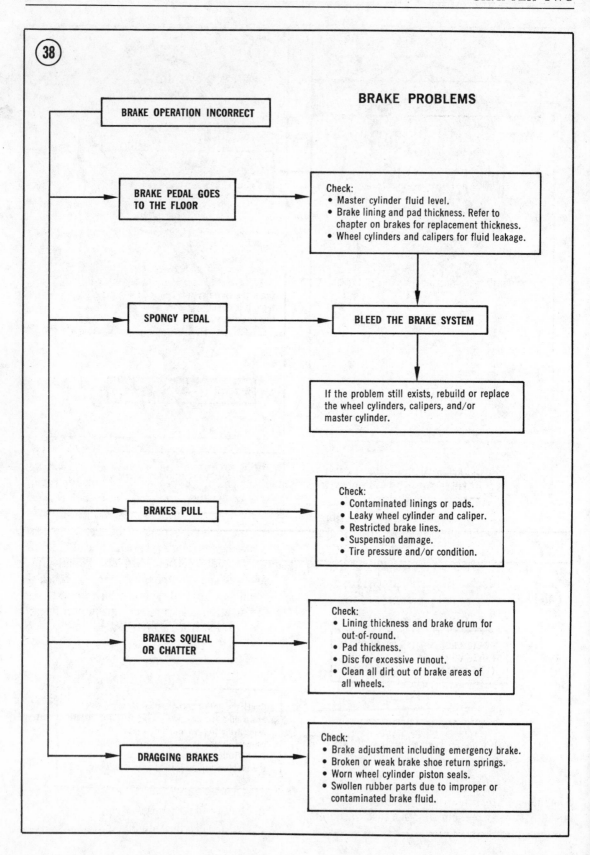

③⑧

BRAKE PROBLEMS

BRAKE OPERATION INCORRECT

BRAKE PEDAL GOES
TO THE FLOOR

Check:
• Master cylinder fluid level.
• Brake lining and pad thickness. Refer to
  chapter on brakes for replacement thickness.
• Wheel cylinders and calipers for fluid leakage.

SPONGY PEDAL

BLEED THE BRAKE SYSTEM

If the problem still exists, rebuild or replace
the wheel cylinders, calipers, and/or
master cylinder.

BRAKES PULL

Check:
• Contaminated linings or pads.
• Leaky wheel cylinder and caliper.
• Restricted brake lines.
• Suspension damage.
• Tire pressure and/or condition.

BRAKES SQUEAL
OR CHATTER

Check:
• Lining thickness and brake drum for
  out-of-round.
• Pad thickness.
• Disc for excessive runout.
• Clean all dirt out of brake areas of
  all wheels.

DRAGGING BRAKES

Check:
• Brake adjustment including emergency brake.
• Broken or weak brake shoe return springs.
• Worn wheel cylinder piston seals.
• Swollen rubber parts due to improper or
  contaminated brake fluid.

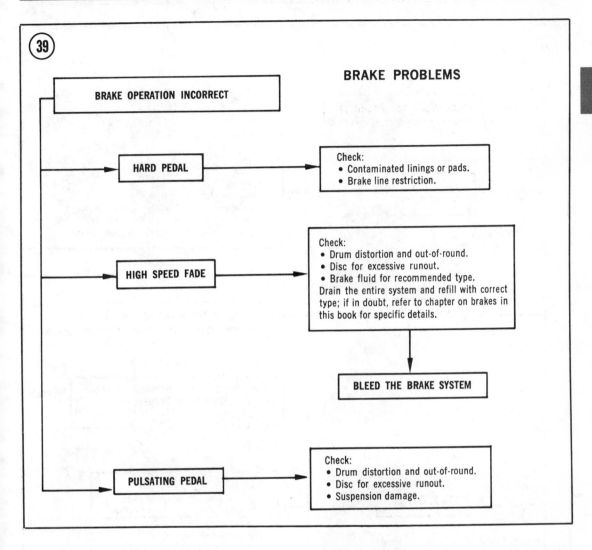

(39)

BRAKE PROBLEMS

BRAKE OPERATION INCORRECT

HARD PEDAL

Check:
• Contaminated linings or pads.
• Brake line restriction.

HIGH SPEED FADE

Check:
• Drum distortion and out-of-round.
• Disc for excessive runout.
• Brake fluid for recommended type.
Drain the entire system and refill with correct type; if in doubt, refer to chapter on brakes in this book for specific details.

BLEED THE BRAKE SYSTEM

PULSATING PEDAL

Check:
• Drum distortion and out-of-round.
• Disc for excessive runout.
• Suspension damage.

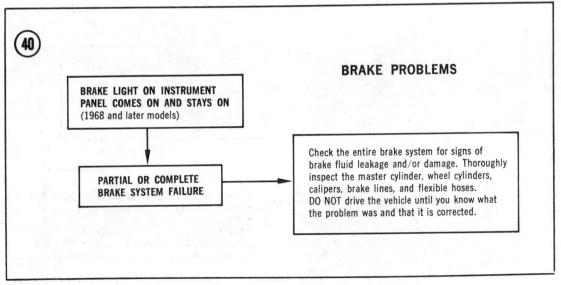

(40)

BRAKE PROBLEMS

BRAKE LIGHT ON INSTRUMENT PANEL COMES ON AND STAYS ON
(1968 and later models)

PARTIAL OR COMPLETE BRAKE SYSTEM FAILURE

Check the entire brake system for signs of brake fluid leakage and/or damage. Thoroughly inspect the master cylinder, wheel cylinders, calipers, brake lines, and flexible hoses.
DO NOT drive the vehicle until you know what the problem was and that it is corrected.

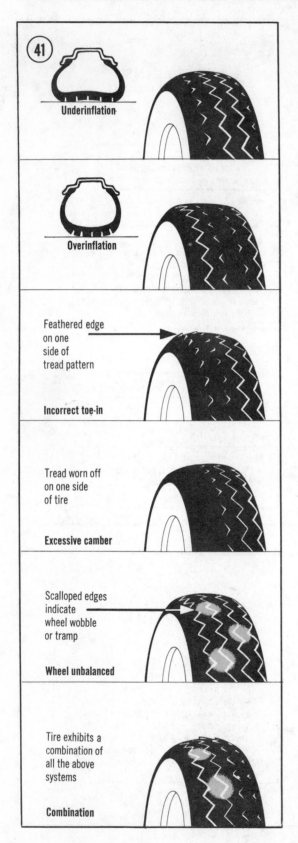

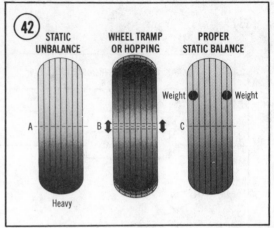

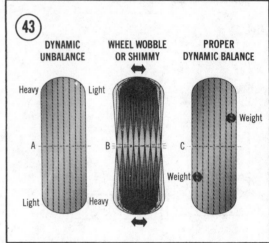

Figure 41 identifies wear patterns and indicates the most probable causes.

WHEEL BALANCING

All four wheels and tires must be in balance along two axes. To be in static balance (**Figure 42**), weight must be evenly distributed around the axis of rotation. (A) shows a statically unbalanced wheel; (B) shows the result — wheel tramp or hopping; (C) shows proper static balance.

To be in dynamic balance (**Figure 43**), the centerline of the weight must coincide with the centerline of the wheel. (A) shows a dynamically unbalanced wheel; (B) shows the result — wheel wobble or shimmy; (C) shows proper dynamic balance.

NOTE: If you own a 1980 or later model, first check the Supplement at the back of the book for any new service information.

3

CHAPTER THREE

LUBRICATION AND MAINTENANCE

To ensure good performance, dependability, and safety, regular preventive maintenance is essential. This chapter outlines periodic maintenance for a vehicle subjected to average use (a combination of urban and highway driving and light-duty off-road use). A vehicle that is driven extensively off-road or used primarily in stop-and-go traffic may require more frequent attention; but even without use, rust, dirt, and corrosion cause unnecessary damage if the vehicle is neglected. Whether maintenance is performed by the owner or a dealer, regular routine attention helps avoid expensive repairs.

ROUTINE CHECKS

The following simple checks should be performed at each fuel stop.

1. Check the engine oil level. The oil should be checked with the engine warm and the vehicle on level ground. The level should be between the 2 marks on the dipstick (**Figure 1**) — never below and never above. If necessary, add oil to bring the level above the lower mark.

Oil being added should be the same viscosity grade as the oil that is in the engine.

2. Check the battery electrolyte level. It should be even with the top of the vertical separators in the case (above the plates). Top up any cells that are low with distilled water; never add electrolyte to a battery that is in service.

3. Check the radiator coolant level. If the vehicle is fitted with a coolant recovery tank, the level should be at the half-full mark or somewhere between the full and low marks (**Figure 2**). On systems without a recovery tank, loosen the radiator cap to the first notch, using a shop rag folded in several thicknesses to protect your hand. Wait until you are certain the pressure in the system has been relieved, then unscrew the cap. The coolant level should be above the tubes in the top radiator tank. If the level is low, add water (or coolant if the vehicle is being operated in sustained low temperatures).

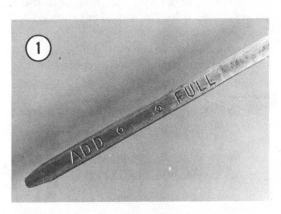

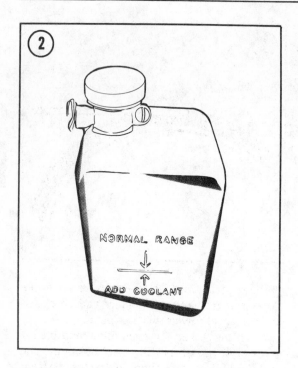

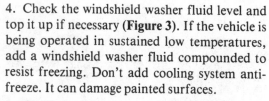

4. Check the windshield washer fluid level and top it up if necessary (**Figure 3**). If the vehicle is being operated in sustained low temperatures, add a windshield washer fluid compounded to resist freezing. Don't add cooling system anti-freeze. It can damage painted surfaces.

5. Check the tire pressures. Refer to **Table 1**.

> NOTE: *Tire pressures should be check-ed when the tires are cold — before the vehicle has been run. For this reason, it is a good idea to keep a tire pressure gauge in the glove compartment. If the tire pressure is checked when the tires are warm, it will be about 3 psi higher following a low-speed drive and about 7 psi higher following a high-speed drive.*

In addition to pressure, the condition of the tire tread and sidewalls should be checked for damage, cracking, and wear. Wear patterns are a good indicator of chassis and suspension alignment (see Chapter Two). If detected early, alignment can be corrected before the tires have worn severely. Checking tire condition is par-ticularly important following hard off-road usage. Pay particular attention to signs of severe rock damage usually evidenced by frac-tures and cuts in the tread and sidewalls. This type of damage presents an extreme driving

Table 1   TIRE PRESSURES

Tire Size and Type	Pressure*	
	Front	Rear
7.35 x 15 B-PT	30 psi	30 psi
7.75 x 15 B-PT	30 psi	30 psi
G-78 x 15 B-PT	30 psi	30 psi
8.25 x 15 B-PT	30 psi	30 psi
8.25 x 15 D-PT	30 psi	32 psi
9.15 x 15 B-PT	30 psi	30 psi
6.50 x 16 6PR-TT	35 psi	40 psi
PT—Passenger type tires B—Load range B		
TT—Truck type tires D—Load range D		

*The tire pressures shown are for original equipment tires. Be-cause of the wide variety of tire types and makes available for FWD, it is impractical to set down all of the tire pressures in this table. When buying tires other than original equipment sizes, check with the manufacturer for recommended pressures. In all cases, never exceed the maximum pressure embossed on the side of the tire.

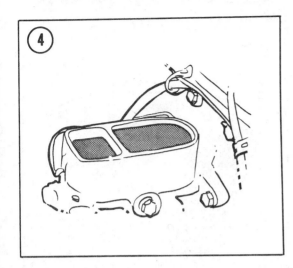

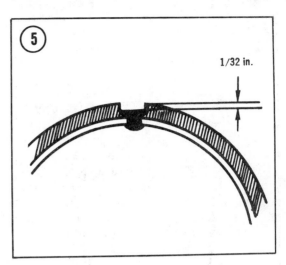

1/32 in.

3

hazard when the vehicle is operated at highway speeds. A damaged tire should be replaced as soon as it is detected.

NOTE
Some 1978-1979 F-100 and F-150 light trucks with 15 x 5.5 or 15 x 6 in. wheel assemblies may be equipped with steel wheels that were improperly manufactured. Return the vehicle to a dealer for inspection and correction, if not already done.

PERIODIC CHECKS AND INSPECTIONS

The following checks and inspections should be made at least once a month or at the intervals indicated. In addition, it is a good idea to perform these checks after the vehicle has been used off-road for an extended period of time.

Brake Fluid Level

Brake fluid level should be checked monthly as well as any time the pedal can be pushed within a couple of inches of the floor. The level should be $\frac{1}{4}$-$\frac{1}{2}$ in. below the top of the reservoir (**Figure 4**). If the level is lower than recommended, clean the area around the filler cap and remove it. Add brake fluid clearly marked SAE J1703, DOT 3, or DOT 4 only to bring the level up to that recommended. In some cases, where the level is extremely low, it may be necessary to bleed the brake hydraulic system as described in Chapter Nine. However, before

the system is filled and bled, refer to *Brake Lines and Hoses* in this chapter and check for and correct any leaks that are found.

When the system has been filled (and bled if necessary), install the filler cap and pump the brake pedal several times to restore system pressure.

Brake Adjustment

Most brakes are self-adjusting (refer to Chapter Nine).

Brake Lining Condition

Drum brake shoe linings should be checked for oil or grease on the friction material and measured to determine their serviceability every 6,000-10,000 miles or when long pedal travel indicates the likelihood of extreme wear. The brake shoe lining should be replaced when the lining has worn down to within $\frac{1}{32}$ in. of the rivet heads (**Figure 5**).

If the friction material is oily or greasy, the linings must be replaced no matter how much material remains.

Parking Brake Adjustment

Adjustment of parking brakes is covered in Chapter Nine.

Brake Lines and Hoses

Brake lines and hoses should be routinely checked for signs of deterioration, chafing, and kinks. This is particularly important following rough, off-road use where the likelihood of brush and rock damage is high. Any line that is less than perfect should be replaced immediately.

Check all the connections for tightness and look for signs of leakage which may indicate a cracked or otherwise unserviceable connection. As with lines and hoses, any connections that are less than perfect should be replaced.

When a line has been replaced, or in any situation where a brake line or hose has been disconnected, refer to Chapter Nine and fill and bleed the brake system.

Manual Transmission Oil Level

The transmission oil level must be checked with the vehicle sitting level. If you do not have access to a hydraulic hoist, a mechanic's "creeper" will be helpful to get beneath the vehicle.

Prior to checking the transmission oil level, the vehicle should be driven for several miles to warm up the oil. Then, unscrew the level plug on the transmission case (**Figure 6**). If the level is correct, a small amount of oil should seep out of the level hole. If necessary, carefully add fresh oil up to the bottom edge of the hole and install the fill/level plug and tighten it securely.

CAUTION
If the vehicle has been operated in deep water, pay particular attention to the condition of the oil. If water droplets are present, indicating that water has entered the transmission, change the oil immediately.

Automatic Transmission Oil Level

The transmission oil level must be checked with the vehicle sitting level and the engine and transmission warmed up to operating temperature. If the level is checked with the transmission cold the level will appear to be low.

1. Set the handbrake, select PARK with the transmission control lever, start the engine, and allow it to run for a couple of minutes to ensure that the fluid coupling is full of fluid. Shift the lever through all positions and return it to PARK.

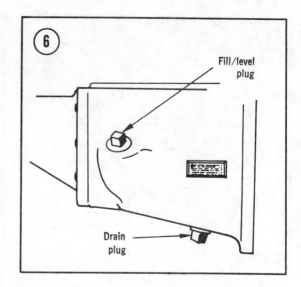

2. Wipe the transmission dipstick handle and filler tube clean with a dry rag. Withdraw the dipstick and wipe it with a clean lint-free cloth. *Do not use the rag that was used to clean the tube and handle.* Any contamination that might find its way into the transmission — even lint from a rag — could cause serious damage.

3. Insert the clean dipstick all the way into the filler tube and then withdraw it again and check the level. The level should be above the ADD mark on the dipstick (**Figure 7**). If the level is below the ADD mark, fresh Type F automatic transmission fluid must be added. Keep in mind that the distance between the marks on the dipstick represents considerably less than a quart. Use a clean funnel fitted with a fine-mesh filter to direct the fluid into the filler tube. Slowly add the fluid, with the engine running, a little at a time. Periodically recheck the level as described above while adding fluid.

If the fluid level is extremely low, foaming that is caused when the fluid pump draws air into the transmission may prevent an accurate reading on the dipstick. In this case, shut off the engine and allow several minutes for the foaming to subside. Then, add oil as described above — about ⅓ quart at a time — checking the level after each addition, until the level is correct. Then, hold the footbrake down and select each of the gear positions for several seconds to allow the servo pistons to fill. Recheck the level as described above and correct it once again if it is necessary.

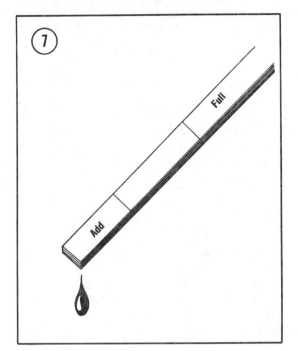

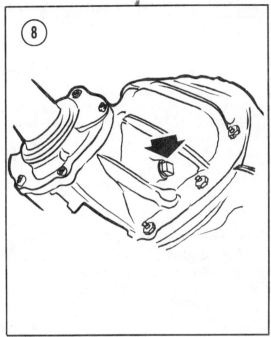

CAUTION
If the vehicle has been operated in deep water, pay particular attention to the condition of the oil. If water droplets are present, indicating that water has entered the transmission, change the oil immediately.

Axle Oil Level

The oil level in the axle differential should be checked and corrected if necessary every 6,000 miles of road use, every 1,000 miles of off-road use, and daily if the vehicle is operated in deep water. (In this instance, the check is essential to determine if water has entered the axle, in which case the contaminated oil must be drained and the axle filled with fresh oil.)

The vehicle must be sitting level when the axle oil level is checked. Wipe the area around the fill/level plug clean. Unscrew the fill/level plug from the differential case (**Figure 8**). If the level is correct, a small amount of oil will begin to seep out of the hole. If it does not, slowly add oil to correct the level. For standard differentials, add hypoid gear oil. For Ford Traction-Lok (limited-slip) differentials, add special hypoid gear oil clearly marked for use in limited-slip differentials.

When the level is correct, screw in and tighten the fill/level plug and wipe any excess oil from the outside of the differential case.

Intake/Exhaust Manifold Nuts and Bolts

The intake/exhaust manifold nuts and bolts should be checked for broken or missing lockwashers and for looseness. Nuts that are snug need be tightened no further, but loose nuts should be tightened to the appropriate torque shown in **Table 2**. Overtightening of nuts can cause studs to break or castings to crack, requiring expensive repairs.

Drive Belts

Check the alternator, water pump, fan, air pump, air conditioning, and steering and brake pump belts for fraying, glazing, or cracking of the contact surfaces. Belts that are damaged or deteriorated should be replaced before they fail and cause serious problems from engine overheating, electrical system failure, or reduction of steering and brake control. Belt replacement is described in Chapter Eight.

In addition to being in good condition, it is important that the drive belts be correctly adjusted. A belt that is too loose will cause the

Table 2   INTAKE AND EXHAUST MANIFOLD FASTENER TORQUE

Engine	Fastener	Torque (ft.-lb.)
170 cid 6, 1969-1972	Exhaust manifold to cylinder head	13–28
240 cid 6, 1970-1974	Exhaust manifold to cylinder head	23–28
240 cid 6, 1970-1971	Intake manifold to exhaust manifold	28–30
240 cid 6, 1972-1974	Intake manifold to exhaust manifold	28–33
300 cid 6, 1970	Exhaust manifold to cylinder head	20–25
300 cid 6, 1970-1971	Intake manifold to exhaust manifold	28–30
300 cid 6, 1971-1975	Exhaust manifold to cylinder head	23–28
300 cid 6, 1972-1975	Intake manifold to exhaust manifold	28–33
300 cid, 1976	Exhaust manifold to cylinder head	23–28
300 cid, 1976	Intake manifold to cylinder head	28–33
300 cid, 1977-1979	Exhaust manifold to cylinder head	28–33
300 cid, 1977-1979	Intake manifold to cylinder head	22–32
302 cid V8, 1969-1974	Exhaust manifold to cylinder head	12–16
302 cid V8, 1975	Exhaust manifold to cylinder head	18–24
302 cid V8, 1969-1975	Intake manifold to cylinder head	23–25
302/351W cid, 1976-1979	Exhaust manifold to cylinder head	18-24
302/351W cid, 1976	Intake manifold to cylinder head	23-25
302/351W cid, 1977-1979	Intake manifold to cylinder head, $\frac{3}{8}$ in.	22-32
302/351W cid, 1977-1979	Intake manifold to cylinder head, $\frac{5}{16}$ in.	17-25
360/390 cid V8, 1969-1975	Exhaust manifold to cylinder head	12-18
360/390 cid V8, 1969-1972	Intake manifold to cylinder head	32-35
360/390 cid V8, 1973-1975	Intake manifold to cylinder head	40-50
360/390, 1976	Exhaust manifold to cylinder head	12-18
360/390, 1976	Intake manifold to cylinder head	40-45
351M/400 cid, 1977-1979	Exhaust manifold to cylinder head	18-24
351M/400 cid, 1977-1979	Intake manifold to cylinder head, $\frac{3}{8}$ in.	22-32
351M/400 cid, 1977-1979	Intake manifold to cylinder head, $\frac{5}{16}$ in.	17-25
460 cid, 1976-1979	Exhaust manifold to cylinder head	28-33
460 cid, 1976-1979	Intake manifold to cylinder head	22-32

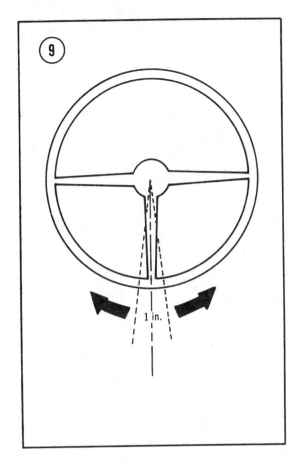

driven components to operate at less than optimum. A belt that is adjusted too tightly will wear rapidly and place unnecessary side loads on the bearings of the driven components, possibly resulting in their premature wear or failure. See Chapter Eight for drive belt adjustment.

Vacuum Fittings and Hoses

Check the vacuum fittings and connection to make sure they are tight, and inspect the hoses for cracking, kinking, or deterioration. Any damaged or deteriorated lines should be replaced.

Coolant Condition

Remove the radiator cap and check the condition of the coolant. If it is dirty, drain and flush the radiator and cooling system and fill it with fresh coolant as described in Chapter Eight. In any case, the coolant should be changed every 24 months regardless of condition or mileage.

Coolant Hoses

Inspect the heater and radiator hoses. Replace any that are cracked, deteriorated, extremely soft, or extremely hard. Make sure the hoses are correctly routed and installed and that all the clamps are tight.

Radiator

Check the radiator for leaks and damage. Blow bugs and dirt out of the fins, from the rear of the radiator, with compressed air. Have a service station pressure test the radiator cap. This is a simple test that takes only a few minutes (see Chapter Eight) with the test equipment on hand at most stations. The cap should maintain pressure and the relief valve remain closed to 13 psi.

The radiator should also be pressure tested, as described in Chapter Eight.

Wheel Alignment

Wheel alignment should be checked periodically by a dealer or an alignment specialist. Misalignment is usually indicated first by incorrect tire wear. See *Tire Wear Analysis* (Chapter Two). Wheel alignment specifications are provided in Chapter Eleven.

Steering

1. With the vehicle on level ground, and with the front wheels lined up straight ahead, grasp the steering wheel and turn it from right to left and check for rotation free play. The free play should not be greater than about one inch (**Figure 9**). If it is, the front wheel bearings should be checked for condition and adjustment (see Chapter Eleven), and the kingpins, steering linkage, and steering arm should be checked as possible causes of excessive play. These checks should be referred to a dealer.

2. Try to move the steering wheel in and out and check for axial play. If any play is felt, check the tightness of the steering wheel center nut.

3. Attempt to move the steering wheel from side to side without turning it. Movement is an indication of loose steering column mounting bolts or worn column bushings. Check and

tighten the mounting bolts if necessary, and if the movement is still present, the vehicle should be referred to a dealer or front end specialist for corrective service.

Power Steering Fluid Level

The power steering fluid level must be checked with the engine and fluid warmed up to operating temperature.

1. Turn the steering wheel to right and left lock several times and then turn the wheels straight ahead. Shut off the engine.

2. Remove the dipstick from the pump reservoir, wipe it clean with a lint-free cloth, reinsert it all the way into the tube, and withdraw it. The fluid level should be between the cross-hatching at the bottom of the stick and the FULL mark (**Figure 10**). If it is not, carefully add power steering fluid (E5W-M2C128-C) and re-check the level. Do not overfill the reservoir. If the level after filling is above the FULL mark, fluid must be siphoned off until the level is correct.

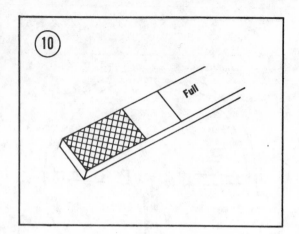

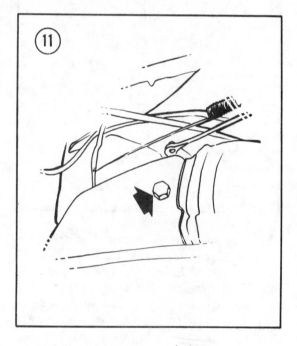

LUBRICATION

Strict adherence to a detailed lubrication schedule is at least as important as timely preventive maintenance. The recommended lubrication schedule (in this chapter) is based on average vehicle use — a combination of highway and urban driving with some light-duty off-road use, in moderate weather and climate. Abnormal use, such as mostly off-road use, in dusty and dirty conditions, or in extremely hot or cold climates, requires that the lubrication schedule be modified so that the lubricants are checked and changed more frequently.

Acids that form in the engine, transmission, and differential oil during short-haul driving, or during operation in extremely cold climates, are injurious to moving parts and will wear out parts as quickly as dirty lubricants.

Engine Oil and Filter Change

For average use, the engine oil and filter should be changed at the intervals shown in the maintenance tables at the end of this chapter. If driving is primarily short distances and in stop-and-go traffic, or if the vehicle is used mostly off-road, the oil and filter should be changed twice as often as for average use. If the vehicle is driven only a few hundred miles each month, the oil and filter should be changed every 6-8 weeks. If the vehicle is driven for long periods in extremely cold climate, where the temperature is frequently below 10°F, the oil and filter should be changed twice as often as for average use.

Recommended oil grades are shown in **Table 3**. Use only a detergent oil with an API rating of SE or SD. These quality ratings are stamped on the top of the can.

Table 3 RECOMMENDED OIL GRADES

Consistent Temperature	Oil Grade
Multigrade oils	
Below 32°F	SAE 5W-30*
—10°F to +90°F	SAE 10W-30, SAE 10W-40
Above +10°F	SAE 20W-40
Monograde oils	
—10°F to 32°F	SAE 10W
10°F to 60°F	SAE 20W, SAE 20
32°F to 90°F	SAE 30
Above 60°F	SAE 40

*If the vehicle is being operated at sustained highway speeds, the next heavier grade of oil should be used.

Table 4 ENGINE OIL CAPACITY

Engine	Capacity*
170 cid 6-cyl.	6 qt.
240 and 300 cid 6-cyl.	5 qt.
All V-8 engines	5 qt.
*Add 1 qt. with filter change.	

Try always to use the same brand of oil. If the oil you select to use is not from one of the major oil companies, it may not always be available when you are traveling and when you are operating the vehicle for extended periods off-road. For these reasons, then, it is a good idea to carry a couple quarts of oil in the vehicle.

The use of oil additives is not necessary nor is it recommended.

1. Before draining the old oil, thoroughly warm up the engine so the oil will drain freely. Place a drip pan beneath the engine and unscrew the drain plug (**Figure 11**). Allow 10-15 minutes for the oil to completely drain and reinstall the drain plug.

2. On a vehicle equipped with an oil cooler, relocate the drip pan beneath the cooler, remove the drain plug, and allow an additional 5 minutes for draining. Then reinstall drain plug.

NOTE: *Not all coolers are equipped with a drain plug. If not, it will be necessary to disconnect the bottom cooler hose and direct it into the drip pan. When the oil has ceased to drain, be sure to install the hose correctly and tighten the clamp or the union.*

3. Relocate the drip pan beneath the oil filter, unscrew the filter, and allow about 5 minutes for the oil to drain. Discard the filter. When the oil has ceased to drain, thoroughly clean the filter mounting flange with solvent and wipe it dry with a clean cloth. Lightly coat the sealing ring of the new filter with fresh oil and screw the filter onto the block. When it contacts with the sealing flange, tighten it ¼ turn by hand.

4. Fill engine with the correct grade (**Table 3**) and amount (**Table 4**) of fresh oil and install the oil filler cap.

5. Start the engine and allow it to idle for several minutes to ensure that the oil has had a chance to circulate throughout the system. On some vehicles, the oil pressure warning light may remain on for several seconds after the engine is first started; this is normal. While the engine is running, check the drain plugs and the filter for leaks and correct them if necessary. Then, shut off the engine and check the oil level with the dipstick. If necessary, add oil to correct level.

Manual Transmission Oil Change

Procedures for checking the oil (fluid) level in both manual and automatic transmissions are presented earlier in this chapter. Oil changes in both transmission types are recommended at the intervals shown in maintenance tables at the end of this chapter (with normal use). If the vehicle is driven only a few hundred miles each month, the oil should be changed more frequently, as is the case if the vehicle is operated in extremely cold climate where the temperture is frequently below 10°F. Acids that form in the transmission during short-haul driving or during operation in extremely cold climates are injurious to moving parts. Also, the oil should be changed if water has entered the transmission.

Prior to draining the transmission, drive the vehicle for several miles to warm the oil so that it will flow freely. Remove the fill/level plug. Place a drip pan beneath the transmission and unscrew the drain plug (**Figure 12**). Allow the oil to drain for 10-15 minutes. Clean the drain plug and install it. Tighten the plug firmly but be careful not to overtighten it and risk stripping the threads on the transmission housing.

Refer to **Table 5** and fill the transmission with the correct amount and grade of oil. The transmission oil level is correct when oil just begins to seep out of the fill/level hole. Screw in and tighten the fill/level plug taking care not to overtighten, and wipe excess oil from the outside of the transmission. Check to make sure the drain plug does not leak.

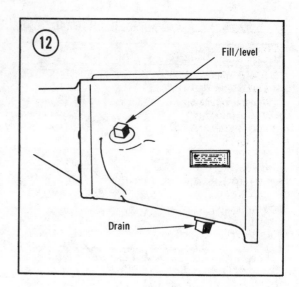

Automatic Transmission Fluid Change

Prior to draining the transmission, drive the vehicle for several miles to warm up the fluid so it will drain freely. The vehicle must sit level during draining and filling. If a hoist or a pit is not available, a mechanic's "creeper" will be helpful for working beneath the vehicle. See **Table 5** for fluid types.

C4 or MX-HD Transmission

1. Place a drip pan beneath the transmission and disconnect the bottom end of the filler tube from the transmission and allow fluid to drain.

2. When the draining is complete, unscrew the bolts which attach the pan to the transmission and remove the pan and the gasket.

3. Thoroughly clean the pan and the screen and blow them dry with compressed air. It may be necessary to remove bits of gasket from the pan and transmission sealing surfaces; use a soft scraper and take care not to damage the sealing surfaces.

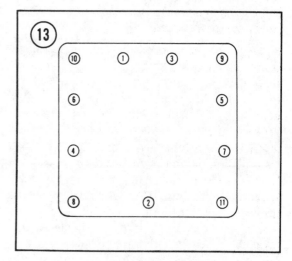

4. Install the pan using a *new gasket*. Screw in and tighten the bolts in a crisscross pattern (**Figure 13**). Reconnect the bottom of the filler tube to the pan, making sure the connection is clean and tight.

5. Using a clean funnel with a fine-mesh filter, pour 3 quarts of fresh automatic transmission fluid (**Table 5**) into the transmission through the filler pipe. Start the engine and allow it to idle for 2 minutes with the gear selector in the P position. Increase the engine speed to a fast

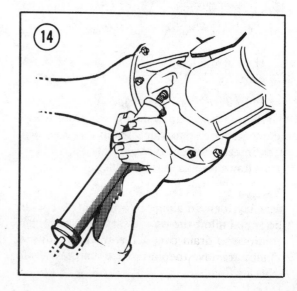

Table 5 TRANSMISSION OIL

Transmission	Oil Grade	Capacity
3-speed manual	Standard transmission lubricant	3.5 pt.
4-speed New Process 435		
Without extension	SAE 50 engine oil	6.5 pt.
With extension	SAE 50 engine oil	7.0 pt.
4-speed Warner T-19	SAE 50 engine oil	7.0 pt.
C4 automatic		
300 cid engine	ATF Type F	20.0 pt.
302 cid engine	ATF Type F	17.5 pt.
351, 400 and 460		
cid engines	ATF Type F	24.5 pt.
C6 automatic		
1969-1977	ATF Type F	25.5 pt.
1978-on	DEXRON II or Type CJ ATF	25.5 pt.

3

idle (no more than about 1,200 rpm) and allow the engine and transmission to reach normal operating temperature.

6. With the handbrake set and the service brake depressed, slowly move the selector through all the gear positions. Return the selector to P and recheck the fluid level. If necessary, add fluid to bring the level midway between the ADD and FULL marks on the dipstick. Remember, do *not* overfill the transmission; too much fluid is harmful. If the level is above the maximum mark on the dipstick, sufficient fluid must be drained to correct the level.

7. When the fluid level is correct, check for and correct any leaks at the filler tube connection and around the edge of the pan. Then road test the vehicle to ensure the transmission operates correctly. After the vehicle has been driven about 125 miles, check the level once again and correct it if necessary.

C6 Transmission

1. Place a drip pan beneath the transmission and loosen the bolts which attach the pan to the transmission several turns. Allow the fluid to drain down level to the pan flange.

2. Beginning at the rear of the flange and working forward along both sides, remove the bolts and allow the pan to tilt so the fluid will continue to drain over the rear of the flange. Finally, remove the pan and pour out the remaining fluid.

3. Refer to Steps 3 through 7 for the C4 and MX-HD transmissions and clean, reassemble, and fill the transmission.

Axle Oil Changing

Prior to draining the oil from the differential, drive the vehicle for several miles to warm up the oil so it will flow freely. With the vehicle sitting level, wipe the area around the fill/level plug clean and unscrew the plug. Remove the old oil with a suction pump (**Figure 14**). If a suction pump is not available, place a drip pan beneath the differential and unscrew the rear cover bolts several turns. With a mallet, tap around the edge of the cover to break it loose so it can be pulled out far enough to allow the oil to drain. Be careful not to damage the cover gasket. (If the gasket is damaged, the cover must be removed and a new gasket installed.)

When the oil has ceased to drain, tighten the cover bolts in a crisscross pattern.

Refer to *Axle Oil Level*, earlier in this chapter and fill the differential with the appropriate type of hypoid gear lubricant until the oil level reaches the bottom of the fill/level hole and just begins to seep out. Then install the fill/level plug and tighten it securely. Wipe any spilled oil from the differential housing.

After the vehicle has been driven for about 100 miles, check for and correct any leaks around the edge of the cover, particularly in the area of the bottom bolt. If leakage is found, recheck and correct the oil level after the leak has been corrected.

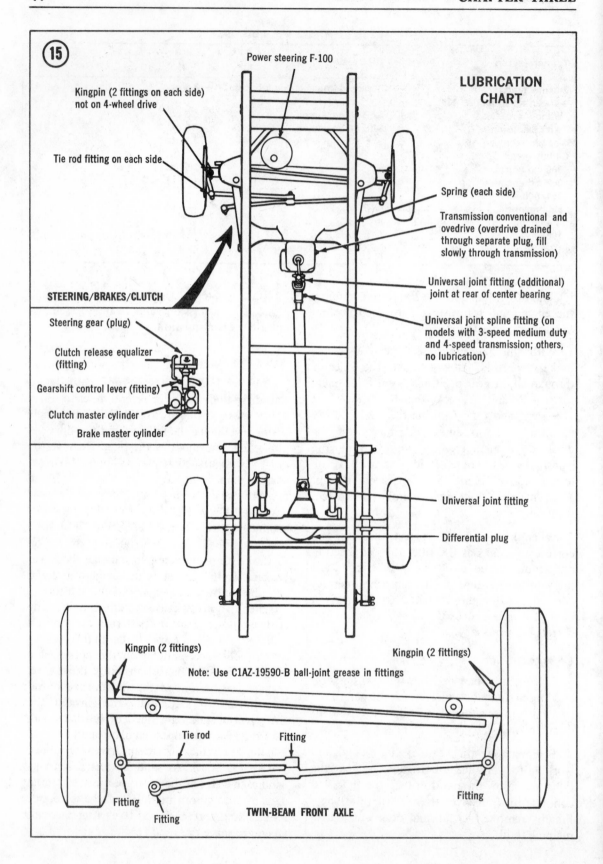

⑮

Power steering F-100

LUBRICATION CHART

Kingpin (2 fittings on each side) not on 4-wheel drive

Tie rod fitting on each side

Spring (each side)

Transmission conventional and ovedrive (overdrive drained through separate plug, fill slowly through transmission)

Universal joint fitting (additional) joint at rear of center bearing

Universal joint spline fitting (on models with 3-speed medium duty and 4-speed transmission; others, no lubrication)

STEERING/BRAKES/CLUTCH

Steering gear (plug)

Clutch release equalizer (fitting)

Gearshift control lever (fitting)

Clutch master cylinder

Brake master cylinder

Universal joint fitting

Differential plug

Kingpin (2 fittings)

Kingpin (2 fittings)

Note: Use C1AZ-19590-B ball-joint grease in fittings

Tie rod

Fitting

Fitting

Fitting

Fitting

Fitting

TWIN-BEAM FRONT AXLE

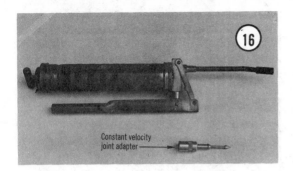

Constant velocity
joint adapter

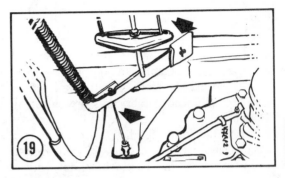

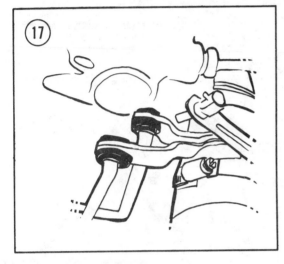

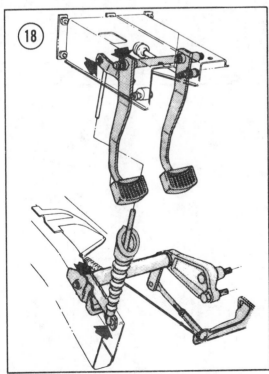

3

Chassis Lubrication

Complete chassis lubrication should be performed at the intervals shown in the maintenance tables at the end of this chapter. For extensive off-road use, the interval should be every 1,000 miles, and if the vehicle is operated in deep water, chassis lubrication should be attended to daily.

Lubrication points and fittings are shown in **Figure 15**. Recommended lubricants are shown in **Table 6** along with Ford part numbers. If Ford-marketed lubricants are not available, equivalent lubricants available through most major oil companies can be substituted. However, make sure the oil dealer knows the specific application so that he can recommend a suitable substitute.

A simple hand-operated grease gun like the one shown in **Figure 16** is a worthwhile investment, particularly if the vehicle is used extensively off-road and in mud, snow, and water.

The chassis lubricant shown in **Table 6** is recommended for ambient temperatures that are consistently above 10°F. For operation in temperatures consistently below 10°F, Ford calcium soap grease is recommended for lube fittings.

Do not overlook items such as gear selector linkage (**Figure 17**), clutch linkage (**Figure 18**), parking brake linkage (**Figure 19**), speedometer cable, clutch release equalizer (**Figure 20**), and the steering gearbox. Lack of lubrication on these items will make control operation difficult in addition to causing premature wear. However, lubricants should be used sparingly and excess oil should be wiped away to prevent it from attracting dirt which will also accelerate wear. Recommended lubricants for the points mentioned are shown in **Table 6**.

Body Lubrication

All hinges, latches, and front seat tracks should be lubricated at the intervals shown in the maintenance tables at the end of this chapter to ensure smooth operation and reduce wear. Recommended lubricants are shown in **Table 6**.

Apply lubricant sparingly, operating the mechanism several times to aid penetration. Then, wipe off the excess lubricant with a clean, dry cloth to prevent it from attracting dirt and from soiling clothes, carpet, or upholstery.

Steering Gear Oil

The oil level in the steering gear should be checked at the intervals shown in the maintenance tables found at the end of this chapter and corrected if necessary.

1. Unscrew the fill plug from the sector shaft cover (**Figure 21**). The lubricant should be visible in the fill plug opening.

2. If lubricant must be added, refer to **Table 6** and add sufficient lubricant to raise the level to about 1 inch from the top of the fill plug opening and install the fill plug.

MAINTENANCE SCHEDULES

Tables 7-9 provide maintenance recommendations and intervals for all vehicles covered in this book.

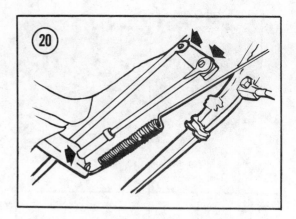

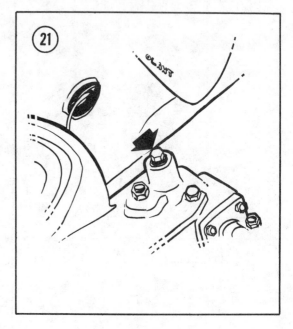

3

Table 6   RECOMMENDED LUBRICANTS

Item	Ford Part Name	Ford Part No.	Ford Specifications
Body hinges, latches, door striker plates and rotors, seat tracks, door checks	Polyethylene grease	C4AZ-19584-B	ESB-M1C106-B
Lock cylinders	Lock lubricant	B4A-19587-A	ESB-M2C20-A
Distributor bushing oil cup	Engine oil, SAE-10W	—	ESE-M2C35-A
Distributor cam	Distributor cam lubricant	C4AZ-19D530-A	ESF-M1C66-A
Front axle spindle pins, steering linkage, front and rear spring shackle pins, clutch linkage fittings, universal joints	Multi-purpose lubricant	C1AZ-19590-B	ESA-M1C75-B
Steering gear	Steering gear lubricant	C3AZ-19578-A	ESW-M1C87-A
Hydraulic clutch master cylinder/brake master cylinder	Extra heavy-duty brake fluid	C6AZ-19542-A or B	ESA-M6C25-A
Spring leaves; transmission linkage pivots; accelerator ball sockets; brake and clutch pedal pivots and clevises; parking brake linkage; pivots, and clevises	Engine oil, SAE 10W	—	ESE-M2C35-A or ESE-M2C101-B
Engine oil	6,000-mile motor oil - MS sequence tested (Canadian - Long Life Super Premium motor oil)	C5AZ-19579-D, E, K, L, M, P, S CC5AZ-19579-A, G, ① CC7AZ-19579-A ①	ESE-M2C101-C
Front and rear wheel bearings (except rear wheel bearings on F-100)	Multi-purpose lubricant	C1AZ-19590-B	ESA-M1C75-B
Automatic transmissions, power steering reservoir (medium, heavy, extra heavy only)	Automatic transmission and power steering fluid	C4, MX-HD: C1AZ-19582-A, C or D C6: Type CJ	M2C33-F (Type F)
Power steering reservoir (light truck only)	Power steering fluid ②	D2AZ-19582-A	ESW-M2C128-A
	(continued)		

① Canadian number.
② If higher power steering efforts are encountered during operation of units below 0°F, flush and fill with low temperature fluid Ford Part No. CD3AZ-19582-A, Ford Spec. No. ESE-M2C140-A.

Table 6   RECOMMENDED LUBRICANTS (continued)

Item	Ford Part Name	Ford Part No.	Ford Specifications
Speedometer and tachometer cables	Speedometer cable lubricant	D2AZ-19581-A	ESF-M1C160-A
Carburetor oil bath air cleaner	Above 32°F - engine oil SAE 30 Below 32°F - engine oil SAE 20	—	ESE-M2C37-A ESE-M2C36-A
Engine oil filter	Autolite or Motorcraft long life oil filter	C1AZ-6731-A	ES-C8AF-6714-A or C
Accelerator linkage	SAE 10W oil	—	ESE-M2C35-A
Rear axle	Hypoid gear lubricant	C6AZ-19580-B	ESW-M2C105-A ③
Ford Traction-Lok axles	Hypoid gear lubricant	C9AZ-19580-A	ESW-M2C119-A
Manual shift transmissions (except Ford 3-speed)	Engine oil, SAE 50 - above 0°F Engine oil, SAE 30 - below 0°F	C6TZ-19C547-A	ESE-M2C39-C ESE-M2C37-C
Exhaust control valve	Rust penetrant and inhibitor	C0AZ-19A501-A (Canadian) C8BA-19579-B	ESR-M99C56-A
Ford 3-speed manual transmissions	Standard transmission lube	C3RZ-19C547-B	ESW-M2C83-B
Transmission remote gearshift levers	Multi-purpose lubricant	C1AZ-19590-B	ESA-M1C75-B
Drive shaft, universal joints, slip spline	Multi-purpose lubricant	C1AZ-19590-B	ESA-M1C75-B

③ For complete refill of Dana limited-slip rear axles, add 4 ounces EST-M2C118-A (friction modifier).

Table 7   NON-SCHEDULED MAINTENANCE — ALL YEARS

The following maintenance operations are not required at definite mileage or time intervals, but should be performed when needed. These services are not covered by the warranty.

Maintenance Operation	Frequency Observation
Clean body/door drain holes.	At least twice annually.
Check the battery and recharge if necessary (specific gravity falls below 1.230). Check connections for tightness. Clean corrosion from terminal and top of battery.	Starter turns engine slower than usual. Headlight brighter when engine is speeded up from idle.
Check headlamp alignment.	Light beam appears too high or too low while driving with a normal load.
Adjust the parking brake.	Parking brake does not hold the vehicle on a reasonable grade.
Adjust automatic transmission neutral switch.	Starter will not engage with shift selector in N (neutral) or P (park); or back-up light does not operate.
Lubricate door and tailgate hinges and checks.	Doors or tailgate bind during opening or closing, or noisy operation.
Check tires, wheel balance and front wheel toe. (Caster and camber are preset at the factory and are not adjustable.)	Poor handling characteristics and/or abnormal tire wear are experienced.
Remove excess mud build-up from wheels, undercarriage and steering linkage. Inspect for and correct any bent or damaged components.	At frequent intervals when operating off-highway or if front wheel shimmy is experienced.
Check windshield washer fluid level — add fluid if required.	If washers do not spray fluid when operated.
Check alternator and regulator output.	Slow engine cranking, hard steering, headlights dim at engine idle speed, early or repeat electrical component failures.
Check operation of lights, horn, turn signals, windshield wipers and washers, instruments, vent system, heater and accessories.	As required.
Check brake warning light operation.	At engine start-up.
Check operation of the clutch.	As required.
Check engine oil level.	As required — at each fuel stop.
Lubricate door locks, door latches, and hood latch.	Difficult to operate or noisy.

(continued)

Table 7   NON-SCHEDULED MAINTENANCE — ALL YEARS   (continued)

Maintenance Operation	Frequency Observation
Adjust steering gear preload, steering linkage or front wheel bearings. Check suspension and frame for loose attachments.	Excessive steering wheel play, loose steering system or front wheel shimmy.
Check wheel nut torque.	Within 500 miles after new vehicle delivery or wheel removal.
Lubricate automatic transmission kick-down linkage.	Abnormal accelerator pressure needed for forced downshift.
Check the drive shaft.	At frequent intervals when operating off-highway.
Lubricate clutch and transmission linkage. To avoid attracting dust or grit to the lube points, do not overlubricate.	Linkage action is sluggish.
Lubricate accelerator linkage lightly with the specified lubricant.	Accelerator linkage is sluggish.
Replace windshield wiper blades.	Wiper blades do not clean windshield after windshield and blades have been properly cleaned.
Check the spring leaves for being evenly stacked and the spring clips or U-bolts, rear spring front eye bolt and shackle bolts for being tight.	While the vehicle is hoisted for lubrication.
Inspect and rotate tires and check tire pressures.	Poor handling characteristics and/or abnormal tire wear are experienced.
Check and adjust transmission controls and shift operation.	When hard shifting is encountered.
Tighten frame mounted fuel tank strap bolts.	Driving conditions or inspection indicates looseness.
Check for fuel, coolant, oil or other fluid leaks.	At frequent intervals.
Check seat and shoulder belt buckles, release mechanisms and belt webbing.	As required.
Inspect the seat back latches for proper operation.	As required.
Inspect the exhaust system for broken, damaged, or missing parts.	Excessive noise or smell of fumes is experienced.
Flush and inspect complete underside of the vehicle.	At least once annually.
Adjust the service brakes.	Unusual sounds when braking, increased brake pedal travel or repeated pulling to one side.

Table 8   SCHEDULED MAINTENANCE — 1969-1971

Maintenance Operation	Service Interval							
Number of months or thousands of miles, whichever comes first.	6	12	18	24	30	36	42	48
Engine								
Change engine oil and filter. ①	X	X	X	X	X	X	X	X
Clean and refill oil bath air cleaner (if so equipped). ①	X	X	X	X	X	X	X	X
Replace dry-type air cleaner filter (6-cylinder). ①		X		X		X		X
Replace dry-type air cleaner filter (8-cylinder). ①				X				X
Test crankcase emission system. Clean system and replace emission control valve if required. ③	X	X	X	X	X	X	X	X
Clean crankcase emission system hoses, tubes, fittings, carburetor spacer and replace if necessary. Replace emission control valve.		X		X		X		X
Clean crankcase filler breather cap. ①	X	X	X	X	X	X	X	X
Replace fuel system filter (gas engine).				X				X
Inspect thermactor exhaust emission control system hoses and replace if required (on trucks so equipped).		X		X		X		X
Drain, flush and refill cooling system. ②								
Check and lubricate exhaust control valve. Free up if necessary. (If so equipped).	X	X	X	X	X	X	X	X
Clean and adjust distributor points — replace as required. (Clean distributor cap).		X		X		X		X
Check and adjust carburetor — idle speed and fuel mixture.		X		X		X		X
Check and clean external choke mechanism.		X		X		X		X
Check and adjust ignition timing — initial timing, mechanical and vacuum advances, and vacuum retard (if so equipped).		X		X		X		X
Inspect ignition wiring (secondary) for proper installation and good condition.		X		X		X		X
Inspect, clean, adjust and test spark plugs — replace as required.		X		X		X		X
Make spark intensity test of each spark plug wire.		X		X		X		X
Inspect fuel lines and filter for leaks.		X		X		X		X
Torque intake manifold bolts to specifications (8-cylinder only).		X		X		X		X
Inspect cooling system hoses for deterioration, leaks and loose clamps. Repair and/or replace as required. ⑥		X		X		X		X
Lubricate distributor bushing (oil cup).				X				X
Check drive belt tension and adjust as required.	X	X	X	X	X	X	X	X
Chassis and Transmission Check exhaust system.	X	X	X	X	X	X	X	X

(continued)

Table 8   SCHEDULED MAINTENANCE — 1969-1971   (continued)

Maintenance Operation	Service Interval							
Number of months or thousands of miles, whichever comes first.	6	12	18	24	30	36	42	48
Check brake master cylinder fluid level.	X	X	X	X	X	X	X	X
Check power steering pump fluid level.	X	X	X	X	X	X	X	X
Lubricate steering linkage.	X	X	X	X	X	X	X	X
Lubricate parking brake linkage, pivots and clevises.	X	X	X	X	X	X	X	X
Repack and adjust front wheel bearings. ⑦				X				X
Repack and adjust rear wheel bearings (Dana axle only). ⑦				X				X
Rotate wheels and tires.	X	X	X	X	X	X	X	X
Inspect brake linings (drum brakes only).				X				X
Check standard transmission fluid level and clean breather.	X	X	X	X	X	X	X	X
Check automatic transmission fluid level.	X	X	X	X	X	X	X	X
Check and adjust automatic transmission intermediate band and reverse band (if so equipped).	X		X			X		X
Drain and refill standard transmission (except 3-speed light and medium duty Ford).				X				X
Check rear axle lube level. ③ ④	X	X	X	X	X	X	X	X
Lubricate parking brake and speedometer cables.				X				X
Drain and refill rear axle lube. ⑤								
Front axle spindle pins.	X	X	X	X	X	X	X	X
Lubricate universal joints. ⑤	X	X	X	X	X	X	X	X
Lubricate universal joint slip yokes. ⑤	X	X	X	X	X	X	X	X
Body								
Lubricate body lock cylinders and door, hood and tailgate hinges and checks.	X	X	X	X	X	X	X	X
Lubricate hood latch and auxiliary catch. ⑧								

① More frequently under continuous stop and go operations or extremely dusty conditions.

② Every 24 months.

③ Every 1,000 miles in off-highway operation.

④ To check these axles, the plug should be backed out slowly. If seepage occurs around the threads, the specified amount of lubricant is present in the axle and the plug should be turned back in immediately to avoid any drainage.

⑤ Perform DAILY when operating in water. Include re-packing the hub-lock bearings if so equipped.

⑥ If coolant is dirty or rusty in appearance, the system should be cleaned and flushed. The radiator cap should be cleaned and system refilled with a 50/50 solution of Rotunda coolant and water.

⑦ Replace front and rear wheel seals whenever a hub assembly is removed.

⑧ Every 6,000 miles.

Table 9   SCHEDULED MAINTENANCE — 1972-1979

Every 5,000 miles or 5 months, whichever comes first

- Clean exterior of engine with engine degreaser.
- Lubricate U-joints and slip yoke.
- Lubricate front axle spindle pins.
- Lubricate steering linkage.
- Check fluid levels in rear axle,[1] transmission (and clean breather), and power steering.
- Inspect exhaust system (including heat shields).
- Inspect brake linings, piston boots, pivot pins, lines, and hoses.
- Inspect clutch linkage and adjust if necessary.
- Change engine oil.
- Adjust idle fuel mixture, fast idle speed, and curb idle speed and TSP off-speed.
- Tighten intake manifold bolts/nuts.
- Replace crankcase emission filter in air cleaner.
- Lubricate and free-up exhaust control valve (if so equipped).
- Inspect distributor points (if so equipped).
- Check fuel lines and connections.
- Clean and refill oil bath air cleaner (if so equipped).
- Check dry-type air cleaner element and replace if necessary.
- Check coolant condition and protection.
- Check cooling hoses and clamps.

Every 10,000 miles or 10 months, whichever comes first

- Perform all procedures under preceding section, plus the following:
- Check master cylinder reservoir fluid level.
- Lubricate parking brake linkage, pivots, and clevises.
- Adjust valve clearance (mechanical lifter models).
- Replace dry-type air cleaner element (if so equipped).
- Check deceleration valve — fuel or spark (if so equipped).
- Adjust idle fuel mixture, fast idle speed, curb idle speed, and TSP off-speed.
- Clean crankcase breather cap (if so equipped).
- Replace engine oil filter.
- Replace spark plugs.
- Adjust initial ignition timing.
- Replace distributor points (if so equipped), and lubricate distributor shaft bushing; inspect distributor cap and rotor.
- Inspect spark plug wires and connections.
- Check spark control systems (CTRS, CTAV, CSC, etc.) and delay valve.
- Check PCV system, hoses, and tubes.
- Check thermactor system (if so equipped).
- Check vacuum throttle position (if so equipped).
- Check fuel deceleration valve (if so equipped).
- Check EGR system and delay valve.
- Inspect drive belts.
- Check engine compression.

(continued)

Table 9   SCHEDULED MAINTENANCE — 1972-1979 (continued)

Every 20,000 miles or 20 months, whichever comes first

Perform all procedures under each preceding section, plus the following:

- Repack and adjust front and rear wheel bearings[2].
- Drain and refill rear axle (Dana axle only)[3].
- Drain and refill automatic transmission (severe service only).
- Lubricate power steering cylinder actuator stud.
- Inspect fuel vapor emission control system (fuel tank filler cap and hoses and vapor lines).
- Replace PCV valve.
- Check air cleaner temperature control and delay valve.
- Check carburetor throttle, choke linkage and delay valve; and air valve.
- Replace fuel system filter.
- Inspect evaporative emission canister.

1. To check the axle lubricant, the plug should be backed out slowly. If seepage occurs around the threads, enough lubricant is present and the plug should be turned back in immediately to avoid any drainage.
2. Replace seals whenever a hub assembly is removed.
3. Perform every 5,000 miles if towing a Class I or III trailer.

NOTE: Emission system abbreviations:
  CTRS = Cold Transmission regulated spark control system
  PCV = Positive crankcase ventilation system
  EGR = Exhaust gas recirculation system
  CSC = Coolant spark control
  TSP = Throttle solenoid positioner
  CTAV = Cold temperature activated vacuum spark system

NOTE: If you own a 1980 or later model, first check the Supplement at the back of the book for any new service information.

CHAPTER FOUR

4

TUNE-UP

To ensure maximum operating economy and service life, and to comply with regulated exhaust emission standards, a complete tune-up should be performed at the intervals shown in **Table 1**.

These recommended intervals are based on normal use — a combination of highway, city, and off-road driving. If the vehicle is used extensively for stop-and-go city driving, more frequent tune-ups may be required. Extensive off-road use should have little effect on tune and the recommended intervals can generally be followed with little degradation of performance or economy.

EXPENDABLE PARTS

The expendable ignition parts (spark plugs, points, and condenser) should be routinely replaced during the tune-up. In addition, some expendable emission control devices on some models must also be replaced if the vehicle is to remain within legal emission standards. These devices are shown in Chapter Three. You should have all of the necessary parts on hand before you begin a tune-up.

TUNE-UP SEQUENCE

Because different systems in an engine interact, the procedures should be done in the following order.

1. Tighten cylinder head bolts.
2. Adjust valve clearance (mechanical lifters).
3. Work on ignition system.
4. Adjust carburetor.

CYLINDER HEAD BOLTS

1. Note the location of breather hoses and disconnect them and the oil fill cap from the valve cover. Unscrew the bolts which hold the valve cover to the cylinder head and remove the valve cover.

2. Tighten the cylinder head bolts in the appropriate pattern shown in **Figure 1** to the torque specified in **Table 2**.

Table 1   TUNE-UP INTERVALS

Year	Interval
1969-1974	12,000 miles or 12 months
1975 and later	Refer to A, B, or C imprinted on engine decal

VALVE CLEARANCE ADJUSTMENT (MECHANICAL LIFTERS)

The valve clearance must be adjusted with the engine warmed up to operating temperature. Because the clearance must be measured and set with the engine idling, it is recommended that a step-type "go/no-go" gauge be used. Valve clearance is shown in **Table 3**.

1. Remove the valve rocker cover as described above. Start the engine and allow it to idle.

2. Insert the go/no-go gauge between the lifter heel and the end of the valve stem (**Figure 2**). The "go" portion of the gauge should enter the gap but the "no-go" portion should not.

If adjustment is required, turn the adjuster nut until the clearance is correct.

3. Continue to adjust the remaining valves in the same manner.

VALVE CLEARANCE ADJUSTMENT (HYDRAULIC LIFTERS)

Correct valve clearance in engines equipped with hydraulic lifters is maintained automatically in many cases throughout the life of the engine. However, if incorrect valve clearance is suspected as a possible cause of poor performance or the engine has logged many thousands of miles, the valve clearance should be checked and corrected by a dealer or automotive shop.

All 1976 and later models covered by this book have engines with hydraulic valve lifters. These lifters do not require periodic adjustment. However, if the engine is performing poorly and the problem cannot be isolated to any other cause, or if the engine has logged many thousands of miles, have your dealer check the valve clearance, and correct it if required.

IGNITION SYSTEM

Two basic types of ignition systems are used on the Ford vehicles covered in this manual; the conventional mechanical contact breaker ignition and the breakerless electronic ignition. The

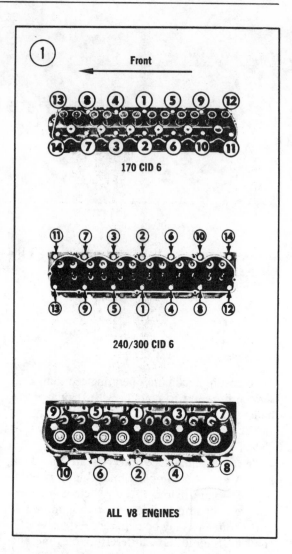

170 CID 6

240/300 CID 6

ALL V8 ENGINES

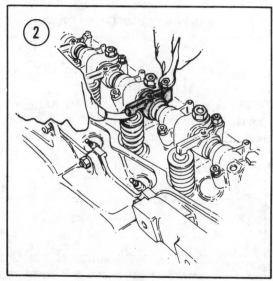

Table 2　CYLINDER HEAD BOLT TORQUE

Engine	Torque (ft.-lb.)		
	Stage 1	Stage 2	Stage 3
170, 240, 300 cid 6-cyl.	55	65	70-85
302 cid V8	55	65	65-72
351M cid V8	75	95	105
360, 390 cid V8	60	70	80-90
400 cid V8	75	95	105
460 cid V8	80	110	130-140

Table 3　VALVE CLEARANCES

Engine	1969	1970	1971	1972
170 cid 6	0.018 in.	0.018 in.	0.018 in.	0.018 in.
240 cid 6; 300 cid 6	0.082-0.152 in.	0.082-0.152 in.	0.082-0.152 in.	0.075-0.175 in.* 0.100-0.150 in.**
302 cid V8	0.067-0.167 in.	0.067-0.167 in.	0.067-0.167 in.	0.067-0.167 in.* 0.067-0.117 in.**
360 cid V8; 390 cid V8	0.100-0.200 in.	0.100-0.200 in.	0.100-0.200 in.	0.119-0.219 in.* 0.119-01.69 in.**

Engine	Year		
	1973	1974	1975
170 cid 6	—	—	—
240 cid 6; 300 cid 6	0.074-0.174 in.* 0.125 in.**	0.100-0.200 in.* 0.100-0.150 in.**	0.100-0.200 in.* 0.125-0.175 in.**
302 cid V8	0.090-0.190 in.* 0.090-0.140 in.**	0.090-0.190 in.* 0.090-0.140 in.**	0.090-0.190 in.* 0.115-0.165 in.**

*Acceptable clearance range.　　**Preferred clearance range.

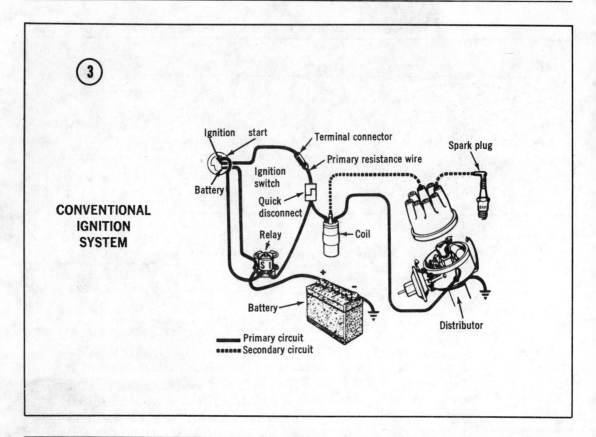

③

CONVENTIONAL
IGNITION
SYSTEM

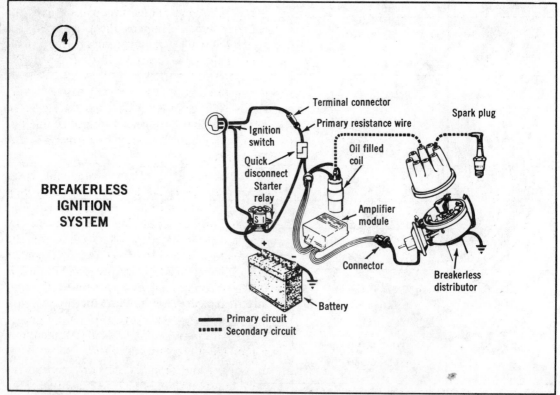

④

BREAKERLESS
IGNITION
SYSTEM

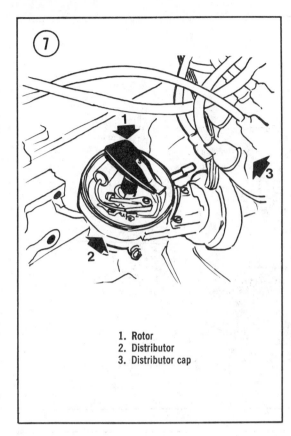

1. Rotor
2. Distributor
3. Distributor cap

two types of systems are shown in **Figures 3 and 4**. The distributors are shown in exploded views in **Figures 5 and 6**.

Service to breakerless ignition systems is limited to replacement of spark plugs, checking and correcting ignition timing, and inspection and repair of wiring. Total ignition service is presented for mechanical contact breaker systems. Procedures are presented separately.

Mechanical Contact Breaker Ignition

The expendable ignition parts (spark plugs, points, and condenser) should be replaced and the contact breaker dwell angle and ignition timing checked and adjusted if necessary at the intervals shown in **Table 1**. If the vehicle is used primarily in stop-and-go city driving, or if it is driven extensively at low engine speeds, replacement, or at least cleaning and adjustment of spark plug electrode and contact breaker gaps should be carried out more frequently.

1. Identify the high-tension spark plug leads and disconnect them from the spark plugs by carefully pulling and twisting the insulated caps; do not pull the leads loose by grasping the wires. Unscrew the spark plugs from the cylinder head(s), keeping them in order. Examine the spark plugs and compare their condition to the color chart in Chapter Two. The condition of the spark plugs is an indication of engine condition, and can warn of developing trouble. For this reason, keep the spark plugs in order until they have been inspected so that unsatisfactory conditions can be further isolated by cylinder.

2. Remove the distributor cap and rotor (**Figure 7**). Clean the high-tension spark plug and coil leads and check them for chafing, melting, or cracked insulation and replace any that are deteriorated or damaged. Clean the distributor cap and rotor and inspect them for cracks, burnt contacts, and arc-over. Pitting of the rotor contact and arc-over between the contacts in the cap generally indicate the presence of resistance, either in the cap or the rotor or both. If excessive pitting or arcing is found, it is a good idea to replace both parts.

3. Loosen the terminal nut on the contact breaker assembly (**Figure 8**) and disconnect the

⑤

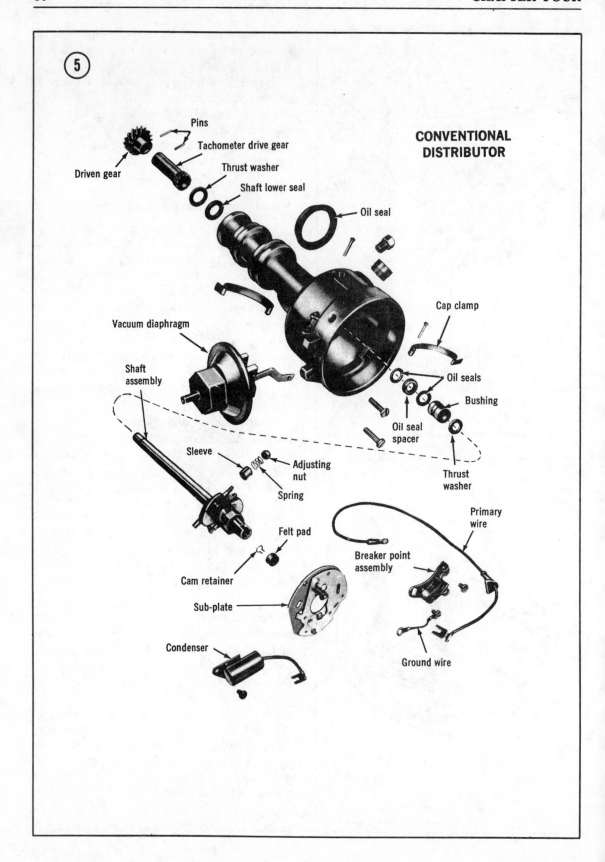

Pins

Tachometer drive gear

Driven gear

Thrust washer

Shaft lower seal

Oil seal

CONVENTIONAL DISTRIBUTOR

Cap clamp

Vacuum diaphragm

Oil seals

Shaft assembly

Bushing

Oil seal spacer

Thrust washer

Sleeve

Adjusting nut

Spring

Primary wire

Felt pad

Breaker point assembly

Cam retainer

Sub-plate

Condenser

Ground wire

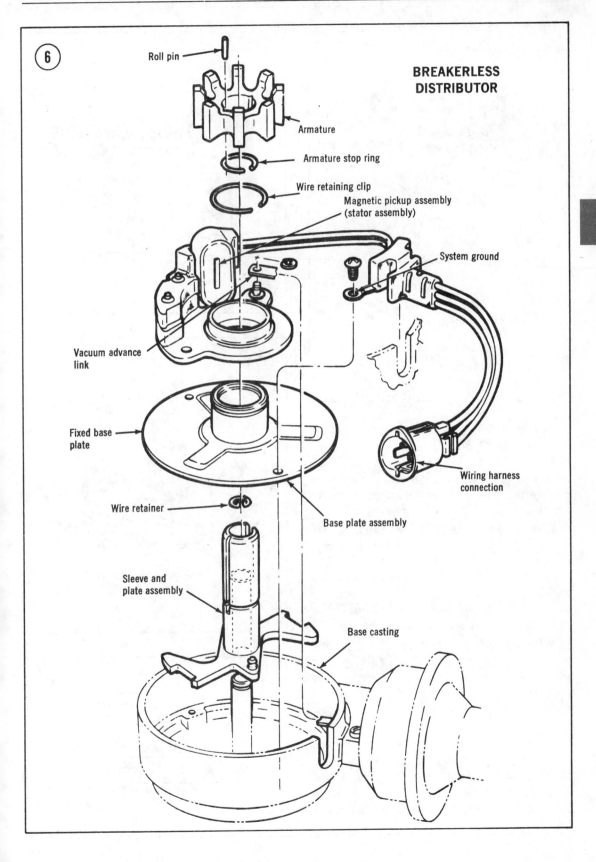

6

Roll pin

BREAKERLESS DISTRIBUTOR

Armature

Armature stop ring

Wire retaining clip

Magnetic pickup assembly (stator assembly)

System ground

Vacuum advance link

Fixed base plate

Wiring harness connection

Wire retainer

Base plate assembly

Sleeve and plate assembly

Base casting

4

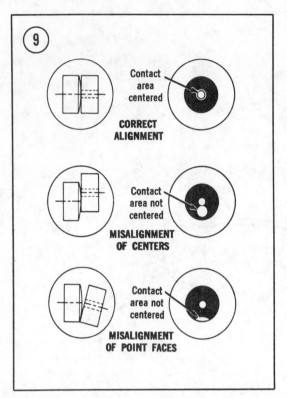

CORRECT
ALIGNMENT

Contact area not centered

MISALIGNMENT
OF CENTERS

Contact area not centered

MISALIGNMENT
OF POINT FACES

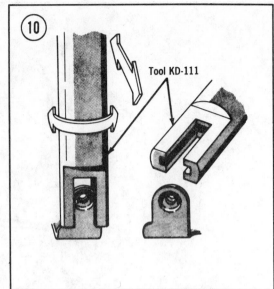

Tool KD-111

primary lead. Unscrew the retaining screw from the condenser and the contact breaker assembly. Note the location of the ground wire so it may be installed in the same place, and remove the condenser and breaker from the distributor.

4. Check the movement of the centrifugal advance mechanism by carefully turning the contact breaker cam by hand and releasing it. It should snap back against spring tension. If it does not, the distributor should be checked for wear or damage. This is a job for a Ford Dealer or an automotive electrical specialist.

5. Wipe cam and breaker plate clean. Lightly coat the cam with special distributor cam grease. Never use oil or common grease; they will break down under the high-temperature and frictional load and are likely to find their way onto the contacts.

6. Install the new contact breaker assembly and condenser in the distributor. Make sure the ground lead, condenser lead, and primary lead are installed exactly as they were before. Double check the connections and screw to ensure that they are tight.

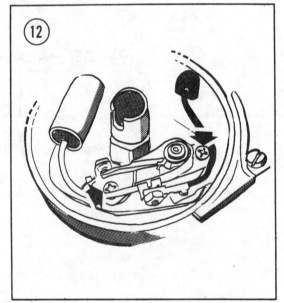

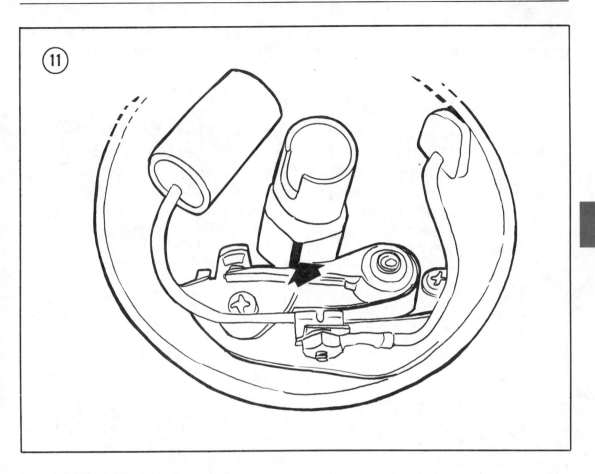

7. With a pivoted contact breaker, rotate the crankshaft to close the breaker contacts and check their alignment (**Figure 9**). This vented-type breaker must be accurately aligned to ensure full service life and performance. If alignment is not correct, carefully bend the stationary contact; do not bend the movable arm. If possible, a tool like the one shown (Ford tool No. KD-111) should be used (**Figure 10**).

> NOTE: *Contact alignment is not necessary for unvented pivotless contact points.*

8. Rotate the crankshaft until the breaker contacts are at their maximum opening and the lifter heel rests on the peak of one of the cam lobes (**Figure 11**). Check the gap with a flat feeler gauge and compare it to **Table 4**. To adjust the contact gap, loosen the screws which attach the contact breaker assembly to the distributor (**Figure 12**) and move the fixed plate as required until the gap is correct. Then,

without further moving the contact breaker plate, tighten the 2 screws and recheck the gap. If a dwell meter is available, connect in accordance with the manufacturer's instructions and measure the dwell angle of the contacts. If the dwell angle is below that shown in **Table 4** the contact gap is too large, and if the dwell angle is greater than specified, the contact gap is too small. If necessary, readjust the contacts.

9. Set the electrode gap on the new spark plugs (**Table 4**). Adjust the gap by bending only the side (ground) electrode (**Figure 13**). Screw the spark plugs into the cylinder head and tighten them to 15-20 ft.-lb.

10. Install the rotor and the distributor cap. Connect the high-tension leads to the spark plugs as shown in **Figure 14A and 14B**.

11. Adjust the ignition timing using a timing light and a tachometer. Connect the instruments according to the manufacturer's instructions (**Figures 15 and 16**). The timing light must be connected to the No. 1 cylinder spark plug

Table 4   IGNITION SPECIFICATIONS

170 CID SIX	1969	1970	1971	1972	1973	1974	1975
Initial ignition timing	6° BTDC	6° BTDC	6° BTDC	6° BTDC	—	—	—
Spark plug Type Gap	Autolite BF82 or equivalent 0.032-0.036 in.	Autolite BF82 or equivalent 0.032-0.036 in.	Autolite BF82 or equivalent 0.032-0.036 in.	Autolite BF82 or equivalent 0.032-0.036 in.	— — —	— — —	— — —
Dwell angle w/ emission control	35-40°	35-40°	35-40°	35-40°	—	—	—
Distributor point gap w/ emission control	0.027 in.	0.027 in.	0.027 in.	0.027 in.	—	—	—
240 CID SIX	**1969**	**1970**	**1971**	**1972**	**1973**	**1974**	**1975**
Initial ignition timing	6° BTDC	6° BTDC	6° BTDC	6° BTDC	6° BTDC	Ⓐ	—
Spark plug Type Gap	Autolite BF42 BTF 42 0.032-0.036 in.	Autolite BTF42 or equivalent 0.032-0.036 in.	Autolite BF42 BTF31 0.032-0.036 in.	Autolite BF42 or equivalent 0.034 in.	Autolite BRF42 or equivalent 0.032-0.036 in.	Ⓐ	—
Dwell angle w/ emission control	35-40° 37-42°	35-40°	35-40° 37-42°	35-39°	33-39°	Ⓐ	—
Distributor point gap w/ emission control	0.027 in. 0.025 in.	0.027 in.	0.027 in. 0.025 in.	0.027 in.	0.027 in.	Ⓐ	—

Ⓐ Specifications for spark plug number and gap, distributor gap, and dwell angle are given on the valve cover decal.

(continued)

Table 4   IGNITION SPECIFICATIONS   (continued)

300 CID SIX	1969	1970	1971	1972	1973	1974	1975–1979
Initial ignition timing	6° BTDC	6° BTDC	6° BTDC	6° BTDC	Ⓐ	Ⓐ	Ⓐ
Spark plug Type Gap	Autolite BTF42 or equivalent 0.032- 0.036 in.	Autolite BTF42 or equivalent 0.032- 0.036 in.	Autolite BF42 BTF31 0.032- 0.036 in.	Autolite BF42 or equivalent 0.034 in.	Ⓐ	Ⓐ	Ⓐ
Dwell angle w/ emission control	35-40° 37-42°	35-40° 37-42°	35-40° 37-42°	35-39°	Ⓐ	Ⓐ	Ⓐ
Distributor point gap w/ emission control	0.027 in. 0.025 in.	0.027 in. 0.025 in.	0.027 in. 0.025 in.	0.027 in.	Ⓐ	Ⓐ	Ⓐ
302 CID V8	**1969**	**1970**	**1971**	**1972**	**1973**	**1974**	**1975–1979**
Initial ignition timing	6° BTDC	6° BTDC	6° BTDC	6° BTDC	Ⓐ	Ⓐ	Ⓐ
Spark plug Type Gap	Autolite BTF31 or equivalent 0.028- 0.032 in.	Autolite BTF31 or equivalent 0.028- 0.032 in.	Autolite BTF31 or equivalent 0.028- 0.032 in.	Autolite BF42 or equivalent 0.034 in.	Autolite BRF42 or equivalent 0.032- 0.036 in.	Ⓐ	Ⓐ
Dwell angle w/ emission control	24-29°	24-29°	24-29°	26-30°	24-30°	Ⓐ	Ⓐ
Distributor point gap w/ emission control	0.021 in.	0.021 in.	0.021 in.	0.017 in.	0.017 in.	Ⓐ	Ⓐ

Ⓐ Specifications for spark plug number and gap, distributor gap, and dwell angle are
   given on the valve cover decal.

(continued)

Table 4   IGNITION SPECIFICATIONS (continued)

351M	See engine decal						
360 & 390 CID V8	1969	1970	1971	1972	1973	1974	1975-1979
Initial ignition timing	6° BTDC	6° BTDC	6° BTDC	6° BTDC	A	A	A
Spark plug Type	Autolite BF32 or equivalent	Autolite BF32 or equivalent	Autolite BF32 or equivalent	Autolite BF42 or equivalent	Autolite BF42 or equivalent	A	A
Gap	0.032-0.036 in.	0.032-0.036 in.	0.032-0.036 in.	0.034 in.	0.032-0.036 in.		
Dwell angle w/emission control	26-31°	24-29°* 26-31°**	24-29°* 26-31°**	26-30°	24-30°	A	A
Distributor point gap w/emission control	0.017 in.	0.017 in.[1]	0.017 in.[1] 0.021 in.[2]	0.017 in.	0.017 in.	A	A
400/460	See engine decal						

*F-100 models.   **F-250 models.

A Specifications for spark plug number and gap, distributor gap, and dwell angle are given on the valve cover decal.

1. For transistorized ignition, set point gap at 0.020 in. and dwell angle at 22-24°.
2. 390 cid V8 in F-100 models.

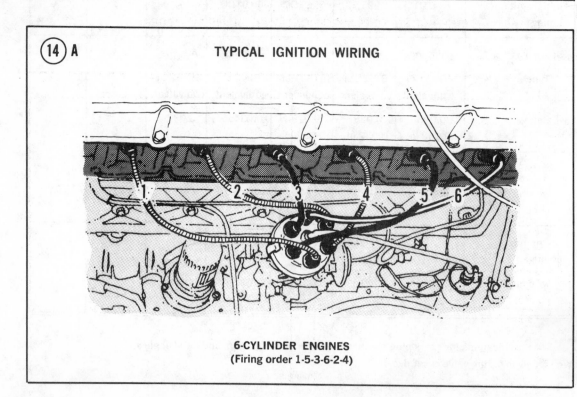

(14) A   TYPICAL IGNITION WIRING

6-CYLINDER ENGINES
(Firing order 1-5-3-6-2-4)

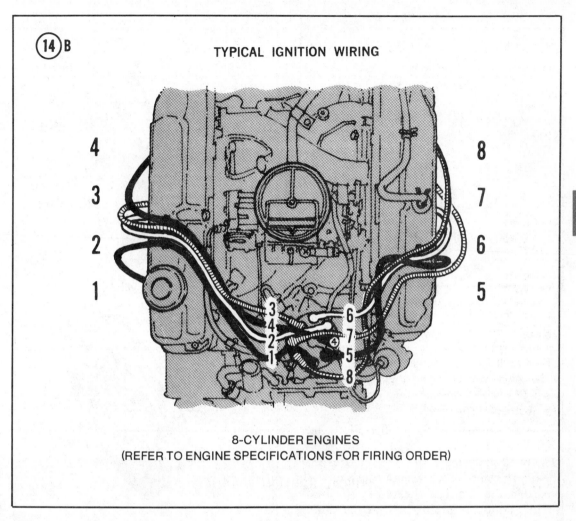

TYPICAL IGNITION WIRING

8-CYLINDER ENGINES
(REFER TO ENGINE SPECIFICATIONS FOR FIRING ORDER)

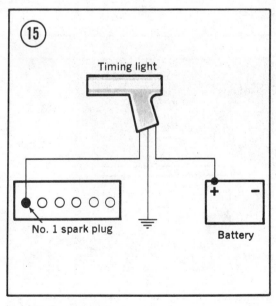

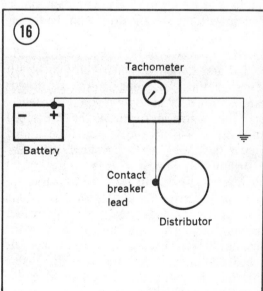

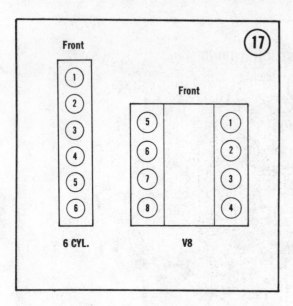

Front   ⑰

①
②
③
④
⑤
⑥

Front

⑤ ①
⑥ ②
⑦ ③
⑧ ④

6 CYL.   **V8**

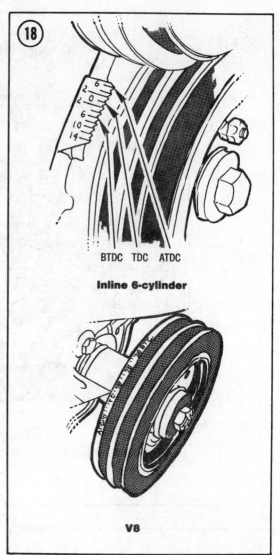

BTDC TDC ATDC

Inline 6-cylinder

V8

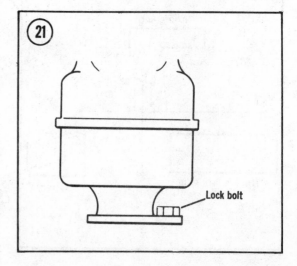

Lock bolt

— front cylinder on 6-cylinder engines, front right cylinder on V8 engines. See **Figure 17**. Clean the timing marks on the crankshaft pulley and the timing plate (**Figure 18**) and mark them with chalk so they can easily be seen. Disconnect the vacuum line(s) from the distributor and plug them.

12. Start the engine and set the idle at 600 rpm with the idle speed adjusting screw (**Figure 19** and **Figure 20**). This ensures that the centrifugal advance has not begun to work and that the timing indicated is the basic timing. Point the timing light at the timing marks. The timing mark on the pulley should line up with the specified mark on the timing plate.

13. If the timing is incorrect, shut off the engine and loosen the distributor lock bolt (**Figure 21**) just far enough so the distributor can be turned by hand with some resistance. Start the engine and recheck the idle speed and correct it if necessary. Point the timing light at the timing marks and slowly rotate the distributor body clockwise or counterclockwise until the timing marks are aligned. Then shut off the engine and tighten the distributor lock bolt without further moving the distributor and disturbing the setting. Start the engine, recheck the idle speed, and double-check the timing to ensure that the distributor did not move when the lock bolt was tightened.

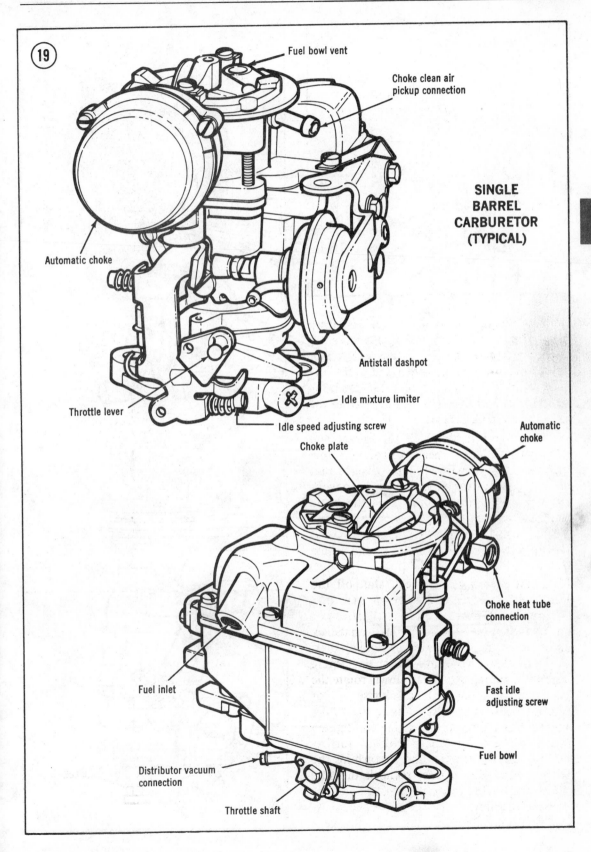

(19)

Fuel bowl vent

Choke clean air
pickup connection

SINGLE
BARREL
CARBURETOR
(TYPICAL)

4

Automatic choke

Antistall dashpot

Throttle lever

Idle mixture limiter

Idle speed adjusting screw

Choke plate

Automatic
choke

Choke heat tube
connection

Fuel inlet

Fast idle
adjusting screw

Fuel bowl

Distributor vacuum
connection

Throttle shaft

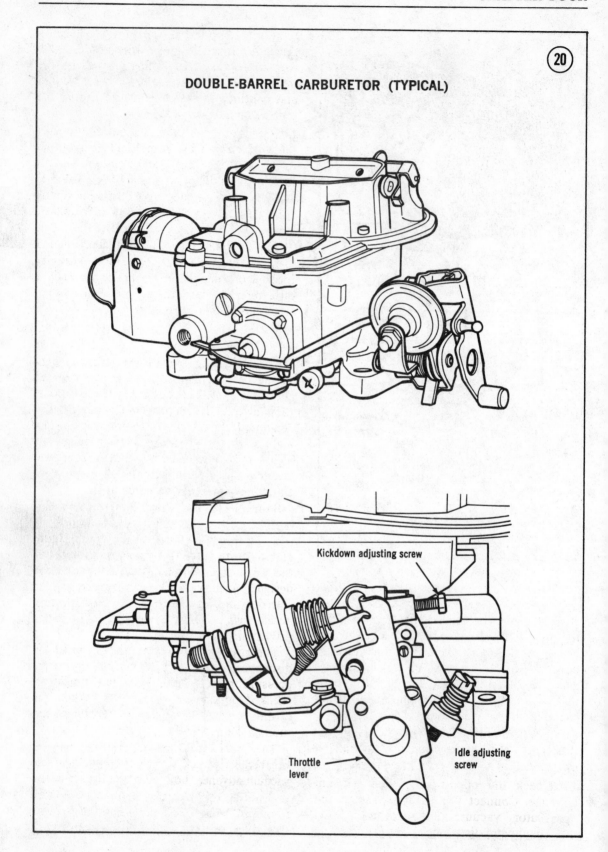

20

DOUBLE-BARREL CARBURETOR (TYPICAL)

Kickdown adjusting screw

Throttle lever

Idle adjusting screw

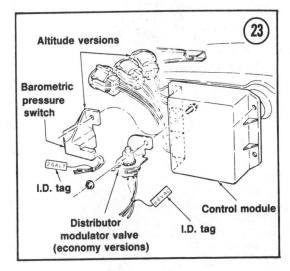

Altitude versions

Barometric
pressure
switch

I.D. tag

Distributor
modulator valve
(economy versions)

Control module

I.D. tag

14. After the initial timing has been set, check the operation of the centrifugal advance mechanism. Start the engine and slowly increase the speed to 2,000 rpm while directing the timing light at the timing marks. The timing should begin to advance between 700 and 1,000 rpm, and at 2,000 rpm, it should be $6\frac{3}{4}$-8° greater than initial timing. If the timing does not advance, or if the values are appreciably lower than specified, the distributor should be entrusted to a Ford dealer or an automotive ignition specialist for bench testing and repair.

15. Check the operation of the vacuum advance. Connect the vacuum line to the distributor vacuum advance unit. (On dual-diaphragm distributors, connect the line to outer diaphragm, **Figure 22**). Slowly increase the engine speed from idle to 2,000 rpm and observe the timing marks with the timing light. Advance should begin sooner and continue farther than it did during the centrifugal advance test.

16. On dual-diaphragm distributors, connect the other vacuum line from the intake manifold to the inner diaphragm and check the retard. Readjust carburetor to normal idle (**Table 5**) and observe the timing marks with the timing light. The timing should retard to about 6° ATDC.

If either the retard or advance functions fail to work correctly, the distributor must be checked on special test equipment. In such a case, refer the work to a Ford dealer or an automotive ignition specialist.

Breakerless Ignition System

The spark plugs should be replaced and the timing checked and adjusted at the intervals shown in **Table 1**. Procedures are the same as those given under *Mechanical Contact Breaker Ignition*. If the vehicle is used primarily in stop-and-go city driving, or if it is driven extensively at low engine speeds, replacement, or at least cleaning and adjustment of the spark plugs should be carried out more frequently.

Some 1978 and later Ford Motor Co. engines use a dual-mode ignition module. It can be identified by an extra module connector and will be designated as such on the VECI decal on the engine. The module is designed to provide a basic timing setting for cranking and can electronically retard timing under certain operating conditions for better driveability.

The module's 3-pin connector must be disconnected from the vacuum or barometric pressure switch before ignition timing is checked or adjusted (**Figure 23**). When the timing is correct, be sure to reconnect the module connector.

The only adjustments possible on the breakerless ignition system are centrifugal and vacuum advance, both of which should be entrusted to a Ford dealer or automotive ignition specialist. Also, suspected ignition trouble should be referred to a dealer or specialist;

Table 5   ENGINE IDLE SPEED

Engine	Idle Speed
170 cid 6	
1969	750 rpm
1970-1971	775 rpm
1972	750 rpm
240 cid 6	
1969	500 rpm (auto.); 775/500 rpm* (manual)
1970 — F-250	550 rpm (auto.); 600 rpm (manual)
F-100	850/500 rpm* (manual), 575/500 rpm* (auto.)
1971 — F-250	550 rpm (auto.); 600 rpm (manual)
F-100	550/500 rpm* (auto.); 775/500 rpm* (manual)
1972	850/500 rpm* (manual); 600/500 rpm* (auto.)
1973-on	See engine decal
300 cid 6	
1969	525 rpm (auto.); 600 rpm (manual)
1970-1972	550 rpm (auto.); 600 rpm (manual)
1973-on	See engine decal
302 cid V8	
1969	550 rpm (auto.); 650 rpm (manual)
1970	600 rpm (auto.); 675 rpm (manual)
1971	600 rpm (auto. w/AC); 600/500 rpm* (auto.)
	800/500 rpm* (manual)
1972	600/500 rpm* (auto.); 800/500 rpm* (manual)
1973-on	See engine decal
351M cid V8	See engine decal
360/390 cid V8	
1969-1972	550 rpm (auto.); 650 rpm (manual)
1973-on	See engine decal
400 cid V8	See engine decal
460 cid V8	See engine decal

*Higher rpm with solenoid energized; lower rpm with solenoid de-energized.

testing of the electronic module requires special equipment and skills and an otherwise good electronic circuit can be irreparably damaged by an incorrect test hookup.

CARBURETOR

Carburetor adjustments include normal idle and fast idle settings. Idle fuel-air mixture settings are not recommended; this affects exhaust emissions levels and cannot be accurately adjusted without the use of an exhaust gas analyzer. The idle air mixture screw is fitted with a limiter cap which prevents adjustments being made that will produce an out-of-specification idle mixture. If the idle cannot be correctly set with the idle speed screws, the carburetor should be referred to a Ford dealer or an automotive tune-up specialist certified to make emission-related adjustments.

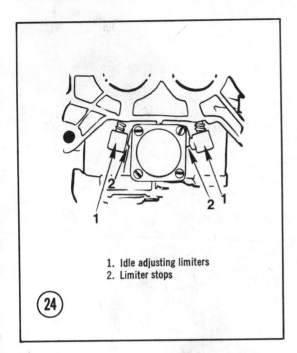

1. Idle adjusting limiters
2. Limiter stops

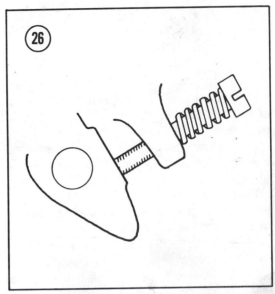

steady stream of fuel should be discharged from the nozzle(s). If this is weak or erratic, it is likely that the accelerator pump is faulty and the carburetor should be referred to a Ford dealer or automotive specialist for major service.

Basic Idle Setting With Engine Off

1. Remove the air cleaner assembly. Carefully turn the idle mixture limiter caps clockwise until they stop (**Figure 24**).

2. Turn the idle speed adjusting screw counterclockwise until the throttle butterfly seats in the throttle bore. If the butterfly does not seat with the idle speed screw backed off, check the plunger on the dashpot or solenoid (**Figure 25**) to make sure that it is not holding the butterfly open. If the plunger is preventing the butterfly from seating, loosen the locknut on the dashpot and screw the dashpot into the bracket until the butterfly seats.

3. Turn the idle speed screw clockwise until it just touches its stop (**Figure 26**). Then turn the screw 1½ additional turns to set the basic idle.

Idle Setting With Engine On (1969-1975 Models)

1. Set the parking brake, start the engine, and allow it to warm up for 20 minutes at 1,500 rpm by positioning the fast idle cam at the center

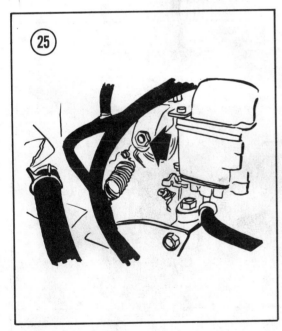

Accelerator Pump Discharge Test

1. Unscrew the wing nut from the top of the air cleaner assembly and remove the top cover.

2. Open the throttle smoothly and at the same time look in the top of the carburetor and observe the discharge from the accelerator pump nozzle (single throat carburetor) or nozzles (2- and 4-throat carburetors). A quick,

notch (**Figure 27**). Do not touch the throttle during warmup or the cam will release and return to normal idle.

2. Connect a tachometer in accordance with the manufacturer's instructions. On vehicles with standard transmission the selector must be in NEUTRAL, and on vehicles with automatic transmission, the selector should be set at DRIVE. *Double check* to make sure the parking brake will prevent the vehicle from moving with the transmission set in DRIVE. If it will not, shut off the engine and adjust the parking brake before proceeding. Check the choke butterfly to make sure it is fully open.

3. Turn on the headlights and select high beam to place a normal alternator load on the engine. If the vehicle is equipped with air conditioning, make sure it is turned off.

4. Reinstall the air cleaner assembly. Set the curb idle speed by turning the idle speed adjusting screw as required, referring to **Table 5** for the correct engine rpm. For Carter YF 1-V carburetors (6-cylinder engines) equipped with a solenoid throttle modulator (**Figure 28**), turn the solenoid plunger in or out until the idle is correct. Then, disconnect the solenoid lead near the loom (do not disconnect it from the carburetor). Turn the idle speed screw as required to bring the idle to 500 rpm. Reconnect the solenoid lead and open the throttle slightly. The plunger should extend and remain extended as long as the ignition is on. Check the operation of the solenoid by turning off the engine and restarting it.

5. When the correct idle has been set with the idle speed screw(s), turn the idle mixture limiter (one on single-throat carburetors, two on 2- and 4-throat carburetors) until the idle is smooth.

> NOTE: *On 2- and 4-throat carburetors, the 2 idle mixture limiters must be turned the same amount.*

Idle Setting (1976 300 cid Engine)

1. Set parking brake, place transmission in NEUTRAL, and remove air cleaner. Remove vacuum lines at the EGR valve and the air cleaner motor and plug lines.

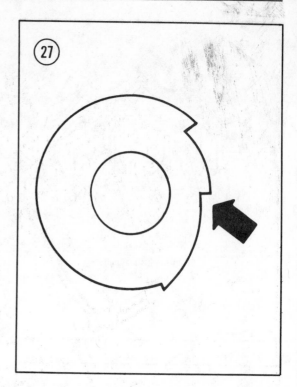

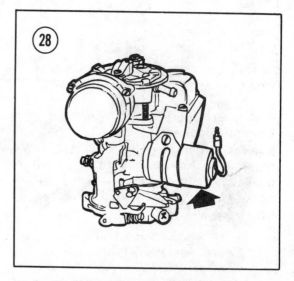

2. Start and warm engine up to normal operating temperature with throttle linkage set on kickdown step of fast idle cam (first step down from highest part of cam). See **Figure 29**.

3. Return engine to idle and remove and plug vacuum line(s) at distributor. Check, and adjust if necessary, initial timing. See Vehicle Emission Control Information (VECI) decal in engine compartment for timing specification.

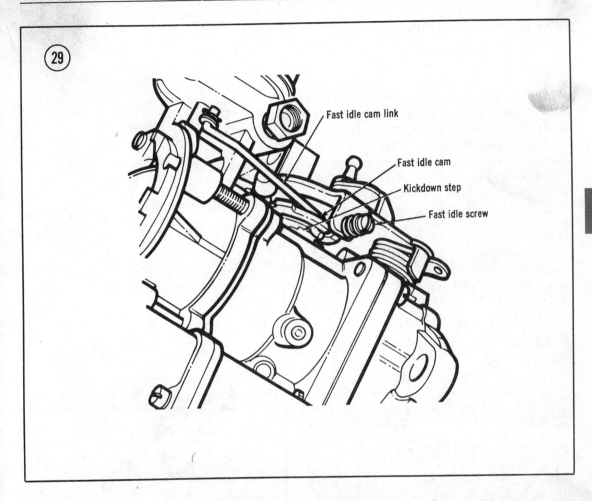

Fast idle cam link

Fast idle cam

Kickdown step

Fast idle screw

4

4. Reconnect distributor vacuum line(s), open the throttle, manually place fast idle cam in high cam position, and allow throttle to close in this position. Now, manually turn the cam so that fast idle adjusting screw falls on kickdown step of cam. Set fast idle speed to specification (see VECI decal).

> NOTE: *A bypass vacuum line should be installed from the distributor primary diaphragm directly to the vacuum source to assure proper vacuum advance during setting of fast idle speed. Remove bypass and replace vacuum hose when proper fast idle speed is obtained.*

5. Allow engine to run for about 5 minutes on the kickdown step. Then open and close throttle, allowing engine to return to idle. Make sure fast idle cam drops and fast idle adjusting screw does not contact the fast idle cam.

6. If dashpot interferes with throttle closing, back off dashpot. Adjust curb idle speed to specification. This adjustment must be made immediately (1 to 2 minutes) after performing Step 5, otherwise engine will become too warm and idle speed will drop off. If necessary, repeat Step 5 to cool off engine, then adjust idle speed to specification.

7. Use a pair of pliers on the shaft to collapse the dashpot. Then adjust the clearance between the collapsed dashpot shaft and the throttle lever pad to specification (see VECI decal).

8. Increase engine speed to 2,000 rpm, then allow it to return to normal and recheck idle speed. If not within +10 rpm of specification, readjust and recheck.

9. Unplug and replace all vacuum lines removed in Step 1. Shut off engine and replace air cleaner.

Idle Setting (1976 302 cid Engines)

1. Start engine and allow it to reach normal operating temperature. Check initial timing and adjust to specification. See Vehicle Emission Control Information (VECI) decal in engine compartment. When timing check is completed, make sure vacuum lines are reinstalled.

2. If so equipped, remove spark delay valve and attach port throttle vacuum line directly to distributor primary spark advance mechanism. If distributor has dual diaphragms, leave the secondary (retard) diaphragm vacuum line in place.

> NOTE: *The secondary diaphragm vacuum inlet is located on top of the diaphragm housing. The other end of the vacuum line connects to the intake manifold.*

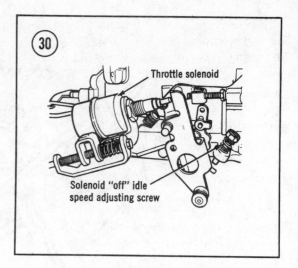

Throttle solenoid

Solenoid "off" idle speed adjusting screw

3. Remove the vacuum line at the EGR valve and plug the line.

4. Set throttle to high step of fast idle cam. Allow engine to run until idle speed stabilizes, then adjust fast idle to specification given on VECI decal.

5a. On models equipped with throttle solenoid positioner (TSP), or solenoid dashpot, disconnect the electrical lead to the TSP or dashpot and set idle speed to the "TSP-off" speed stated on the VECI decal, using the idle adjusting screw.

5b. Connect the electrical lead to the TSP or solenoid dashpot and set the curb idle speed to specification (see VECI decal) by adjusting the TSP body (**Figure 30**) or the solenoid plunger (**Figure 31**). Adjustment should be made with manual transmission in NEUTRAL or automatic transmission in DRIVE (with parking brake set).

6. On models without throttle positioner solenoid or dashpot, set curb idle speed to specification (see VECI decal), using the idle speed adjustment screw. Automatic transmission should be in DRIVE and manual transmission should be in NEUTRAL.

7. If vehicle has an automatic transmission, place in NEUTRAL and increase engine speed to about 2,200 rpm for about 5 seconds and allow engine to return to idle. Place transmission in DRIVE and recheck curb idle speed, readjusting if required.

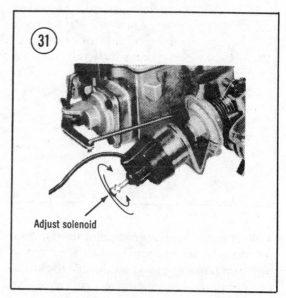

Adjust solenoid

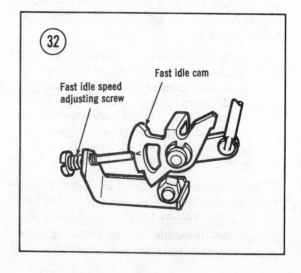

Fast idle cam

Fast idle speed adjusting screw

8. Repeat Step 7 until proper curb idle speed is obtained within a 6-second time span.

9. If spark delay valve was bypassed, correctly reinstall it. Also reconnect vacuum line to EGR valve.

Idle Setting (1976 351 cid Engines)

1. Remove air cleaner and plug vacuum lines from intake manifold. Start engine and allow it to reach normal operating temperature.

2. Check and adjust, if required, initial timing according to specification given on Vehicle Emission Control Information (VECI) decal in engine compartment. Be sure vacuum line is replaced on distributor after check.

3. If vehicle is equipped with spark delay valve, remove valve from vacuum line and connect line directly to primary side of distributor vacuum advance mechanism. If distributor is equipped with dual-diaphragm advance mechanism, leave secondary (retard) diaphragm vacuum line in place.

NOTE: *The secondary diaphragm vacuum inlet is located on top of the diaphragm housing. The other end of the vacuum line connects to the intake manifold.*

4. Remove the vacuum line from the EGR valve and plug it.

5a. On carburetors equipped with dashpot, set throttle to high step on choke cam (**Figure 32**) and allow the engine to run until idle speed stabilizes. Then adjust idle speed to fast idle speed specified on VECI decal.

5b. Set dashpot clearance to 0.090-0.140 and then set idle speed to the rpm specified on the VECI decal, using the curb idle speed setscrew (**Figure 31**). With transmission in NEUTRAL, rev engine to 2,200 rpm for 5 seconds, allow engine to return to idle, and check speed again. Readjust, if necessary, to obtain specified curb idle, always resetting dashpot clearance to specification each time rpm is adjusted. Repeat this step as often as required to obtain a return to specified rpm within a 6-second time span.

6a. On models equipped with throttle solenoid positioner (TSP), set throttle to kickdown step

on choke cam and adjust fast idle speed to rpm specified on the VECI decal. Set throttle to high step on choke cam and allow engine to run for about 5 seconds, then rotate choke cam until adjusting screw falls to kickdown step on cam. Recheck fast idle speed and if not to specification, readjust as required. Repeat this procedure until specification is obtained and can be repeated.

6b. Allow engine to return to curb idle speed and disconnect electrical lead to TSP. Set idle speed to "TSP-off" speed specified on the VECI decal. Reconnect electrical lead to energize TSP and set idle speed to curb idle rpm specified on the VECI decal. Make sure automatic transmission is in DRIVE or manual transmission is in NEUTRAL when making this adjustment. If vehicle is equipped with automatic transmission, place in NEUTRAL, increase engine speed to 2,200 rpm for 5 seconds, and release the throttle. Immediately place transmission in DRIVE and recheck idle speed. Readjust, if necessary, to obtain specified speed. Repeat procedure until proper curb idle rpm can be repeated within a 6-second time span.

7. Replace spark delay valve to original positions and hookup, and reconnect vacuum line to EGR valve.

Idle Setting (1976 360 cid Engines)

1. Block front wheels and set parking brake. If vehicle has automatic transmission, place it in DRIVE; if manual transmission, in NEUTRAL.

2. Check timing and, if necessary, adjust to specification. See Vehicle Emission Control Information (VECI) decal in engine compartment. Also see *Ignition System*, earlier in this chapter.

3. Remove air cleaner, start engine, and allow it to warm up to normal operating temperature. Make sure automatic choke plate is in vertical (OFF) position.

4. On manual transmission models, make sure solenoid is energized and extended, then adjust idle speed to the "curb idle" speed specified on the VECI decal with transmission in NEUTRAL. Turn solenoid adjusting screw to make adjustment. Accelerate engine to 2,000 rpm for 10 seconds and allow engine to return to idle. After 60 seconds, recheck idle speed and read-

just to specification if required. Repeat this step as often as required until repeatable specified rpm is obtained.

5. Place automatic transmission in DRIVE and make sure solenoid is energized and extended. Set idle speed to the "curb idle" rpm specified on the VECI decal. Place transmission in NEUTRAL, accelerate engine to 2,000 rpm for a few seconds, release accelerator and place transmission in DRIVE. Recheck curb idle speed. Redjust to specified curb idle speed, if necessary. Repeat this step as often as required to obtain a repeatable curb idle specified speed within a few seconds.

6. To obtain the "TSP-off" or "off solenoid" idle speed specified on the VECI decal, disconnect the electrical lead to the TSP or solenoid, place the transmission in NEUTRAL (all models), and adjust rpm to specification using idle speed screw.

7. To set fast idle speed (all models), place transmission in NEUTRAL and connect manifold vacuum directly to advance side of distributor diaphragm, bypassing any spark delay or cold temperature cutout valve(s). Disconnect and plug vacuum line at EGR valve. Make sure engine is running at normal operating temperature.

8. Rotate fast idle cam so that adjusting screw is resting on the "kickdown" step of the cam (**Figure 32**). Note that the kickdown step is indicated by a "V" stamped on the cam. Use the fast idle speed adjusting screw to adjust rpm to the speed specified on the VECI decal. Accelerate slightly and recheck fast idle speed, making certain the adjusting screw has remained on the kickdown step of the cam.

9. Unplug and restore all vacuum lines to their original positions. Reconnect the TSP or solenoid electrical connector and recheck curb idle speed. Replace the air cleaner and tighten fasteners. Stop engine.

Idle Setting (1976 460 cid Engines)

1. Start engine, allow it to reach normal operating temperature, and check initial timing (see *Ignition Service*, earlier in this chapter).

2. Remove the top and center vacuum lines from the cold start spark advance (CSSA) system

ported vacuum switch (PVS) located in the heater elbow and connect the vacuum lines together. Disconnect the EGR vacuum hose at the carburetor and plug the carburetor port. Do not remove the choke pulldown hose.

3. Remove the air cleaner and remove and plug the cleaner vacuum hose. Set throttle on choke cam kickdown step and adjust engine speed to fast idle speed specified on Vehicle Emission Control Information (VECI) decal. Open throttle briefly and release, allowing idle speed to stabilize with throttle still resting on kickdown step of cam. Recheck fast idle rpm and readjust as required. Repeat this step as often as required until specified rpm can be repeated.

4. Replace hoses moved in Step 2 to their original positions.

5. With the electrical connector to the throttle positioner solenoid (TSP) disconnected, set low idle to the speed specified on the VECI decal, using the low idle speed adjusting screw (see **Figure 33**).

6. Reconnect the TSP and set engine speed to the curb idle rpm specified on the VECI decal (see **Figures 33 and 34**). If vehicle is equipped with automatic transmission, make the curb idle adjustment with the transmission in DRIVE. If transmission is manual, make adjustment in NEUTRAL.

7. Place transmission in NEUTRAL and rev engine to 2,000 rpm for 15 seconds, then allow engine to return to curb idle. If transmission is automatic, place in DRIVE. Recheck curb idle speed and readjust to specification, if required.

8. Repeat Steps 6 and 7 until specified rpm can be repeated. Replace air cleaner and reconnect vacuum hose.

Idle Setting (All 1977-1979 Models)

1. Apply parking brake and block wheels. Remove air cleaner and plug all vacuum lines to cleaner.

2. On vehicles with V8 engines, and equipped with thermactor systems, revise dump valve vacuum lines as follows:

   a. If dump valve has one or two vacuum lines at the side, disconnect and plug lines.

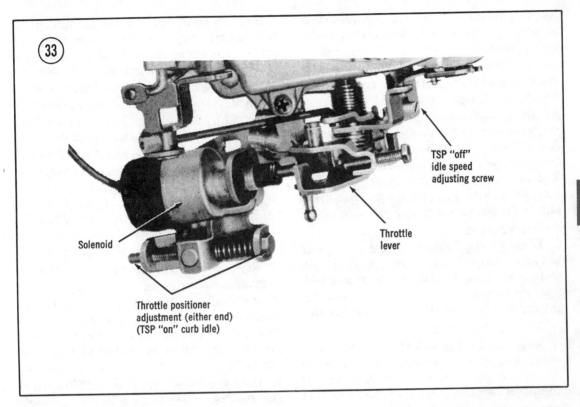

(33)

TSP "off"
idle speed
adjusting screw

Solenoid

Throttle
lever

Throttle positioner
adjustment (either end)
(TSP "on" curb idle)

4

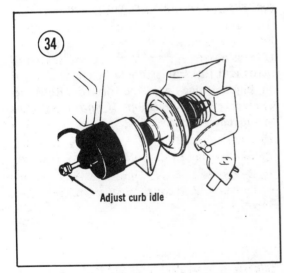

(34)

Adjust curb idle

b. If dump valve has one line at top, check to see if line connects to intake manifold. If not, use a bypass line to connect the valve directly to the intake manifold, first removing and plugging the existing vacuum line at the dump valve.

3. Make sure throttle and choke linkages are working freely and properly.

4. If the vehicle has a spark delay valve, bypass it by connecting a vacuum line directly to the advance side of the distributor vacuum advance mechanism.

5. If vehicle has a fuel decel valve, disconnect and plug the vacuum hose to the valve.

6. Remove the vacuum line from the EGR valve and plug it.

7. Make sure all lights and accessories are turned off. Start the engine and allow it to reach normal operating temperature. Make sure the choke plate is fully open.

8. Place transmission in NEUTRAL and set the choke linkage on the specified step of the fast idle cam. See Vehicle Emission Control Information (VECI) decal. Measure fast idle speed and adjust to specification if necessary. Accelerate engine to about 2,500 rpm for 15 seconds, then recheck fast idle speed, making sure linkage is still on specified step of fast idle cam. Repeat as often as required until repeatable specified fast idle speed is obtained.

9. Reconnect EGR, spark decel valve, and spark delay valve as appropriate, to their original positions.

10. Collapse the throttle solenoid positioner (TSP) plunger by forcing the throttle lever against it and check the "TSP-off" speed against the specification on the VECI decal. Adjust if required, using the "TSP-off" idle speed adjustment screw (see **Figure 33**).

11. Accelerate engine to 2,500 rpm for about 15 seconds and allow it to return to idle. Place automatic transmission in DRIVE, or leave manual transmission in NEUTRAL. Allow idle speed to stabilize, then check speed against that specified on VECI decal. Adjust, if required. Repeat this step and recheck idle speed, readjusting if required.

12. Install air cleaner assembly and unplug and reconnect vacuum lines. Recheck curb idle speed with automatic transmission in DRIVE and manual transmission in NEUTRAL. If curb idle speed is not as specified on VECI decal, remove air cleaner and repeat Step 11.

13. Stop engine, remove test equipment, and torque air cleaner wing nuts.

Additional Checks

If the correct carburetor idle speed cannot be achieved as described above, and after the preceding recommended tune-up steps have been performed, the vacuum lines and fittings should be carefully inspected for leaks, and if leaks are found, they should be corrected before idle speed adjustment is attempted again.

If the above idle speed adjustment procedure is being used only to correct an unsatisfactory idle condition, the following areas (which are covered earlier in this chapter) must also be checked before the idle speed adjustment is attempted.

a. Electrical continuity in ignition system
b. Spark plug condition and electrode gap
c. Contact breaker and condenser condition and adjustment (dwell angle)
d. Ignition timing
e. Valve clearance
f. Engine compression

If, after all of the services and adjustments described above have been accurately carried out and the idle speed is still not adjustable within specifications, three probable areas of investigation remain — carburetor fuel level, crankcase ventilation system condition, and idle air/fuel ratio. The vehicle should then be referred to a Ford dealer or automotive tune-up specialist for diagnosis and correction.

FILTERS

Air and fuel filters should be changed when an engine tune-up is performed. Refer to Chapter Six, *Emission Control System Maintenance* section.

NOTE: If you own a 1980 or later model, first check the Supplement at the back of the book for any new service information.

CHAPTER FIVE

ENGINE

The engines covered in this book include the 170 cid inline 6-cylinder (**Figures 1 and 2**), the 240 and 300 cid inline 6-cylinder (**Figures 3 and 4**), the 302 and 460 cid V-8 (**Figures 5 and 6**), the 351M and 400 cid V-8 (**Figures 7 and 8**) and the 360 and 390 cid V-8 (**Figures 9 and 10**).

The 302 and 460 cid V-8 engines utilize the same basic design. The cylinder blocks are made of a high grade cast iron with thin wall construction. A precision cast nodular iron crankshaft turns on 5 main bearings. The pistons are made from an aluminum alloy, then tin plated. The rocker arms are individually bolt mounted and are actuated by hydraulic lifters. The 460 cid V-8 engine's valves are chrome plated.

All 6-cylinder engines use a cast iron cylinder block. The 170 cid engine uses a cast iron crankshaft turning in 4 main bearings; the 240 and 300 cid engines use 7 main bearings. Mechanical tappets are used in the 170 cid engine, hydraulic tappets in the 240 and 300 cid engines.

The 351M and 400 cid V-8 engines share the same basic design and structure. The cast iron cylinder block uses thin wall construction. A precision cast nodular iron crankshaft turns in 5 main bearings. Pistons are aluminium alloy,

tin plated. Rocker arms are pedestal mounted and lifters are hydraulically actuated. The 351M has a shorter stroke than the 400, and altered pistons, crankshaft, and camshaft. Otherwise the two engines, both of which are offered as options for F-100 through F-350 trucks, are basically the same.

The 360 and 390 cid V-8 engines share the same basic design, the major difference being in the stroke. Otherwise the engines share the same features with the other V-8 engines in this book.

Engine fastener torque recommendations are given in **Table 1** (end of chapter); specifications for all engines are given in **Tables 2-4** at the end of this chapter.

ENGINE REMOVAL/INSTALLATION

Removal

The following procedure is for the engine only (transmission not attached).

1. Drain cooling system and crankcase, then remove hood or tilt the cab.

2. Remove air cleaner (refer to *Emission Control System Maintenance* section, Chapter Six), then remove air conditioner compressor and condenser.

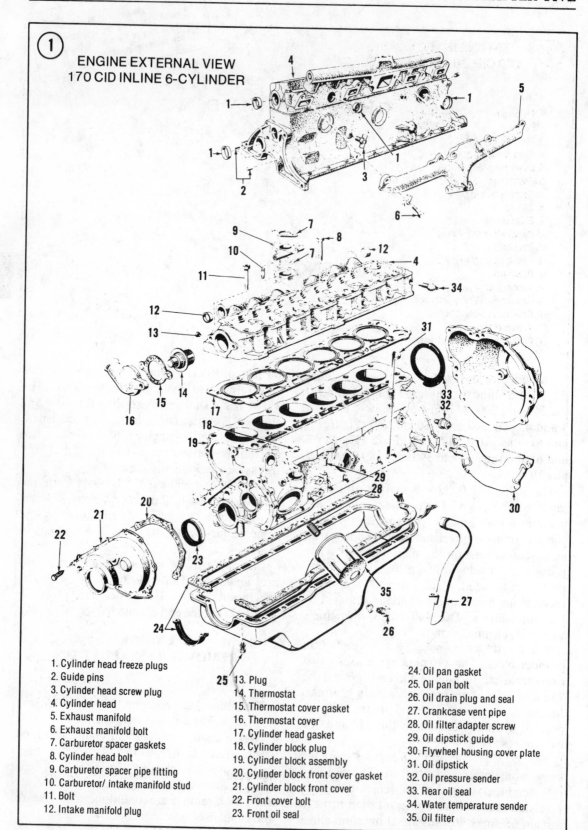

① ENGINE EXTERNAL VIEW
170 CID INLINE 6-CYLINDER

1. Cylinder head freeze plugs
2. Guide pins
3. Cylinder head screw plug
4. Cylinder head
5. Exhaust manifold
6. Exhaust manifold bolt
7. Carburetor spacer gaskets
8. Cylinder head bolt
9. Carburetor spacer pipe fitting
10. Carburetor/ intake manifold stud
11. Bolt
12. Intake manifold plug

13. Plug
14. Thermostat
15. Thermostat cover gasket
16. Thermostat cover
17. Cylinder head gasket
18. Cylinder block plug
19. Cylinder block assembly
20. Cylinder block front cover gasket
21. Cylinder block front cover
22. Front cover bolt
23. Front oil seal

24. Oil pan gasket
25. Oil pan bolt
26. Oil drain plug and seal
27. Crankcase vent pipe
28. Oil filter adapter screw
29. Oil dipstick guide
30. Flywheel housing cover plate
31. Oil dipstick
32. Oil pressure sender
33. Rear oil seal
34. Water temperature sender
35. Oil filter

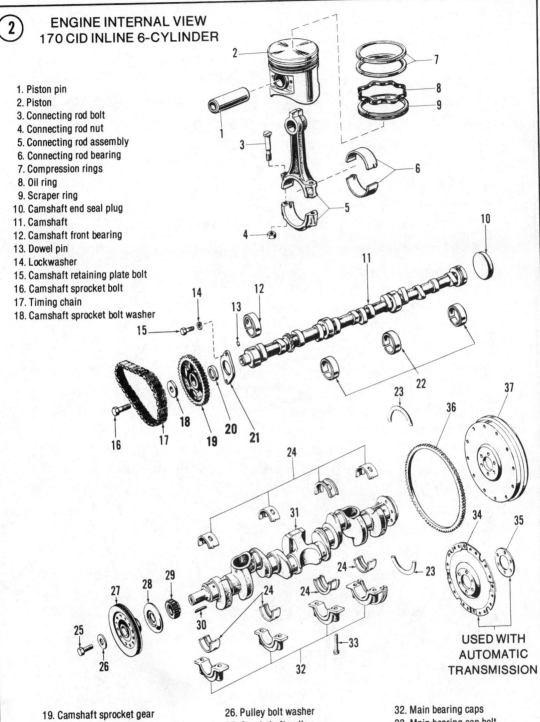

② ENGINE INTERNAL VIEW
170 CID INLINE 6-CYLINDER

1. Piston pin
2. Piston
3. Connecting rod bolt
4. Connecting rod nut
5. Connecting rod assembly
6. Connecting rod bearing
7. Compression rings
8. Oil ring
9. Scraper ring
10. Camshaft end seal plug
11. Camshaft
12. Camshaft front bearing
13. Dowel pin
14. Lockwasher
15. Camshaft retaining plate bolt
16. Camshaft sprocket bolt
17. Timing chain
18. Camshaft sprocket bolt washer

USED WITH
AUTOMATIC
TRANSMISSION

19. Camshaft sprocket gear
20. Sprocket gear spacer
21. Camshaft retaining plate
22. Camshaft bearings
23. Rear oil seals
24. Crankshaft main bearings
25. Crankshaft pulley bolt

26. Pulley bolt washer
27. Crankshaft pulley
28. Oil slinger
29. Crankshaft timing gear
30. Crankshaft Woodruff key
31. Crankshaft

32. Main bearing caps
33. Main bearing cap bolt
34. Torque converter drive plate
35. Torque converter plate bolt
36. Flywheel ring gear
37. Flywheel

5

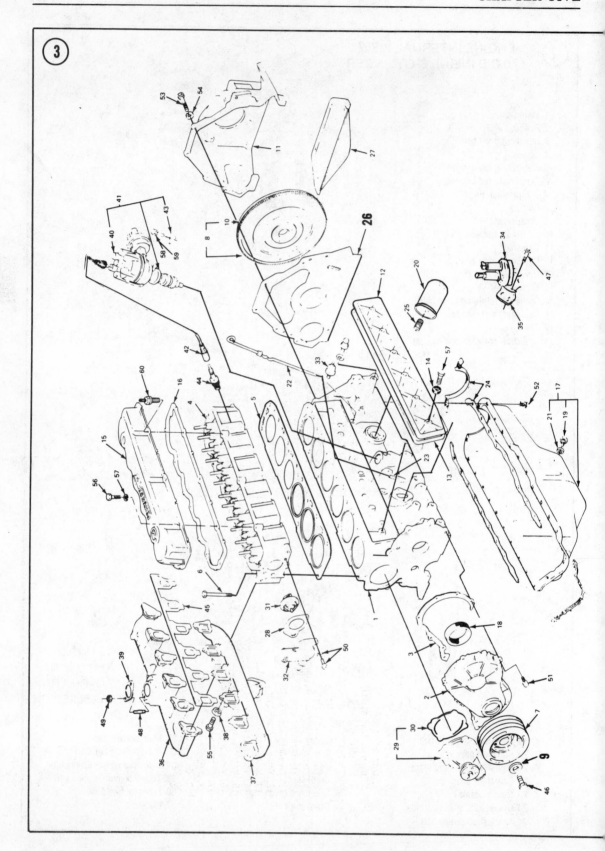

5

ENGINE EXTERNAL VIEW
240/300 CID INLINE 6-CYLINDER

1. Cylinder assembly (includes internal parts)
2. Cylinder front cover assembly
3. Cylinder front cover gasket
4. Cylinder head
5. Cylinder head gasket
6. Cylinder head bolt
7. Crankshaft pulley assembly (includes damper)
8. Flywheel assembly
9. Crankshaft pulley retaining washer
10. Flywheel ring gear
11. Flywheel housing assembly
12. Valve pushrod cover
13. Valve pushrod cover gasket
14. Valve pushrod cover bolt grommet
15. Valve rocker arm cover assembly
16. Valve rocker cover gasket
17. Oil pan assembly
18. Cylinder front cover seal
19. Oil pan drain plug
20. Oil filter element assembly

21. Oil pan drain plug gasket
22. Oil level indicator
23. Oil level indicator tube assembly
24. Oil pan gasket set
25. Oil filter mounting bolt insert
26. Engine rear plate assembly
27. Clutch housing dust cover
28. Water outlet connection gasket
29. Water pump assembly
30. Water pump housing gasket
31. Thermostat
32. Water outlet connection
33. Oil pressure engine unit gauge assembly
34. Fuel pump assembly
35. Fuel pump mounting gasket
36. Intake manifold
37. Exhaust manifold
38. Manifold gasket set
39. Carburetor gasket
40. Distributor cap
41. Distributor assembly

42. Spark plug wire set
43. Distributor hold-down
44. Spark plug assembly
45. Intake manifold-to-cylinder head gasket
46. Bolt
47. Screw and washer assembly
48. Carburetor-to-manifold stud screw
49. Hexagon jamb nut
50. Washer head bolt
51. Washer head bolt
52. Bolt
53. Bolt
54. Lockwasher
55. Bolt
56. Bolt
57. Lockwasher
58. Bolt
59. Lockwasher
60. Stud and washer

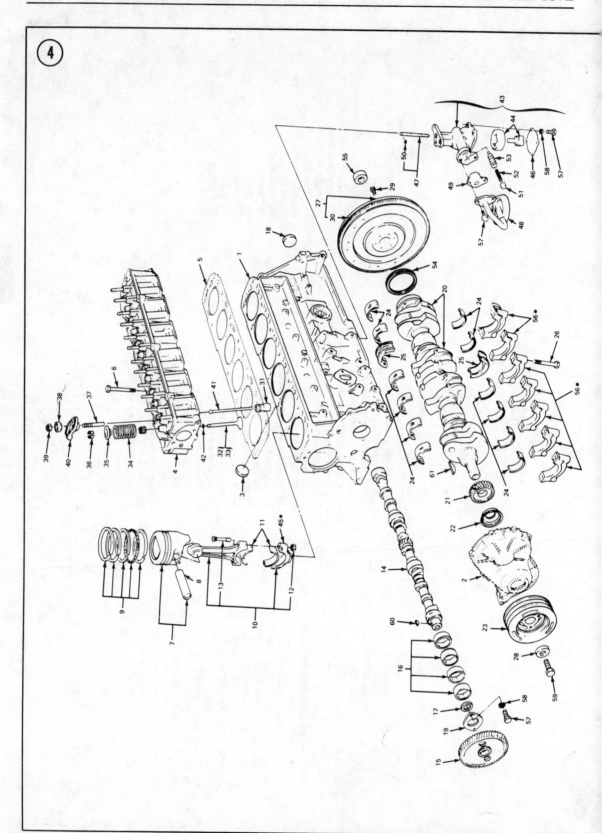

5

ENGINE INTERNAL VIEW
240/300 CID INLINE 6-CYLINDER

1. Block assembly (internal parts not included)
2. Cylinder front cover assembly
3. Engine plug
4. Cylinder head
5. Cylinder head gasket
6. Cylinder head bolt
7. Piston assembly
8. Piston pin
9. Piston ring set
10. Connecting rod assembly
11. Connecting rod bearing
12. Connecting rod nut
13. Connecting rod bolt
14. Camshaft
15. Camshaft gear
16. Camshaft bearing
17. Camshaft gear spacer
18. Camshaft rear bearing plug
19. Camshaft thrust plate
20. Crankshaft assembly
21. Crankshaft gear
22. Crankshaft oil slinger

23. Crankshaft pulley assembly (includes damper)
24. Crankshaft main bearing
25. Crankshaft main bearing (thrust)
26. Crankshaft main bearing cap bolt
27. Flywheel assembly
28. Crankshaft pulley retaining washer
29. Flywheel-to-crankshaft bolt
30. Flywheel ring gear
31. Valve hydraulic tappet assembly
32. Exhaust valve
33. Intake valve
34. Valve spring
35. Valve spring retainer
36. Valve spring retainer key
37. Valve rocker arm support stud
38. Valve rocker arm fulcrum seat
39. Valve rocker arm stud nut
40. Valve rocker arm
41. Valve pushrod
42. Valve stem (I and E) seal
43. Oil pump assembly
44. Oil pump drive rotor and shaft assembly

45. Rod cap (supplied with 6200 rod assembly)
46. Oil pump drive plate
47. Oil pump intermediate shaft assembly
48. Oil pump screen, tube, and cover assembly
49. Oil pump inlet tube gasket
50. Oil pump intermediate shaft ring
51. Oil pump relief valve plug
52. Oil pump relief valve spring
53. Oil pump relief valve plunger
54. Crankshaft rear packing
55. Clutch pilot bearing
56. Main bearing cap (supplied in 6010 block assembly)
57. Bolt
58. Lockwasher
59. Bolt
60. Woodruff key
61. Woodruff key

88

CHAPTER FIVE

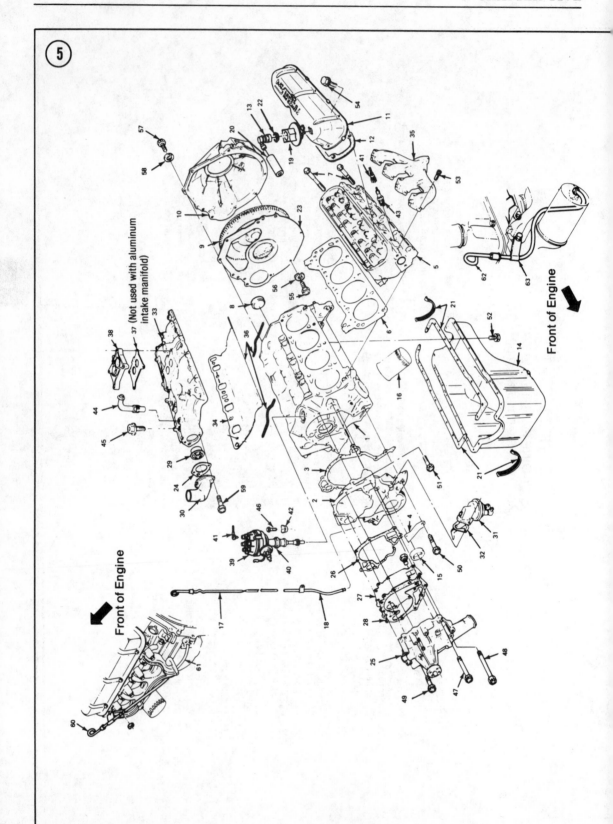

ENGINE EXTERNAL VIEW
302/460 CID V-8

1. Cylinder assembly (includes internal parts)
2. Cylinder front cover assembly
3. Cylinder front cover gasket
4. Timing pointer
5. Cylinder head
6. Cylinder head gasket
7. Cylinder head bolt
8. Camshaft rear bearing plug
9. Flywheel assembly
10. Flywheel housing assembly
11. Valve rocker arm cover assembly
12. Valve rocker arm cover gasket
13. Positive crankcase ventilation (PCV) elbow and valve assembly
14. Oil pan assembly
15. Cylinder front cover seal
16. Oil filter element assembly
17. Oil level indicator
18. Oil level indicator tube assembly
19. Oil filler cap assembly
20. Positive crankcase ventilation hose
21. Oil pan gasket set
22. Crankcase ventilation retainer grommet
23. Engine rear plate assembly
24. Water outlet connection gasket
25. Water pump assembly
26. Water pump housing gasket
27. Water pump cover
28. Water pump cover gasket
29. Water thermostat
30. Water outlet connection
31. Fuel pump assembly
32. Fuel pump mounting gasket
33. Intake manifold
34. Intake manifold-to-cylinder block seal
35. Exhaust manifold
36. Manifold gasket set
37. Carburetor gasket
38. Carburetor-to-intake manifold spacer
39. Distributor parts
40. Distributor assembly
41. Spark plug wire set
42. Distributor clamp
43. Spark plug assembly
44. Hot water connection elbow
45. Head bolt washer
46. Bolt
47. Bolt
48. Bolt
49. Bolt
50. Bolt
51. Bolt or screw
52. Bolt
53. Bolt
54. Bolt
55. Bolt
56. Lockwasher
57. Bolt
58. Lockwasher
59. Bolt
60. Oil level indicator
61. Oil level indicator tube assembly
62. Oil level indicator
63. Oil level indicator tube assembly

5

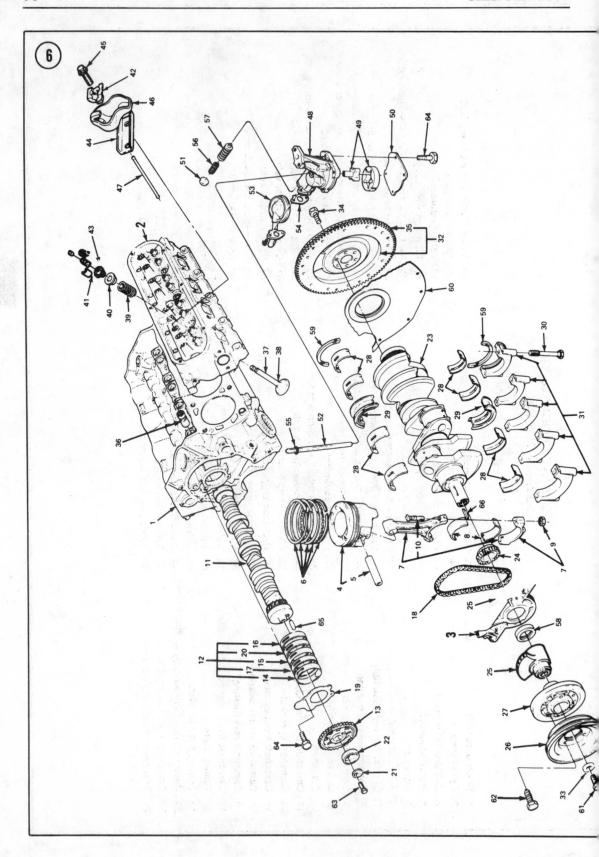

5

ENGINE INTERNAL VIEW
302/460 CID V-8

1. Block assembly
2. Cylinder head
3. Cylinder front plate
4. Piston assembly
5. Piston pin
6. Piston ring set
7. Connecting rod assembly
8. Connecting rod bearing
9. Connecting rod nut
10. Connecting rod bolt
11. Camshaft
12. Camshaft bearing kit (standard)
13. Camshaft sprocket
14. Camshaft front bearing
15. Camshaft center bearing
16. Camshaft rear bearing
17. Camshaft front intermediate bearing
18. Timing chain
19. Camshaft thrust plate
20. Camshaft rear intermediate bearing
21. Camshaft sprocket washer
22. Two-piece fuel pump eccentric

23. Crankshaft assembly
24. Crankshaft sprocket
25. Crankshaft oil slinger
26. Pulley assembly
27. Crankshaft damper assembly
28. Crankshaft main bearing (except center)
29. Crankshaft bearing (center)
30. Crankshaft main bearing cap bolt
31. Main bearing cap
32. Flywheel assembly
33. Crankshaft pulley retaining washer
34. Flywheel-to-crankshaft bolt
35. Flywheel ring gear
36. Hydraulic tappet assembly
37. Exhaust valve
38. Intake valve
39. Valve spring
40. Valve spring retainer
41. Valve spring retainer key
42. Valve rocker arm fulcrum seat
43. Valve stem seal
44. Valve pushrod valley baffle

45. Valve rocker arm attaching bolt
46. Valve rocker arm
47. Valve pushrod
48. Oil pump assembly
49. Oil pump drive rotor and shaft assembly
50. Oil pump body plate
51. Oil pump relief valve plug
52. Oil pump intermediate shaft assembly
53. Oil pump screen, tube, and cover assembly
54. Oil pump inlet tube gasket
55. Oil pump intermediate shaft O-ring
56. Oil pump relief valve spring
57. Oil pump relief valve plunger
58. Cylinder front seal
59. Crankshaft rear packing
60. Engine rear plate
61. Bolt
62. Bolt
63. Bolt
64. Bolt
65. Dowel pin
66. Woodruff key

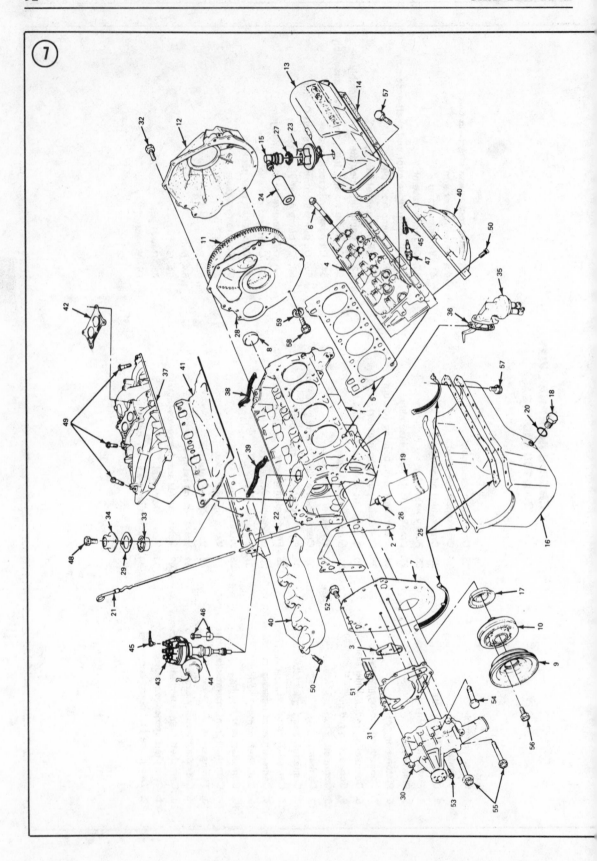

5

ENGINE EXTERNAL VIEW
351 M/400 CID V-8

1. Block assembly (internal parts not included)
2. Cylinder front cover plate gasket
3. Timing pointer
4. Cylinder head
5. Cylinder head gasket
6. Cylinder head bolt
7. Cylinder front cover plate
8. Camshaft rear bearing plug
9. Crankshaft pulley assembly
10. Engine crankshaft damper assembly
11. Flywheel assembly
12. Flywheel housing assembly
13. Valve rocker arm cover assembly
14. Valve rocker arm cover gasket
15. Positive crankcase elbow and valve assembly
16. Oil pan assembly
17. Cylinder front cover oil seal
18. Oil pan drain plug
19. Oil filter element assembly

20. Oil pan drain plug gasket
21. Oil level indicator
22. Oil level indicator tube assembly
23. Oil filler cap assembly
24. Crankcase ventilation hose
25. Oil pan gasket set
26. Oil filter mounting bolt insert
27. Crankcase ventilation grommet retainer
28. Engine rear plate assembly
29. Water outlet connection gasket
30. Water pump assembly
31. Water pump housing gasket
32. Bolt
33. Water thermostat
34. Water outlet connection
35. Fuel pump assembly
36. Fuel pump mounting gasket
37. Intake manifold
38. Intake manifold to cylinder block (rear) seal
39. Intake manifold to cylinder

block (front) seal
40. Exhaust manifold
41. Intake manifold to cylinder head gasket
42. Carburetor gasket
43. Distributor cap
44. Distributor assembly
45. Spark plug wire set
46. Distributor clamp
47. Spark plug assembly
48. Screw and lockwasher
49. Bolt hex washer head
50. Washer head bolt
51. Bolt
52. Self-tapping screw
53. Self-tapping screw
54. Washer head bolt
55. Washer head bolt
56. Bolt
57. Washer head bolt
58. Bolt
59. Lockwasher

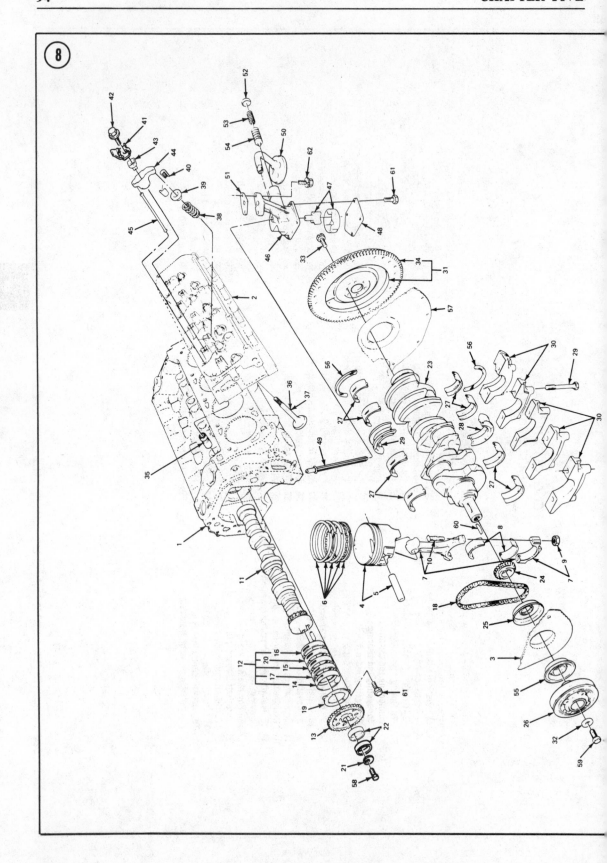

ENGINE INTERNAL VIEW
351 M/400 CID V-8

1. Block assembly (internal parts not included)
2. Cylinder front cover assembly
3. Cylinder head
4. Piston assembly
5. Piston pin
6. Piston ring set
7. Connecting rod assembly
8. Connecting rod bearing
9. Connecting rod nut
10. Connecting rod bolt
11. Camshaft
12. Standard camshaft bearing kit
13. Camshaft (nylon) sprocket
14. Camshaft front bearing
15. Camshaft center bearing
16. Camshaft rear bearing
17. Camshaft front intermediate bearing
18. Timing chain
19. Camshaft thrust plate
20. Camshaft rear intermediate bearing
21. Camshaft sprocket washer
22. Camshaft fuel pump eccentric

23. Crankshaft assembly
24. Crankshaft sprocket
25. Damper spacer
26. Crankshaft damper assembly
27. Crankshaft main (except center)
28. Crankshaft main (center) bearing
29. Crankshaft main bearing cap bolt
30. Main bearing cap
31. Flywheel assembly
32. Crankshaft pulley retaining washer
33. Flywheel to crankshaft bolt
34. Flywheel ring gear
35. Hydraulic tappet assembly
36. Exhaust valve
37. Intake valve
38. Valve spring
39. Valve spring retainer
40. Valve spring retainer key
41. Fulcrum
42. Rocker arm attach bolt
43. Guide
44. Valve rocker arm
45. Valve pushrod

46. Oil pump assembly
47. Oil pump drive rotor and shaft assembly
48. Oil pump body plate
49. Oil pump intermediate shaft assembly
50. Oil pump screen, tube and cover assembly
51. Oil pump inlet tube gasket
52. Oil pump relief valve plug
53. Oil pump relief valve spring
54. Oil pump relief valve plunger
55. Cylinder front cover oil seal
56. Crankshaft rear packing
57. Engine rear plate
58. Bolt
59. Bolt
60. Woodruff key
61. Bolt
62. Bolt

5

⑨

ENGINE EXTERNAL VIEW
360/390 CID V-8

1. Cylinder block assembly
2. Cylinder front cover
3. Cylinder front cover gasket
4. Engine core plug
5. Cylinder head
6. Cylinder head gasket
7. Cylinder head bolt
8. Valve spring oil baffle
9. Bolt
10. Oil pan assembly
11. Front cover seal
12. Oil pan gasket
13. Oil pan drain plug
14. Drain plug gasket
15. Dipstick
16. Dipstick tube assembly
17. Oil filler cap
18. Oil filler tube
19. Clutch housing
20. Clutch release lever trunnion
21. Clutch housing dust cover

22. Intake manifold
23. Rear seal
24. Front seal
25. Right exhaust manifold
26. Left exhaust manifold
27. Manifold gasket
28. Carburetor gasket
29. Heater hose fitting
30. Carburetor spacer
31. Water temperature sender adaptor
32. Pipe plug
33. Fitting connector
34. Bolt
35. Bolt
36. Bolt
37. Flat washer
38. Bolt
39. Lockwasher
40. Bolt
41. Lockwasher

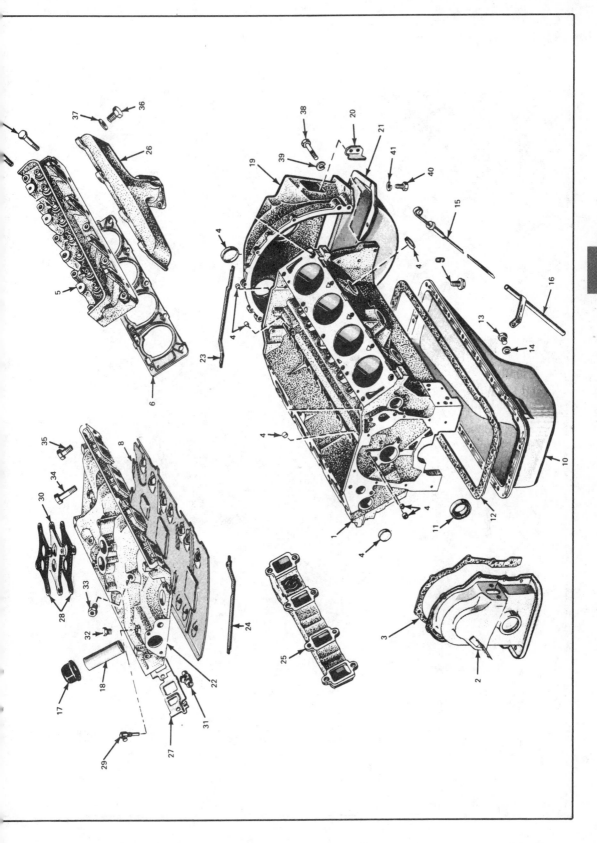

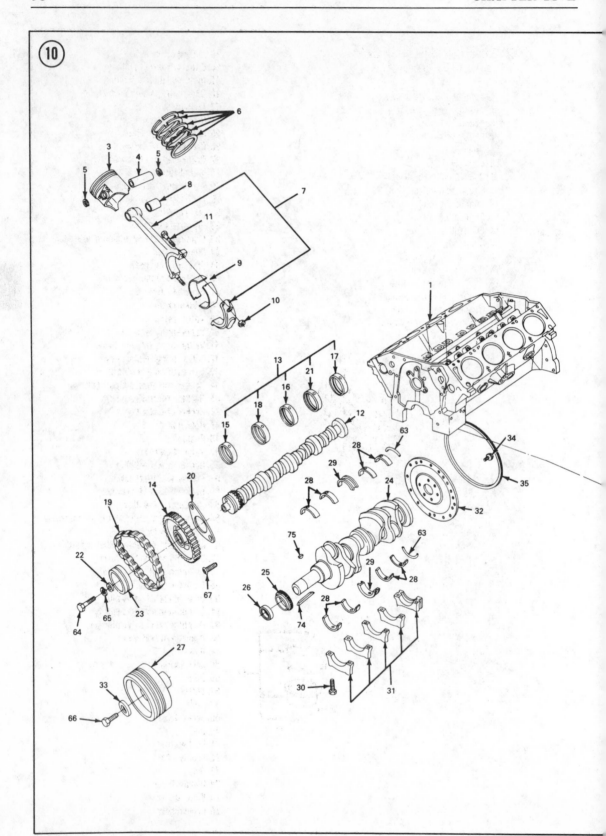

ENGINE INTERNAL VIEW
360/390 CID V-8

1. Cylinder block assembly
2. Cylinder head assembly
3. Piston
4. Piston pin
5. Snap ring
6. Piston ring set
7. Connecting rod assembly
8. Connecting rod bushing
9. Connecting rod bearing
10. Connecting rod nut
11. Connecting rod bolt
12. Camshaft
13. Camshaft bearing set
14. Camshaft sprocket
15. Front camshaft bearing
16. Center camshaft bearing
17. Rear camshaft bearing
18. Intermediate rear bearing

19. Timing chain
20. Camshaft thrust plate
21. Intermediate rear bearing
22. Camshaft sprocket washer
23. Fuel pump runner
24. Crankshaft assembly
25. Crankshaft sprocket
26. Crankshaft oil slinger
27. Crankshaft pulley assembly
28. Main bearing
29. Center main bearing
30. Main bearing cap bolt
31. Main bearing cap
32. Flywheel assembly
33. Crankshaft pulley retaining washer
34. Flywheel bolt
35. Flywheel ring gear
36. Hydraulic tappet assembly
37. Exhaust valve
38. Intake valve
39. Valve spring
40. Valve spring retainer
41. Valve spring retainer sleeve
42. valve spring retainer key
43. Valve spring oil baffle
44. Rocker arm shaft support bolt
45. Rocker arm shaft support
46. Rocker arm shaft
47. Rocker arm
48. Pushrod
49. Valve stem seal
50. Rocker arm shaft plug
51. Rocker arm shaft spring
52. Rocker arm shaft washer
53. Oil pump assembly
54. Oil pump drive rotor and shaft assembly
55. Oil pump body plate
56. Oil pump intermediate shaft assembly
57. Oil pump screen tube cover
58. Oil pump inlet tube gasket
59. Oil pump gasket
60. Oil pump relief valve plug
61. Oil pump relief valve spring
62. Oil pump relief valve plunger
63. Crankshaft rear seal
64. Bolt
65. Lockwasher
66. Bolt
67. Screw
68. Bolt
69. Lockwasher
70. Bolt
71. Lockwasher
72. Lockwasher
73. Bolt
74. Woodruff key
75. Woodruff key
76. Lockwasher

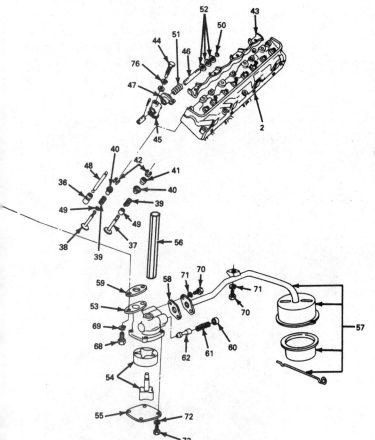

3. Disconnect battery positive (+) cable, heater hose from water pump and coolant outlet housing, and flexible fuel line from fuel pump.

4. Remove radiator, cooling fan, water pump pulley, and fan drive belt (refer to Chapter Eight, *Radiator, Fan, Water Pump,* and *Drive Belts* sections).

5. Disconnect accelerator cable and choke cable at carburetor and remove cable retracting spring. (On a vehicle equipped with power brakes, disconnect vacuum line at intake manifold; on a vehicle equipped with automatic transmission, disconnect transmission kickdown rod at bellcrank assembly.)

6. Disconnect exhaust manifold from muffler inlet pipe, then disconnect body ground strap and battery ground cable at engine.

7. Disconnect engine wiring harness at ignition coil, coolant temperature sending unit and oil pressure sending unit, and position harness out of the way.

8. Remove alternator mounting bolts and place the alternator out of the way (leave wires attached). On a vehicle with power steering, remove power steering pump from its mounting brackets and place it right side up, to one side (leave wires attached). On air conditioner equipped cars, bleed the air system and disconnect the 2 air pressure lines at the compressor.

9. Raise the vehicle and remove the starter (and the fluid filler tube bracket on automatic transmission equipped trucks). Remove the engine's rear plate upper right bolt.

10. Remove flywheel housing lower attaching bolts (on manual transmission equipped models), then disconnect clutch retracting spring.

11. Remove converter housing access cover assembly (on automatic transmission equipped models), then remove flywheel-to-converter nuts and secure the converter assembly in the housing. Remove transmission oil cooler lines from engine's retaining clip. Remove housing-to-engine lower attaching bolts.

12. Remove insulator-to-intermediate support bracket nut from each engine front support.

13. Lower vehicle and place a transmission jack under the transmission to support it. Remove the remaining flywheel or converter housing engine bolts.

14. Attach engine lifting sling and raise engine slightly. Carefully pull it from the transmission and lift it out of the chassis (**Figure 11**).

Installation

1. Install a new muffler inlet pipe gasket.

2. Lower engine into chassis. Engage the dowels in the block with the holes in the converter housing or flywheel. On an automatic transmission equipped car, start the converter pilot into the crankshaft, then remove the retainer holding the converter in the housing. On a manual transmission equipped car, start the transmission input shaft into the clutch disc. (It may be necessary to adjust the attitude of the transmission slightly if the transmission input shaft will not enter the clutch disc. If the engine hangs up after the shaft enters, turn the crankshaft, with the transmission in gear, until the shaft splines mesh with the clutch disc splines.)

3. Install the flywheel housing or converter upper attaching bolts, then remove the jack supporting the transmission.

4. Lower engine until it rests on the engine supports and remove the lifting sling (refer to **Figure 11**).

5. Install left and right engine support insulator-to-intermediate support bracket attaching nuts and washers.

6. Install automatic transmission oil cooler lines bracket.

7. Install remaining flywheel housing or converter attaching bolts, then connect clutch return spring.

8. Install starter and connect starter cable. On models so equipped, attach automatic transmission fluid filler tube bracket; then install transmission oil cooler lines in cylinder block bracket.

9. Install exhaust manifold-to-muffler inlet pipe lockwashers and nuts.

10. Connect engine ground strap and battery ground cable.

11. On vehicles so equipped, connect automatic transmission kickdown rod to bellcrank assembly on intake manifold.

12. Connect accelerator linkage to carburetor and install retracting spring. Connect choke cable to carburetor and hand throttle (if so equipped).

13. On vehicles with power brakes, connect brake vacuum line to intake manifold.

14. Connect coil primary wire, oil pressure and coolant temperature sending unit wires, heater hoses, flexible fuel lines, and battery positive (+) cable.

15. Install alternator on mounting bracket (on vehicles with power steering, install power steering pump on mounting brackets also).

16. Install water pump pulley, spacer, cooling fan and drive belt, then adjust drive belts to specifications (refer to Chapter Eight).

17. Install radiator, then connect lower radiator-to-water pump hose, and upper radiator-to-coolant outlet housing (refer to Chapter Eight).

18. Connect air compressor lines, compressor, and condenser (if removed).

19. On automatic transmission models, connect oil cooler lines.

20. Install the hood.

21. Fill and bleed cooling system (refer to Chapter Eight, *Coolant Change* section).

22. Fill crankcase, then operate engine at fast idle and check all connections and gaskets for leakage.

23. Adjust carburetor idle speed and mixture (refer to Chapter Four, *Carburetor* section).

24. On standard transmission models, adjust clutch pedal free travel (refer to Chapter Ten, *Clutch* section).

25. On automatic transmission models, adjust transmission control linkage (refer to Chapter Ten, *Automatic Transmission* section). Then check the fluid level and add as necessary to bring to proper level (refer to Chapter Three, *Periodic Checks and Inspections* section under *Automatic Transmission Oil Level* procedure).

26. Install air cleaner (refer to Chapter Six, *Emission Control System Maintenance* section.

INTAKE MANIFOLD (V-8 ENGINES)

Removal

1. Drain cooling system, then remove air cleaner and intake duct assembly, including crankcase ventilation hose.

2. Disconnect all carburetor linkage, electrical wires, vacuum lines, fuel lines, water hoses, and evaporative hoses (anything that would impede removal of the intake manifold). Mark each item with masking tape to make installation simple.

3. Remove distributor hold-down bolt and remove distributor (refer to Chapter Seven, *Distributor* section).

4. Remove intake manifold attaching bolts, then remove intake manifold and carburetor as a unit. Discard old gaskets and seals (including intake manifold attaching bolt sealing washers).

Installation

1. Clean mating surfaces of the intake manifold, cylinder heads, and cylinder block with a solvent such as Ford Spot Remover or equivalent. Apply a 1/8 in. bead of silicone

sealer (available at any auto parts jobber) at points shown in **Figure 12**.

2. Apply a 1/16 in. bead of silicone sealer to the outer end of each intake manifold seal for the full width of the seal (4 places). Refer to **Figure 12**.

> *NOTE*
> *It is important to complete assembly promptly, as this sealer sets up in 15 minutes. Do not drip sealer into engine valley.*

3. Position seals on cylinder block and new gaskets on cylinder heads with gaskets interlocked with seal tabs. Be sure that the holes in the gaskets are aligned with the holes in the cylinder heads.

> *NOTE*
> *Some V-8's use a valley baffle and the end seals as shown in **Figure 13**. Clean the mating surfaces of the intake manifold, cylinder heads, cylinder block, and cylinder block end seal rails with Ford Spot*

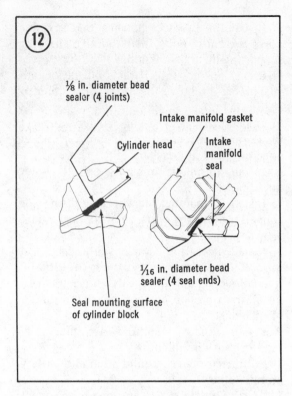

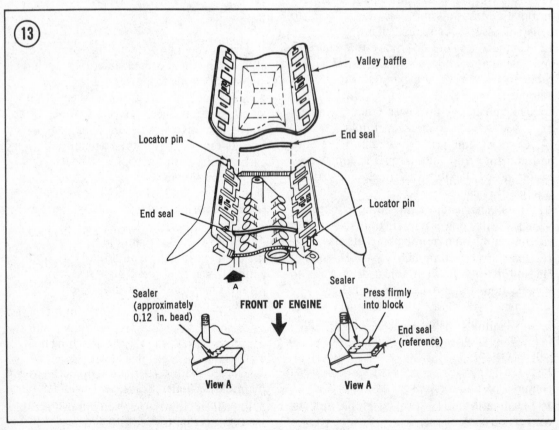

Remover solvent (or equivalent). Install 2 locator pins in the holes shown in Figure 13, and hand-tighten. Apply sealer. Install front and rear seals as shown, then install the valley baffle. Remove the locator pins.

4. Lower intake manifold into position on cylinder block and cylinder heads. After intake manifold is in place, run your finger around the seal area to be sure that seals are in place. If not, remove intake manifold and reposition the seals.

5. Check to be sure that holes in manifold gaskets and manifold are in alignment. Install intake manifold attaching nuts and bolts and tighten evenly (refer to **Table 1** at the end of the chapter and to **Figure 14**).

6. Complete installation by reversing Steps 1-3 under *Removal* procedure, preceding.

NOTE
When installation is complete, start engine and run at fast idle. Check all hose connections and gaskets for leaks. Retighten intake manifold bolts (refer to Figure 14).

MANIFOLD ASSEMBLY (INLINE ENGINES)

Removal

1. Remove air cleaner, then disconnect all carburetor 1inkage, fuel lines, vacuum lines, and anything else that would impede removal of the manifold.

2. Remove manifold nuts and bolts and lift manifold assemblies from engine. Remove and discard gaskets.

3. To separate manifolds, remove nuts holding intake and exhaust manifolds together.

Installation

1. Clean cylinder head/manifold mating surfaces.

2. If manifolds have been separated, coat mating surfaces lightly with graphite grease and place exhaust manifold over studs on intake manifold. Install lockwashers and nuts and tighten finger-tight.

3. Install new intake manifold gasket. Coat mating surfaces lightly with graphite grease,

then place manifold assemblies in position against cylinder head. Be sure that gaskets do not become dislodged. Install attaching washers, bolts, and nuts. Tighten evenly (refer to **Figure 14** and to **Table 1**).

NOTE
If manifolds were separated, install nuts joining them.

4. Install a new gasket on the muffler inlet pipe and connect inlet pipe to exhaust manifold. Tighten nuts evenly 25-38 ft.-lb (35-52 N•m).

5. Finish installation by connecting all vacuum lines, fuel lines, carburetor linkage, and other items which were disconnected during the removal procedure.

6. Install air cleaner and adjust engine idle speed and fuel mixture (refer to Chapter Four, *Carburetor* section).

EXHAUST MANIFOLDS (V-8 ENGINES)

Removal

1. Remove air cleaner and intake duct assembly, including crankcase ventilation hose.

2. Remove bolts holding air cleaner inlet duct (on models so equipped).

3. Disconnect muffler inlet pipe.

4. Remove heat shields and attaching bolts and flat washers, then remove exhaust manifold.

Installation

1. Clean mating surfaces with a flat scraper.

2. Position exhaust manifolds on cylinder heads, then install heat shields and attaching bolts and flat washers. Tighten bolts securely, working from the center toward the ends.

3. Install new gaskets on the muffler inlet pipes and position muffler inlet pipes into the manifolds. Install and tighten attaching nuts.

4. Position air cleaner inlet duct (if so equipped) and install and tighten attaching bolt evenly (refer to **Table 1**).

5. Install air cleaner and intake duct assembly, including crankcase ventilation hose.

5

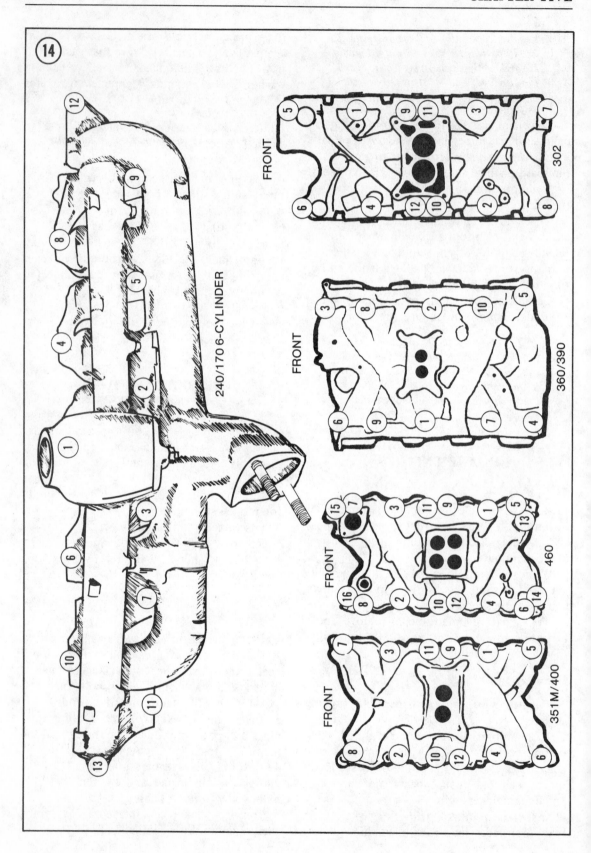

14

240/170 6-CYLINDER

302

360/390

460

351M/400

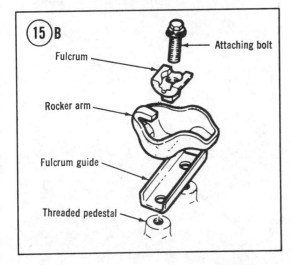

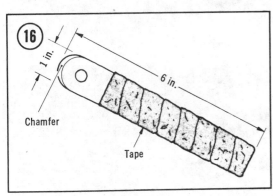

ROCKER ARM COVERS
(ALL MODELS)

Removal/Installation

1. Remove air cleaner and disconnect all lines, pipes, etc., which impede removal of the rocker arm covers.

2. Remove rocker arm cover hold-down bolts and pull covers off.

3. To install, clean all gasket surfaces and place new gaskets in the covers (be sure that the gasket tabs engage the notches in the cover). Position the covers and install and tighten the bolts evenly to the values listed in **Table 1**. After ten minutes, tighten the bolts to the same value again.

CYLINDER HEAD

Removal

1. Remove intake manifold and carburetor as a unit (refer to *Intake Manifold* section, earlier in this chapter).

2. Remove rocker arm covers (refer to *Rocker Arm Covers* section earlier in this chapter).

3. Loosen rocker arm fulcrum bolts so that the rocker arms can be rotated to one side (**Figure 15A** and **Figure 15B**). Remove pushrods in sequence so that they may be installed in their original position.

4. Remove the cylinder head attaching bolts evenly, a few turns at a time to avoid distorting the head, then lift the cylinder head off the block. Remove and discard the old head gasket.

Disassembly/Assembly

1. Remove carbon from the combustion chambers with a wire brush or homemade scraper (**Figure 16**).

2. Compress the valve spring with a spring compressor (**Figure 17**), then remove the spring retainer locks and release the spring (**Figures 18A and 18B**).

3. Remove the spring retainer, sleeve, spring, stem seal, and valve (**Figures 19-22**).

4. To assemble the cylinder head components, reverse the preceding steps, and observe the following:

   a. Be sure to install each valve in the port from which it was removed.

   b. Install a new stem seal on the valve (use a 5/8 in. deep wall socket and light hammer or mallet to seat the seal on the valve stem).

   c. Install the valve spring over the valve, then the spring retainer and sleeve.

5

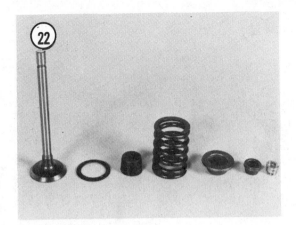

d. Compress the spring with a spring compressor and install the retainer locks.

Installation

1. Clean all mating surfaces thoroughly, then install a new gasket over the cylinder dowels on the block (**Figure 23**).

> *NOTE*
> *When you purchase the head gasket from your dealer, take note to see if it is a specially treated composition gasket (ask your dealer to be sure). These gaskets have a narrow colored bead running around the gasket edges (**Figure 24**). Do not use sealer on these gaskets.*

2. Set the cylinder head in place and snug all bolts down evenly in the sequence shown in **Figure 25**. Tighten all cylinder bolts to specifications (refer to **Table 5** and to **Figure 26**).

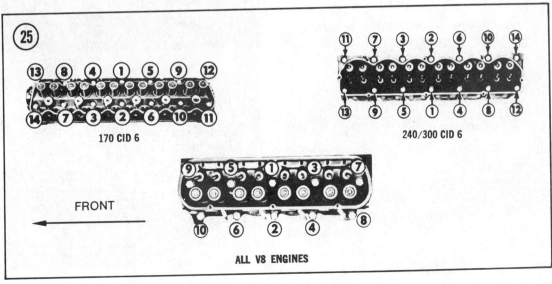

170 CID 6

240/300 CID 6

FRONT

ALL V8 ENGINES

3. Clean pushrods in solvent and blow out oil passages with compressed air. Check pushrod ends for nicks, grooves, roughness, or excessive wear. Check pushrods for straightness. Always replace an obviously bent pushrod.

4. Lubricate end of pushrod with Lubriplate or equivalent, then install them in their original positions (**Figure 27**). Install exhaust valve stem cap on engines so equipped.

5. Lubricate rocker arms and fulcrum seats with Lubriplate or equivalent, then install rocker arms (refer to **Figures 15A and 15B**).

6. Complete assembly by performing procedures given under *Rocker Arm Covers* and *Intake Manifold* sections, earlier in this chapter.

VALVE MECHANISM

Reconditioning of the intake and exhaust valves is best left to a qualified machine shop or to your Ford dealer. However, considerable money can be saved by removing the cylinder head and taking it to your dealer. The procedure for this can be found in the *Cylinder Head* section, preceding.

OIL PAN

Removal/Installation

1. Remove bolts holding oil pan to crankcase, then lift pan off.
2. Scrape all mating surfaces clean.
3. Install a new oil pan gasket and cylinder block seals (**Figure 28**). Install oil pan retaining bolts and tighten evenly.

OIL PUMP

Removal/Installation

1. Remove oil pan (refer to *Oil Pan* section, preceding).
2. Remove oil pump inlet tube and screen assembly (**Figure 29**).
3. Remove oil pump attaching bolts (**Figure 30**), then remove the oil pump gasket and intermediate drive shaft.
4. To install, reverse preceding steps.

CRANKSHAFT

Removal

1. Remove engine (refer to *Engine Removal/Installation* sections earlier in this chapter).

2. Remove crankshaft pulley from crankshaft vibration damper. Remove damper with a puller (**Figure 31**).

3. Remove oil pan (refer to *Oil Pan* section, preceding).

4. Remove oil pan-to-cylinder front cover attaching bolts. Cut oil pan gasket flush with cylinder block face prior to separating cover from cylinder block. Remove cylinder front cover and water pump as an assembly (**Figure 32**).

5. Turn crankshaft over with a bar (**Figure 33**) until timing marks on sprockets are as shown in **Figure 34**. Slide both sprockets and timing chain forward and remove them as an assembly (**Figure 35**).

6. Invert engine on engine stand, then remove oil pump (refer to *Oil Pump* section, preceding).

7. Mark bearing caps so that when you reassemble them they match.

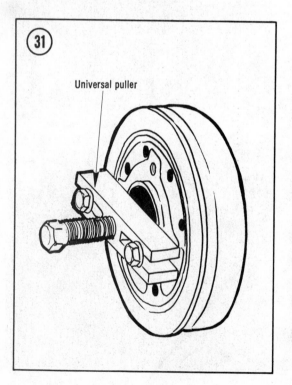

Universal puller

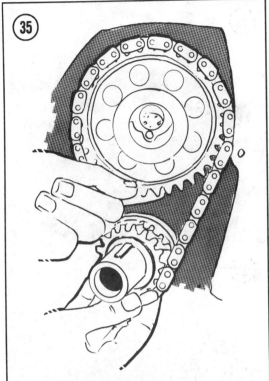

8. Turn crankshaft with a bar (**Figure 36**) until connecting rod from which the cap is to be removed is down (**Figure 37**), then remove bearing cap (**Figure 38**). Push connecting rod and piston up into the cylinder until the rod bolts clear the crankshaft journal. (Remove any ridge or deposits from the upper end of the cylinder bore with a ridge cutter. Follow the manufacturer's instructions.) Repeat this procedure with all connecting rods.

9. Remove main bearing caps (**Figure 39**), then lift crankshaft out of the block.

Inspection

1. Clean crankshaft thoroughly in solvent. Blow out oil passages with compressed air.

2. Examine crankpins and main bearing journals for wear, scoring, or cracks. Check all journals against specifications (**Table 2, 3, or 4**). If necessary, have crankshaft reground.

3. Measure crankshaft end play. Insert a feeler gauge between thrust bearing (**Figure 40**) and compare to **Table 2, 3, or 4**. Replace thrust bearing if gap exceeds specifications.

Installation

1. Remove rear journal oil seal from block and rear main bearing cap, then clean all mating surfaces of the block and rear main bearing cap, and the rear journal oil seal groove, with Ford Spot Remover or equivalent.
2. If so equipped, remove oil seal retaining pin from bearing cap. (This pin is not used with a split-lip seal).
3. Dip split lip-type seal halves in clean engine oil, then install upper seal (cylinder block) into its groove with undercut side of seal facing the front of the engine.

CAUTION
Do not allow oil to get into sealer area.
Also, no traces of solvent should be left
prior to installation of the new seal.

4. Apply an even 1/16 in. bead of Ford silicone rubber sealer (or equivalent) to the areas shown in **Figure 41**.
5. If new main bearings are to be installed, remove old bearing halves from the crankcase, then install new shells in their place (**Figure**

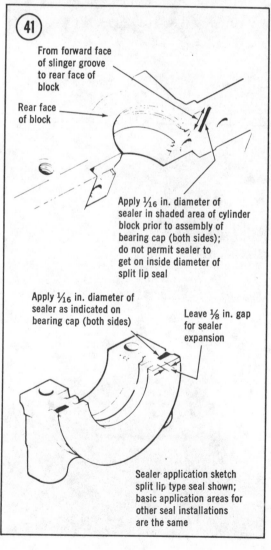

From forward face of slinger groove to rear face of block

Rear face of block

Apply ⅟₁₆ in. diameter of sealer in shaded area of cylinder block prior to assembly of bearing cap (both sides); do not permit sealer to get on inside diameter of split lip seal

Apply ⅟₁₆ in. diameter of sealer as indicated on bearing cap (both sides)

Leave ⅛ in. gap for sealer expansion

Sealer application sketch split lip type seal shown; basic application areas for other seal installations are the same

42

42). If crankshaft main bearings have to be reground, be sure that the new bearings match the journal sizes (your Ford dealer or machine shop will give you the correct sizes).

6. Lubricate the bearing shells with engine assembly lubricant (**Figure 43**), then set crankshaft in place.

7. Install all bearing caps except the thrust bearing and tighten to specifications (**Table 1**).

NOTE
Be sure that the main bearing caps are installed in their original locations.

8. Install the thrust bearing cap and tighten bolts finger-tight. Pry crankshaft forward against the thrust surface of the upper half of the bearing. Hold the crankshaft forward and pry the thrust bearing cap to the rear. This will align the thrust surfaces of both halves of the bearing. Retain the forward pressure on the crankshaft and tighten the thrust bearing cap bolts to specifications (refer to **Table 1**, and to **Figure 44**).

9. Install new rod bearings after removing the old shells. Coat the bearing surfaces with engine assembly lubricant (**Figure 45**).

10. Turn crankshaft throw to the bottom of its stroke with a lever. Push piston all the way down until the rod bearing seats on the

5

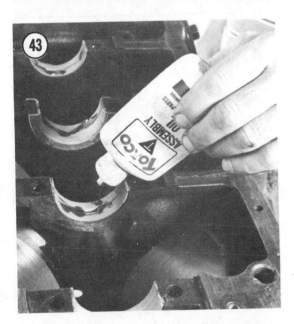

43

44

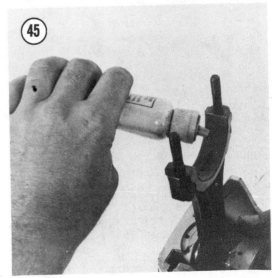

45

crankshaft journal. Install the connecting rod cap and tighten to specifications (refer to **Table 1** and **Figure 46**).

> *NOTE*
> *Always rotate the crankshaft after installing each bearing to be sure that no binding exists.*

11. After the piston and connecting rod assemblies have been installed, check side clearance between connecting rods on each connecting rod crankshaft journal (**Figure 47**).

12. Install the crankshaft key, then slide the timing chain and sprocket on so that the timing marks are as shown in **Figure 34**.

13. Install the cylinder front cover, crankshaft pulley, and adapter.

14. Install oil pan (refer to *Oil pan* section, earlier this chapter).

PISTONS/CONNECTING RODS

Removal

1. Remove cylinder head(s). Refer to *Cylinder Head* section, earlier this chapter.

2. Remove oil pan (refer to *Oil Pan* section, earlier this chapter).

3. Turn crankshaft until piston to be removed is at bottom of its travel, then stuff a cloth into the cylinder opening to catch any residue.

4. Remove any ridge or deposits from the upper end of the cylinder bore with a ridge cutter (follow the instructions furnished by the tool manufacturer).

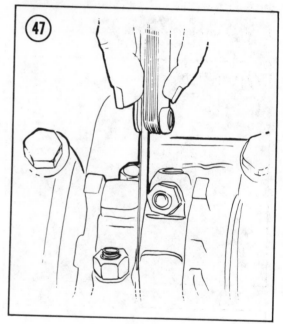

> *CAUTION*
> *Never cut into the ring travel area in excess of 1/32 in. when removing ridges.*

5. Be sure all connecting rod caps are marked so that they can be installed in their original positions.

6. Turn crankshaft until connecting rod being removed is all the way down, then remove connecting rod nuts and cap (refer to **Figures 37 and 38**). Push connecting rod and piston assembly out of the top of the cylinder with a hammer handle.

7. Install the cap on the connecting rod from which it was removed. If new bearings are to be installed, do so at this time (refer to *Crankshaft* section, preceding).

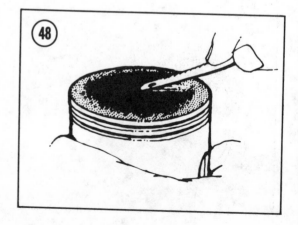

Inspection

1. Clean pistons in solvent. Scrape carbon deposits from top and grooves. Take care to avoid damage to pistons (**Figure 48**).

CAUTION
Do not use wire brush on piston skirts.

2. Examine grooves for burrs, dented edges, and side wear. Pay particular attention to top compression ring groove, as it usually wears more than the others.

3. If damage or wear indicates piston replacement, select a new piston as described in *Piston Clearance and Selection* procedure, following.

Piston Clearance and Selection

1. Make sure cylinder walls are clean and dry.

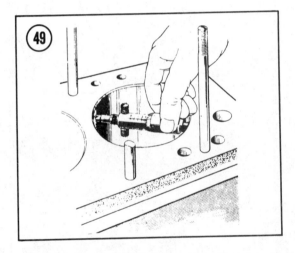

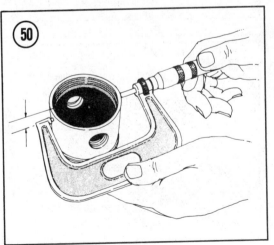

2. Measure cylinder bore 2 1/2 in. from top of bore (**Figure 49**).

3. Measure outside diameter of piston at bottom of skirt (**Figure 50**).

4. The difference between the two readings is the piston clearance.

Piston Ring Installation

1. Select new rings of proper size for piston being used.

NOTE
All compression rings have marks on their upper sides. Install these rings with marks toward top of piston.

2. Insert compression ring into cylinder bore about 1/4 in. above ring travel. Square the ring with the cylinder wall by tapping with a piston. Use a feeler gauge and measure gap (**Figure 51**). Compare to specifications (**Table 2, 3, or 4**). If too large, fit another ring; if smaller than specified, hold a small file in a vise, grip the ends of the ring with fingers, and carefully enlarge the gap as shown in **Figure 52**.

3. Roll each ring around its piston groove as shown in **Figure 53**. Minor binding may be cleaned up with a fine cut file (use care).

4. Install rings with a ring expander tool and position as shown in **Figure 54**.

Installation

1. Coat cylinder walls, pistons, rings, and bearing halves with engine assembly oil (**Figure 55**).

5

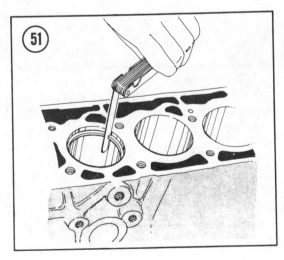

2. Compress the piston rings on the piston being installed with a ring compressor and push into bore with a hammer handle (**Figures 56 and 57**). The notch in the piston should face the front of the engine (**Figure 58**).

> *CAUTION*
> *Be careful that the connecting rod bolts do not gouge the crankshaft journal as you insert the piston and rod assembly.*

3. Install new bearings (if necessary) in rod and cap halves, then position the cap and install and tighten bolts to specifications (refer to **Table 1** and **Figure 59**).

> *CAUTION*
> *Always rotate the crankshaft after installing each bearing to be sure that no binding exists.*

4. Install oil pan (refer to *Oil Pan* section, this chapter), and cylinder heads (refer to *Cylinder Head* section, this chapter).

CYLINDER FRONT COVER AND TIMING CHAIN (V-8)

Removal

1. Refer to Chapter Eight *Water Pump* section, and perform all steps under *Removal*

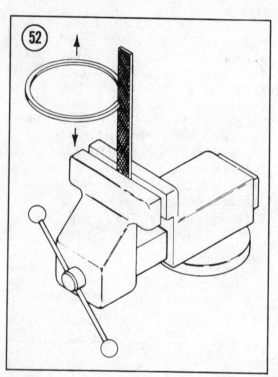

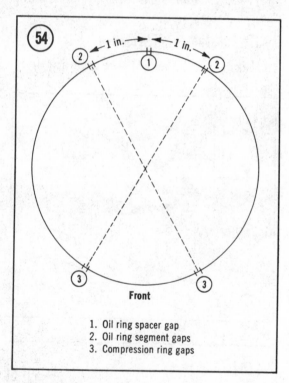

1. Oil ring spacer gap
2. Oil ring segment gaps
3. Compression ring gaps

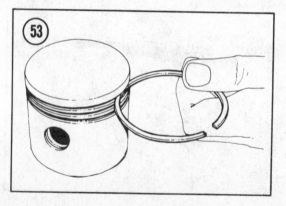

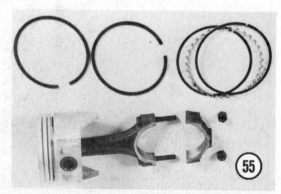

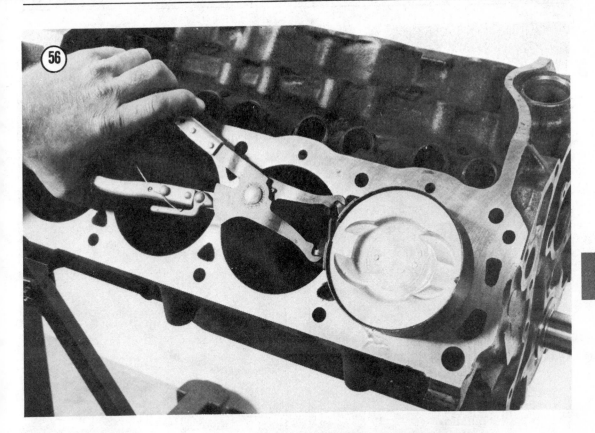

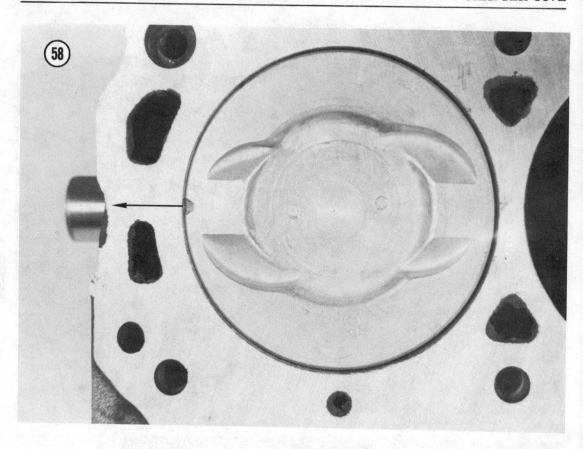

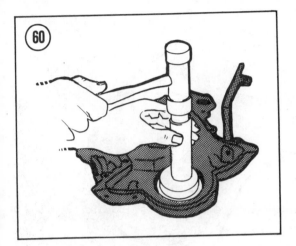

procedure, except removal of the pump (leave it attached to the front cover).

2. Remove crankshaft pulley from crankshaft vibration damper, then remove damper with a puller (refer to **Figure 31**).

3. Disconnect fuel pump outlet line from fuel pump, then remove fuel pump and set to one side with the flexible fuel lines attached.

4. Remove oil level dipstick and bolt holding the dipstick tube to the exhaust manifold.

5. Remove oil pan-to-cylinder front cover attaching bolts. Cut oil pan gasket flush with cylinder block face prior to separating cover from cylinder block. Remove cylinder front cover and water pump as an assembly (refer to **Figure 32**).

6. Discard old cylinder front cover gasket. Remove crankshaft front oil slinger.

7. Turn crankshaft over with a bar (refer to **Figure 33**), until timing marks on sprockets are as shown in **Figure 34**.

8. Remove camshaft sprocket capscrew, washers and fuel pump eccentric, then slide both sprockets and timing chain forward and remove them as an assembly (refer to **Figure 35**).

Installation

1. Install sprockets and timing chain on camshaft (refer to **Figure 35**). Be sure that timing marks on sprockets are as shown in **Figure 34**.

2. Install fuel pump, eccentric washers and camshaft sprocket cap screw. Install crankshaft front oil slinger.

3. Clean all mating surfaces, then install a new oil seal as follows:

   a. Drive out old seal with a drift.

   b. Coat the new seal with grease, then install it in the cover (**Figure 60**). Drive the seal in squarely until it is fully seated in the recess.

   c. Check the seal after installation to be sure that the spring is properly positioned in the seal.

4. Lubricate the timing chain and sprockets with heavy engine oil, then apply heavy engine oil (SE) to the fuel pump eccentric.

5. Coat the gasket surface of the oil pan with Ford silicone rubber sealer (or equivalent), then cut and position the required sections of a new gasket at the corners. Install the pan seal as required (coat the gasket surfaces of the cover and block with sealer and position a new gasket on the block).

6. Install the cylinder front cover on the cylinder block.

CAUTION
Use special care when positioning the cylinder front cover to avoid damaging the seal or mislocating the gasket.

7. Coat the threads of the attaching screws with oil-resistant sealer, then install the screws. Tighten the oil pan-to-cylinder front cover, and the cylinder front cover-to-cylinder block screws evenly.

8. Apply Lubriplate or equivalent to the oil seal rubbing surface of the vibration damper inner hub, to prevent seal damage. Then apply Lubriplate or equivalent to the front of the crankshaft for the damper installation.

9. Line the crankshaft vibration damper keyway with the crankshaft key. Install the damper on the crankshaft and secure it with the capscrew and washer. Then install the crankshaft pulley.

10. Lubricate the fuel pump lever with heavy engine oil, then install the fuel pump (use a new gasket). Connect fuel pump outlet pipe.

11. Refer to Chapter Eight, and perform the *Installation* procedure in the *Water Pump* section.

12. Fill and bleed cooling system (refer to Chapter Eight, *Coolant Change* section).

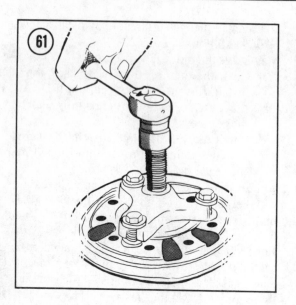

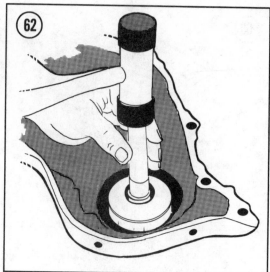

CYLINDER FRONT COVER
(6-CYLINDER)

Removal

1. Drain cooling system (refer to Chapter Eight, *Coolant Change* section).
2. Remove radiator (refer to Chapter Eight, *Radiator* section).
3. Remove alternator adjusting arm bolt, loosen drive belt, and swing the adjusting arm aside. Remove fan, drive belts and pulleys (refer to Chapter Eight, *Fan* and *Drive Belts* sections).
4. Remove screw and washer from end of crankshaft and remove the damper (**Figure 61**).
5. Remove front oil pan and front cover attaching screws.

> *CAUTION*
> *Be sure that no foreign matter enters the crankcase during this procedure.*

6. Remove the cylinder front cover and discard the old gasket.
7. Drive out oil seal with a drift. Clean seal bore in the cover.

Installation

1. Coat the new crankshaft oil seal with grease, then install it in the cover (**Figure 62**).

> *NOTE*
> *Drive the seal in until it is fully seated in the seal bore.*

2. Cut the old front oil pan seal flush at the cylinder block/pan junction point. Remove old seal material, then clean all gasket surfaces on the block, oil pan, and front cover.
3. Cut and fit the new pan seal flush with the cylinder block/pan junction point.

> *NOTE*
> *The old seal can be used as a pattern.*

4. Coat the block and cover gasket surfaces with oil resistant sealer, then position a new front cover gasket on the block.
5. Align the pan seal locating tabs with the holes in the pan, then pull the seal tabs through until the seal is seated firmly. Apply silicone sealer or equivalent to the block/pan junction point (**Figure 63**).
6. Place front cover assembly over the end of the crankshaft and push it against the cylinder block. Start the pan and cover attaching screws.
7. Install the alternator adjusting arm, then tighten all attaching front cover and oil pan screws evenly.

> *NOTE*
> *Tighten the oil pan screws first in order to obtain proper cover alignment.*

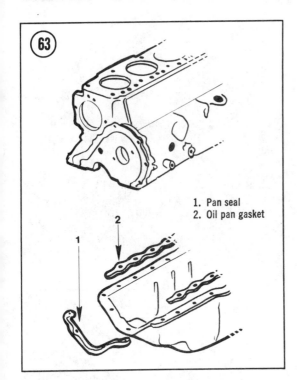

1. Pan seal
2. Oil pan gasket

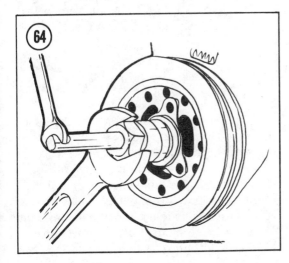

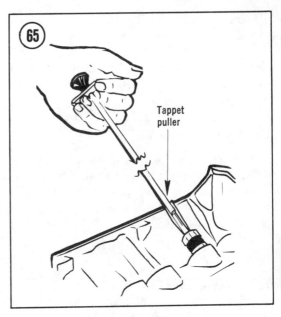

Tappet puller

5

12. Fill the cooling system (refer to Chapter Eight, *Coolant Change* section).

13. Operate engine at a fast idle and check for leaks.

CAMSHAFT (V-8)

Removal

1. Drain cooling system (refer to Chapter Eight, *Coolant Change* section). Disconnect radiator hoses, then disconnect transmission oil cooler lines (if so equipped). Remove radiator (refer to Chapter Eight, *Radiator* section).

2. Remove cylinder front cover and timing chain (refer to *Cylinder Front Cover and Timing Chain* section, preceeding).

3. Remove intake manifold and carburetor assembly (refer to appropriate *Intake Manifold* section earlier in this chapter).

4. Remove tappets as follows:
   a. Remove rocker arm covers (refer to *Rocker Arm Covers* section earlier in this chapter).
   b. Loosen valve rocker arm stud nut and turn rocker arms to one side.
   c. Remove valve pushrods in sequence so that you can install them in their original locations.
   d. Lift tappets out of their bores (**Figure 65**).

8. Lubricate the crankshaft stub, damper hub ID, and seal rubbing surface with Lubriplate or equivalent. Be sure that the damper keyway is aligned with the key on the crankshaft. Install the damper (**Figure 64**).

9. Install the washer and capscrew.

10. Install the pulley(s), drive belt(s), and fan (refer to Chapter Eight, *Fan* and *Drive Belts* sections).

11. Install radiator (refer to Chapter Eight, *Radiator* section).

Place them in a rack so that you can install them in their original bores.

5. Remove camshaft thrust plate (**Figures 66 and 67**), then pull camshaft carefully out of the engine to avoid damaging the camshaft bearings.

Bearing Replacement

If camshaft bearings are scored or otherwise damaged, have your Ford dealer or engine rebuilder replace them at this time (bearing replacement requires a special puller, and precision installation).

Installation

1. Oil the camshaft journals and apply Lubriplate or equivalent to the camshaft lobes. Slide the camshaft through the bearings.
2. Coat the camshaft thrust plate with heavy engine oil (SE) and install the camshaft thrust plate with the groove facing the cylinder block.
3. Coat the tappets and tappet bores with heavy engine oil (SE) and install the tappets in their original bores.
4. Coat ends of the pushrods with Lubriplate or equivalent and install them in their original locations (apply lubricant to the valve stem tips at this time). Also, lubricate the rocker arms and fulcrum seats and position the rocker arms over the pushrods.
5. Install the intake manifold (refer to *Intake Manifold* section earlier in this chapter).
6. Replace the crankshaft front oil seal (refer to *Crankshaft* section earlier in this chapter).
7. Install timing chain and cylinder front cover (refer to *Cylinder Front Cover and Timing Chain* section earlier in this chapter).
8. Adjust valves (refer to Chapter Four, *Valve Adjustment* section) then install valve rocker arm covers. Refer to *Rocker Arm Covers (All Models)* section earlier in this chapter.
9. Install crankcase ventilation system (refer to *Crankcase Ventilation System* section earlier in this chapter.
10. Install radiator and hoses (refer to Chapter Eight, *Radiator* section).
11. Connect oil cooler lines (if so equipped).
12. Fill and bleed cooling system (refer to Chapter Eight, *Coolant Change* section).

13. Fill crankcase with engine oil, then start engine and check for oil leaks.
14. Adjust ignition timing (refer to Chapter Four, *Ignition Timing* section).
15. Connect the distributor and intake manifold vacuum hoses.
16. Adjust engine idle speed and fuel mixture (refer to Chapter Four, *Carburetor* section).
17. Check all intake manifold nuts and bolts for tightness.
18. Install air cleaner and intake duct assembly, including crankcase ventilation hose (refer to Chapter Seven, *Emission Control Systems Maintenance* section).

CAMSHAFT (6-CYLINDER)

Removal

1. Drain cooling system (refer to Chapter Eight, *Coolant Change* section), then drain crankcase.

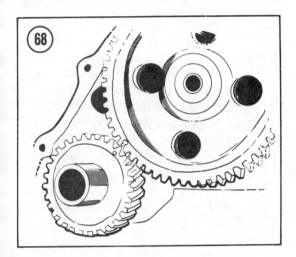

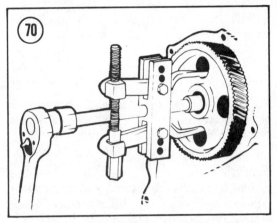

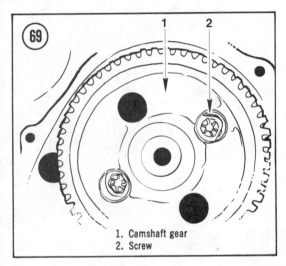

1. Camshaft gear
2. Screw

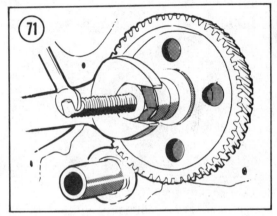

2. Remove radiator (refer to Chapter Eight, *Radiator* section).

3. Remove valve lifters, cylinder front cover, oil pump, and oil pan, following procedures outlined in their respective sections earlier in this chapter.

4. Disconnect fuel pump outlet lines at fuel pump, then remove fuel pump mounting bolts (refer to Chapter Six, *Fuel Pump* section) and see the pump to one side.

5. Disconnect vacuum line at distributor and the primary wire at the ignition coil.

6. Remove the distributor (refer to Chapter Seven, *Distributor* section).

7. Turn crankshaft to align the timing marks as shown in **Figure 68**.

8. Remove camshaft thrust plate screws (**Figure 69**), then remove camshaft gear as shown in **Figure 70**. Remove the key, thrust plate, and spacer.

9. Carefully remove the camshaft.

CAUTION
When removing camshaft, avoid nicking the camshaft bearings.

Bearing Replacement

If camshaft bearings are scored or otherwise damaged, have your Ford dealer replace them at this time (bearing replacement requires a special puller, and precision installation).

Installation

1. Oil camshaft bearings and apply Lubriplate or equivalent to the camshaft lobes. Slide the camshaft through the bearings.

2. Assemble key, spacer and thrust plate to camshaft. Align the gear keyway with the key, then install the camshaft gear on the camshaft (**Figure 71**).

3. Install the camshaft, gear and thrust plate as an assembly. Rotate the crankshaft if necessary to align the timing marks as shown in **Figure 68**. *Do not turn the crankshaft again until the distributor is installed.*

4. Clean cylinder front cover and cylinder block gasket surfaces and install a new front oil seal in the cylinder front cover (refer to *Cylinder Front Cover and Timing Chain* section, preceding).

5. Install cylinder front cover and damper, oil pump, oil pan, and valve lifters, following the procedures found in the appropriate sections earlier in this chapter.

6. Install radiator (refer to Chapter Eight, *Radiator* section).

7. Set distributor rotor so that the points are about to open for the No. 1 cylinder firing position. Install the distributor (refer to Chapter Seven, *Distributor* section). Check the breaker points. If the timing marks are still aligned (refer to Step 7 under *Removal* procedure, this section), the points should be fully open in the No. 1 cylinder firing position. If they are not, remove the distributor and rotate the shaft in the proper direction (clockwise), and install the distributor again.

8. Clean fuel pump and cylinder block gasket surfaces, then install the fuel pump with a new gasket (refer to Chapter Six, *Fuel Pump* section). Connect the fuel outlet line to the fuel pump.

9. Fill crankcase, then fill cooling system (refer to *Coolant Change* section in Chapter Eight).

10. Start engine and check for leaks.

11. Adjust ignition timing (refer to Chapter Four, *Ignition System* section).

12. Connect distributor vacuum line to distributor.

13. Adjust carburetor idle speed and fuel mixture (refer to Chapter Four, *Carburetor* section).

Table 1   ENGINE FASTENER TORQUE RECOMMENDATIONS (Ft.-lb.)

	170	240/300	302/460	360/390	351M/400
Camshaft sprocket	35-45	N/A	40-45	45-57	40-45
Camshaft thrust plate	12-15	19-20	9-12	12-18	9-12
Carburetor attach. nuts	12-15	12-15	12-15	12-15	12-15
Connecting rod	19-24	40-45	19-24	40-45	40-45
Front cover	7-9	15-20(240) 12-15(300)	12-18(302) 15-21(460)	10-15(15/16) 19-27(3/8)	12-18
Vibration damper	85-100	130-150	70-90	130-150(5/8) 150-175(3/4)	70-90
PVS valve	N/A	15-18	12-18(302) 15-18(460)	15-18	10-15
EGR valve	N/A	12-18	12-18	12-18	12-18
Flywheel	75-85	75-85	75-85	75-85	75-85
Main bearings	60-70	60-70	60-70	95-105	95-105
Oil filter insert	N/A	20-30	20-30(302) 45-55(460)	50-60	20-30
Oil pump inlet	N/A	10-15	10-15	10-15	10-15
Oil pan	7-9	10-12	9-11	8-10	7-9
Oil pump	12-15	12-15	23-32	17-27	35-50
Crankshaft pulley	N/A	35-50	35-50	35-50	35-50
Rocker arm	30-35	17-23	18-25	40-45	18-25
Spark plug	10-15	15-25	10-15	15-25	10-15
Valve cover	5-8	4-7	3-5(302) 5-6(460)	4-7	4-7
Water outlet	12-15	12-18	9-12(302) 10-15(460)	12-18	12-18
Water pump	12-15	12-18	12-18(302) 15-21(460)	17-27	12-18

5

Table 2   ENGINE SPECIFICATIONS — 170 L6 & 240/300 L6

	170 L6	240/300 L6
General		
Bore	3.50 in.	4.00 in.
Stroke	2.94 in.	3.18 in. (240 cid)
		3.98 in. (300 cid)
Firing order	1-5-3-6-2-4	1-5-3-6-2-4
Cylinder bore		
Diameter	3.5000-3.5024 in.	4.0000-4.0048 in.
Out-of-round, new	0.005 in.	0.005 in.
(wear limit)		
Piston		
Clearance in bore	0.0014-0.0020 in.	0.0014-0.0022 in.
Piston rings		
Number per cylinder	3	3
Ring end gap		
Top	0.010-0.020 in.	0.010-0.020 in.
Bottom	0.010-0.020 in.	0.010-0.020 in.
Oil control	0.015-0.055 in.	0.015-0.055 in.
Ring side clearance		
Top	0.0019-0.0036 in.	0.0019-0.0036 in.
Bottom	0.0020-0.0040 in.	0.0020-0.0040 in.
Oil control	Snug	Snug
Piston pin		
Diameter	0.9119-0.9124 in.	0.9749-0.9754 in.
Clearance		
In piston	0.0003-0.0005 in.	0.0002-0.0004 in.
In rod	Interference fit	Interference fit
Crankshaft		
End play	0.004-0.008 in.	0.004-0.008 in.
Main bearing journal		
Diameter	2.2482-2.2490 in.	2.3982-2.3990 in.
Taper	0.0003 in. max.	0.0003 in. max. (through 1974)
		0.0005 in. max. (1975 on)
Out-of-round	0.0004 in. max.	0.0006 in. max.
Main bearing clearance	0.0010-0.0015 in.	0.0008-0.0015 in.
Connecting rod journal		
Diameter	2.1232-2.1240 in.	2.1228-2.1236 in.
Taper, new	0.0003 in. max.	0.0003 in. max. (through 1974
(wear limit)		0.0006 in. max. (1975 on)
Out-of-round, new	0.0004 in.	0.0006 in. max.
(wear limit)		
Connecting rods		
Side clearance	0.0035-0.0105 in.	0.006-0.013 in.
Bearing clearance	0.0010-0.0015 in.	0.0008-0.0015 in.
Camshaft		
Journal diameter	1.8095-1.8105 in.	2.017-2.018 in.
Runout	0.010 in.	0.008 in.

(continued)

Table 2   **ENGINE SPECIFICATIONS — 170 L6 & 240/300 L6** (continued)

	170 L6	240/300 L6
Valve system		
Lifter type	Mechanical	Hydraulic
Rocker arm ratio	1.50:1	1.61:1 (through 1974)
		1.62:1 (1975 on)
Valve lash	0.018 in. (hot)	0.100-0.150 in. (through 1974)
(intake and exhaust)		0.125-0.175 in. (1975 on)
Intake valve		
Face angle	44°	44°
Seat angle	45°	45°
Seat width	0.070-0.080 in.	0.060-0.080 in.
Stem-to-guide	0.008-0.0025 in.	0.0010-0.0027 in.
clearance		
Seat runout	0.0015-0.0020 in.	0.0020 in.
Exhaust valve		
Face angle	44°	44°
Seat angle	45°	45°
Seat width	0.070-0.090 in.	0.070-0.090 in.
Stem-to-guide	0.0010-0.0027 in.	0.0010-0.0027 in.
clearance		
Seat runout	0.0015-0.0020 in.	0.0020 in.
Valve springs		
Free length	N/A	1.99 in. (intake);
		1.87 in. (exhaust)
Load @ length		
(lbs. @ in.)		
Closed	N/A	76-84 @ 1.700 (intake);
		77-85 @ 1.580 (exhaust)
Open	N/A	187-207 @ 1.300 (intake)
		182-202 @ 1.180 (exhaust)
Installed height	N/A	$1 \frac{11}{16} - 1 \frac{23}{32}$ (intake);
		$1 \frac{9}{16} - 1 \frac{19}{32}$ (exhaust)

N/A = Not available

5

128   **CHAPTER FIVE**

Table 3   ENGINE SPECIFICATIONS — 302 V8 & 460 V8

	302 V8	460 V8
General		
Bore	4.00 in.	4.36 in.
Stroke	3.00 in.	3.85 in.
Firing order	1-5-4-2-6-3-7-8	1-5-4-2-6-3-7-8
Cylinder Bore		
Diameter	4.0004-4.0052 in.	4.3600-4.3636 in.
Out-of-round, new (wear limit)	0.0015 in.	0.005 in.
Piston		
Clearance in bore	0.0018-0.0026 in.	0.0022-0.0030 in.
Piston rings		
Number per cylinder	3	3
Ring end gap		
Top	0.010-0.020 in.	0.010-0.020 in.
Bottom	0.010-0.020 in.	0.010-0.020 in.
Oil control	0.015-0.035 in.	0.010-0.035 in.
Ring side clearance		
Top	0.0019-0.0036 in.	0.0019-0.0036 in.
Bottom	0.002-0.004 in.	0.0020-0.0040 in.
Oil control	Snug	Snug
Piston pin		
Diameter	0.9119-0.9124 in.	1.0398-1.0403 in.
Clearance		
In piston	0.0002-0.0004 in.	0.0002-0.0004 in.
In rod	Interference fit	Interference fit
Crankshaft		
End play	0.004-0.008 in.	0.004-0.008 in.
Main bearing journal		
Diameter	2.2482-2.2490 in.	2.9994-3.0002 in.
Taper	0.0005 in.	0.0005 in.
Out-of-round	0.0006 in.	0.0006 in.
Main bearing clearance	0.0008-0.0015 in.	0.0008-0.0015 in.
Connecting rod journal		
Diameter	2.1228-2.1236 in.	2.4992-2.5000 in.
Taper, new (wear limit)	0.0006 in.	0.0006 in.
Out-of-round, new (wear limit)	0.0006 in.	0.0006 in.
Connecting rods		
Side clearance	0.010-0.020 in.	0.010-0.020 in.
Bearing clearance	0.0008-0.0015 in.	0.0008-0.0015 in.
Camshaft		
Journal diameter	No. 1, 2.0805-2.0815 in.; No. 2, 2.0655-2.0665 in.; No. 3, 2.0505-2.0515 in.; No. 4, 2.0355-2.0365 in.; No. 5, 2.0205-2.0215 in.;	2.1238-2.1248 in.
Runout	0.005 in.	0.005 in. max.

(continued)

Table 3 ENGINE SPECIFICATIONS — 302 V8 & 460 V8 (continued)

	302 V8	460 V8
Valve system		
Lifter type	Hydraulic	Hydraulic
Rocker arm ratio	1.61:1	1.73:1
Valve lash (intake & exhaust)	0.096-0.165 in.	0.100-0.150 in.
Intake valve		
Face angle	44°	44°
Seat angle	45°	45°
Seat width	0.060-0.080 in.	0.060-0.080 in.
Stem-to-guide clearance	0.0010-0.0027 in.	0.0010-0.0027 in.
Seat runout	0.0020 in.	0.0020 in.
Exhaust valve		
Face angle	44°	44°
Seat angle	45°	45°
Seat width	0.060-0.080 in.	0.060-0.080 in.
Stem-to-guide clearance	0.0015-0.0032 in.	0.0010-0.0027 in.
Seat runout	0.0020 in.	0.0020 in.
Valve springs		
Free length	2.04 in. (intake) 1.85 in. (exhaust)	2.06 in.
Load @ length (lbs. @ in.)		
Closed	74-82 @ 1.78 (intake); 76-84 @ 1.60 (exhaust)	76-84 @ 1.81
Open	196-212 @ 1.36 (intake); 190-210 @ 1.20 (exhaust)	218-240 @ 1.33
Installed height	$1\frac{43}{64}$ - $1\frac{51}{64}$ in. (intake); $1\frac{37}{64}$ - $1\frac{39}{64}$ in. (exhaust)	$1\frac{51}{64}$ - $1\frac{53}{64}$ in.

5

Table 4 ENGINE SPECIFICATIONS — 360/390&351M/400V8

	360/390 V8	351M/400 V8
General		
Bore	4.05 in.	4.00 in.
Stroke	3.50 in. (360)	3.50 in. (351)
	3.78 in. (390)	4.00 in. (400)
Firing order	1-5-4-2-6-3-7-8	1-3-7-2-6-5-4-8
Cylinder bore		
Diameter	4.0500-4.0524 in.	4.0000-4.0048 in.
Out-of-round, new	0.005 in.	0.005 in.
(wear limit)		
Piston		
Clearance in bore	0.0015-0.0023 in.	0.0014-0.0022 in.
Piston rings		
Number per cylinder	3	3
Ring end gap		
Top	0.015-0.023 in.	0.010-0.020 in.
Bottom	0.010-0.020 in.	0.010-0.020 in.
Oil control	0.015-0.055 in.	0.010-0.035 in.
Ring side clearance		
Top	0.0019-0.0036 in.	0.0019-0.0036 in.
Bottom	0.0020-0.0040 in.	0.0020-0.0040 in.
Oil control	Snug	Snug
Piston pin		
Diameter	0.9750-0.9753 in.	0.9745-0.9754 in.
Clearance		
In piston	0.0001-0.0003 in.	0.0003-0.0005 in.
In rod	0.0001-0.0005 in.	Interference fit
Crankshaft		
End play	0.004-0.010 in.	0.004-0.008 in.
Main bearing clearance		
Connecting rod journal	2.7484-2.7492 in.	2.9994-3.0002 in.
Diameter	0.0003 in. per in.	0.0005 in. per in.
Out-of-round	0.0004 in.	0.0006 in.
Main bearing clearance	0.0010-0.0015 in.	0.0008-0.0015 in.
Crankpin		
Diameter	2.4380-2.4388 in.	2.3103-2.3111 in.
Taper, new	0.0003 in. per in.	0.0006 in. per in.
(wear limit)		
Out-of-round, new	0.0005 in.	0.0006 in.
(wear limit)		
Connecting rods		
Side clearance	0.010-0.020 in.	0.010-0.020 in.
Bearing clearance	0.0010-0.0015 in.	0.0008-0.0015 in.
Camshaft		
Journal diameter	2.1238-2.1248 in.	No. 1, 2.1248-2.1328 in.
		No. 2, 2.0655-2.0665 in.
		No. 3, 2.0505-2.0515 in.
		No. 4, 2.0355-2.0365 in.
		No. 5, 2.0205-2.0215 in.
Runout	0.008 in.	0.005 in.

(continued)

Table 4 ENGINE SPECIFICATIONS — 360/390 & 351M/400V8 (continued)

	360/390 V8	351M/400 V8
Valve system		
Lifter type	Hydraulic	Hydraulic
Rocker arm ratio	1.73:1	1.73:1
Valve lash (intake & exhaust)	N/A	0.125 in. (351M)
		0.175 in. (400)
Intake valve		
Face angle	44°	44°
Seat angle	45°	45°
Seat width	0.060-0.080 in.	0.060-0.080 in.
Stem-to-guide clearance	0.0010-0.0270 in.	0.0010-0.0027 in.
Seat runout	0.0015 in.	0.002 in.
Exhaust valve		
Face angle	44°	44°
Seat angle	45°	45
Seat width	0.070-0.090 in.	0.070-0.090 in.
Stem-to-guide clearance	0.0020-0.0034 in.	0.0015-0.0032 in.
Seat runout	0.0015 in.	0.002 in.
Valve springs (outer)		
Free length	2.12 in.	2.06 in. (intake)
		1.93 in. (exhaust)
Load @ length (lb. @ in.)		
Closed	85-95 @ 1.820 in.	Intake: 76-84 @ 1.82 in.
		Exhaust: 79-87 @ 1.68 in.
Open	209-231 @ 1.38 in.	Intake & exhaust, 215-237 @ 1.39 in.
Installed height ($\pm \frac{1}{32}$in.)	$1\frac{13}{16}$-$1\frac{27}{32}$ in.	Intake: $1\frac{13}{16}$-$1\frac{27}{32}$ in.
		Exhaust: $1\frac{11}{16}$-$1\frac{23}{32}$ in.

N/A = Not available

Table 5 CYLINDER HEAD BOLT TORQUE

	Torque (ft.-lb.)		
Engine	Stage 1	Stage 2	Stage 3
170, 240, 300 cid 6-cyl.	55	65	70-85
302 cid V8	55	65	65-72
351M cid V8	75	95	105
360, 390 cid V8	60	70	80-90
400 cid V8	75	95	105
460 cid V8	80	110	130-140

5

NOTE: If you own a 1980 or later model, first check the Supplement at the back of the book for any new service information.

CHAPTER SIX

FUEL, EXHAUST, AND EMISSION CONTROL SYSTEMS

This chapter offers removal/installation procedures for the carburetor and fuel pump, and a description of each emission-related fuel system component used on vehicles covered in this manual. Refer to the vehicle emission control information label which can usually be found on the glove compartment door, driver door opening, or in the engine compartment (**Figure 1**). Most emission system work is best left to your dealer, since expensive and specialized equipment is needed. However, a few components can be serviced routinely and procedures are given in the *Emission Control System Maintenance* section of this chapter.

ELECTRICALLY ASSISTED CHOKE

An electrically-heated choke thermostatic spring housing is used to aid fast choke release and improve emission characteristics during engine warm-up (**Figure 2**). The heater operates only when the engine is actually running, and operates off of the center tap of the alternator.

The electric choke system consists of a thermostatic spring, choke cap, bi-metal temperature sensing disc (switch), and a positive temperature coefficient (PTC) ceramic heater. The choke receives its power from the center tap of the alternator (**Figure 3**). The system is grounded through a ground strap connected to the carburetor body; current is constantly supplied to the temperature sending switch.

The electric choke system aids in reducing vehicle exhaust emissions by matching choke operation to engine requirement over a wide range of conditions. The choke system's engine temperature sending control switch is connected in series with the PTC ceramic mentioned previously. The switch/heater device optimizes choke function depending upon "soak temperature," length of "soak," and prior vehicle operation/parking conditions. (Vehicle cold drive-away requirements vary, depending upon the overall vehicle operating temperature.) The electric choke heater and switch satisfies these requirements by allowing increased choke enrichment (no heating) after low temperature soaks of sufficient length to reduce engine temperature to ambient temperature. The choke heater and switch also provide reduced choke enrichment (heating) when the vehicle has soaked in low temperatures for a period of time that is insufficient to reduce engine temperatures below the switching requirements; and when the vehicle has not soaked at temperatures below the switching temperature.

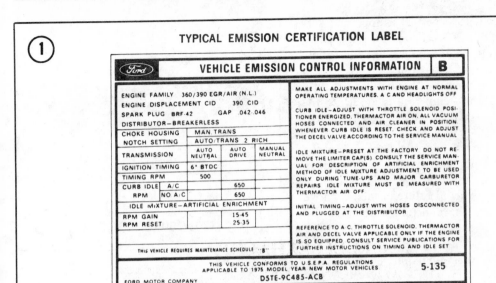

TYPICAL EMISSION CERTIFICATION LABEL

VEHICLE EMISSION CONTROL INFORMATION **B**

ENGINE FAMILY 360/390 EGR/AIR (N.L.)
ENGINE DISPLACEMENT CID   390 CID
SPARK PLUG BRF-42   GAP .042-.046
DISTRIBUTOR—BREAKERLESS

CHOKE HOUSING	MAN. TRANS		
NOTCH SETTING	AUTO/TRANS 2 RICH		
TRANSMISSION	AUTO NEUTRAL	AUTO DRIVE	MANUAL NEUTRAL
IGNITION TIMING	6° BTDC		
TIMING RPM	500		
CURB IDLE A/C		650	
RPM NO A/C		650	

IDLE MIXTURE—ARTIFICIAL ENRICHMENT

| RPM GAIN | 15-45 |
| RPM RESET | 25-35 |

THIS VEHICLE REQUIRES MAINTENANCE SCHEDULE ··B··

MAKE ALL ADJUSTMENTS WITH ENGINE AT NORMAL OPERATING TEMPERATURES. A C AND HEADLIGHTS OFF

CURB IDLE—ADJUST WITH THROTTLE SOLENOID POSITIONER ENERGIZED, THERMACTOR AIR ON, ALL VACUUM HOSES CONNECTED AND AIR CLEANER IN POSITION WHENEVER CURB IDLE IS RESET. CHECK AND ADJUST THE DECEL VALVE ACCORDING TO THE SERVICE MANUAL

IDLE MIXTURE—PRESET AT THE FACTORY. DO NOT REMOVE THE LIMITER CAP(S). CONSULT THE SERVICE MANUAL FOR DESCRIPTION OF ARTIFICIAL ENRICHMENT METHOD OF IDLE MIXTURE ADJUSTMENT TO BE USED ONLY DURING TUNE-UPS AND MAJOR CARBURETOR REPAIRS. IDLE MIXTURE MUST BE MEASURED WITH THERMACTOR AIR OFF

INITIAL TIMING—ADJUST WITH HOSES DISCONNECTED AND PLUGGED AT THE DISTRIBUTOR

REFERENCE TO A. C. THROTTLE SOLENOID, THERMACTOR AIR AND DECEL VALVE APPLICABLE ONLY IF THE ENGINE IS SO EQUIPPED. CONSULT SERVICE PUBLICATIONS FOR FURTHER INSTRUCTIONS ON TIMING AND IDLE SET

THIS VEHICLE CONFORMS TO U.S.E.P.A. REGULATIONS APPLICABLE TO 1975 MODEL YEAR NEW MOTOR VEHICLES   5-135

FORD MOTOR COMPANY   D5TE-9C485-ACB

6

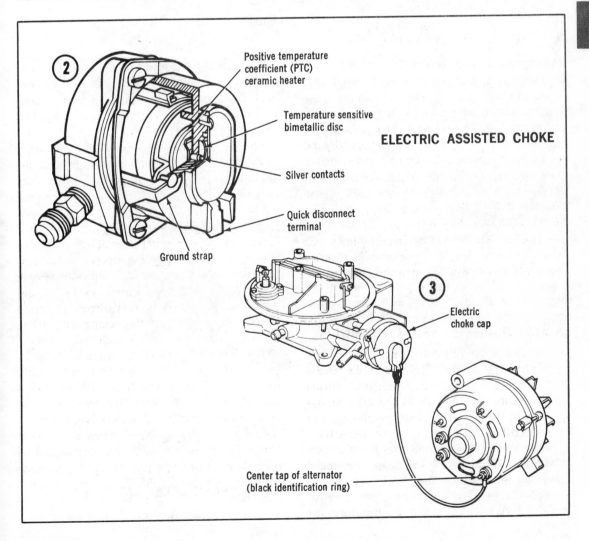

Positive temperature coefficient (PTC) ceramic heater

Temperature sensitive bimetallic disc

ELECTRIC ASSISTED CHOKE

Silver contacts

Quick disconnect terminal

Ground strap

Electric choke cap

Center tap of alternator (black identification ring)

The switch senses the gas temperature surrounding the bi-metal. The temperature sensed is the manifold heated choke hot air supply used to operate the bimetallic choke control thermostat. When the choke is properly calibrated to this temperature gradient, the choke functions efficiently during all ambient warm-up.

Choke "come off time" is decreased by the switch supplying current to the positive temperature coefficient (PTC) heater, which in turn increases the temperature inside the choke cap and, hence, the bimetallic choke control thermostat. The system allows the choke calibration to be as ideally matched to the engine starting/warm-up requirements as possible.

EMISSION SYSTEM CONTROL COMPONENTS

PVS (Ported Vacuum Switch)

Ported vacuum switches are used in several locations in the emission control systems. Two or more ports are used (**Figure 4**), as the valves can be used to turn vacuum on and off, or switch between 2 vacuum sources for a third delivery point.

The typical 3-port PVS switch, when cold, provides a path through the center and top holes. When hot, the top port is closed off and the center and bottom ports are connected. On a "cooling" PVS switch, the distributor vacuum advance diaphragm receives its vacuum signal from the carburetor spark port. If the engine overheats while idling, the PVS connects the distributor to full intake manifold vacuum, thereby increasing the engine speed until cooldown occurs. When the temperature drops once again, the PVS connects the distributor to the spark port.

Vacuum Delay Valves

Delay valves are used in several places on the engine. Basically, the valve slows air flow in the vacuum lines, thus providing time delay control on vacuum operated equipment. The SDV (spark delay valve) is used to delay the opening func-

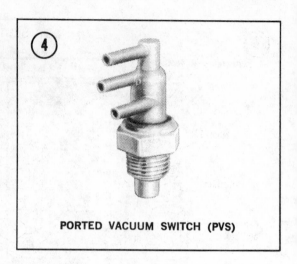

PORTED VACUUM SWITCH (PVS)

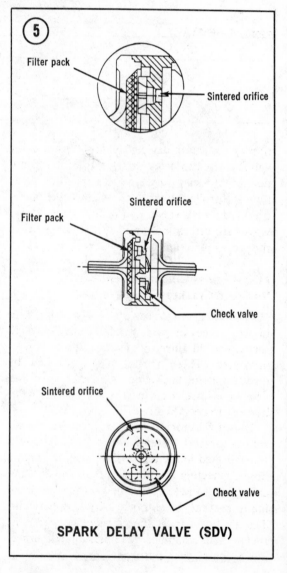

Filter pack

Sintered orifice

Sintered orifice

Filter pack

Check valve

Sintered orifice

Check valve

SPARK DELAY VALVE (SDV)

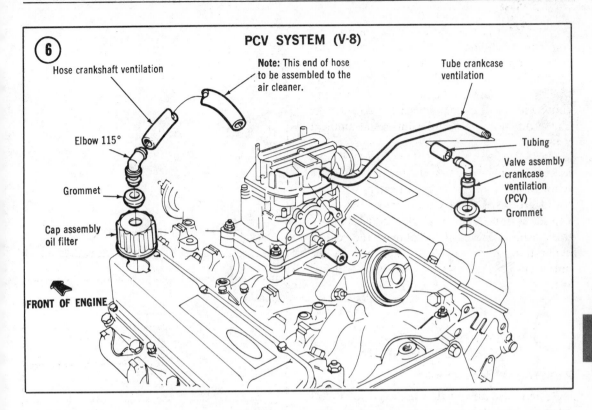

PCV SYSTEM (V-8)

6

Hose crankshaft ventilation

Note: This end of hose to be assembled to the air cleaner.

Tube crankcase ventilation

Elbow 115°

Tubing

Valve assembly crankcase ventilation (PCV)

Grommet

Grommet

Cap assembly oil filter

FRONT OF ENGINE

tion of a vacuum device; the RDV (retard delay valve) is used to delay the closing of a vacuum device. All delay valves have a specified delay time controlled by a porous sintered metal orifice, a check valve, and a filter pack. Delay valves are directional and must be installed in the proper direction (**Figure 5**).

PCV (Positive Crankcase Ventilation) Valve and Crankcase Vent Cap

The closed ventilation system is designed to prevent fumes or gases from escaping through the engine oil filler or breather cap to the atmosphere. These vapors are controlled by directing them back into the intake manifold where they are consumed in the normal combustion process (**Figure 6**).

The carburetor air cleaner provides the air source for this system. Air passes through a filter located in the air cleaner, then through a hose connecting the air cleaner to the oil filler cap. The air filler cap is sealed at the filler opening to prevent the entrance of atmospheric air. The air flows from the oil filler cap into the rocker arm chamber. Ventilating air moves down past the pushrods into the lower

crankcase. The air/crankcase gas mixture flows from the crankcase through a flow-regulating valve (PCV valve) into the intake manifold through the crankcase vent hose, tube, and fittings. This process goes on constantly while the engine is running.

Exhaust Heat Control Valve (6-Cylinder Engines Only)

The air/fuel ratio fluctuates if fuel condenses on the cold surfaces of the induction system, causing uneven acceleration and increased emission levels. The exhaust control valve is designed to provide quick induction system warm-up and improved cold engine air/fuel ratio control. The thermostatically-controlled valve is located in the exhaust manifold.

When the engine is cold, the valve is closed and routes hot exhaust gas through a passage to the riser pad under the carburetor. This warms the air/fuel mixture delivery passages, providing improved air/fuel ratio control. When the engine warms up and the valve opens, this action reduces exhaust gas flow through the warm-up passage to prevent excessive heat.

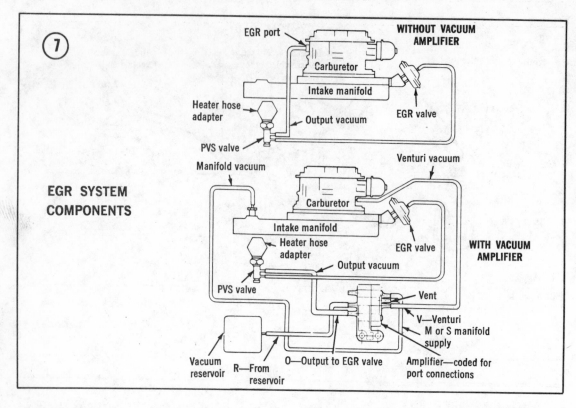

⑦

**EGR SYSTEM
COMPONENTS**

EGR port

**WITHOUT VACUUM
AMPLIFIER**

Carburetor

Intake manifold

Heater hose
adapter

Output vacuum

EGR valve

PVS valve

Manifold vacuum

Venturi vacuum

Carburetor

Intake manifold

Heater hose
adapter

EGR valve

**WITH VACUUM
AMPLIFIER**

Output vacuum

PVS valve

Vent

V—Venturi
M or S manifold
supply

Vacuum
reservoir

R—From
reservoir

O—Output to EGR valve

Amplifier—coded for
port connections

Fuel Filler Cap

The filler cap used with vapor emission control systems on all 350 models has a pressure-vacuum valve that vents air into the tank as fuel is used to prevent tank collapse. Fuel vapor cannot vent to the outside atmosphere unless a pressure of 2 psi above atmosphere is attained.

The filler cap used on all vehicles except 350 models (49-states), which use the same filler cap as evaporative emission control system equipped vehicles without vapor emission control, incorporates an anti-surge mechanism that prevents fuel from spilling through the cap due to surge when cornering. Atmospheric air and fuel vapor are free, normally, to pass in and out of the fuel system, preventing tank collapse and/or excessive pressure build up. In some instances the anti-surge mechanism prevents fuel vapor from passing through the cap. However, pressure cannot build in excess of 2 psi above atmospheric.

Orifice Valve

An orifice valve is situated on top of the fuel tank. The restricted size of the orifice meters the amount of vapor and restricts the fuel from passing out of the tank. The orifice valve connects into the vent line that runs forward to the carbon-filled storage canister in the engine compartment (refer to following section, *Carbon Canister*). Some valves have a float system to reduce further the chance of liquid fuel passing into the vent line.

Carbon Canister

A carbon-filled canister stores fuel vapors vented from the fuel tank (and in some installations, from the carburetor). The canister outlet is connected to the carburetor air cleaner so that the stored vapors can be sucked into the engine and burned.

NOTE: *California models are equipped with a carburetor fuel bowl vent line to the carbon canister in addition to the fuel vapor emission control system on the fuel tank.*

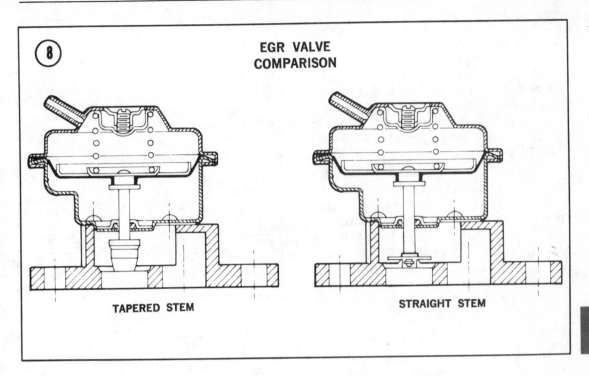

⑧   EGR VALVE COMPARISON

TAPERED STEM   STRAIGHT STEM

6

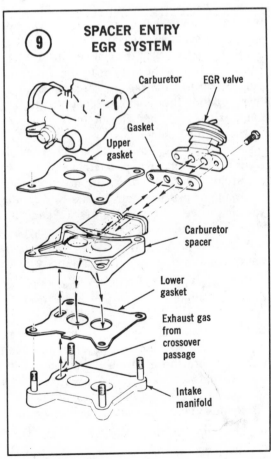

⑨   SPACER ENTRY EGR SYSTEM

Carburetor

EGR valve

Gasket

Upper gasket

Carburetor spacer

Lower gasket

Exhaust gas from crossover passage

Intake manifold

EXHAUST GAS RECIRCULATION SYSTEM

The EGR (exhaust gas recirculation) system is designed to re-introduce exhaust gas into the combustion cycle, reducing the amount of NOX (nitrous oxides) emitted into the atmosphere. The amount of exhaust gas re-introduced and the cycle timing are controlled by various factors such as engine vacuum and temperature. A typical system is shown in **Figure 7**.

EGR (Exhaust Gas Recirculation) Valve

The EGR valve shown in **Figure 8** is operated by vacuum, and is attached to a spacer mounted between the carburetor and intake manifold. When the valve opens, exhaust gas enters the intake manifold. When the valve closes it prevents the exhaust gases from entering the intake passages. Refer to **Figure 9**.

Venturi Vacuum Amplifier

The EGR venturi vacuum amplifier uses a weak venturi vacuum signal in the carburetor throat to shape a strong intake manifold vacuum signal to operate the EGR valve. This provides an accurate, repeatable, and almost exactly proportioned venturi air and EGR flow, which controls oxides of nitrogen emissions with minimal sacrifice in vehicle driveability.

The amplifier may have an exterior vacuum reservoir and check valve to maintain adequate vacuum supply regardless of engine manifold vacuum variations.

A relief valve is used to cancel the output EGR signal when the intake manifold vacuum is low. This allows the EGR valve to close at or near wide-open throttle acceleration when maximum power is required from the engine.

On certain engine applications, the amplifier is calibrated with an output bias. When the venturi vacuum signal is at zero, the output signal already has a pre-determined output (approximately 1-2 in. Hg.). This permits a rapid system response in overcoming the EGR valve spring closing force.

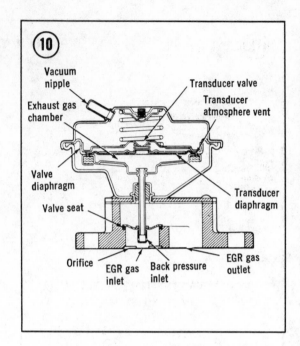

Integral Transducer — EGR System

This valve performs approximately the same function as the separate back pressure transducer and EGR valves used on some systems. The valve assembly (**Figure 10**) has an internal exhaust gas chamber with a transducer diaphragm which senses exhaust backpressure through a hollow valve stem. When the backpressure is low, vacuum is bled through the transducer valve and the EGR valve stays closed. When the backpressure increases, the transducer diaphragm moves up and closes the transducer valve vacuum bleed hole. With the vacuum bleed closed, the EGR valve opens, allowing exhaust gas to flow into the intake manifold. Since the EGR output passage is always exposed to manifold vacuum and EGR gas inlet flow is restricted by an orifice, backpressure at the transducer drops when the EGR valve opens. When it drops, the vacuum bleed hole opens, closing the EGR valve and allowing pressure to build up again. The cycle is continually repeated, modulating the flow of exhaust gas into the intake manifold.

THERMACTOR SYSTEM

A "Thermactor" air injection system is installed on certain engines to reduce carbon monoxide and hydrocarbon content of combustion by-produce gases by injecting fresh air into

the hot exhaust gas stream as it leaves the combustion chamber. A pump supplies air under pressure to the exhaust port near the exhaust valve by either an external air manifold or internal drilled passages in the cylinder head or exhaust manifold. The oxygen in the fresh air, plus the heat of the exhaust gases, causes further oxidation (burning) which converts the exhaust gases into carbon dioxide and water.

The major components of a typical thermactor system are shown in **Figure 11**. They include the air supply pump; external air injection manifold; cylinder head/exhaust manifold with internal air passages; air bypass valve; idle vacuum valve (also see **Figures 12 and 13**); check valve; and hoses, clamps, and brackets.

Air Pump

The air pump is belt-driven (**Figure 14**) and draws air with an impeller-type centrifugal air filter fan, eliminating the need for a separate air filter. Dust and dirt particles cannot enter the pump because these heavier-than-air contaminants are thrown from the air intake by centrifugal force.

Air Bypass Valve

Three types of bypass valves are used, as described below:

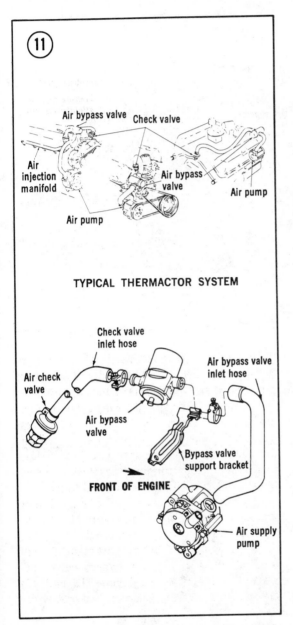

TYPICAL THERMACTOR SYSTEM

FRONT OF ENGINE

rise of intake manifold vacuum under the diaphragm overcomes spring pressure and pulls the valve downward. Air is diverted to the atmosphere momentarily, because vacuum is equalized again on both sides of the diaphragm through a small orifice in the diaphragm.

2. *Normally closed valves* operate as follows: When no vacuum signal is applied to the bypass valve diaphragm, air from the pump is diverted and dumped to the atmosphere for catalytic converter protection (the valve is normally closed). When a vacuum signal (as calibrated) is applied to the bypass valve diaphragm, the air is directed to the engine. The valve also performs a relief function to protect the air pump in the event an excessive downstream restriction occurs (**Figure 16**).

3. *Timed and vented valves* function as follows: As long as signal vacuum is 4 in. Hg. or more (**Figure 17**), this valve functions as a "timed" valve until vented (auxiliary controlled) and will continuously bypass.

Thermactor Idle "Dump"

Thermactor pump air is directed past open relief valve and "dumped" into the atmosphere through vent openings. This condition exists during idle periods of ½-1 minute or more.

Exhaust Check Valve

The exhaust gas check valve (**Figure 18**) germits fresh air to flow into the exhaust port, but prevents the reverse flow of exhaust gases in the event of improper operation of the air pump or low pressure. The valve is situated on the air manifold for "external" systems; on the air crossover manifold for engines using "internal" systems (drilled cylinder heads).

Idle Vacuum Valve

This valve, in conjunction with a vacuum delay valve, provides backfire control, full-time idle air dump, cold temperature catalyst protection, and cold EGR lockout (**Figure 12**). The idle air dump of the secondary air pump output during extended engine idle periods of ½-1 minute or more, helps prevent excessive underbody temperatures caused by the exhaust system. EGR port vacuum at the carburetor moves

1. *Timed bypass function (normally open) valves* prevent backfiring during engine deceleration when larger amounts of unburned gases flow into the exhaust manifold, which cause rapid burning when mixed with fresh air. To prevent this backfire condition, the bypass valve momentarily diverts air from the pump to the atmosphere (**Figure 15**). During normal operation, vacuum is equalized on both sides of the diaphragm. The return spring holds the valve closed, allowing fresh air to flow to the air outlet port. During deceleration, the sudden

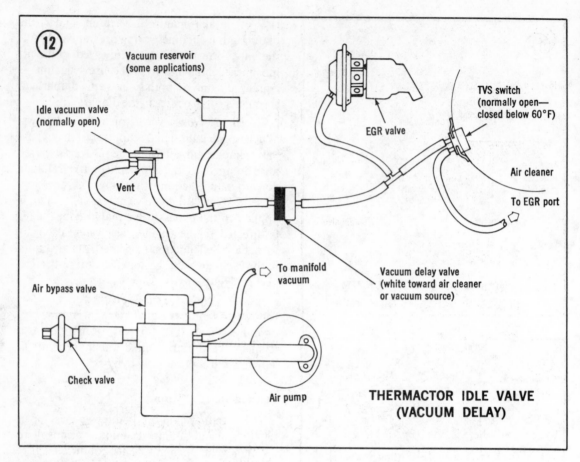

⑫

Vacuum reservoir
(some applications)

Idle vacuum valve
(normally open)

EGR valve

TVS switch
(normally open—
closed below 60°F)

Vent

Air cleaner

To EGR port

Air bypass valve

To manifold
vacuum

Vacuum delay valve
(white toward air cleaner
or vacuum source)

Check valve

Air pump

**THERMACTOR IDLE VALVE
(VACUUM DELAY)**

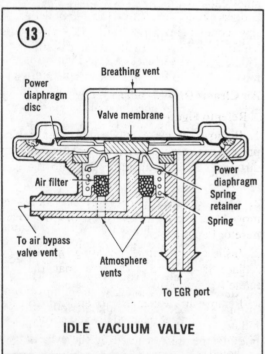

⑬

Power
diaphragm
disc

Breathing vent

Valve membrane

Air filter

Power
diaphragm
Spring
retainer
Spring

To air bypass
valve vent

Atmosphere
vents

To EGR port

IDLE VACUUM VALVE

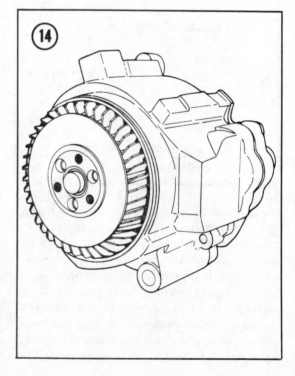

⑭

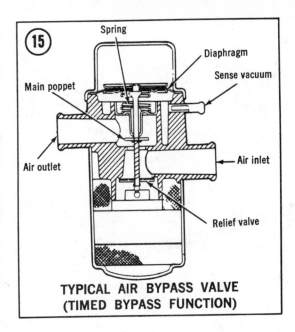

TYPICAL AIR BYPASS VALVE (TIMED BYPASS FUNCTION)

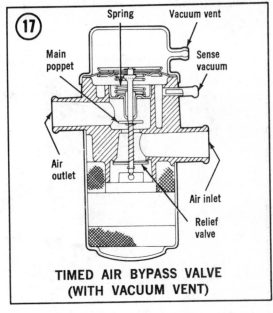

TIMED AIR BYPASS VALVE (WITH VACUUM VENT)

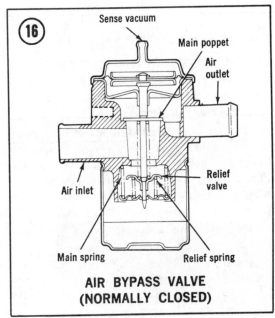

AIR BYPASS VALVE (NORMALLY CLOSED)

the power diaphragm, which closes or opens vents to the atmosphere by moving the valve membrane (**Figure 13**). Vacuum from the EGR port switches off the thermactor at idle because no vacuum is present at closed throttle conditions. The idle vacuum valve is open to atmosphere to dump thermactor air during cold engine operation, extended idle periods of ½-1 minute or more, and deceleration. During warm engine or normal operation, the vacuum valve closes to the atmosphere to allow passage of thermactor air.

EMISSION CONTROL SYSTEM MAINTENANCE

Most emission control system components should be serviced by your dealer, who has the proper devices and latest factory bulletins. A few components, however, can be serviced routinely without special tools, and the procedures are given in this section.

Air Cleaner (Dry Element Type)

Refer to **Figure 19**.

1. Remove air cleaner assembly from engine prior to removing air cleaner element to prevent dirt from accidentally dropping into the carburetor.

2. After air cleaner assembly has been removed, carefully wipe away any dirt from carburetor flange area.

3. Inspect carburetor mounting gasket and replace if damaged. Be sure that the red (adhesive) side is on carburetor flange.

4. Remove air cleaner element and clean the inside of the air cleaner assembly and cover.

5. Install air cleaner body on carburetor flange (it should seat freely on the carburetor gasket).

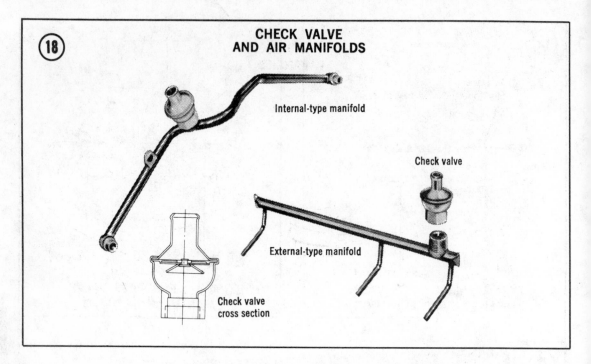

CHECK VALVE AND AIR MANIFOLDS

18

Internal-type manifold

Check valve

External-type manifold

Check valve cross section

6. Install air cleaner element and air cleaner cover, then connect all vacuum or electrical lines.

> NOTE: *When reconnecting crankcase closure lines to the air cleaner, be sure that the joint between the elbow and filter pack is secure and fully engaged.*

7. Install wing nut or screw and tighten firmly. On air cleaners using support brackets, tighten the wing nut prior to securing the support bracket. This will ensure a good seal between the air cleaner and carburetor.

Air Cleaner Replacement (Oil Bath Type)

Refer to **Figure 19**.

1. Remove air cleaner assembly.

2. Remove air cleaner cover and drain oil from reservoir. Wash all parts in solvent, then dry with compressed air.

3. Inspect gasket between oil reservoir chamber and air cleaner body. Replace if necessary.

4. Fill oil reservoir to the full mark with clean engine oil.

5. Install air cleaner assembly and tighten wing nut firmly.

Crankcase Emission Filter Replacement

1. Remove air cleaner cover.

2. Detach retaining clip from crankcase filter pack assembly, then remove filter pack assembly from air cleaner tray.

3. Remove (and discard) filter pad from housing. Wash the housing with solvent, then lightly oil a new filter pad and install it in the housing. (The lamination line of the filter must be visible after installation.) Install sponge gasket over the male nipple of the filter pack housing.

4. Install filter pack assembly in the air cleaner tray and secure with the retaining clip.

5. Install air cleaner cover and (when applicable) the rubberbacked wing nut washer.

6. Connect closure line to filter pack.

**Fuel Filter Replacement
(Integral With Fuel Pump)**

1. Clean the filter case sealing joint area, then remove the filter case while supporting the in-line filter cover or fuel pump adapter.

2. Remove and discard filter cartridge and case gasket.

3. Clean filter case (interior and exterior), then check filter gasket sealing surfaces for residue build-up. Clean as required.

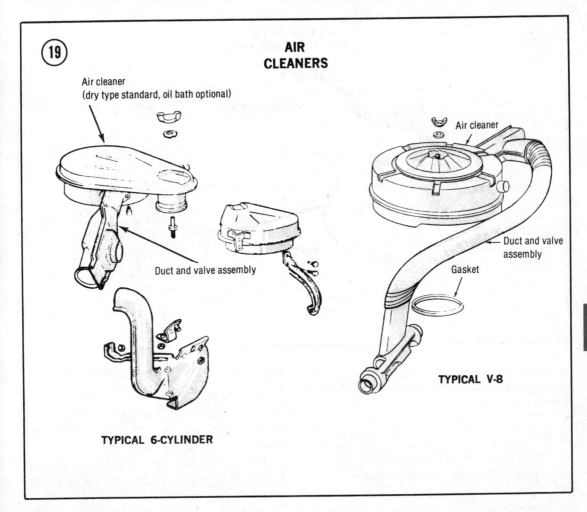

(19) AIR CLEANERS

Air cleaner
(dry type standard, oil bath optional)

Air cleaner

Duct and valve assembly

Duct and valve assembly

Gasket

TYPICAL 6-CYLINDER

TYPICAL V-8

4. Install new filter cartridge over the spout in the filter cover or fuel pump filter adapter. Place a new gasket on the filter case and lubricate it with clean engine oil.

5. Install filter case (with gasket) to mating cover or adapter and tighten enough to make firm gasket contact, then tighten ⅓ turn more.

6. Start engine and check for leaks.

Fuel Filter Replacement
(Carburetor Mounted Throw-away Type)

1. Remove air cleaner.

2. Loosen retaining clamp holding the fuel filter hose to the fuel filter.

3. Remove hose and discard retaining clamp.

4. Unscrew fuel filter from carburetor, then install a new filter and tighten firmly.

5. Install a new clamp on inlet hose and connect hose to new filter. Position the fuel line hose clamp (crimp it securely).

6. Start engine and check for fuel leaks.

7. Install air cleaner.

Fuel Filter Replacement
(Integral With Carburetor)

Refer to **Figure 20**.

1. Disconnect fuel line at carburetor.

2. Remove fuel filter retaining nut, gasket, filter gasket, filter, and spring. Discard filter and gaskets.

3. Install spring, new filter and gaskets, and retaining nut, as follows:

    a. Install new gasket in retaining nut recess.

    b. Install retaining nut gasket over retainer threads.

c. Install filter spring in carburetor fuel inlet filter recess.

d. Place new filter against spring with cone end pointing out.

e. Install retaining nut with gaskets and tighten securely.

f. Push against filter with a small screwdriver. If spring tension does not hold filter against seat the spring is incorrectly assembled. Repeat Steps a-f if necessary.

4. Install fuel line, then start engine and check for leaks.

PCV System Maintenance

1. Remove PCV system components from engine (filler cap, PCV valve, tubes, hoses, fittings).

2. Clean rubber hoses by pushing a cleaning brush through them. Wash hoses in petroleum base solvent, then blow dry with compressed air. Replace any hoses which show obvious wear or damage.

3. Wash crankcase breather in solvent, then shake dry.

4. Be sure all tubes, fittings, and connections are free of obstructions. Check all components for damage or wear and replace if necessary.

5. Install PCV valve, then install all PCV system components in their original positions.

PCV Valve Replacement

The PCV valve should be checked and replaced if necessary at each tune-up.

1. Pull PCV valve from rocker cover (**Figure 21**), but leave it connected to the vent hose. If valve is clear, a hissing sound will be heard when engine is idling, and a strong vacuum will be felt when a finger is placed over valve.

2. Install valve in rocker cover and disconnect crankcase inlet air cleaner from rocker cover. Hold a piece of stiff paper over the opening. After a minute or so, when the crankcase pressure has subsided, the paper should be sucked down against the hole. Shut engine off and once again disconnect PCV valve from rocker cover. Shake and listen for a clicking

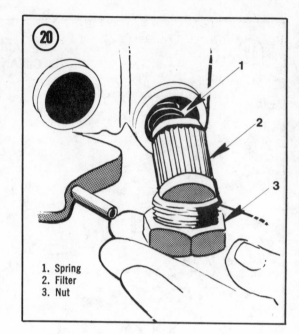

1. Spring
2. Filter
3. Nut

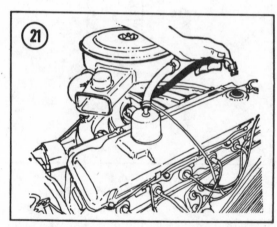

sound that indicates the valve is free. If not, replace it as follows:

a. Disconnect hose(s) and remove PCV valve.

b. Install new PCV valve and connect hose(s).

> NOTE: *If replacement PCV valve requires a plastic fitting for additional vacuum lines, soak new fitting in hot water prior to installation.*

CARBURETOR

If your carburetor becomes unserviceable, it is advisable to install a reconditioned carburetor, as outlined in the following procedure. Refer to **Figures 22 through 26** for exploded views.

Removal

1. Remove the air cleaner (refer to the appropriate *Air Cleaner* section earlier in this chapter).

2. Remove throttle cable or rod from throttle lever. Disconnect vacuum lines, tubes, hoses, and electric wiring.

3. Remove carburetor-to-intake manifold mounting nuts, then remove carburetor, gasket, spacer (if so equipped), and lower gasket.

Installation

1. Clean gasket mounting surfaces. Place spacer (if so equipped) between the 2 new gaskets, then place spacer and gaskets on the intake manifold. Place carburetor on the spacer and gasket and install and evenly tighten the carburetor-to-intake manifold mounting nuts.

2. Connect vacuum lines, tubes, hoses, and electric wiring.

3. Install air cleaner (refer to appropriate *Air Cleaner* section earlier in this chapter).

4. Adjust carburetor (refer to Chapter Four, *Carburetor* section).

FUEL PUMP

Single-action mechanical fuel pumps are standard on all engines. On 6-cylinder engines, the pump is mounted on the lower left-center of the engine cylinder block; on V-8 engines, the pump is located on the left side of the cylinder front cover.

If the fuel pump is suspected of a malfunction, perform the *Fuel Pump Test* described in Chapter Two and compare the results to the specifications shown in **Table 1**.

Removal/Installation

1. Disconnect inlet and outlet fuel lines at the fuel pump.
2. Remove pump-to-cylinder block mounting screws, then remove pump and gasket.
3. Discard old gasket and clean gasket mating surfaces. Install a new gasket (coat it on both sides with oil-resistant sealer; also coat the screw threads).
4. Hold pump in position against the mounting pad (with the gasket held in place on the pump flange by the sealer). Be sure that the rocker arm rides on the camshaft eccentric. (Turn engine over until the fuel pump eccentric is on the low side of the stroke, if necessary.)
5. Push the pump tightly against the mounting pad and install the attaching screws. Snug them down evenly to 19-27 ft.-lb.
6. Connect inlet and outlet fuel lines to the pump.
7. Operate engine and check for leaks.

6

Table 1   FUEL PUMP SPECIFICATIONS (1)

Engine	Pressure (psi)
All I6	5.5-6.5 (2)
302 cid	5.5-6.5 (3)
351M/400 cid	6.5-7.5 (3, 4)
360/390 cid	5-7
460 cid	5-7

NOTES
1. All pumps should flow approximately one pint in 30 seconds at normal curb idle speed and engine temperature.
2. 1969-1973; 4-6 psi
3. 1974-1975; 5.5-6.5 psi
4. 1969-1973; 5-7 psi

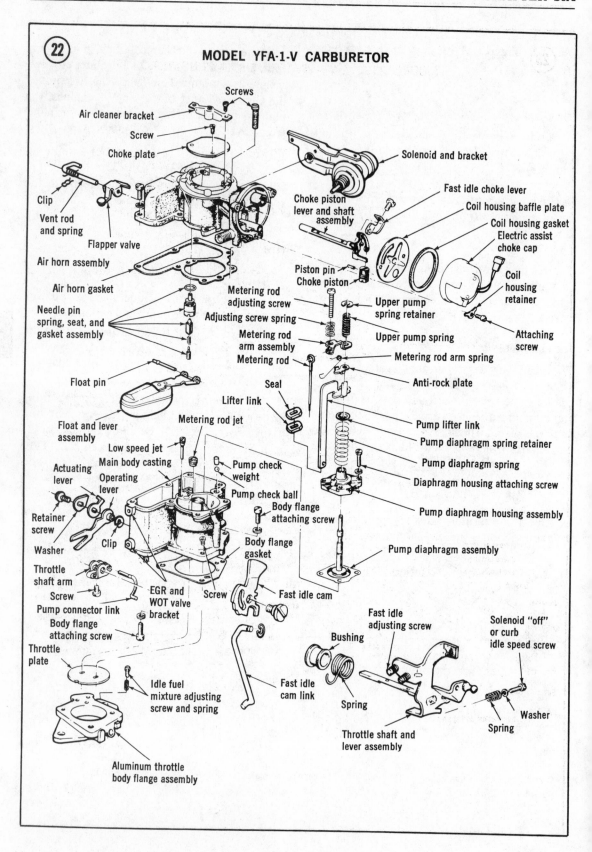

MODEL YFA-1-V CARBURETOR

(22)

- Screws
- Air cleaner bracket
- Screw
- Choke plate
- Solenoid and bracket
- Clip
- Vent rod and spring
- Flapper valve
- Choke piston lever and shaft assembly
- Fast idle choke lever
- Coil housing baffle plate
- Coil housing gasket
- Electric assist choke cap
- Air horn assembly
- Air horn gasket
- Needle pin spring, seat, and gasket assembly
- Piston pin
- Choke piston
- Metering rod adjusting screw
- Adjusting screw spring
- Metering rod arm assembly
- Metering rod
- Upper pump spring retainer
- Upper pump spring
- Metering rod arm spring
- Coil housing retainer
- Attaching screw
- Float pin
- Seal
- Lifter link
- Anti-rock plate
- Float and lever assembly
- Metering rod jet
- Low speed jet
- Main body casting
- Actuating lever
- Operating lever
- Pump check weight
- Pump check ball
- Pump lifter link
- Pump diaphragm spring retainer
- Pump diaphragm spring
- Diaphragm housing attaching screw
- Pump diaphragm housing assembly
- Retainer screw
- Washer
- Clip
- Body flange attaching screw
- Body flange gasket
- Pump diaphragm assembly
- Throttle shaft arm
- Screw
- Pump connector link
- Body flange attaching screw
- EGR and WOT valve bracket
- Screw
- Fast idle cam
- Fast idle adjusting screw
- Solenoid "off" or curb idle speed screw
- Throttle plate
- Idle fuel mixture adjusting screw and spring
- Fast idle cam link
- Bushing
- Spring
- Spring
- Washer
- Throttle shaft and lever assembly
- Aluminum throttle body flange assembly

(23) MODEL 2150 2-V — WITHOUT COMPENSATOR

Fuel bowl vent valve

Booster venturi screw

Yoke

Air horn

Yoke screw

Choke plate screw
(2 required)

Metering rods

Gasket

Lift rod

Gasket

Choke plate

Support and booster assembly

Gasket

Choke plate shaft

Weight

Spring

Pump check ball

Retainer

Float

Lever retaining screw

Float shaft

Choke plate lever

Float shaft retainer

Choke plate rod

Choke arm adjustment screw

Fuel inlet needle

Retainer

Inlet needle seat

Throttle shaft and
lever assembly

Idle speed
adjusting screw

Shield

Positive closure spring

Retainer

Spring

Filter screen

Retaining clip

Screw (2 required)

Main body

Main jets

Choke pulldown
diaphragm assembly

Vacuum hose

Elastomer
valve

Accelerator
pump rod

Nylon choke arm

Return spring

Linkage lever

Pump diaphragm

Accelerator
pump cover

Diaphragm link

Fast idle cam link

Spring

Shaft retainer

Fast
idle
cam

Choke housing shaft

Choke housing

Spring

Fast
idle
lever

Gasket

Choke lever

Enrichment
valve

Idle
limiter
cap

Pin

Gasket

Gasket

Fast
idle
adjustment
screw

Gasket

Idle
mixture
needle

Cover screw
(4 required)

Retainer

Pump operating
lever

Lever screw

Housing screw
(3 required)

Shield

Throttle
plates

Cover

Actuating
lever spring

Vent valve
actuating lever

Hot air inlet

High-speed
bleed cam

Screw (3 required)

Shield screw
(2 required)

Vent valve
bracket

Thermostatic spring housing

Cover screw

6

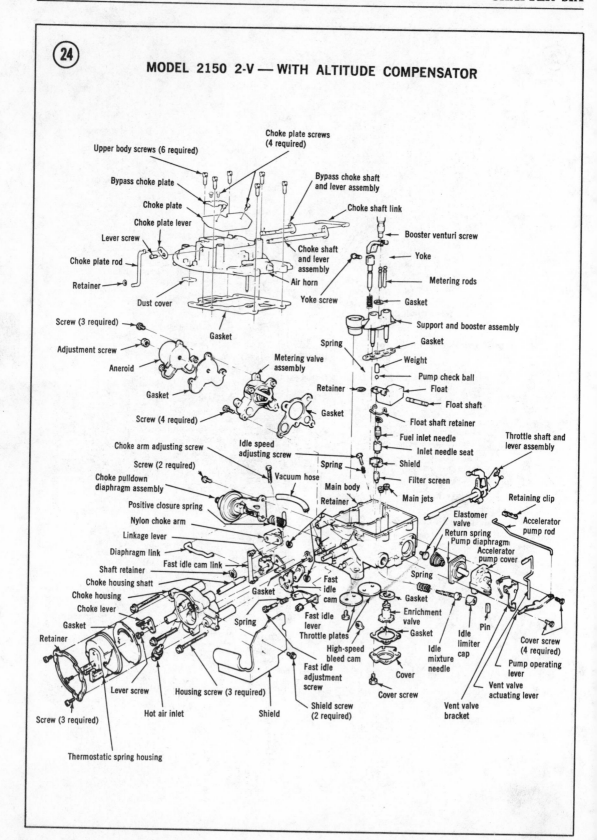

(24) MODEL 2150 2-V — WITH ALTITUDE COMPENSATOR

Upper body screws (6 required)

Choke plate screws (4 required)

Bypass choke plate

Bypass choke shaft and lever assembly

Choke plate

Choke shaft link

Choke plate lever

Lever screw

Booster venturi screw

Choke plate rod

Choke shaft and lever assembly

Yoke

Retainer

Air horn

Metering rods

Dust cover

Yoke screw

Gasket

Gasket

Support and booster assembly

Screw (3 required)

Spring

Gasket

Adjustment screw

Weight

Aneroid

Metering valve assembly

Pump check ball

Gasket

Retainer

Float

Float shaft

Screw (4 required)

Gasket

Float shaft retainer

Idle speed adjusting screw

Fuel inlet needle

Choke arm adjusting screw

Inlet needle seat

Throttle shaft and lever assembly

Screw (2 required)

Spring

Shield

Retaining clip

Choke pulldown diaphragm assembly

Vacuum hose

Filter screen

Positive closure spring

Retainer

Elastomer valve

Accelerator pump rod

Nylon choke arm

Main body

Main jets

Return spring

Linkage lever

Pump diaphragm

Diaphragm link

Fast idle cam link

Spring

Accelerator pump cover

Shaft retainer

Choke housing shaft

Gasket

Fast idle cam

Gasket

Choke housing

Choke lever

Fast idle lever

Gasket

Enrichment valve

Pin

Idle limiter cap

Gasket

Spring

Gasket

Cover screw (4 required)

Retainer

Throttle plates

High-speed bleed cam

Idle mixture needle

Pump operating lever

Lever screw

Housing screw (3 required)

Fast idle adjustment screw

Cover

Vent valve actuating lever

Screw (3 required)

Hot air inlet

Shield

Shield screw (2 required)

Cover screw

Vent valve bracket

Thermostatic spring housing

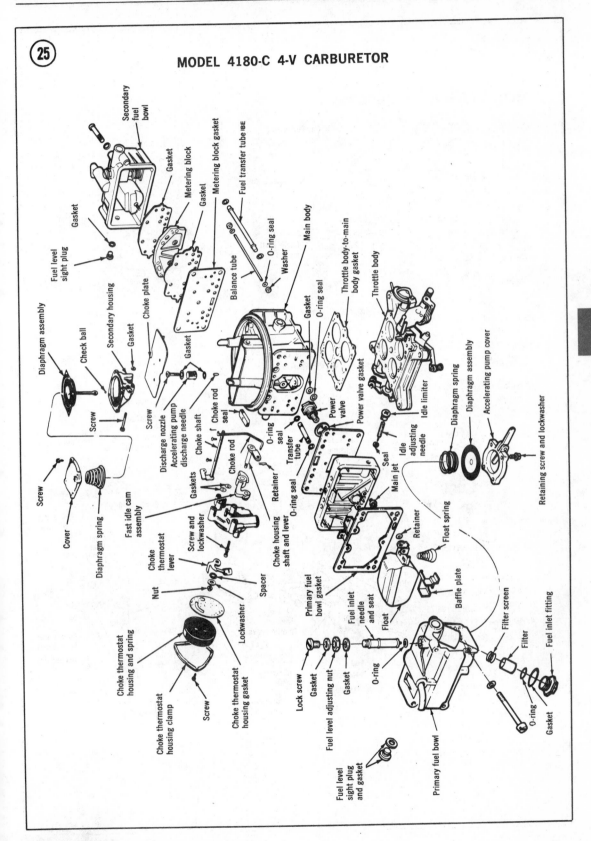

25

MODEL 4180-C 4-V CARBURETOR

26

MODEL 2100-2V CARBURETOR

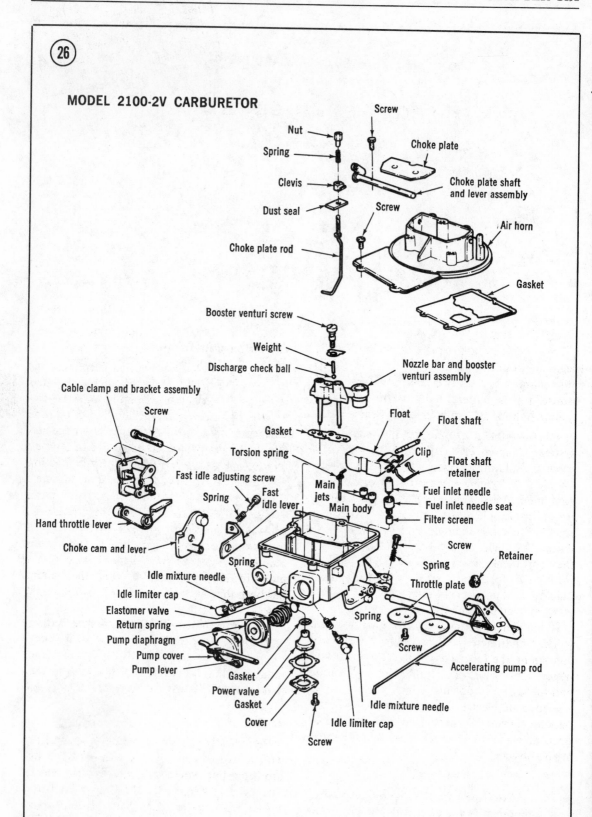

Nut
Spring
Clevis
Dust seal
Choke plate rod
Screw
Choke plate
Screw
Choke plate shaft and lever assembly
Air horn
Gasket

Booster venturi screw
Weight
Discharge check ball
Nozzle bar and booster venturi assembly

Cable clamp and bracket assembly
Screw
Gasket
Torsion spring
Float
Float shaft
Clip
Float shaft retainer

Fast idle adjusting screw
Spring
Fast idle lever
Main jets
Main body
Fuel inlet needle
Fuel inlet needle seat
Filter screen

Hand throttle lever
Choke cam and lever
Spring
Screw
Spring
Retainer
Throttle plate

Idle mixture needle
Idle limiter cap
Elastomer valve
Return spring
Pump diaphragm
Pump cover
Pump lever
Spring
Screw
Accelerating pump rod

Gasket
Power valve
Gasket
Cover
Screw
Idle mixture needle
Idle limiter cap

CHAPTER SEVEN

ELECTRICAL SYSTEM

Ford vehicles are equipped with 12-volt, negative-ground electrical systems. Included in this chapter are service and checkout procedures for the battery, fuses, starter, charging system, lighting system, and instruments.

When trouble is experienced in the electrical system, Chapter Two can prove valuable as a guide to isolating problem areas as well as explaining the functions and uses of electrical test equipment. Very often, electrical trouble can be traced to a simple cause, such as a blown fuse, a loose or corroded connection, a loose alternator drive belt, or a frayed wire. But, while these problems are easily correctable and of seemingly no major importance, they can quickly lead to serious difficulty if they are allowed to go uncorrected.

If you plan to do much of your own electrical work, a multimeter (described in Chapter Two) combining the functions of an ohmmeter, ammeter, and voltmeter, is essential to locating and sorting out problems.

Above all, electrical system repair requires a patient, thorough approach to find true causes of trouble and then correct all of the faults that are involved.

BATTERY

The battery is perhaps the single most important component in the electrical system — and commonly it is the most neglected.

Cleaning and Inspection

In addition to checking and correcting the battery electrolyte level at each gas stop (Chapter Three), the battery should be frequently cleaned with a solution of baking soda and water to remove corrosion from the terminals. Liberally coat the entire top of the battery as well as the terminals with the solution and allow it to stand for several minutes. Carefully flush the residue away with clean water; while the baking soda will neutralize the acids in the corrosion deposits, there's no need in risking unneutralized acid getting onto painted surfaces by rinsing the battery with a high-pressure water spray. When the battery has been thoroughly flushed, dry it with an old rag.

Inspect the battery case for damage, chafing, and cracks. Pay particular attention to moisture on the outside of the case; often this is an indication that the case is damaged to the extent that the battery is leaking electrolyte.

Testing

Periodically test the condition of the battery with a hydrometer. If you don't have a hydrometer but would consider buying one (a nominal investment), select one with numbered graduations rather than with a color-band scale; it's important to know the true condition of the battery — not just good, bad, or so-so. Draw enough electrolyte from each cell — one at a time — to raise the float in the hydrometer. Read it as shown in **Figure 1**. If the specific gravity is less than that indicated in **Table 1**, taking into account the temperature, and if the differences in specific gravity from one cell to another are close (less than 0.050), the battery requires a charge.

However, if the difference in specific gravity from one cell to another is greater than 0.050, one or more cells may be sulfated or otherwise poor. In such a case, the battery should be replaced before it causes trouble.

NOTE: *When testing the battery with a hydrometer, always return the electrolyte to the cell from which it was removed before testing the next cell.*

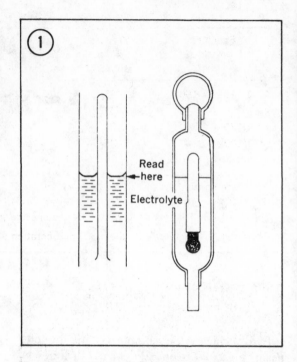

Charging

There's no need to remove the battery from the vehicle to charge it. Just make certain that the area is well ventilated and that there is no chance of sparks or open flame being in the vicinity of the battery; during charging, highly explosive hydrogen is produced by the battery.

Disconnect the ground lead from the battery. Remove the caps from the battery cells and top up each cell with distilled water. Never add electrolyte to a battery that is already in service. The electrolyte level in the cells should be about ¼ in. above the plates.

Connect the charger to the battery — negative to negative, positive to positive (**Figure 2**). If the charger output is variable, select a low setting (5-10 amps), set the voltage selector to 12 volts, and plug the charger in. If the battery is severely discharged (below 1.125), allow it to charge for at least 8 hours. Less charge deterioration requires less charging time.

NOTE: *If time permits, charge at the lower rate and for a long period of time; however, if there is not sufficient time for slow charging, follow the high-rate charging times and rates shown in Table 2.*

After the battery has charged for a suitable period of time, unplug the charger and discon-

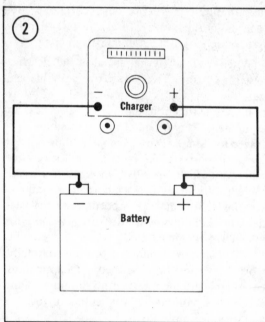

Table 1   ELECTROLYTE SPECIFIC GRAVITY

	Permissible Value	Full Charge Value at 68°F
Moderate climate	Over 1.20	1.26
Cold climate	Over 1.22	1.28
Warm climate	Over 1.18	1.23

Table 2 HIGH-RATE CHARGING TIMES

Specific Gravity Reading	Charge Rate Amperes	Battery Capacity — Ampere Hours				
		45	55	70	80	85
1.125 — 1.150 ①	35	65 min.	80 min.	100 min.	115 min.	125 min.
1.150 — 1.175	35	50 min.	65 min.	80 min.	95 min.	105 min.
1.175 — 1.200	35	40 min.	50 min.	60 min.	70 min.	75 min.
1.200 — 1.225	35	30 min.	35 min.	45 min.	50 min.	55 min.
Above 1.225	5	②	②	②	②	②

① If the specific gravity is below 1.125, use the indicated high rate of charge for the 1.125. specific gravity, then charge at 5 amperes until the specific gravity reaches 1.250 at 80°F.

② Charge at 5 ampere rate only until the specific gravity reaches 1.250 at 80°F.

Warning: At no time during the charging operation should the electrolyte temperature exceed 130°F.

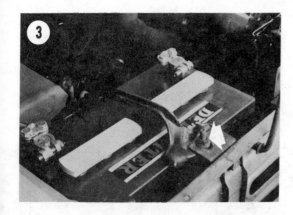

nect it from the battery. Be extremely careful about sparks. Test the condition of each cell with a hydrometer as described above and compare the results with **Table 1**.

If the specific gravity indicates that the battery is fully charged, and if the readings remain the same after one hours, the battery can be considered to be in good condition and fully charged. Check the electrolyte level and add distilled water if necessary, install the vent caps, and reconnect the ground lead.

Removal/Installation

1. Loosen the bolts in the terminal clamps for enough so the clamps can be spread slightly. Lift straight up on the clamps (negative first) to remove them from the posts. Twisting or prying on the clamps or posts can result in serious damage to a battery that may otherwise be in good condition.

2. Unscrew the nuts from the hold-down bolts (**Figure 3**) and remove the hold-down frame. If the battery is retained by a single lug that locks into a recess in the lower part of the case, unscrew the bolt that holds the lug to the battery box. Lift the battery out of the engine compartment.

3. Reverse these steps to install the battery. Before setting the battery in place, clean the battery holder with a solution of baking soda and water to neutralize any acids that may have formed. Allow the solution to stand for several minutes then carefully flush it away with clean water, and dry it with an old rag. Set the battery into the holder making sure it is squarely seated. Install the hold-down frame and screw on the nuts snugly.

First connect the positive lead to the battery, then the negative. Tighten the clamp bolts securely and check their tightness by trying to rotate them on the posts by hand. Coat the terminals liberally with Vaseline to inhibit corrosion and formation of ash-like acid deposits.

ALTERNATOR

The alternator is a self-rectifying three-phase current generator consisting of a stationary armature (stator), a rotating field (rotor), and a three-phase rectifying bridge of silicon diodes. The alternator generates alternating current which is converted to direct current by the silicon diodes for use in the vehicle's electrical

7

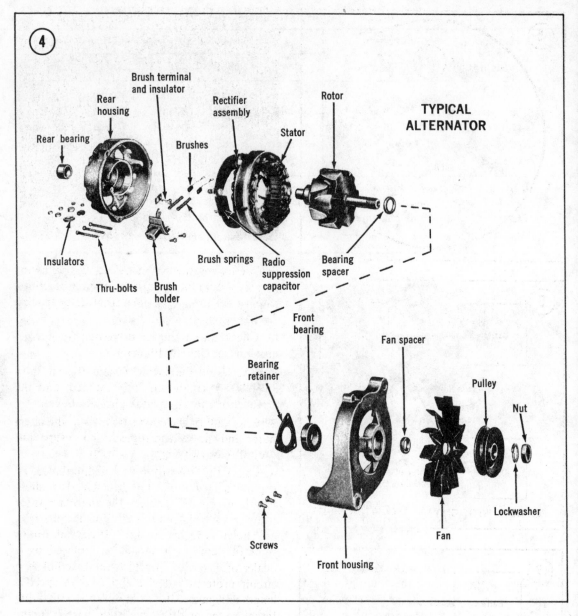

④

TYPICAL ALTERNATOR

Rear bearing

Rear housing

Brush terminal and insulator

Brushes

Rectifier assembly

Stator

Rotor

Insulators

Thru-bolts

Brush holder

Brush springs

Radio suppression capacitor

Bearing spacer

Front bearing

Fan spacer

Bearing retainer

Pulley

Nut

Lockwasher

Screws

Front housing

Fan

circuits. The output of the alternator is regulated by a voltage regulator to keep the battery charged. The alternator is mounted on the front of the engine and is driven through a belt by the crankshaft pulley. A typical alternator is shown in exploded view in **Figure 4**.

When working on the alternator, make sure the connections are not reversed. Current flow in the wrong direction will damage the diodes and render the alternator unserviceable. The alternator B terminal must be connected to battery voltage (**Figure 5**). When charging the battery in the vehicle, disconnect the battery leads before connecting the charger. This is a precaution against incorrect current bias and heat reaching the alternator.

Testing

The first indication of charging system trouble is usually slow engine cranking speed during starting. This will often occur long before the charge warning light or ammeter indicates that there is potential trouble. When charging system trouble is first suspected, it should be carefully tested, either by a Ford dealer or an automotive electrical specialist. However,

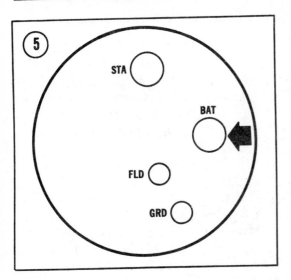

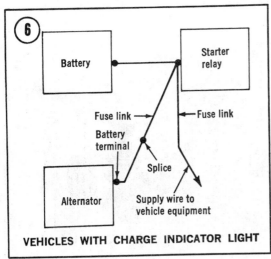

VEHICLES WITH CHARGE INDICATOR LIGHT

before having the system tested, the following checks should be made to make sure something else is not the cause of what seems to be trouble in the charging system.

1. Check the alternator drive belt for correct tension (see Chapter Eight).

2. Check the battery to ensure that it is in satisfactory condition, fully charged, and the connections are clean and tight (see above).

3. Check all of the connections from the alternator and the voltage regulator to ensure that they are clean and tight.

4. Check the fuse link for burned, bubbled, or expanded insulation. The fuse link is a short length of wire that protects the alternator from heavy reverse currents. Fuse link installations are shown in **Figures 6 and 7**. If the link shows signs of damage, it should be replaced by a dealer or electrical specialist; the fuse link is a circuit protection device and is of a specific length and gauge. If it were replaced with a different gauge or different length wire it might not function (burn through) when necessary.

When each of the above points have been carefully checked and unsatisfactory conditions corrected, and there are still indications that the charging system is not performing as it should, have it checked.

Removal/Installation

1. Disconnect the negative battery cable at the battery (**Figure 8**). Unplug the connector from the rear of the alternator (**Figure 9**).

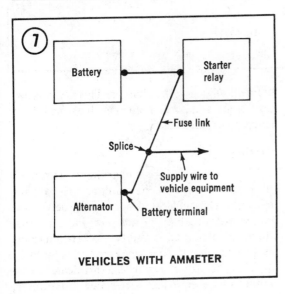

VEHICLES WITH AMMETER

2. Loosen the belt tension adjuster at the alternator (**Figure 10**). Swing the alternator toward the engine and remove the drive belt from the pulley.

3. Unscrew the adjuster bolt and pivot bolt and remove the alternator.

4. Reverse these steps to install the alternator. Make certain the alternator plug has been connected before connecting the negative battery lead. Refer to Chapter Eight and adjust the drive belt tension.

CHARGE INDICATOR RELAY

If the alternator and voltage regulator are operating satisfactorily and the charge indicator warning light remains on, or the ammeter registers discharge, the charge indicator relay (located inside the voltage regulator) must be tested. This is a job for a Ford dealer or an automotive electrical specialist.

STARTER

Service to the starter requires experience and special tools. The service procedure described below consists of removal and installation. Any repairs on the unit itself should be entrusted to a Ford dealer or an automotive electrical specialist.

Removal/Installation

1. Disconnect the negative cable at the battery (**Figure 8**).

2. Disconnect the positive battery cable and the starter control cable at the starter (**Figure 11**).

3. Thoroughly clean the outside of the starter and the area at which it is attached to the bell housing. Unscrew the starter mounting bolts

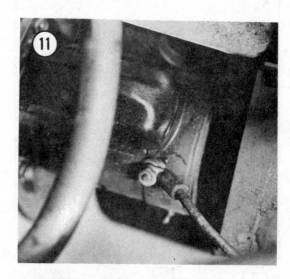

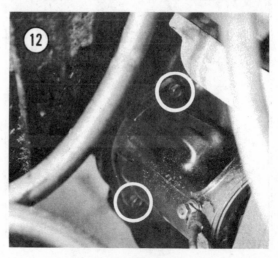

(Figure 12) and pull the starter out of the bell housing.

4. Install the starter by reversing these steps. Make sure the connections are tight to ensure good electrical contact.

DISTRIBUTOR

Removal/Installation
(V-8 Engines)

1. Remove air cleaner.

2. Disconnect distributor primary wiring at coil or quick disconnect.

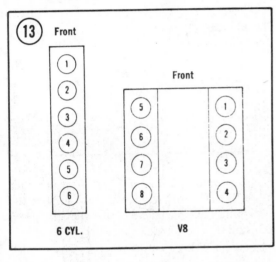

6 CYL.   **V8**

3. Disconnect vacuum advance lines at distributor.

4. Remove distributor cap and position to one side, out of the way.

5. On models equipped with an adapter beneath the rotor, remove the rotor and adapter, then reinstall the rotor.

6. Scribe an alignment mark on the distributor body and cylinder block to indicate the position of the rotor in the distributor, and the distributor in the block. (These marks will be used as guides when installing the distributor.)

7. Remove distributor hold-down bolt and clamp. Lift distributor out of block.

NOTE: *Do not rotate engine while distributor is out of block or it will be necessary to retime the engine.*

8. If crankshaft was accidentally rotated while distributor was out of the engine, proceed as follows:

    a. Rotate crankshaft until No.1 piston is on TDC after compression stroke (refer to **Figure 13** for location of No. 1 cylinder).

    b. Align correct initial timing mark on timing pointer with the timing pointer on the crankshaft damper (refer to **Figure 14**).

7

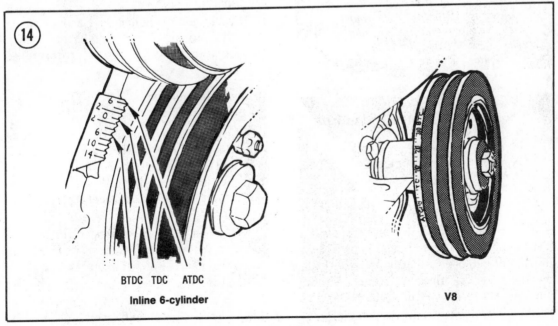

BTDC TDC ATDC

Inline 6-cylinder   **V8**

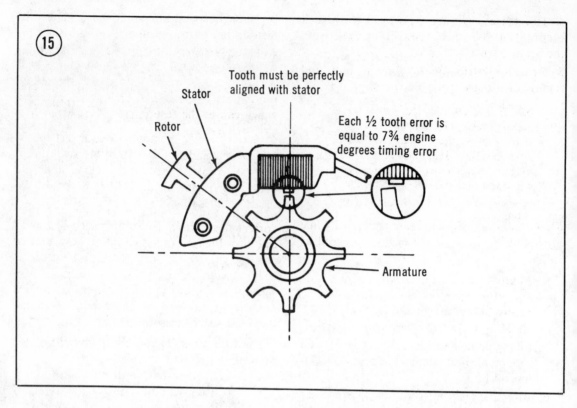

Stator

Rotor

Tooth must be perfectly
aligned with stator

Each ½ tooth error is
equal to 7¾ engine
degrees timing error

Armature

c. Position the distributor in the block with the rotor at the No. 1 firing position (**Figure 15**).

NOTE: *The cap is marked with an embossed "No. 1" at the No. 1 terminal.*

It may be necessary to crank the engine with the starter after the distributor drive gear is partially engaged in order to engage the oil pump intermediate shaft. If this is required, return crankshaft to the initial timing alignment. Install (but do not tighten) the retaining clamp and bolt. Rotate the distributor to advance the timing to a point where the armature tooth is aligned properly, then tighten the clamp.

9. If crankshaft has not been moved since distributor was removed, simply install distributor in block with rotor aligned with the mark previously scribed on distributor body, and the marks on the distributor body and cylinder block aligned.

10. On models equipped with an adapter beneath the rotor, remove the rotor from the distributor and install the base adapter. Then reinstall the rotor and cap.

11. Connect distributor wiring at coil or quick disconnect.

12. Check ignition timing with a timing light and adjust to specifications (refer to Chapter Four, *Ignition System* section for procedure).

Removal/Installation
(6-Cylinder Engines)

1. On engines equipped with a Thermactor pump, remove one of the pump's mounting bolts and the drive belt, then swing the pump to one side to allow distributor access. (It might also be necessary to disconnect the Thermactor air filter and lines.)

2. Rotate engine until the proper timing mark on the engine crankshaft damper is aligned with the timing pointer (refer to **Figure 14**).

3. Remove distributor cap and check to be sure that the rotor is aligned with the mark on the side of the distributor body (refer to **Figure 15**).

4. Disconnect vacuum hose(s) from distributor, then disconnect the ignition lead from the wiring harness.

5. Remove distributor hold-down bolt and remove distributor from block.

> NOTE: *The hex shaft that drives the oil pump might stick in the distributor shaft and be accidentally withdrawn from the pump. Don't lose it. To install it again, coat one end with heavy grease and insert that end into the hex hole in the distributor shaft.*

6. If crankshaft was accidentally rotated while distributor was out of the engine, proceed as follows:

   a. Rotate crankshaft until No. 1 piston is on TDC after compression stroke (refer to **Figure 13** for location of No. 1 cylinder).

   b. Align correct initial timing mark on timing pointer with the timing pointer on the crankshaft damper (refer to **Figure 14**).

   c. Align the distributor rotor with the mark on the distributor (refer to **Figure 15**). Slide the distributor into the engine. Be sure that the oil pump drive shaft is fully seated in the pump, and that the distributor rotor and body are in the proper position.

7. Install the distributor hold-down bolt and clamp.

8. Install the adapter (if used), rotor, and distributor cap.

9. On models so equipped, install the Thermactor belt, hoses, and filter.

10. Connect distributor wiring at coil or quick disconnect.

11. Check ignition timing with a timing light and adjust to specifications (refer to Chapter Four, *Ignition System* section for procedure).

FUSES

Whenever a failure occurs in any part of the electrical system, always check the fuse box to see if a fuse has blown. If one has, it will be evidenced by a blackening of the fuse or by a break in the metal link in the fuse. Usually the trouble can be traced to a short circuit in the wiring connected to the blown fuse. This may be caused by worn-through insulation or by a wire which has worked loose and shorted to ground. Occasionally, the electrical overload which causes the fuse to blow may occur in a switch or a motor.

A blown fuse should be treated as more than a minor annoyance; it should serve also as a warning that something is wrong in the electrical system. Before replacing a fuse, determine what caused it to blow and then correct the trouble. Never replace a fuse with one of a higher amperage rating than that of the one originally used. Never use tinfoil or other metallic material to bridge fuse terminals. Failure to follow these basic rules could result in heat or fire damage to major parts, or loss of entire vehicle.

The fuse panel (**Figure 16**) is located on the firewall, to the left of the pedals.

7

LIGHTS

All lighting elements, with the exception of instrument illumination bulbs, are easily replaced. Individual replacement procedures follow.

Headlight Replacement

The headlights are replaceable sealed-beam units. Both the high- and low-beam circuits and filaments are included in one unit. Failure of one circuit requires replacement of the entire unit.

> NOTE: *If both filaments in the lamp unit fail at the same time it is possible that there is a short in the wiring to that particular lamp. Check the fuse to make sure it is the correct amperage rating and replace it if it is not. Carefully inspect the wiring and connector too for chafing or damage and correct any breaks in the insulation.*

1. Unscrew the screws which hold the headlight trim ring in place and remove the ring.

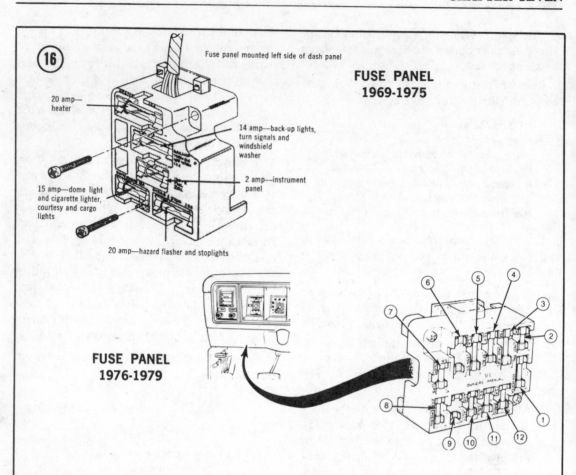

⑯ Fuse panel mounted left side of dash panel

**FUSE PANEL
1969-1975**

20 amp—heater

14 amp—back-up lights, turn signals and windshield washer

2 amp—instrument panel

15 amp—dome light and cigarette lighter, courtesy and cargo lights

20 amp—hazard flasher and stoplights

**FUSE PANEL
1976-1979**

Fuse No.	Circuit Protected	Amps
1	Heater/defroster and/or air conditioner	30^1 or 35^2
2	Instrument panel and cluster lamps, ashtray, transmission indicator lamp, radio lamp, heater, air conditioner lamp, headlamp, and windshield wiper illuminator	3.0
3	Auxiliary tank solenoid	7.5
4	Seat belt buzzer	7.5
5	Throttle solenoid, emission control circuitry	7.5
6	Not used	
7	Dome, cargo, courtesy lamps, cigarette lighter, glove box lamp, underhood lamp	15
8	Emergency flashers, stop lamps	20
9	Not used	
10	Accessory feed, heated backlite relay, speed control, 4 x 4 indicator light, dual battery relay	20
11	Back-up lamps, turn signal flasher, windshield washer	15
12	Radio	7.5

1. 1976 models   2. 1977-1979 models

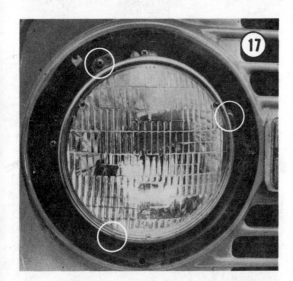

2. Loosen the 3 headlight retaining screws (**Figure 17**), turn the light unit counterclockwise to line up the large cutouts with the screws, and remove the unit. Unplug the connector from the rear of the light.

> NOTE: *Do not turn the headlight beam adjusting screws (**Figure 18**). Otherwise the setting will be disturbed and the headlight beam will require adjustment.*

3. Reverse the above to install a new light unit. Make sure the connector is firmly seated before installing the unit. Set the light in place, making sure the lugs on the light engage the recesses in the lamp holder (**Figure 19**). Set the retainer ring in place and turn it clockwise so the small end of each cutout engages a screw. Tighten the screws and install the outer trim ring.

Signal Light Replacement

To change bulbs in a rear combination light (**Figure 20**), license plate light, parking/turn indicator lights (**Figure 21**), or side marker lights, unscrew the screws which hold the lens in place. Remove the lens and the bulb that is being replaced by pressing in on it, turning counterclockwise, and pulling it out of the socket. Wipe clean the inside of the lens and the lamp reflectors. Press the new bulb into the socket and turn it clockwise to lock it into the socket. Install the lens taking care not to overtighten the screws and crack the lens.

> NOTE: *The mounting screw for the license plate light is a self-threading type that will cut the threads out of the tailgate unless it is properly started. Set the screw in the hole and slowly turn it counterclockwise until it "clicks" into engagement with the threads. Then screw it in snugly.*

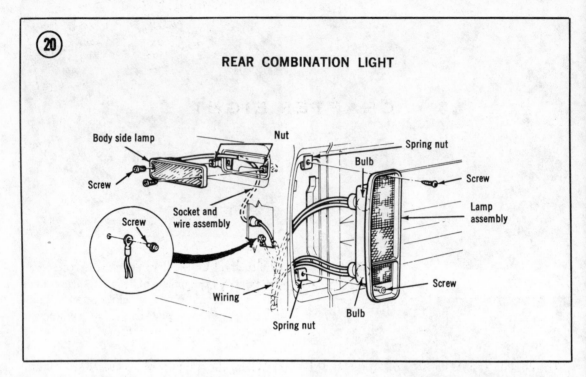

20

REAR COMBINATION LIGHT

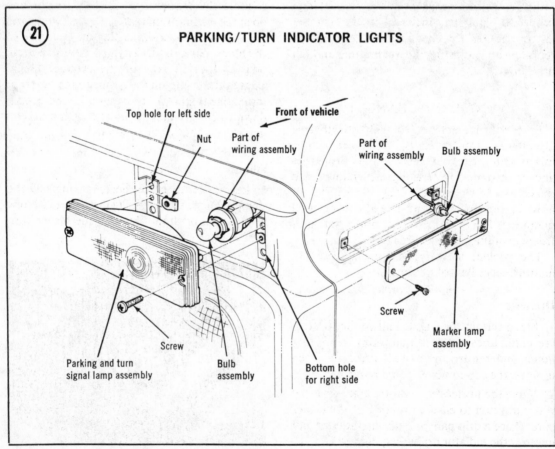

21

PARKING/TURN INDICATOR LIGHTS

NOTE: If you own a 1980 or later model, first check the Supplement at the back of the book for any new service information.

CHAPTER EIGHT

COOLING, HEATING, AND AIR CONDITIONING

The cooling system consists of a pressurized radiator, thermostat, water pump, fan, and appropriate plumbing. Included in this chapter are procedures for changing the coolant and replacing and adjusting the water pump and fan drive belts.

COOLANT CHANGE

Ford vehicles are cooled with an ethylene glycol-based anti-freeze. The anti-freeze can be mixed with water to alter its cooling properties and its resistance to freezing, depending upon the climate in which the vehicle is operated. In most cases, however, anti-freeze can be used undiluted. If it is to be mixed, follow the anti-freeze manufacturer's instructions.

The coolant should be changed every 12 months, regardless of mileage.

Draining

1. Make certain the engine and cooling system are cool. Loosen the radiator cap to its first notch and release the system pressure. Then unscrew the cap completely and remove it.

2. Move the heater temperature control to the WARM position to ensure draining of the heater core. Place a drip pan beneath the radiator and unscrew the radiator drain plug (**Figure 1**).

3. When the radiator has ceased to drain, relocate the drip pan beneath the engine and open the engine drain tap(s). **Figure 2** illustrates a V-8, which has a drain plug on each side of the block. Six-cylinder engines have one drain plug at the left rear of the cylinder block. Loosen the clamp on the IN line to the heater at the engine (**Figure 3**), disconnect it, and bend it down to aid draining the heater. Allow several minutes for the system to drain.

Filling

1. Reconnect the heater hose, making sure the clamp is tight. Close the engine taps and screw in the radiator drain plug. Set the heater controls at WARM.

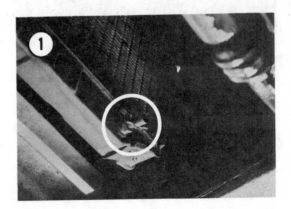

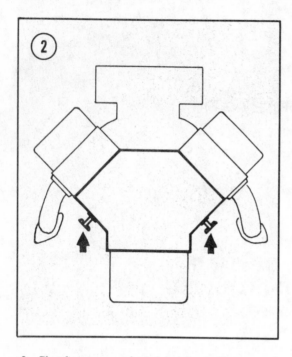

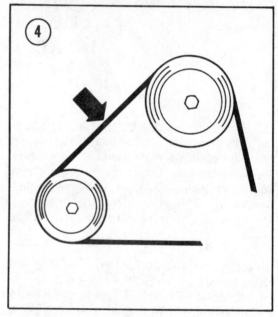

2. Slowly pour coolant into the radiator until the level is at the mark in the filler neck. Start the engine and allow it to idle for about one minute with the radiator cap off.

3. Check the level in the radiator and top it up as required. Install the radiator cap and check for (and correct) any leaks.

PRESSURE CHECK

If the cooling system requires repeated topping up, it probably has a leak. One of the most likely causes of cooling system leakage is the radiator cap, which can be tested as described in Chapter Three. The cooling system test described below can also be made at the time the radiator cap is tested. Have it done by a Ford dealer or a service station if you do not have access to a tester.

> **CAUTION**
> *The engine and cooling system must be cold when the pressure test is carried out.*

1. Remove the radiator cap and, if necessary, top up the coolant to the level mark in the filler neck.

2. Install the pressure tester and pump it to pressurize the system to 18-21 psi.

3. Thoroughly inspect the radiator, hoses, and all the connections for leaks. If any leaks are found at the hose connections, tighten the clamps and pressurize the system again. If a leak is found in a hose, replace the hose and pressure test the system again.

> **CAUTION**
> *Any hoses that are brittle, spongy, or swollen should be replaced routinely. If they do not leak now, they soon will or may, in fact, rupture. This type of hose failure, particularly during high-speed or off-road driving, could result in extensive engine damage or, at the least, considerable inconvenience.*

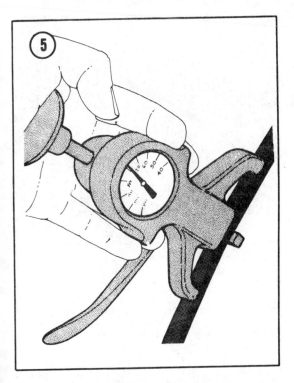

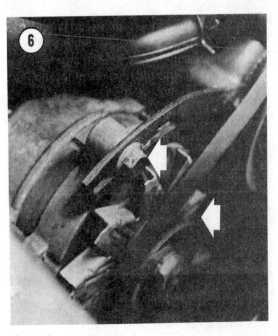

If a leak is found in the radiator core or in the top and bottom tanks, have the radiator repaired by a Ford dealer or radiator specialist. When the repaired radiator has been reinstalled, pressure test the system to make sure all connections are water-tight.

DRIVE BELTS

The water pump/fan drive belt, as well as the belts which drive the alternator, air conditioning, power steering pump, etc., should be inspected monthly for condition and adjustment.

Worn, frayed, cracked, or glazed belts should be replaced at once. The components to which they direct power are essential to the safe and reliable operation of the vehicle. If correct adjustment is maintained on the belts, they will usually all enjoy the same service life. For this reason, and because of the labor involved in replacing an inboard belt (requiring the removal of the outer belts), it is a good idea to replace all belts as a set. The low added expense is well worth the time involved in doing the job twice, to say nothing of the consequences of a failed belt.

In addition to being in good condition, it is important that the drive belts be correctly ad-justed. A belt that is too loose will not permit the driven components to operate at maximum efficiency. In addition, the belt will wear rapidly because of increased friction caused by slipping. A belt that is adjusted too tight will be overstressed and tend to be pulled apart, and it in turn will overstress bearings in driven components resulting in their premature wear or possible failure.

Drive belt tension (adjustment) is measured by deflection of the belt midway between two pulleys at the belt's longest run (**Figure 4**).

Alternator/Fan-Water Pump Belt (Without Air Conditioning)

For maximum belt life and component efficiency, the belt tension should be checked with a tester like that shown in **Figure 5**. The tension for a new belt should be 140 lb. and for a used belt (one that has been in operation for more than 10 minutes) the tension should be 110 lb. As a temporary setting, until the actual tension can be adjusted, a deflection of about ½ in. with moderate force applied to the belt is a reasonable compromise.

To adjust the tension, loosen the pivot bolt located beneath the alternator and then loosen the lock bolt (**Figure 6**). Move the alternator toward or away from the engine as required until the tension is correct, then tighten the lock bolt and then the pivot bolt without further moving the alternator. When the adjustment has been made, double check to ensure that it is correct.

To replace the belt, loosen the alternator bolts as just described and swing the alternator toward the engine as far as it will go so the belt can be removed from the pulleys.

Alternator Belt (With Air Conditioning)

Adjust the alternator drive belt as described above, using a belt tension tester (**Figure 5**). The tension for a new belt should be 140 lb. and for a used belt (one that has been in operation for more than 10 minutes), the tension should be 110 lb.

Air Conditioning Belt

Measure the belt tension with a tester, midway betwen the crankshaft pulley and the air conditioning compressor pulley (**Figure 7**). The tension for a new belt should be 140 lb. and for a used belt (one that has been in service for more than 10 minutes), the tension should be 110 lb.

To adjust the belt tension, loosen the bolts on the idler pulley (**Figure 8**) and move the idler as required until the tension is correct. Then, without further moving the idler pulley, tighten the bolts securely and recheck the tension.

To replace the belt, loosen the idler pulley bolts and swing the pulley toward the air conditioning compressor as far as it will go so the belt can be removed.

Power Steering Pump Belt

Measure the tension of the power steering pump belt with a tester, midway between the fan-water pump pulley and the power steering pump pulley (**Figure 9**). The tension for a new belt should be 120-150 lb. For a used belt (one that has been in service for more than 10 minutes), the tension should be 90-120 lb.

To adjust the tension of the belt, loosen the bolts which attach the pump or pump mounting bracket to the adjusting bracket (**Figure 10**) and move the pump by applying pressure at the web behind the pulley.

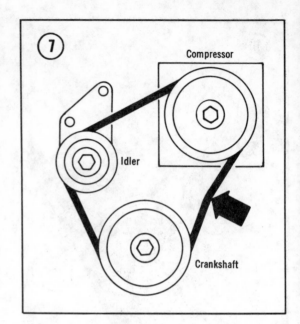

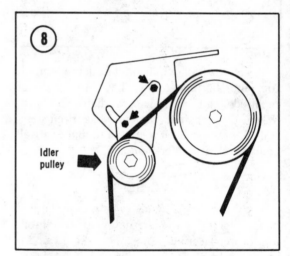

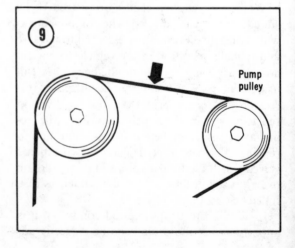

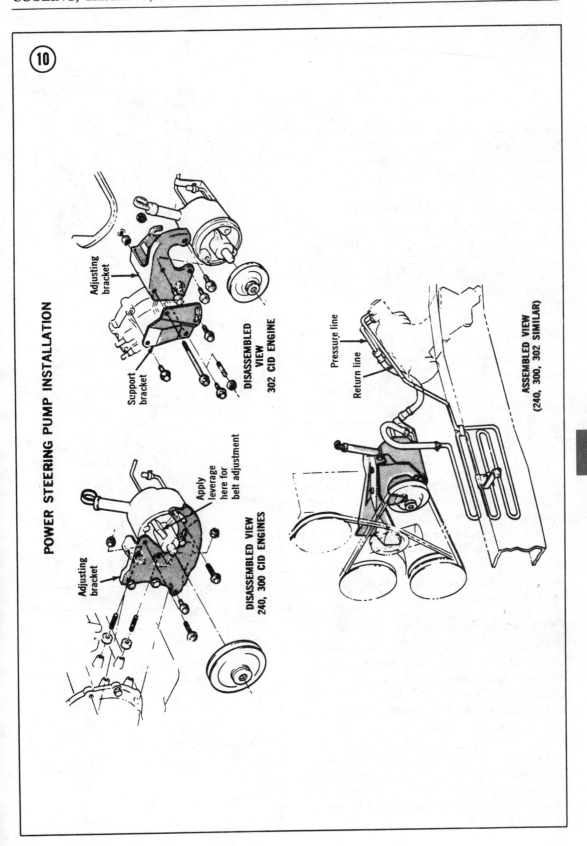

(10)

POWER STEERING PUMP INSTALLATION

Adjusting
bracket

Support
bracket

DISASSEMBLED
VIEW
302 CID ENGINE

Apply
leverage
here for
belt adjustment

Adjusting
bracket

DISASSEMBLED VIEW
240, 300 CID ENGINES

Pressure line

Return line

ASSEMBLED VIEW
(240, 300, 302 SIMILAR)

8

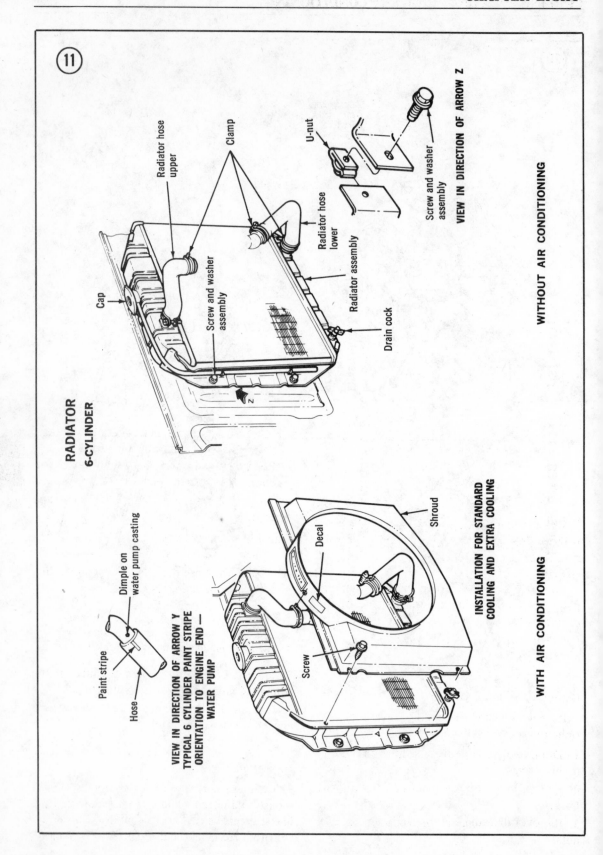

11

RADIATOR
6-CYLINDER

Cap

Radiator hose
upper

Clamp

Screw and washer
assembly

Radiator hose
lower

Radiator assembly

Drain cock

U-nut

Screw and washer
assembly

VIEW IN DIRECTION OF ARROW Z

WITHOUT AIR CONDITIONING

Paint stripe

Dimple on
water pump casting

Hose

VIEW IN DIRECTION OF ARROW Y
TYPICAL 6 CYLINDER PAINT STRIPE
ORIENTATION TO ENGINE END —
WATER PUMP

Decal

Shroud

Screw

INSTALLATION FOR STANDARD
COOLING AND EXTRA COOLING

WITH AIR CONDITIONING

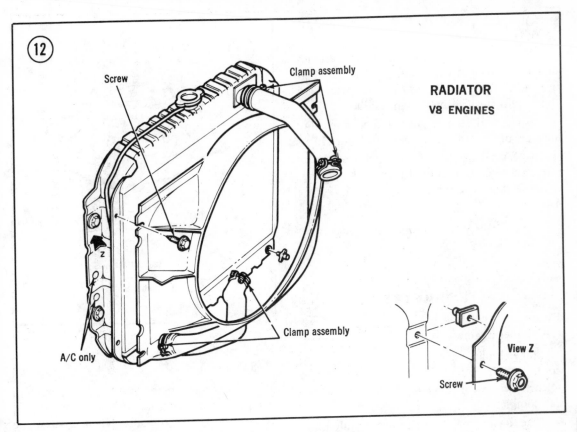

RADIATOR

V8 ENGINES

Screw

Clamp assembly

Clamp assembly

A/C only

View Z

Screw

8

CAUTION

Do not apply pressure to the reservoir; it will bend and leak.

When the tension is correct, tighten the bolts without further moving the pump. Then recheck the tension to make sure it has not changed.

To replace the belt, loosen the adjusting and pivot bolts and swing the pump toward the engine as far as it will go so the belt can be removed.

RADIATOR

Removal/Installation

Refer to **Figures 11 and 12** for the various radiator connection points.

1. Drain cooling system as outlined previously in this chapter.

2. Loosen radiator hose clamps and disconnect hoses.

3. Remove all radiator connection bolts and nuts.

4. Remove and inspect radiator (refer to *Inspection* section, following).

5. To install, reverse the preceding steps and observe the following points:

   a. Position the clamps on each end of the hose.

   b. Slide the hose over the connections, then tighten the clamps.

   NOTE: *If the connections have a bead around the edges, be sure that the clamps are located beyond the beads.*

6. Fill the cooling system as outlined in the *Coolant Change* section of this chapter.

7. Operate the engine for a few minutes to check for leaks.

Inspection

1. Check general appearance of radiator. If obviously damaged (badly bent cooling fins, leaks, excessive rust or scale deposits inside the radiator, etc.), take the radiator to a radiator

specialist and have it flushed and repaired, if possible.

2. Check radiator cap for rust or dirt particles under the vacuum valve and rubber seal (**Figure 13**). Rinse with warm tap water to thoroughly flush away foreign residue.

3. Inspect and remove rust or dirt on sealing surfaces of the rubber seal (refer to **Figure 13**).

4. Inspect radiator filler neck for rust or dirt on sealing surface at bottom of filler neck opening. Wipe sealing surface clean with a cloth (**Figure 14**).

> NOTE: *Remove any paint on the filler neck sealing surface with paint thinner.*

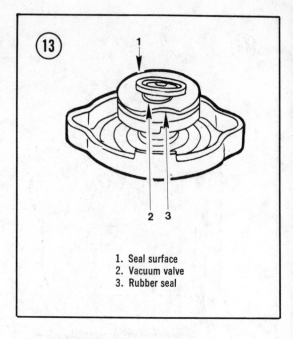

1. Seal surface
2. Vacuum valve
3. Rubber seal

THERMOSTAT

Removal/Installation
(6-Cylinder Engines)

1. Make certain engine and cooling system are cool. Loosen radiator cap to first notch to release the system pressure. Then unscrew the cap completely.

2. Place a catch pan under radiator drain plug, then unscrew the drain plug (refer to **Figure 1**). Drain radiator until coolant level falls below the thermostat housing.

3. Remove coolant outlet elbow attaching bolts, then pull elbow away from the cylinder head far enough to provide access to the thermostat. Remove thermostat and old gasket.

4. Check thermostat (refer to *Inspection* procedure, following).

5. Clean gasket mating surfaces, then coat new gasket with water-resistant sealer. Position gasket on cylinder head opening.

> NOTE: *The coolant outlet elbow has a locking recess into which the thermostat is turned and locked. Be sure to install the thermostat with the bridge section in the outlet elbow. Turn the thermostat clockwise to lock it in position.*

6. Place coolant outlet elbow against cylinder head. Install and tighten attaching bolts securely.

7. Fill cooling system, then operate engine to check for leaks.

Removal/Installation
(V-8 Engines)

1. Make certain engine and cooling system are cool. Loosen radiator cap to first notch to release the system pressure. Then unscrew the cap completely.

2. Place a catch pan under radiator drain plug, then unscrew the drain plug (refer to **Figure 1**). Drain radiator until coolant level falls below the thermostat housing.

3. Disconnect the by-pass hoses at the water pump and intake manifold. Remove the by-pass tube, then remove water outlet housing attaching bolts and bend upper radiator hose upward and remove the thermostat and gasket.

4. Check thermostat (refer to *Inspection* procedure, following).

5. Clean gasket mating surfaces, then coat new gasket with water-resistant sealer. Position water outlet housing gasket on intake manifold opening.

6. Install thermostat in intake manifold opening.

> NOTE: *Position the thermostat so that the copper pellet or element is toward the engine and the thermostat flange is positioned in the recess. (If the thermostat is improperly installed, coolant flow will be retarded.)*

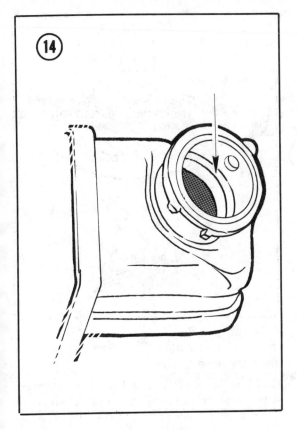

7. Place the water outlet housing against the intake manifold and install and tighten attaching bolts securely. Install the water bypass line and tighten hose connections.

8. Fill cooling system, then operate engine to check for leaks.

Inspection

1. Place thermostat in a 33% solution of glycol heated to 25°F above the temperature stamped on the thermostat.

2. Submerge thermostat and agitate liquid. Valve should open fully.

3. Remove valve and place in another 33% glycol solution heated to 10°F under the temperature stamped on thermostat.

4. Thermostat should close completely when completely submerged and liquid is agitated.

5. If thermostat fails the above test it should be replaced. If OK, reinstall in housing, using a new gasket. Tighten bolts securely.

6. Replace radiator hose and refill with coolant.

FAN

Removal/Installation

Refer to **Figures 15 and 16** for the following procedure.

1. Remove all drive belts, if necessary (refer to *Drive Belts* section, earlier in this chapter).

2. Remove fan retaining bolts, then remove fan.

3. To install, reverse the preceding steps, and refer to *Drive Belts* section earlier in this chapter for belt adjustment.

WATER PUMP

Removal
(6-Cylinder Engines)

1. Drain cooling system (refer to *Coolant Change* section earlier in this chapter).

2. Loosen alternator adjusting arm bolt, then remove alternator drive belt. (On vehicles equipped with air conditioning, remove compressor belt).

3. Remove fan and pulley (refer to *Fan* section, preceding).

4. Disconnect heater hose, radiator supply line at water pump, and lower radiator hose.

5. Remove water pump attaching bolts, then remove water pump and old gasket.

Installation
(6-Cylinder Engines)

1. Remove old water pump fittings and install them on new pump (coat bolt threads with waterproof sealer).

2. Clean old gasket material from mating surfaces, then position a new gasket, coated with sealer on both sides, on water pump.

3. Position water pump on the block, install attaching bolts (coat bolt threads with waterproof sealer), and tighten securely.

4. Install lower radiator hose, heater hose, and radiator supply line, then install pulley and fan.

5. Install all belts and adjust belt tension (refer to *Drive Belts* section earlier in this chapter).

6. Fill cooling system (refer to *Coolant Change* section earlier in this chapter).

7. Start engine and check cooling system for leaks.

8

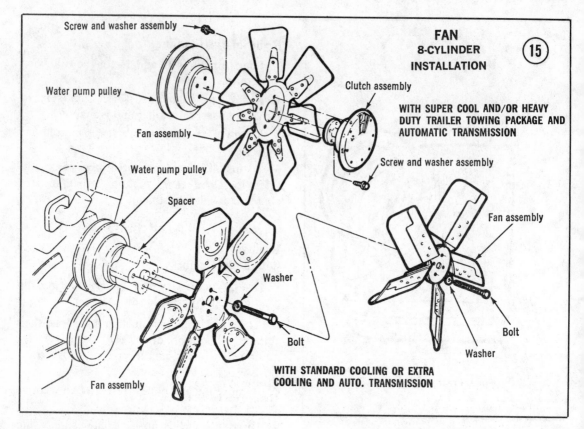

Screw and washer assembly

FAN
8-CYLINDER
INSTALLATION
(15)

Water pump pulley

Clutch assembly

Fan assembly

**WITH SUPER COOL AND/OR HEAVY
DUTY TRAILER TOWING PACKAGE AND
AUTOMATIC TRANSMISSION**

Screw and washer assembly

Water pump pulley

Spacer

Fan assembly

Washer

Bolt

Washer

Bolt

Fan assembly

**WITH STANDARD COOLING OR EXTRA
COOLING AND AUTO. TRANSMISSION**

Removal
(V-8 Engines)

1. Drain cooling system (refer to *Coolant Change* section earlier in this chapter) and disconnect battery.

2. Remove fan shroud attaching bolts and slide shroud rearward.

3. Remove fan and spacer from water pump shaft (refer to *Fan* section earlier in this chapter).

4. If so equipped, remove air conditioner compressor drive belt idler pulley and compressor mount to water pump bracket.

5. Loosen alternator and remove drive belt (refer to *Drive Belts* section earlier in this chapter).

6. If so equipped, loosen power steering pump and remove drive belt (refer to *Drive Belts* section earlier in this chapter).

7. Remove water pump pulley, alternator bracket from water pump, power steering pump bracket from water pump, and heater hose from the water pump.

8. Disconnect lower radiator hose at the water pump, then remove all bolts holding water pump to engine.

9. Remove water pump and old gasket (discard gasket).

10. To install, remove old gasket material from mating surfaces, coat a new gasket on both sides with sealer, then place it on the cylinder front cover.

11. Coat the water pump attaching bolt threads with waterproof sealer. Place the pump in position and install it with the bolts.

12. Reverse Steps 1 through 8 to conclude the installation.

> NOTE: *After installation, adjust all drive belts (refer to **Drive Belts** section earlier in this chapter), and fill the cooling system (refer to **Coolant Change** section earlier in this chapter).*

13. Operate engine and check for cooling system leaks.

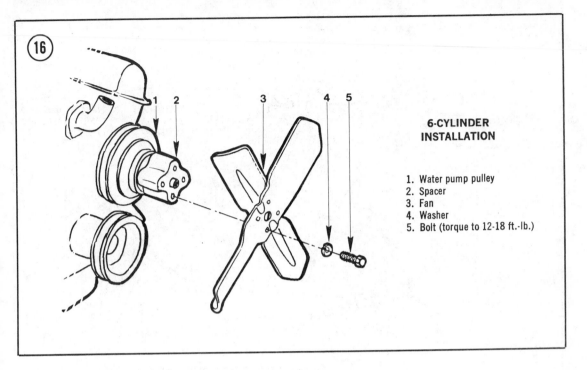

6-CYLINDER INSTALLATION

1. Water pump pulley
2. Spacer
3. Fan
4. Washer
5. Bolt (torque to 12-18 ft.-lb.)

HEATING SYSTEM

All F-series vehicles are equipped with a standard fresh air heater or optional Deluxe Hi-Lo heater. Removal and installation procedures for each type are given in the following sections.

STANDARD FRESH AIR HEATING SYSTEM

The standard fresh air heater draws air from the cowl top area. The heater is mounted under the right side of the instrument panel (**Figure 17**). Air for the heater comes from the right outside air vent, which is attached to the heater and the cowl side panel.

An air door in the heater controls the air flow through the heater. This door is controlled by the lower function control lever (**Figure 18**). When this lever is in the OFF position, air through the heater is shut off (including ram air). When the lever is in the HEAT position, air is directed to the floor; when it is positioned between HEAT and DEFROST, air is directed to the floor and the windshield.

The air temperature is controlled by the upper (temperature) control lever.

Heater Assembly Removal/Installation

1. Disconnect temperature and function control cables from the heater housing.

2. Disconnect wires from blower resistor (refer to **Figure 18**).

3. Remove screws holding air inlet (vent) duct to heater housing (**Figure 19**).

4. Disconnect blower wires (**Figure 20**).

5. Drain radiator (refer to *Coolant Change* section earlier in this chapter), then remove heater hoses from heater core.

6. Remove stud retaining nuts, then remove heater (refer to **Figure 20**).

7. Remove gasket between heater hose ends and dash panel at core tubes.

8. To install, position heater assembly in vehicle and install stud retaining nuts.

9. Connect heater hoses to heater core.

10. Fill radiator (refer to *Coolant Change* section earlier in this chapter).

11. Connect blower motor wires.

12. Place defroster nozzle on heater so that heater and defroster openings are in the up position, and there is no air leakage around the seal (**Figure 21**).

8

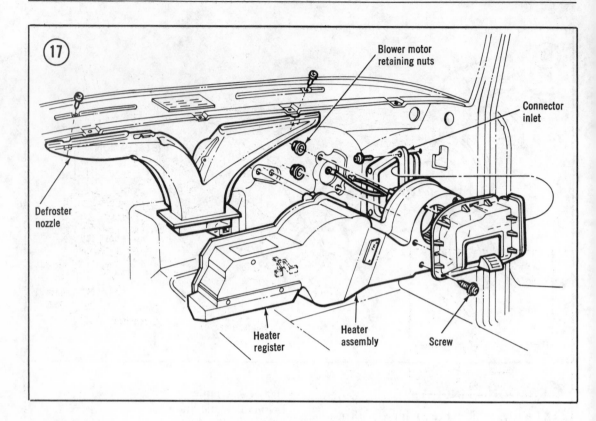

⑰

Blower motor
retaining nuts

Connector
inlet

Defroster
nozzle

Heater
register

Heater
assembly

Screw

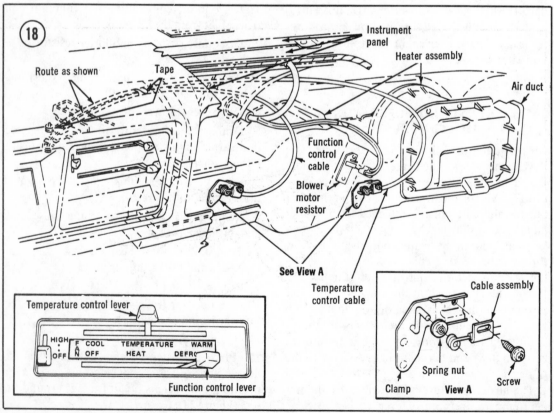

⑱

Instrument
panel

Heater assembly

Route as shown

Tape

Air duct

Function
control
cable

Blower
motor
resistor

See View A

Temperature
control cable

Temperature control lever

HIGH F COOL   TEMPERATURE   WARM
·
OFF   N OFF   HEAT   DEFRO

Function control lever

Cable assembly

Spring nut

Screw

Clamp   View A

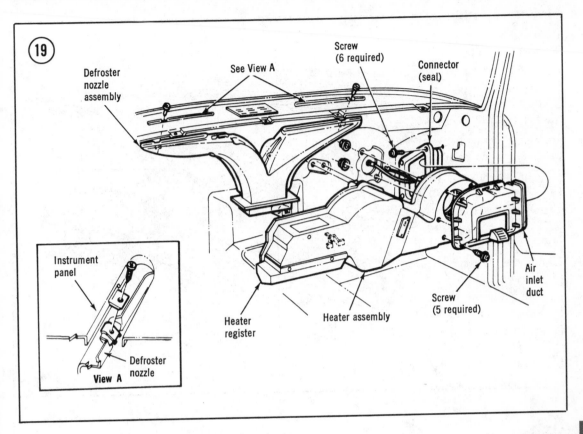

19

Defroster nozzle assembly

See View A

Screw (6 required)

Connector (seal)

Instrument panel

Defroster nozzle

View A

Heater register

Heater assembly

Screw (5 required)

Air inlet duct

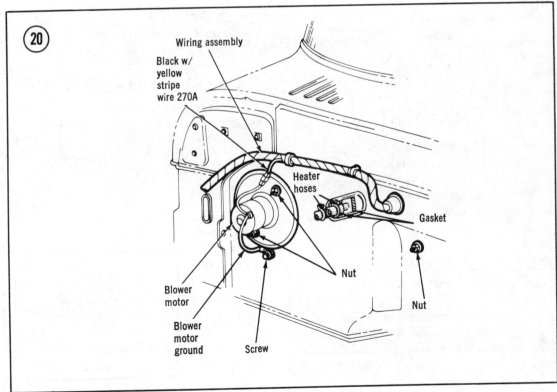

20

Wiring assembly

Black w/ yellow stripe wire 270A

Heater hoses

Gasket

Nut

Blower motor

Blower motor ground

Screw

Nut

13. Install air inlet (vent) duct to heater, then push duct firmly against seal on side cowl. Tighten attaching screws.

14. Connect wires to blower motor resistor.

15. Connect temperature and function control cables to heater. Adjust cables (refer to **Figure 18**).

16. Install gasket between heater hose ends and dash panel at core ends.

17. Fill cooling system (refer to *Coolant Change* section earlier in this chapter).

18. Check heater operation.

Heater Core Replacement

1. Remove heater assembly as outlined in previous section.

2. Remove heater core cover and gasket, then pull heater core and lower support from heater.

3. Install foam gaskets on heater core and install in heater assembly.

4. Install core seal and cover plate.

5. Install heater in vehicle.

Heater Blower Motor Removal/Installation

Refer to **Figure 17** for the following procedure.

1.Remove heater assembly as outlined previously.

2. Remove screws and nuts holding blower to heater.

3. Remove blower fan from motor shaft, then remove motor from mounting plate.

4. Install new motor on mounting plate and install blower fan on motor shaft.

5. Install blower and motor in heater. Install heater.

Heater Blower Resistor Replacement

To replace the resistor, which is mounted on the heater near the temperature door cable attachment (refer to **Figure 18**), disconnect the wire connector and remove the two 2-piece snap clips holding the resistor to the heater. Remove the center of the snap clip first, then the rest of the clip.

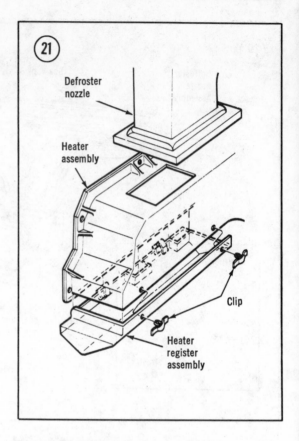

(21)

Defroster nozzle

Heater assembly

Clip

Heater register assembly

Heater Hose Routings

Refer to **Figure 22** for typical heater hose routing for the models covered in this book.

DELUXE HI-LO HEATING SYSTEM

This heating system features a heater core through which engine coolant flows; a water valve which controls this flow through the heater core; a blower; and control doors which regulate air flow into the vehicle.

Fresh outside air is drawn into the system via an air intake duct. The air passes through and around the heater core (**Figure 23**). From the blower housing, the air is channeled into the plenum chamber and discharged through defroster outlets, floor ducts, and/or instrument panel registers. (The control doors determine the amount of air that passes through the heater core and the outlets.)

Plenum Chamber Removal/Installation

Refer to **Figure 24** for the following procedure.

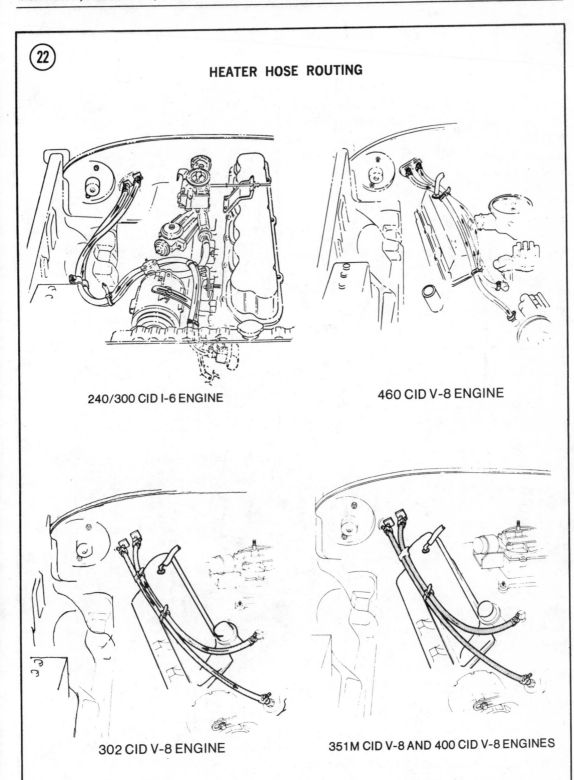

HEATER HOSE ROUTING

240/300 CID I-6 ENGINE

460 CID V-8 ENGINE

302 CID V-8 ENGINE

351M CID V-8 AND 400 CID V-8 ENGINES

8

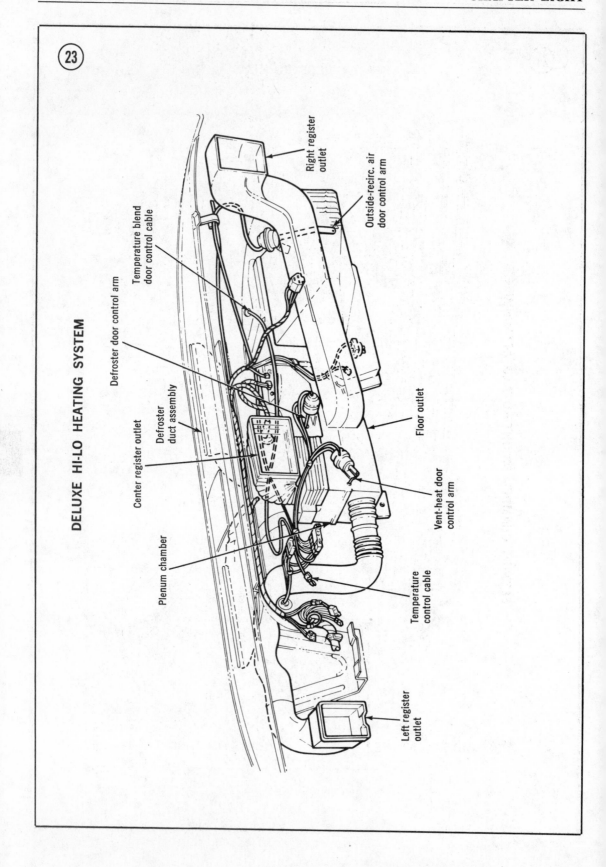

(23)

DELUXE HI-LO HEATING SYSTEM

Right register outlet

Outside-recirc. air door control arm

Temperature blend door control cable

Defroster door control arm

Floor outlet

Center register outlet

Defroster duct assembly

Plenum chamber

Vent-heat door control arm

Temperature control cable

Left register outlet

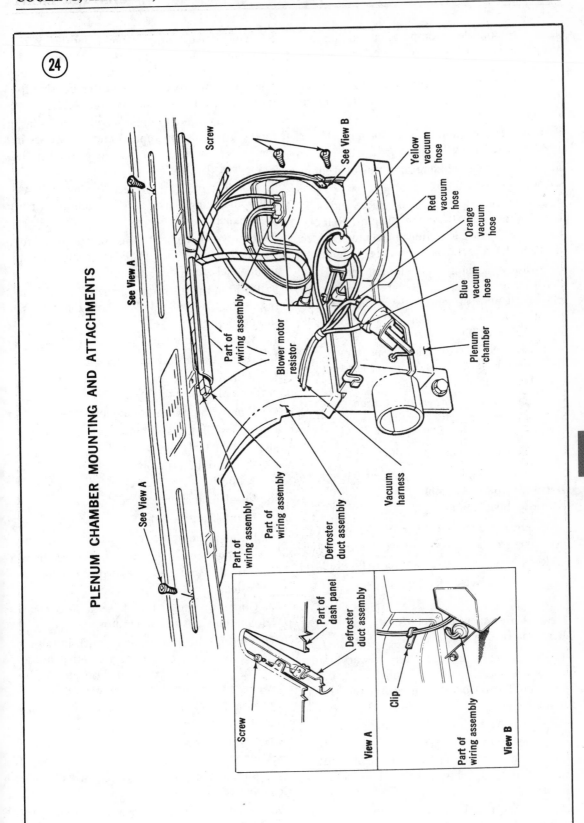

PLENUM CHAMBER MOUNTING AND ATTACHMENTS

24

Screw

See View B

Yellow vacuum hose

Red vacuum hose

Orange vacuum hose

Blue vacuum hose

Plenum chamber

Part of wiring assembly

Blower motor resistor

Vacuum harness

See View A

See View A

Part of wiring assembly

Part of wiring assembly

Defroster duct assembly

View A

Screw

Part of dash panel

Defroster duct assembly

View B

Clip

Part of wiring assembly

8

1. Remove the glove compartment and disconnect the vacuum hoses from the heat/defrost door and vent heat door vacuum motors and the 2 wire connectors from the blower motor resistor. Remove the 2 wires from the clip on the right side of the plenum.

2. Remove bolt holding the plenum lower bracket-to-dash panel.

3. Remove screws holding right side of plenum to the heater assembly.

4. Disconnect right register duct and left register hose duct from the plenum. Remove plenum while disconnecting the center register duct and defroster nozzles from the plenum.

5. Position plenum in vehicle, connecting the defroster nozzle and center register duct to the plenum. Connect right register duct to the plenum and install screws to retain plenum at the heater assembly.

6. Install one bolt to hold the plenum lower bracket to the dash panel. Connect left register hose duct to the plenum.

7. Connect vacuum hoses to vacuum motors, and the wire connectors to the blower motor resistor.

8. Install glove compartment liner.

Defroster Nozzle Assembly Removal/Installation

1. Remove plenum chamber as described in preceding section.

2. Remove defroster nozzle (refer to **Figure 24**).

3. To install, reverse preceding steps.

Heater Core and/or Blower Motor Removal/Installation

1. Disconnect battery cable, remove carburetor air cleaner, and partially drain the coolant system (refer to *Coolant Change* section earlier in this chapter).

2. Remove heater hoses from heater core.

3. Remove glove box liner and the register duct by pulling from the instrument panel register and releasing the clip at the plenum (refer to **Figure 25**).

4. Disconnect right cowl outside air intake vacuum hose from the outside-recirculating door vacuum motor.

5. Remove rear housing from under the instrument panel (refer to **Figure 26**). Remove outside air intake duct from the rear housing and install one upper nut to hold the heater housing-to-dash after the rear housing is removed.

6. Remove screws holding the plenum-to-dash (above transmission tunnel) and the screws in the heater housing. Remove the plenum (refer to **Figure 24**).

7. Install a piece of protective tape on "A" pillar inner cowl panel, at lower right of instrument panel.

8. Remove lower right instrument panel-to-"A" pillar bolt, then lower the center instrument panel brace, bolt, and nut.

9. Position the instrument panel rearward and install the "A" pillar bolt to hold the panel in this position.

10. Remove heater core.

11. Remove temperature blend door.

12. Remove temperature blend door arm support and pivot arm retainer.

13. Remove blower motor and blower wheel.

14. To install, transfer blower wheel to blower motor and panel assembly.

15. Install door arm pivot retainer and door arm support.

16. Install temperature blend door.

17. Install heater core.

18. Install plenum, then connect blower wires.

19. Remove heater housing upper retaining nut; install heater outlet; and position the air intake duct.

20. Connect white vacuum hose to the outside-recirculating door vacuum motor.

21. Reposition the instrument panel, install retaining bolts, and remove the protective tape at the "A" pillar inner cowl panel (located at the lower right corner of instrument panel).

22. Install right register duct assembly and install glove box liner.

23. Connect heater hoses to heater core assembly.

24. Fill cooling system (refer to *Coolant Change*, earlier in this chapter).

25. Install air cleaner, then connect battery cable to battery.

26. Check blower motor operation.

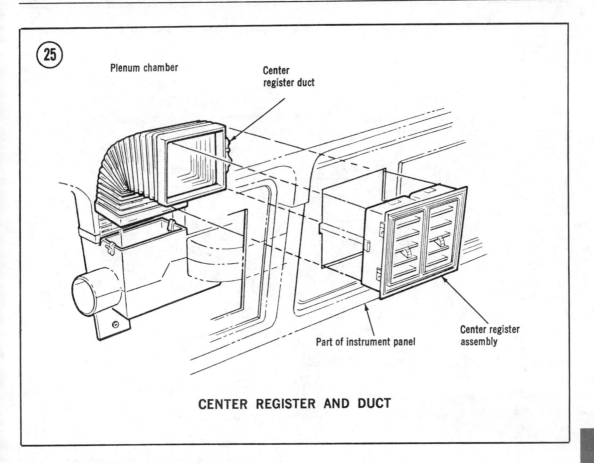

(25)

Plenum chamber

Center
register duct

Part of instrument panel

Center register
assembly

CENTER REGISTER AND DUCT

8

Duct Assemblies and Extensions

Refer to **Figure 26** for removal and installation of duct assemblies and extensions.

AIR CONDITIONING

Major service and repair to air conditioning systems requires specialized training and tools, and the difficulty of the work is compounded in the late heating/air conditioning systems. However, most air conditioning problems do not involve major repair; they are well within the ability of an experienced hobbyist mechanic, armed with an understanding of how the system works.

SYSTEM OPERATION

A typical air conditioning system is shown in **Figure 27**. (Actual component locations may differ, depending on model.)

The five basic components are common to all air conditioning systems:

a. Compressor
b. Condenser
c. Receiver-drier
d. Expansion valve
e. Evaporator

The components, connected with high-pressure hoses and tubes, form a closed loop. A refrigerant, dichlorodiflouromethane (more commonly referred to as R-12), circulates through the system under high pressure — as much as 300 psi. As a result, work on the air conditioning system is potentially hazardous if certain precautions are ignored. For safety's sake *read this entire section* before attempting any troubleshooting, checks, or work on the system.

A typical system is shown schematically in **Figure 28**. For practical purposes, the cycle begins at the compressor. The refrigerant, in a warm, low-pressure vapor state, enters the low-pressure side of the compressor. It is compressed to a high-pressure hot vapor and pumped out of the high-pressure side to the condenser.

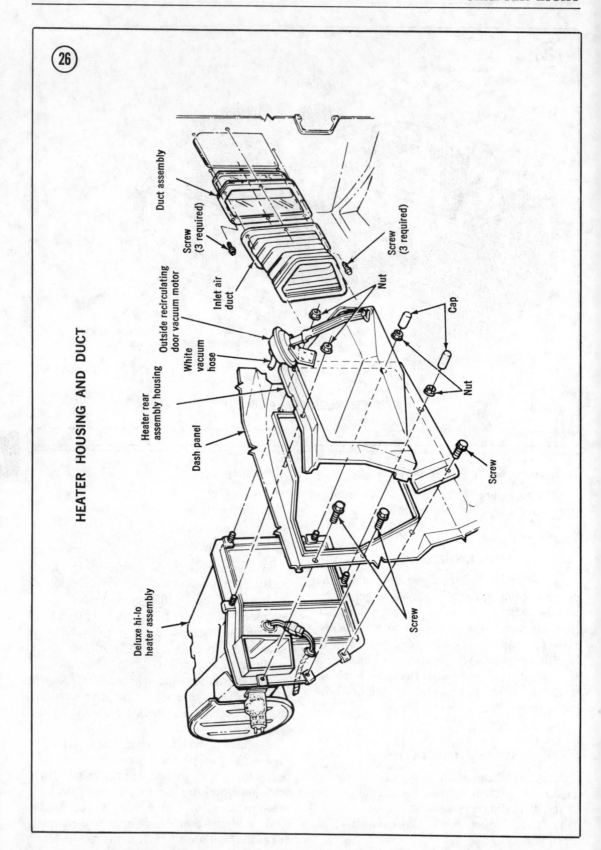

㉖

HEATER HOUSING AND DUCT

Duct assembly

Screw
(3 required)

Screw
(3 required)

Inlet air
duct

Outside recirculating
door vacuum motor

White
vacuum
hose

Heater rear
assembly housing

Dash panel

Nut

Cap

Nut

Screw

Screw

Deluxe hi-lo
heater assembly

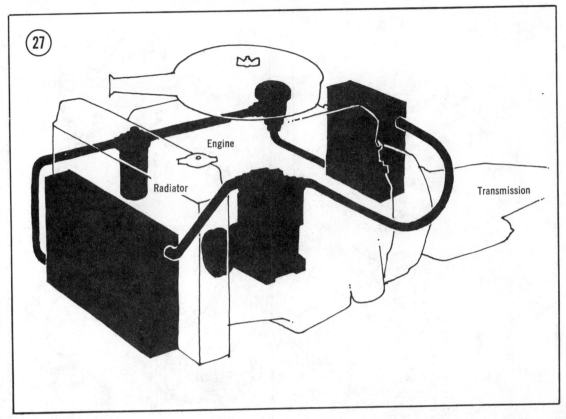

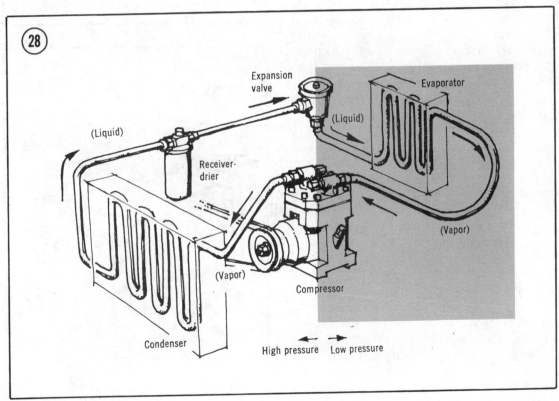

8

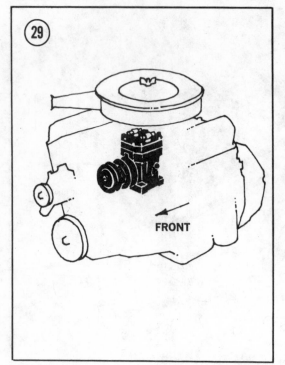

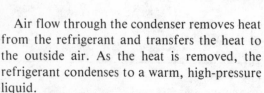

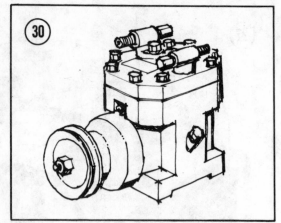

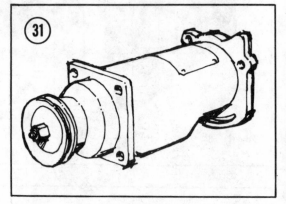

Air flow through the condenser removes heat from the refrigerant and transfers the heat to the outside air. As the heat is removed, the refrigerant condenses to a warm, high-pressure liquid.

The refrigerant then flows to the receiver/drier where moisture is removed and impurities are filtered out. The refrigerant is stored in the receiver/drier until it is needed. Generally, the receiver/drier incorporates a sight glass that permits visual monitoring of the condition of the refrigerant as it flows. This is discussed later.

From the receiver/drier, the refrigerant flows to the expansion valve. The expansion valve is thermostatically controlled and meters refrigerant to the evaporator. As the refrigerant leaves the expansion valve it changes from a warm, high-pressure liquid to a cold, low-pressure liquid.

In the evaporator, the refrigerant removes heat from the cockpit air that is blown across the evaporator's fins and tubes. In the process, the refrigerant changes from a cold, low-pressure liquid to a warm, high-pressure vapor which flows back to the compressor where the refrigeration cycle began.

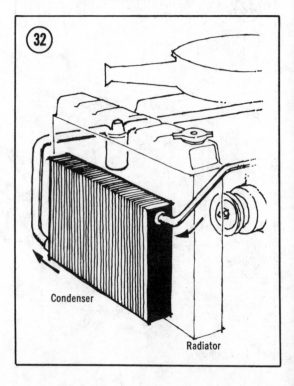

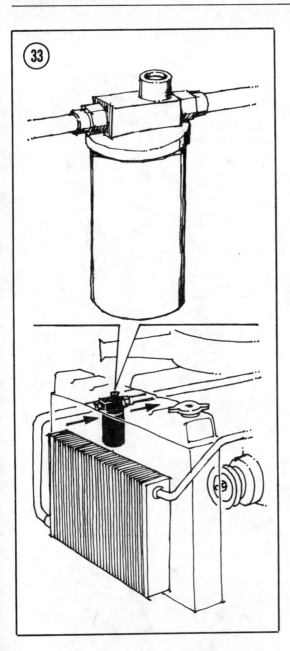

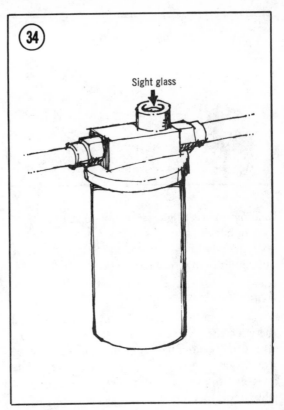

Sight glass

GET TO KNOW
YOUR VEHICLE'S SYSTEM

With **Figure 27** as a guide, begin with the compressor and locate each of the following components in turn:

   a. Compressor

   b. Condenser

   c. Receiver/drier

   d. Expansion valve

   e. Evaporator

Compressor

The compressor is located on the front of the engine, like an alternator, and is driven by one or two drive belts **(Figure 29)**. The large pulley on the front contains an electromagnetic clutch that is activated and operates the compressor when the air conditioning controls are switched on. There are two compressor types — piston-and-crank **(Figure 30)** and swashplate (axial plate, see **Figure 31**).

Condenser

In most cases, the condenser is mounted in front of the radiator **(Figure 32)**. Air passing through the fins and tubes removes heat from the refrigerant, in the same manner it removes heat from the engine coolant as it passes through the radiator.

The receiver/drier is a small tank-like unit **(Figure 33)**, usually found mounted to one of the wheel wells. Many receiver/driers incorporate a sight glass through which refrigerant flow can be seen when the system is operating **(Figure 34)**. Some systems have an in-

8

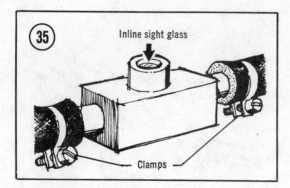

Inline sight glass

Clamps

line sight glass (**Figure 35**). Some early systems do not have a sight glass but it's not essential to system operation — just handy to help diagnose air conditioning troubles.

Expansion Valve

The expansion valve (**Figure 36**) is located between the receiver/drier and the evaporator. It is usually mounted on or near the firewall, in the engine compartment. In some very late systems, the valve is concealed in a housing on the firewall.

Evaporator

The evaporator is located in the passenger compartment, beneath the dashboard, and is hidden from view by the fan shrouding and ducting (**Figure 37**). Warm air from the passenger compartment is blown across the fins and tubes in the evaporator where it is cooled and dried and then ducted back into the compartment through the air outlets.

ROUTINE MAINTENANCE

First rate preventative maintenance for your air conditioning system couldn't be simpler; at least once a month, even in cold weather, start your engine and turn on the air conditioner and operate it at each of the switch and control settings. Allow it to operate for about five minutes. This will ensure that the compressor seal will not deform from sitting in the same position for a long period of time. If this occurs, the seal is likely to leak.

The efficiency of your air conditioning system depends in great part on the efficiency of your engine cooling system. Periodically

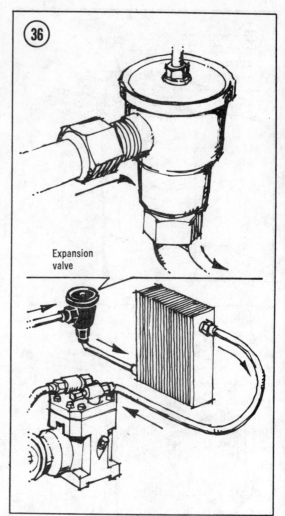

Expansion valve

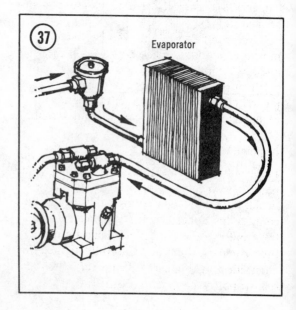

Evaporator

REFRIGERANT : R-12
CAPACITY : 1.70 KG (3.75 lb)

(38)

check the coolant for its level and cleanliness. If it is dirty, drain and flush the system and fill it with fresh coolant and water, following the coolant manufacturer's instructions for coolant/water ratio. Have your radiator cap pressure tested and replace it if it will not maintain 13 psi pressure. If the system requires repeated topping up and the radiator cap is in good condition, it is likely that there is a leak in the system. Pressure test it as described earlier in this chapter.

With an air hose and a soft brush, clean the radiator fins and tubes to remove bugs, leaves, and any other imbedded debris.

Check and correct drive belt tension as described earlier.

If the condition of the cooling system thermostat is in doubt, check it as described earlier and replace it if it is faulty.

When you are confident that the engine cooling system is working correctly, you are ready to inspect and test the air conditioning system.

Inspection

1. Clean all lines, fittings, and system components with solvent and a clean rag. Pay particular attention to the fittings; oily dirt around connections almost certainly indicates a leak. Oil from the compressor will migrate through the system to the leak. Carefully tighten the connection, taking care not to overtighten and risk stripping the threads. If the leak persists it

will soon be apparent once again as oily dirt accumulates. Clean the sight glass with a clean, dry cloth.

2. Clean the condenser fins and tubes with a soft brush and an air hose, or with a high-pressure stream of water from a garden hose. Remove bugs, leaves, and other imbedded debris. Carefully straighten any bent fins with a screwdriver, taking care not to dent or puncture the tubes.

3. Check the condition and tension of the drive belts and replace or correct as necessary.

4. Start the engine and check the operation of the blower motor and the compressor clutch by turning the controls on and off. If either the blower or the clutch fails to operate, shut off the engine and check the condition of the fuses. If they are blown, replace them. If not, remove them and clean the fuse holder contacts. Then, recheck to ensure that the blower and clutch operate.

Testing

1. With the transmission in PARK (automatic) or NEUTRAL (manual) and the handbrake set, start the engine and run it at a fast idle.

2. Set the temperature control to its coldest setting and turn the blower to high. Allow the system to operate for 10 minutes with the doors and windows open. Then close them and set the blower on its lowest setting.

3. Place a thermometer in a cold-air outlet. Within a few mintues, the temperature should be 35-45°F. If it is not, it's likely that the refrigerant level in the system is low. Check the appearance of the refrigerant flow through the sight glass. If it is bubbly, refrigerant should be added.

REFRIGERANT

The majority of automotive air conditioning systems use a refrigerant designated R-12. However, a commercial grade, designated R-20, is used in heavy-duty systems. The two are not compatible. Look for an information sticker, usually mounted near the compressor, to determine which refrigerant your system uses **(Figure 38)**. Also, check the system capacity in-

8

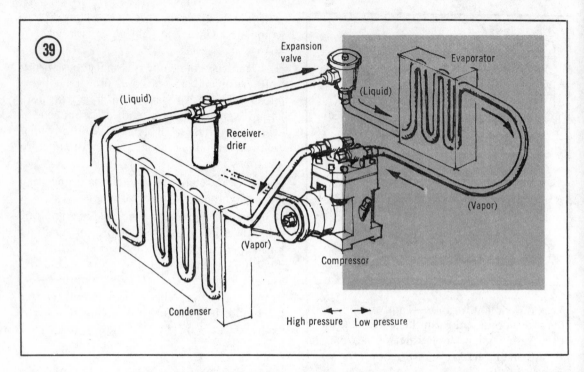

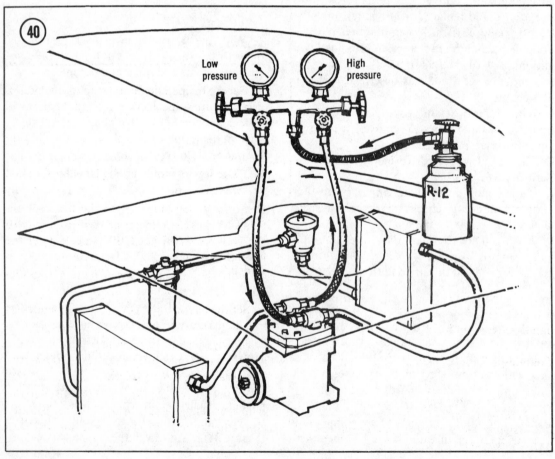

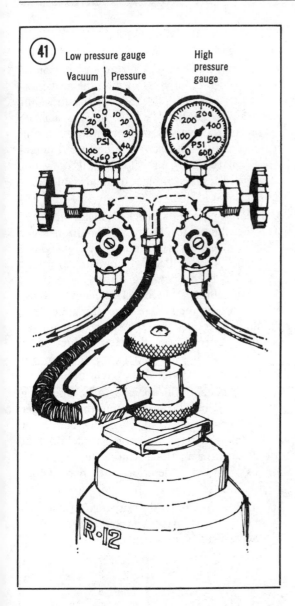

41 Low pressure gauge   High pressure gauge
Vacuum | Pressure

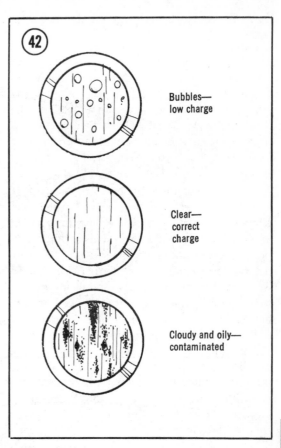

42 Bubbles—low charge

Clear—correct charge

Cloudy and oily—contaminated

dicated on the sticker. Capacity can range from two to five pounds, depending on the system.

That harmless-looking little can of refrigerant is potentially hazardous. If it is hooked up to the high-pressure side of the compressor, or is hooked up without a gauge set, it becomes a hand grenade.

Charging

WARNING
Do not attempt to add refrigerant to the system without using a gauge set; it's essential that the system pressure during charging does not exceed 50 psi.

1. Carefully read and understand the gauge manufacturer's instructions before charging the system.

2. Remove the cap from the Schrader valve on the low-pressure side of the compressor (**Figure 39**). The low-pressure side is labelled SUCTION, SUCT., or SUC.

3. Connect the gauge set to the low-pressure Schrader valve. Connect the refrigerant can to the gauge set and hang the gauge set on the hood (**Figure 40**).

4. Start the engine and run it at a fast idle (about 1,000 rpm).

5. Set the temperature control at its coldest setting. Set the blower at its lowest setting.

6. Slowly open the refrigerant feed valve on the gauge set (**Figure 41**). Do not allow the refrigerant pressure to exceed 50 psi.

7. Watch the refrigerant as it flows through the sight glass (**Figure 42**). When it's free of bubbles, the system is charged. Shut off the refrigerant feed valve on the gauge set.

TROUBLESHOOTING

Preventive maintenance, like that just described, will help to ensure that your system is working efficiently. Still, trouble can develop and while most of it will invariably be simple and easy to correct, you must first locate it. The following sequence will help to diagnose system troubles when your air conditioning ceases to cool the passenger compartment.

1. First, stop the vehicle and look at the control settings. One of the most common sources of air conditioning trouble occurs when the temperature control is set for maximum cold and the blower is set on low. This arrangement promotes ice buildup on the fins and tubes of the evaporator, and particularly so in humid weather. Eventually, the evaporator will ice over completely, and restrict air flow. Turn the blower on high and place a hand over an air outlet. If the blower is running but there is little or no air flowing through the outlet, the evaporator is probably iced up. Leave the blower on high and turn off the temperature control or turn it down to its lowest setting — and wait; it will take 10 or 15 minutes before the ice begins to melt.

2. If the blower is not running, the motor may be burned out, there may be a loose connection, or the fuse may be blown. First check the fuse panel for a blown or incorrectly seated fuse. Then, check the wiring for loose connections.

3. Shut off the engine and check the condition and tension of the compressor drive belt. If it is loose or badly worn, tighten or replace it.

4. Start the engine and check the condition of the compressor clutch by turning the air conditioner on and off. If the clutch does not energize, it may be defective, its fuse may be blown, or the evaporator temperature-limiting switches may be defective. If the fuse is defective, replace it. If the clutch still does not energize, refer the problem to an air conditioning specialist.

5. If all components checked so far are OK, start the engine, turn on the air conditioner and watch the refrigerant through the sight glass; remember, if it's filled with bubbles after the system has been operating for a few seconds, the refrigerant level is low. If the sight glass is oily or cloudy, the system is contaminated and should be serviced by an expert as soon as possible. Corrosion and deterioration occur rapidly and if it's not taken care of at once it will result in a very expensive repair job.

6. If the system still appears to be operating satisfactorily but the air flow into the passenger compartment is not cold, check the condenser and cooling system radiator for debris that could block the air flow. And recheck the cooling system as described earlier under *Inspection*.

7. If the above steps do not uncover the difficulty, have the system checked and corrected by a specialist as soon as possible.

NOTE: If you own a 1980 or later model, first check the Supplement at the back of the book for any new service information.

CHAPTER NINE

BRAKES

BRAKE SYSTEM CHECKS AND ADJUSTMENT

The brake systems on all Ford vehicles covered in this handbook have two independent hydraulic circuits. The normal or primary circuit operates all four brakes. The secondary circuit operates the rear wheel brakes in the event the primary brake circuit fails.

Brake Failure

Failure of one of the brake circuits will normally be indicated by the brake warning light turning on. However, if the light is burned out or the wiring faulty, the first indication of a brake failure may occur when the brakes are applied.

If the warning light comes on, carefully slow and stop the vehicle, taking into account that the braking effectiveness is greatly reduced. Remove the cap from the master cylinder reservoir (**Figure 1**) and check to see if there is fluid in both reservoirs. If the level is low in one, or it is empty, check further for leaks along the brake lines and at each wheel. If the level is correct in both reservoirs, the fault may lie in the switch, wiring, or the differential pressure valve in the master cylinder. In any case, drive the vehicle with extreme care until the system can be checked and the trouble corrected.

Brake Fluid Level

The brake fluid level in the master cylinder reservoir should be checked routinely every 6,000 miles or at any time there is suspected leakage in the brake hydraulic system.

The fluid level must be within ¼ in. of the tops of the reservoirs (**Figure 2**). If the fluid level is extremely low in one or both reservoirs, inspect the lines and fittings for leakage, and check the wheel cylinders as described in *Brake Lining Inspection*. Correct any leaks before adding fluid and bleed the system as described later.

Add only Ford Extra Heavy-Duty Brake Fluid or equivalent fluid. This fluid grade is

9

identified by its blue color and is recommended for all conditions.

CAUTION
Never add low-temperature brake fluid to the fluid that is already in the system.

Brake Fluid Changing

After long usage, brake fluid absorbs sufficient atmospheric moisture to significantly reduce its boiling point and make it prone to vapor lock during repeated hard brake applications (such as in mountain driving). While no hard and fast rule exists for changing the fluid in the system, it should be checked at least annually by bleeding fluid from one of the wheel cylinders and inspecting it for signs of moisture. If moisture is present, the entire system should be drained and bled as described below.

Brake System Bleeding

The brake system must be bled following any repairs in which a portion of the system is disconnected, after a leak has been corrected, or when water is present in the hydraulic fluid. The system can be bled using a pressure tank type bleeder or manually with the aid of an assistant. Because it is unlikely that a home mechanic will have a pressure tank bleeder, the second method is described.

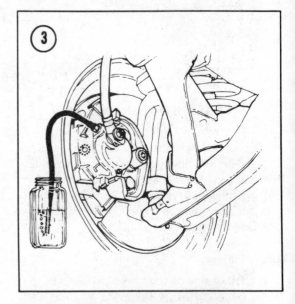

It is a good idea to bleed the system beginning with the brake located farthest from the master cylinder and then working toward the master cylinder. As with adding fluid to the system, use only the fluid specified earlier.

1. Check the brake fluid level in the reservoirs and top them up with fresh fluid to within ¼ in. of the top. Leave the cap and diaphragm off the master cylinder, but cover it with clean, lint-free shop rags to prevent fluid from being ejected and getting onto painted surfaces.

2. Wipe any dirt or oil from the bleeder screw (**Figure 3**) of the first brake to be bled and attach a length of hose to the screw. The hose must fit snugly over the screw. Place the other end of the hose in a container partially filled with fresh brake fluid.

3. Using the commands "down" and "up" to guide your assistant, open the bleeder valve

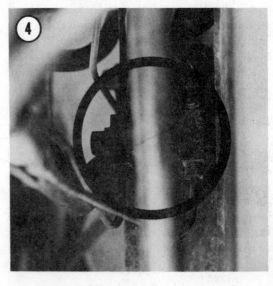

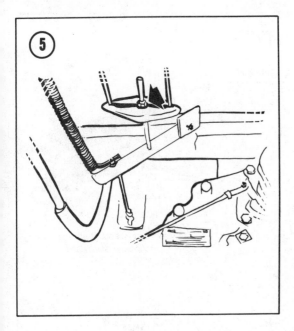

about ½ turn and have your assistant depress the brake pedal and hold it. Close the bleeder valve and instruct the assistant to release the brake pedal. When the brake pedal is all the way up, open the bleeder valve and have the brake depressed once again. Close the bleeder valve and have the brake released. Continue this sequence until the brake fluid running out of the hose and into the container is free of air bubbles. Then close the bleeder valve; tighten it, and remove the bleeder hose. Top up the fluid in the master cylinder reservoirs and recover the reservoir with the rags.

4. Bleed the other brakes in the same manner, topping up the reservoir with fresh fluid after each unit has been bled. When the entire system has been bled and the fluid levels in the master cylinder reservoirs have been topped up to within ¼ in. of the top, check the feel of the brake pedal. If it is not firm, some air remains in the system and it must be bled again in the manner just described.

5. When the pedal feel is correct, road test the vehicle to ensure that the brakes operate correctly. Begin checking at low speed until you are confident that the braking action is good.

> NOTE: *If the brake warning light remains on after the brake system has been bled and the braking action is satisfactory, the pressure differential*

valve is probably not centered. In such case, loosen the tube connector of the pressure differential valve opposite the circuit that was bled last *(Figure 4)*. Slowly depress the brake pedal until the brake warning light goes off, signaling that the pressure differential valve is centered. Then tighten the tube connector and recheck and correct the fluid level in master cylinder reservoirs.*

Service Brake Adjustment

The service brakes are self-adjusting. Adjustment occurs when the vehicle is driven in reverse and the brakes are applied. If the brake pedal can be pushed within a couple of inches of the floor, the brakes should be adjusted by backing the vehicle up several times and sharply applying the brakes. Test the adjustment by driving the vehicle at about 20 mph and braking to a smooth stop. If the pedal travel is still long, adjust them once again as just described.

Parking Brake Adjustment

The parking brake should be adjusted whenever the foot control can be depressed six or more clicks. Before adjusting the parking brake, adjust the service brakes as described earlier.

1. Depress the parking brake pedal 2 clicks.
2. Adjust the cable tension by turning the adjusting nut **(Figure 5)**.

> NOTE: *Before tightening the adjuster nut, check to see if the equalizer is fitted with a locknut and if it is, loosen it before tightening the adjuster. When the adjustment is correct, tighten the locknut.*

3. Release the parking brake control and check the cables to make sure they are still not tight.

If a brake cable tension gauge is not available, a temporary adjustment can be made by progressively tightening the adjuster nut and checking the movement of the foot control until it can be depressed three to five clicks with moderate pressure. Make sure, however, that the brake is released when the foot control is released. Have the brake adjusted with a tension gauge at the earliest opportunity.

9

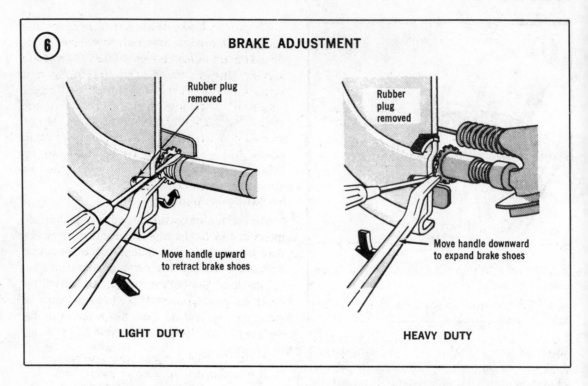

BRAKE ADJUSTMENT

⑥

Rubber plug
removed

Move handle upward
to retract brake shoes

LIGHT DUTY

Rubber
plug
removed

Move handle downward
to expand brake shoes

HEAVY DUTY

BRAKE DRUMS

Removal (100/150 Models)

1. Raise vehicle so wheel clears floor, then install jackstands for safety.

2. Remove hub cap and wheel, then remove 3 retaining nuts and remove brake drum.

> NOTE: *If drum will not come off, insert a narrow screwdriver through the brake adjusting lever from the adjusting screw. While holding the adjusting lever away from the adjusting screw, loosen the adjusting screw with the brake adjusting tool (Figure 6).*

Installation (100/150 Models)

1. Remove protective coating from new brake drum (if one is to be installed) with degreaser.

2. Adjust brakes (refer to *Service Brake Adjustment* section, preceding).

3. Install brake drum and brake drum retaining nuts (tighten evenly).

Removal (250/350 Models)

1. Raise vehicle so wheel clears floor, then install jackstands for safety.

2. Remove hub cap and wheel, then remove 3 retaining nuts and remove brake drum.

> NOTE: *If drum will not come off, insert a narrow screwdriver through the brake adjusting lever from the adjusting screw. While holding the adjusting lever away from the adjusting screw, loosen the adjusting screw with the brake adjusting tool (Figure 6).*

3. Remove the rear axle retaining bolts and lockwashers, axle shaft, and gasket.

4. Remove wheel bearing locknut, lockwasher, and adjusting nut. Then remove hub and drum from axle.

5. Remove brake drum-to-hub retaining screws, bolts, or bolts and nuts. Remove brake drum from hub.

6. Check drum for damage or wear, and have drum turned down by your Ford dealer, or install a new one if necessary. (If a new drum must be installed, remove wheel studs and brake drum from the hub.)

Installation (250/350 Models)

1. If a new drum is to be installed, remove protective coating with degreaser.

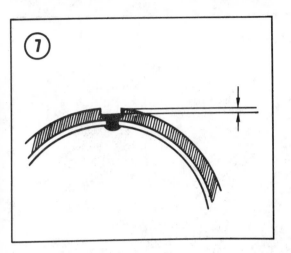

2. If wheel and hub was removed, install new grease retainer seals.

3. Install brake drum on hub with attaching screws, or wheel studs.

4. Check brake surface runout. If runout exceeds 0.007 in., have the hub and drum assembly turned at your Ford dealer.

5. Place hub and drum as a unit on the axle, and start the adjusting nut.

6. Adjust wheel bearing nut and install wheel bearing lockwasher and locknut.

7. Install a new gasket and install bolts and lockwashers.

8. Install wheel and tighten wheel nuts evenly.

9. Adjust brakes (refer to *Service Brake Adjustment* earlier in this chapter).

10. Remove jackstands and lower vehicle to floor.

Inspection (All Models)

1. Remove brake drum (one side only, see following NOTE), as outlined in preceding section.

> NOTE: *If the brakes are simply being inspected for lining condition and remaining service life, it is not necessary to remove the drums and wheels from both sides; the condition of the linings and drums on one side is indicative of the condition of those on the opposite side. However, if the drums and linings on the first side require cleaning and dressing, this service should be carried out on the opposite side also.*

2. Wipe the brake shoes and insides of the drums with a clean dry cloth to remove sand, dirt, and any other foreign matter. *Do not use solvent.* Inspect the drums for scoring and scratches. Any score sufficiently deep to snag a fingernail is reason enough for having the drums turned and the linings replaced. Minor scoring and scratches can be removed with fine emery cloth, following which the drum must be thoroughly cleaned with compressed air to remove any abrasive.

3. Inspect the linings for dirt, oil, grease, and brake fluid. Dirt and foreign particles that are imbedded in the lining can be removed with a wire brush, but if the lining is grease-soaked with oil, or brake fluid, it must be replaced.

4. Measure the depth of the rivet holes with a depth gauge (**Figure 7**). If the lining is worn to within $\frac{1}{32}$ in. of the rivet heads, it must be replaced.

> NOTE: *It is important that brakes be reconditioned at least in pairs—both fronts or both rears—or all 4 wheels at the same time. In addition, if the linings are replaced, they must be arced to the contour of the drums which in most cases will require truing. This is a job for a Ford dealer or automotive brake specialist.*

5. Install the drum and tighten the nuts securely (75-105 ft.-lb.). Then install the wheel on the drum and tighten the lug nuts to the same torque.

If a brake adjuster was loosened prior to drum removal, refer to the adjusting procedure described earlier and adjust the brake.

BRAKE SHOE REPLACEMENT (LIGHT DUTY)

Removal

1. Remove the brake drum as described above. Lift up on the adjusting lever (**Figure 8**) and disengage it from the adjusting screw. Run the adjusting screw in as far as it will go. Pull back on the adjuster lever until it can be unhooked from the hole in the secondary shoe. *Do not pry it out of the hole.*

2. Disconnect the adjuster spring and the lever. Disconnect retracting springs from the anchor

9

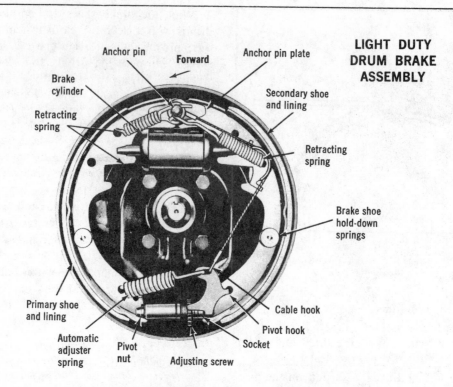

LIGHT DUTY
DRUM BRAKE
ASSEMBLY

⑧

Anchor pin

Forward

Anchor pin plate

Brake cylinder

Secondary shoe and lining

Retracting spring

Retracting spring

Brake shoe hold-down springs

Primary shoe and lining

Cable hook

Pivot hook

Automatic adjuster spring

Pivot nut

Socket

Adjusting screw

FRONT BRAKE

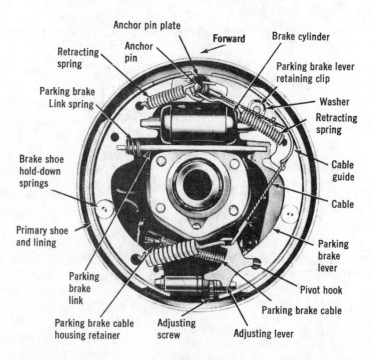

Anchor pin plate

Forward

Brake cylinder

Retracting spring

Anchor pin

Parking brake lever retaining clip

Parking brake Link spring

Washer

Retracting spring

Brake shoe hold-down springs

Cable guide

Cable

Primary shoe and lining

Parking brake lever

Parking brake link

Pivot hook

Parking brake cable

Parking brake cable housing retainer

Adjusting screw

Adjusting lever

REAR BRAKE

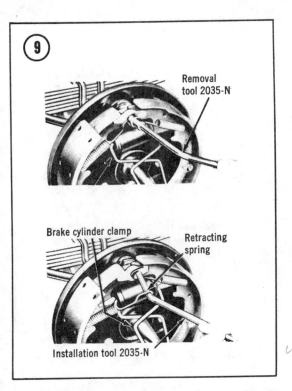

(9)

Removal
tool 2035-N

Brake cylinder clamp

Retracting
spring

Installation tool 2035-N

pin (**Figure 9**) using a tool (Ford No. 2035-N) like the one shown. Remove the cable anchor and the cable guide.

3. Press in on the shoe hold-down spring cups, remove the pins, and remove the cups and springs. Note the color coding on the springs so they may be installed in their correct positions.

4. Remove the parking brake link and spring (rear brakes) and disconnect the cable from the lever. With the shoes removed from the backing plate, remove the clip and spring washer from the secondary shoe and disconnect the parking brake lever.

Inspection

1. Carefully pry back the lower edge of each wheel cylinder boot and check for leakage. A slight film of brake fluid on the rods is normal, but if there is an excessive amount of fluid in the boots, the wheel cylinder should be rebuilt or replaced. (Refer to *Wheel Cylinders* section later in this chapter.)

2. Inspect the backing plate for oil that may have leaked past the axle seal. If oil is present, the seals should be replaced (see Chapter Eleven).

3. Check and tighten the bolts that attach the backing plate to the axle housing. Thoroughly clean the backing plate and all of the brake components. If a solvent must be used, use only denatured alcohol or brake fluid. Do not use mineral-based detergents. Clean the shoe contact surfaces on the backing plate with emery cloth. Make certain all loose dirt, rust, and abrasives are removed.

4. Check the operation of the adjuster screw. If it does not turn smoothly, disassemble, clean, and lubricate it.

5. Work on the drums and shoes should be entrusted to a dealer or a brake specialist. The drums must be measured for roundness and the contact surface checked for serviceability. Often, they must be trued with a brake drum lathe. In addition, the shoes and new linings must be arced to the contour of the drums.

Installation

1. Clean your hands thoroughly and check the new linings to make sure they are not nicked or burred. If they are bonded linings, check for and remove any bonding cement along the edges.

2. Use brake lubricant to lubricate the following items:

   a. Parking brake cable
   b. Fulcrum end of parking brake lever
   c. Adjusting screw
   d. Shoe contact points on the backing plate

3. Attach the parking brake lever to the secondary shoe using the spring washer and the retaining clip.

4. Install the shoes on the backing plate using the hold-down springs, cups, and pins. (The purple spring is used on the secondary shoe.)

5. Install the parking brake link, spring, and washer and connect the brake cable to the lever (rear brake). Install the anchor pin plate and attach the cable anchor to the pin with the crimped side of the cable collar toward the backing plate.

6. Connect the primary shoe retracting spring to the anchor pin (**Figure 9**). Install the cable guide in the secondary shoe; the flanged holes in the guide must fit into the hole in the web.

9

Route the cable around the guide, making sure it is in the groove and not between the guide and shoe.

7. Connect the secondary shoe retracting spring to the anchor pin. Check to make sure that the anchor pin plate, cable anchor, and the hooks on the primary and secondary shoe retracting springs are all stacked flat on the anchor pin.

8. Assemble the adjuster, making sure it is the correct one for the brake on which you are working. The adjusting screw and the lever are stamped either R or L for right or left. The right pivot nut has 2 machined identification lines (**Figure 10**); the left one, one line. If an adjuster is installed on the wrong brake it will retract the shoes rather than expand them each time the automatic adjuster operates.

9. Screw the adjusting screw all the way into the nut then back it off ½ turn. Install the socket on the end of the screw. Install adjuster between shoes with screw toward secondary shoe.

10. Attach the cable to the adjusting lever, engage the hook on the lever in the hole in the secondary shoe, and connect the adjuster spring. Check the action of the adjuster by pulling the cable (between the guide and the adjuster lever) toward the secondary shoe far enough to lift the adjuster out of engagement with the notches in the adjuster screw. Then release the cable. The adjuster lever should engage the next notch in the screw and the adjuster spring should pull the lever down to its original position, turning the screw one notch.

If the adjuster does not operate correctly, check the following points:

    a. Make sure the cable ends are not pulled out of the crimped collars. If they are, the cable should be replaced.

    b. Make sure the groove in the cable guide is smooth and the groove is parallel to the shoe and it lies flat against the shoe web. If it is damaged, replace it.

    c. Make sure the hook on the lever is square and parallel with the lever. If it is not, it may be possible to bend it until it is correct. If not, replace the lever.

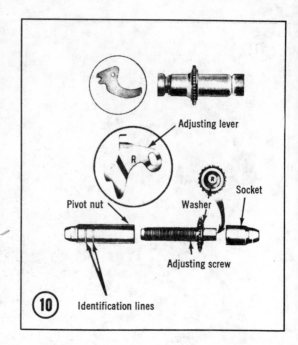

    d. Make sure the adjusting screw socket is seated in the notch in the secondary shoe.

11. When both brakes on an axle have been assembled, make a preliminary adjustment; pull the adjuster lever away from the adjusting screw just far enough to disengage it. Do not bend it. Turn the adjuster screw to expand the brakes just far enough so the drum can be installed with a slight drag. Then, loosen the adjuster screw 1¼ turns to retract the shoes. Install the drums and wheels.

12. Make a final brake adjustment by repeatedly driving the vehicle backward and forward and stopping with firm pedal pressure until the pedal height and resistance are satisfactory.

BRAKE SHOE REPLACEMENT (HEAVY DUTY)

Removal

Refer to **Figure 11** for the following procedure.

1. Remove the brake drum as described above. On front brakes, remove the spring clip from the anchor pin. On rear brakes, from the back of the backing plate, unscrew the nut from the parking brake lever pivot bolt (**Figure 12**) and remove the lever.

⑪ **HEAVY DUTY DRUM BRAKE ASSEMBLY**

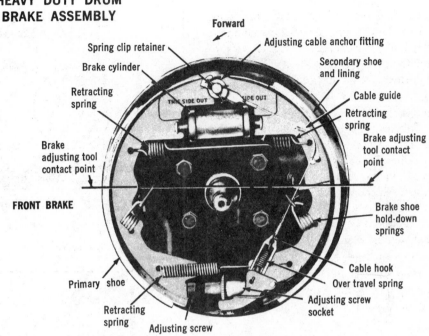

Forward

Spring clip retainer
Brake cylinder
Retracting spring
Brake adjusting tool contact point
FRONT BRAKE
Primary shoe
Retracting spring
Adjusting screw

Adjusting cable anchor fitting
Secondary shoe and lining
Cable guide
Retracting spring
Brake adjusting tool contact point
Brake shoe hold-down springs
Cable hook
Over travel spring
Adjusting screw socket

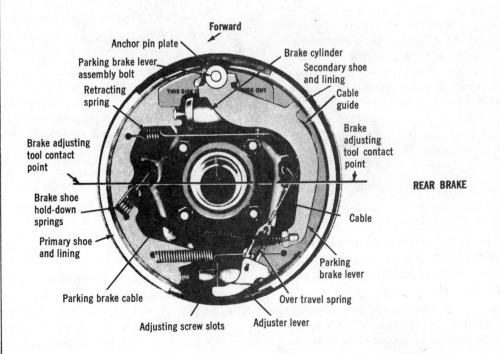

Forward

Anchor pin plate
Parking brake lever assembly bolt
Retracting spring
Brake adjusting tool contact point
Brake shoe hold-down springs
Primary shoe and lining
Parking brake cable
Adjusting screw slots

Brake cylinder
Secondary shoe and lining
Cable guide
Brake adjusting tool contact point
REAR BRAKE
Cable
Parking brake lever
Over travel spring
Adjuster lever

9

⑫

HEAVY DUTY REAR DRUM BRAKE

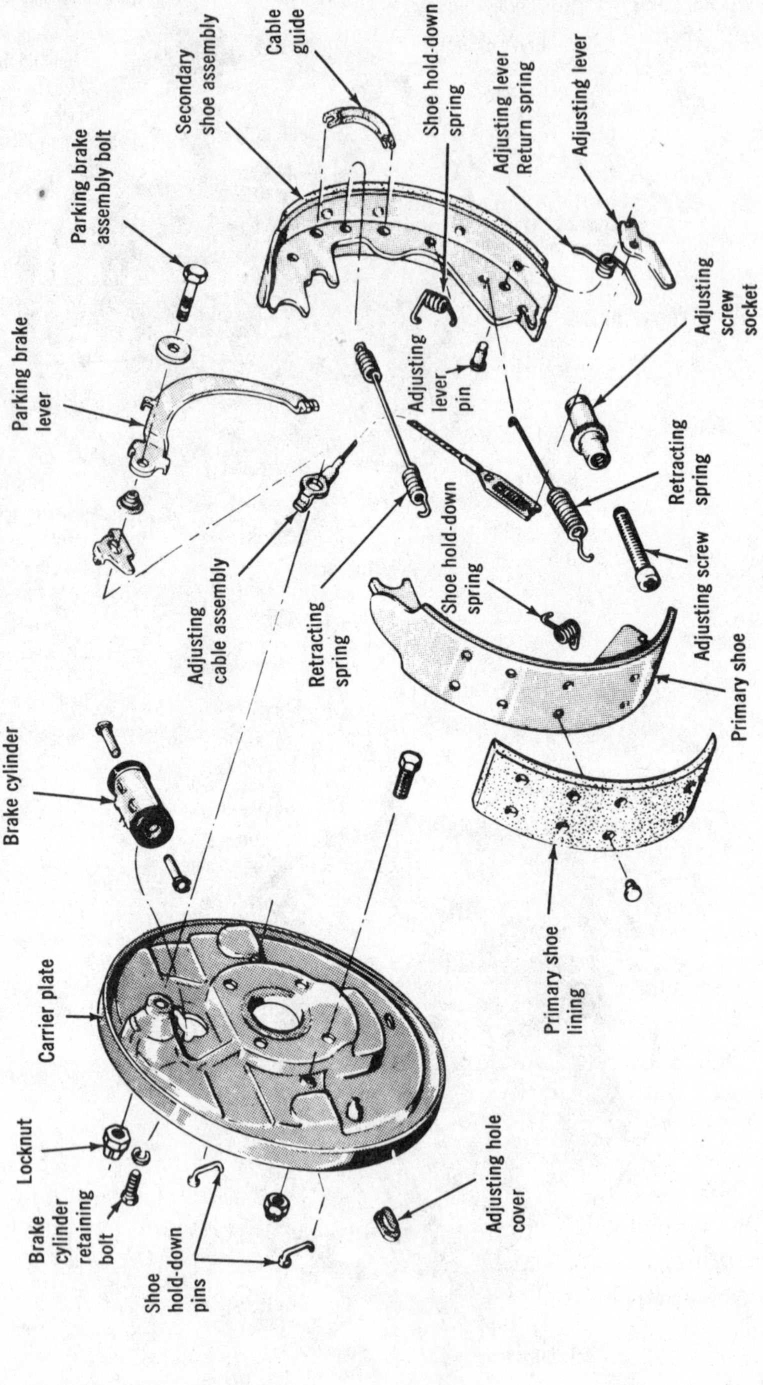

Parking brake assembly bolt

Secondary shoe assembly

Cable guide

Shoe hold-down spring

Adjusting lever Return spring

Adjusting lever

Parking brake lever

Adjusting screw socket

Adjusting lever pin

Retracting spring

Adjusting cable assembly

Retracting spring

Shoe hold-down spring

Retracting spring

Adjusting screw

Primary shoe

Brake cylinder

Primary shoe lining

Carrier plate

Locknut

Brake cylinder retaining bolt

Shoe hold-down pins

Adjusting hole cover

2. Disconnect the adjuster cable from the anchor pin and the adjuster lever. Disconnect and remove the brake shoe retracting springs.

3. Unhook the brake hold-down springs from the eyes on the backing plate and remove the adjuster and shoes from the backing plate. Unscrew the adjuster and disassemble them.

Inspection

Refer to the inspection steps for the brakes described above. In addition, burnish the shoe contact points on the backing plate and remove any residue.

Installation

1. Clean your hands thoroughly and check the new linings to make sure they are not nicked or burred. If they are bonded linings, check for and remove any bonding cement along edges.

2. Use brake lubricant to lubricate the following items:

    a. Parking brake cable

    b. Fulcrum end of parking brake lever

    c. Adjusting screw

    d. Shoe contact points on the backing plate

    e. Spring eyes on shoes and backing plate

3. Attach the upper retracting spring to both shoes and then set the assembly in place on the backing plate with the notches in the shoes engaged in the slots in the wheel cylinder pistons. Install the brake hold-down springs to hold the shoes to the backing plate.

4. Install the adjuster assembly, making sure it is the correct one for the brake being worked on; the parts are stamped either R or L (for right or left) and the adjuster nuts are identified with machined grooves — two for right and one for left.

The slot in the adjuster screw must be toward the primary shoe.

5. Install the bottom retracting spring, the adjuster lever spring, and the adjuster lever. Connect the adjuster cable to the adjuster lever, making sure the cable engages the groove in the cable guide. Then, connect the upper end of the cable to the anchor pin.

6. On rear brakes, connect the parking brake cable to the parking brake lever, then install the lever in the anchor pin. Screw on and tighten the nut at the rear of the backing plate to hold the parking brake lever in place.

7. Refer to Steps 10 and 11 in *Installation* procedure of the *Brake Shoe Replacement (Regular Duty)* section, preceding.

WHEEL CYLINDERS

Removal

1. Remove wheel, drum, and brake shoes, as outlined previously.

2. Remove cylinder-to-shoe connecting links.

3. Disconnect hydraulic brake line from the brake cylinder.

4. Remove brake cylinder retaining bolts and lockwashers, then remove cylinder from backing plate.

> NOTE: *If brake cylinder is leaking, replace it with a reconditioned one available from your Ford dealer or local parts supply house.*

Installation

1. Place brake cylinder on backing plate and install retaining bolts and lockwashers.

2. Install a new gasket on brake line fitting (if so equipped), then connect brake line to brake cylinder.

3. Install brake shoes and connecting links between shoes and cylinder. Install drum and wheel as outlined previously.

4. Adjust brakes as outlined previously, then bleed brakes (refer to *Brake System Bleeding*, this chapter).

DISC BRAKE PAD REPLACEMENT (HEAVY DUTY RAIL SLIDER CALIPER)

The brake shoe and lining assemblies should be replaced when the lining is worn to $\frac{1}{32}$ in. above the backing plate. Always replace both shoes and lining assemblies on an axle (**Figure 13**).

Removal

1. To avoid brake fluid overflow when caliper pistons are pressed into cylinder bores, siphon

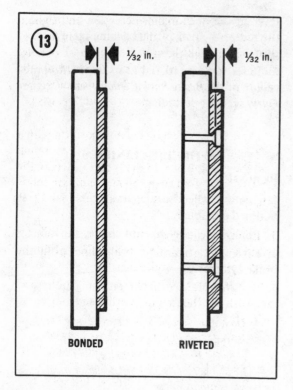

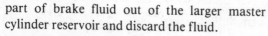

BONDED   RIVETED

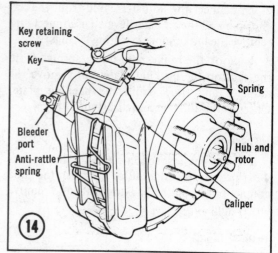

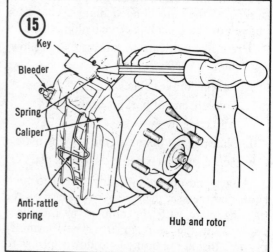

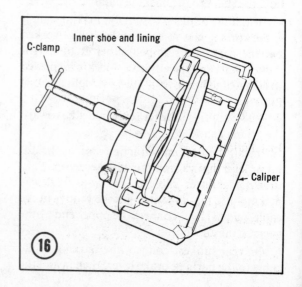

part of brake fluid out of the larger master cylinder reservoir and discard the fluid.

2. Raise vehicle, remove front wheel, and install jackstand for safety.

3. Remove key retaining screw (**Figure 14**), then drive out the key and spring with a brass rod and hammer (**Figure 15**).

> NOTE: *It is not necessary to disconnect hydraulic brake line from caliper.*

4. Remove caliper from its support assembly by rotating key and spring end out and away from the rotor. Slide the opposite end of the caliper clear of the slide in the support, and off the rotor. Lay the caliper on the tie rod or axle, or support it with a piece of wire.

> CAUTION
> *Never let the caliper hang by the brake hose, or the hose might become stretched or twisted.*

5. Remove caliper brake shoe anti-rattle spring and inner and outer shoe/lining assemblies.

6. Clean areas of the caliper and support that come in contact during the sliding action of the caliper.

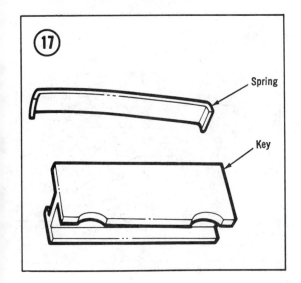

Spring

Key

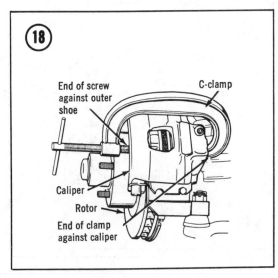

End of screw
against outer
shoe

C-clamp

Caliper

Rotor

End of clamp
against caliper

7. Install a C-clamp on the caliper housing between the piston bores (**Figure 16**). Using the older inner shoe and lining over the pistons, tighten the clamp to the bottom of the caliper pistons in the cylinder bores. Remove clamp and inner shoe lining assembly.

Installation

1. Be sure that caliper pistons are bottomed in the cylinder bore.

2. Install new inner and outer shoes, then install anti-rattle spring.

3. Place the caliper rail into the slide on the support and rotate the caliper onto the rotor. Position the key and spring (**Figure 17**) and

start the subassembly between the caliper and support. The spring must be between the key and caliper, and the spring tangs must overlap the ends of the key (**Figure 15**). Hold up the caliper with a brake adjusting tool or screwdriver, if necessary, against the support assembly.

4. Drive the key and spring into position with a light hammer. Be sure to align the correct notch with the existing hole in the support. Secure the key to the support with the key retaining screw (**Figure 14**), then tighten the screw to 12-20 ft.-lb.

5. Lower the vehicle and check the master cylinder reservoirs. If necessary, fill with brake fluid. Depress the brake pedal several times to seat the linings on the rotor.

> WARNING
> *Do not drive vehicle until brake pedal is firm. It should not be necessary to bleed the brakes, as the hydraulic brake line system was not opened for this procedure. However, if there is reason to suspect air in the brakes, bleed the systems immediately (refer to **Brake System Bleeding**, this chapter).*

DISC BRAKE PAD REPLACEMENT (LIGHT DUTY SLIDING CALIPER)

The brake shoe and lining assemblies should be replaced when the lining is worn to $\frac{1}{32}$ in. above the backing plate. Always replace both shoes and lining assemblies on an axle. Refer to **Figure 13**.

Removal

1. Perform Steps 1 and 2 under *Disc Brake Pad Replacement (Heavy Duty Rail Slider Caliper)* section, preceding.

2. Install an 8-inch C-clamp on caliper (**Figure 18**), then tighten clamp to bottom the caliper piston in the bore. Remove the clamp.

3. Remove the key retaining screw (**Figure 19**), then drive out the caliper support key and caliper support spring with a brass rod and light hammer (**Figure 20**).

> NOTE: *It is not necessary to disconnect the hydraulic brake line to the caliper.*

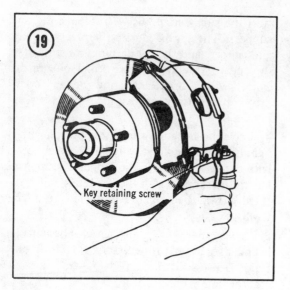

Key retaining screw

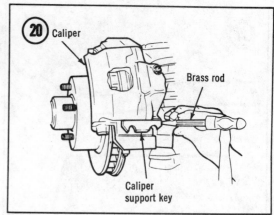

Caliper

Brass rod

Caliper
support key

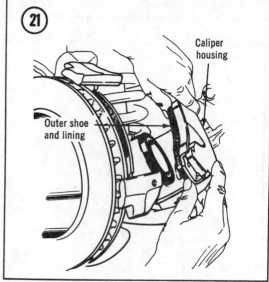

Caliper
housing

Outer shoe
and lining

4. Push the caliper downward against the spindle assembly, then rotate the upper end upward and out of the spindle assembly. After the caliper is removed, lay it on a tie rod or axle.

WARNING
Never hang the caliper by the brake hose, or the hose might be stretched or twisted.

5. Remove the outer shoe and lining from the caliper (**Figure 21**).

NOTE: *It might be necessary to tap the shoe to loosen the flange from the caliper.*

6. Remove the inner shoe and lining (**Figure 22**), then remove the shoe anti-rattle clip from the lower end of the shoe.

7. Clean areas of the caliper and spindle assembly that come in contact during the sliding action of the caliper. Apply a thin coat of high-temperature grease on both surfaces.

CAUTION
Do not get lubricant on rotors or linings. Wipe off excess lubricant after assembly.

Installation

1. Install a new anti-rattle clip on the lower end of the inner shoe (**Figure 23**). Be sure that the tabs on the clip are correctly positioned and that the clip is fully seated.

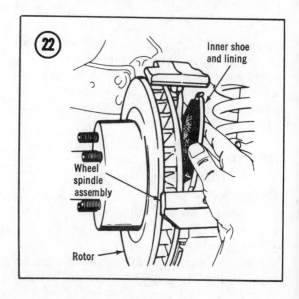

Inner shoe
and lining

Wheel
spindle
assembly

Rotor

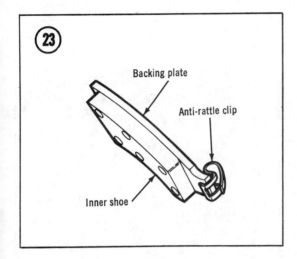

Figure 23

Backing plate

Anti-rattle clip

Inner shoe

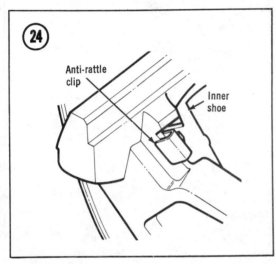

Figure 24

Anti-rattle clip

Inner shoe

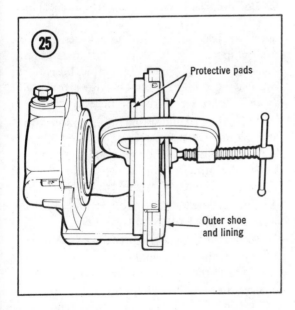

Figure 25

Protective pads

Outer shoe and lining

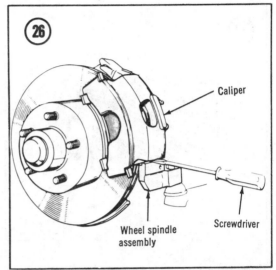

Figure 26

Caliper

Wheel spindle assembly

Screwdriver

2. Place the inner shoe and anti-rattle clip in the shoe abutment with the clip tab against the shoe abutment and the loop-type spring facing away from the rotor (**Figure 24**). Compress the anti-rattle clip and slide the upper end of the shoe into position.

3. Be sure that the caliper piston is bottomed in the cylinder bore. If necessary, use a large C-clamp.

4. Place the outer shoe and lining on the caliper (use your fingers to press the shoe tabs into place; if this is not possible, use a C-clamp as shown in **Figure 25**).

CAUTION
Be careful not to damage the brake lining with the C-clamp.

5. Place the caliper on the spindle assembly (pivot the caliper around the support upper mounting surface). Do not tear or cut the boot when it slips over the inner shoe.

6. Hold the upper machined surface of the caliper against the surface of the support assembly with a brake adjusting tool or screwdriver (**Figure 26**). Install a new caliper support spring and key (**Figures 27 and 28**). Drive the key and spring assembly into position with a soft plastic mallet (**Figure 28**), then install the key retaining screw and tighten it to 12-20 ft.-lb.

7. Lower the vehicle and check the master cylinder reservoirs. If necessary, fill with brake

9

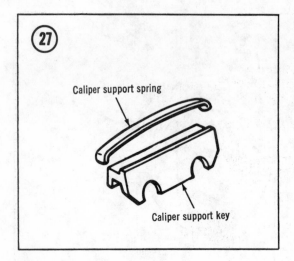

Caliper support spring

Caliper support key

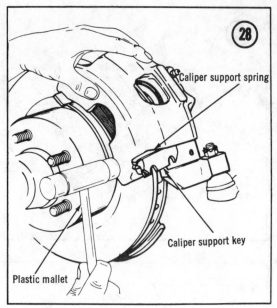

Caliper support spring

Caliper support key

Plastic mallet

fluid. Depress the brake pedal several times to seat the linings on the rotor.

WARNING
*Do not drive vehicle until brake pedal is firm. It should not be necessary to bleed the brakes, as the hydraulic brake line system was not opened for this procedure. However, if there is reason to suspect air in the brakes, bleed the system immediately (refer to **Brake System Bleeding**, this chapter).*

CALIPER REMOVAL/INSTALLATION (HEAVY DUTY RAIL SLIDING CALIPER)

Removal

1. Raise front end of vehicle and remove front wheel assembly. Install jackstand for safety.

2. Disconnect brake hose from caliper. Plug inlet port on caliper and outlet on hose to prevent dirt from entering.

3. Remove key retaining screw (**Figure 14**), then drive out the key and spring with a brass rod and light hammer (**Figure 15**).

4. Remove caliper from the support assembly by rotating the key and spring end out and away from the rotor. Slide the opposite end of the caliper clear of the slide in the support and off the rotor.

5. Clean the caliper and support where they make contact during the sliding action of the caliper. Add a light coat of high-temperature grease to both sliding surfaces.

WARNING
Do not get lubricant on rotors or linings. Braking force will be drastically reduced. Wipe off any excess grease after assembly.

6. Clean brake fluid, grease, dirt, etc., off the rotor braking surfaces.

Installation

1. Place the caliper rail into the slide on the support and rotate it onto the rotor.

2. Position the key and spring (**Figure 17**) and start the subassembly between the caliper and support. The spring must be between the key and caliper, and the tangs must overlap the ends of the key (**Figure 15**). Hold the caliper against the support assembly with a brake adjusting tool or screwdriver, if necessary.

3. Drive the key and spring into position with a soft hammer. The correct notch must line up with the existing hole in the support. Secure the key to the support with the key retaining screw (**Figure 14**), then tighten the screw to 20 ft.-lb.

4. Connect the hydraulic hose to the caliper inlet port (use new copper washers).

5. Install the wheel and lower the vehicle.

6. Fill the master cylinders with brake fluid, then bleed the brake system (refer to *Brake System Bleeding*, this chapter).

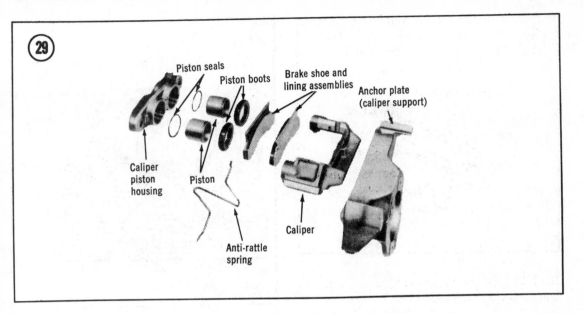

Piston seals
Piston boots
Brake shoe and
lining assemblies
Anchor plate
(caliper support)
Caliper
piston
housing
Piston
Caliper
Anti-rattle
spring

CALIPER REMOVAL/INSTALLATION (LIGHT DUTY SLIDING CALIPER)

Removal

1. Raise the vehicle and install jackstands for safety. Remove wheel.

2. Disconnect brake hose from caliper inlet port. Cap hose and plug the inlet port to prevent brake fluid leakage.

3. Remove caliper as outlined in previous section, *Caliper Removal/Installation (Heavy Duty Rail Sliding Caliper)*. Then remove brake pads as outlined in *Disc Brake Pad Replacement (Light Duty Sliding Caliper)* section, earlier in this chapter.

4. Inspect caliper housing for leakage. Overhaul the caliper if any leakage is present. Refer to following section, *Caliper Overhaul (Light Duty Sliding Caliper)*.

> NOTE: *A small amount of brake fluid wetness inside the boot is normal.*

5. Remove rust or corrosion from the machined surfaces of the support assembly and caliper, with a wire brush. Clean areas of the caliper and spindle assembly that make contact during the sliding action of the caliper.

Installation

1. Install the brake pads and caliper as outlined in previous sections.

2. Connect hydraulic hose to caliper inlet port (use new copper washers).

3. Bleed the brake system (refer to *Brake System Bleeding*, this chapter).

4. Install wheels, remove jackstands, and lower car.

CALIPER OVERHAUL (HEAVY DUTY RAIL SLIDING CALIPER)

Refer to **Figure 29** for the following procedure.

1. Replace piston assemblies if caliper assembly has been leaking. If bores are scored, corroded, or worn, replace cylinder housing.

> CAUTION
> *Never hone cylinder bores; piston assemblies are not available for oversize bores.*

Disassembly

1. Remove caliper, then remove brake shoe and lining assemblies from caliper, as outlined in previous sections. Drain brake fluid from caliper.

2. Secure caliper assembly in a vise (protect the caliper with a piece of soft wood placed on each side).

9

3. Place a piece of wood between the caliper bridge and cylinders, then apply low air pressure to the brake hose inlet to force the pistons out (**Figure 30**). Remove the wood block, and the pistons.

> WARNING
> *Never use high air pressure as the pistons could be ejected with enough force to cause personal injury or damage to the pistons.*

4. Remove bolts and washers holding the caliper to the cylinder housing and separate the caliper from the housing.

5. Remove and discard old piston seals.

Cleaning and Inspection

1. Remove rust or corrosion from machined surfaces of the caliper housing with a wire brush.

> CAUTION
> *Do not use a wire brush on the cylinder bore or damage to the machined surfaces will result.*

2. Clean caliper housing and piston with denatured alcohol. Clean and dry the grooves and passages with clean compressed air. Be sure that cylinder bore is free of foreign matter.

3. Check cylinder bore, seal groove, and boot groove in the bore and piston for damage or excessive wear. Replace piston if it is pitted, scored, or worn.

4. Remove corrosion from the boot groove and machined surfaces of the spindle assembly.

> NOTE: *If you have any doubts about your own ability to determine wear or damage, take the disassembled caliper to your Ford dealer. He will inspect it for a minimal amount.*

5. Replace the anti-rattle clip, caliper support spring and caliper support key, piston seal, and dust boots with new components.

Assembly

1. Lubricate new piston seals with clean brake fluid and install them in the seal grooves in the cylinder bores.

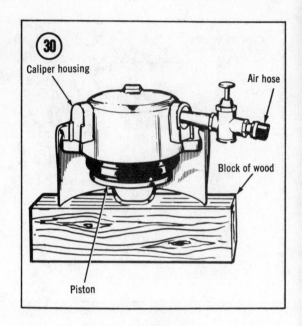

3️⃣0️⃣
Caliper housing
Air hose
Block of wood
Piston

> WARNING
> *Never use old piston seals and dust boots.*

2. Coat the cylinder bores with clean brake fluid, then lubricate the retaining lips of the dust boots with clean brake fluid and install them in the boot retaining grooves in the cylinder bores.

3. Coat pistons with clean brake fluid, then insert them into the dust boots and start them into the cylinders by hand until they are beyond the piston seals.

> CAUTION
> *Do not damage or dislodge the piston seal.*

4. Place a wood block over one piston, then press the piston into the cylinder.

> CAUTION
> *Do not cock the piston in the cylinder.*

5. Install the second boot in the same manner. Be sure that they are correctly seated.

6. Place the piston housing on the caliper and install the piston housing-to-caliper mounting bolts and washers. Tighten the bolts to 155-185 ft.-lb.

7. Install the shoe and lining assemblies in the caliper, then install the caliper as outlined previously.

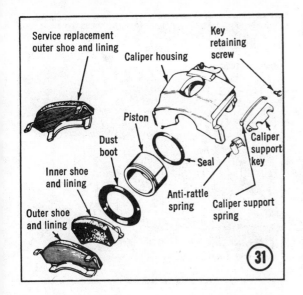

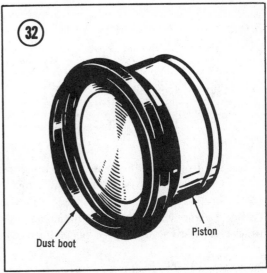

8. Install flexible brake hose, then bleed hydraulic system. Refer to *Brake System Bleeding*, this chapter.

CALIPER OVERHAUL
(LIGHT DUTY SLIDING CALIPER)

Refer to **Figure 31** for the following procedure.

Disassembly

1. Clean the exterior of the caliper in denatured alcohol.

2. Remove plug from caliper inlet port, then drain fluid from caliper housing.

3. Secure caliper assembly in a vise (protect the caliper with a piece of soft wood placed on each side).

4. Place a piece of wood between the caliper legs and the piston as shown in **Figure 30**. Apply low air pressure to the brake hose inlet to force the piston out. Remove the wood block, then the piston.

WARNING
Never use high air pressure as the piston could be ejected with enough force to cause personal injury or damage to the piston.

NOTE: *If the piston is damaged or cocked and will not come out, discontinue the air pressure and tap the piston*

sharply with a soft brass hammer. Never use a sharp instrument to pry the piston out.

5. Remove the boot from the piston and the seal from the caliper cylinder bore (refer to **Figure 31**).

Cleaning and Inspection

Refer to *Cleaning and Inspection* procedure, previous section.

Assembly

Refer to **Figure 31** for the following procedure.

1. Lubricate piston seal with clean brake fluid, then position the seal in the groove in the cylinder bore. Coat the outside of the piston and both dust boot beads with clean brake fluid.

2. Insert piston through dust boot until boot is around the bottom (closed end) of the piston (**Figure 32**).

3. Hold piston and dust boot above the caliper cylinder bore, then work the bead of the dust boot into the groove near the top of the cylinder bore with your fingers.

4. After bead is seated in groove, press straight down on piston until it bottoms in the bore. If necessary, bottom the piston with a C-clamp and a block of wood inserted between the clamp and piston.

CAUTION
Do not cock piston in bore.

5. Install caliper as outlined previously.

6. Bleed hydraulic brake system (refer to *Brake System Bleeding* section in this chapter).

BRAKE DISCS

Inspection

1. Loosen front wheel lug nuts. Jack up front end of car, place it on jackstands, and remove wheel.

2. Check front wheel bearing adjustment (refer to Chapter Eleven, *Wheel Bearing Adjustment* section).

3. Attach a dial indicator to some part of the suspension so that the indicator's stylus touches the rotor surface approximately 1 in. from the outer edge of the rotor (**Figure 33**).

> NOTE: *It is best to have the wheel bolts installed in order to obtain more accurate readings.*

4. Set the dial indicator to zero, then slowly turn the brake disc one complete revolution. Note the high and low readings on the dial. The total between the high and low readings must not exceed 0.003 in. (0.076mm). Have the disc refinished by your Ford dealer, or replace it if the wear is excessive.

5. Inspect disc for deep scratches. Small marks are not important, but deep radial scratches reduce brake effectiveness and increase pad wear. If disc is deeply scratched, it can be turned on a lathe to smooth the surface. However, the disc must not be cut more than 0.020 in. (0.508mm) on each side of the disc.

6. Use a micrometer to measure the thickness of the disc at several points around the circumference and at varying distances from the center. If disc measures less than the minimum thickness stamped on the side of the brake disc (**Figure 34**), replace it.

Removal

1. Raise front of vehicle and install jackstands for safety.

2. Remove wheel.

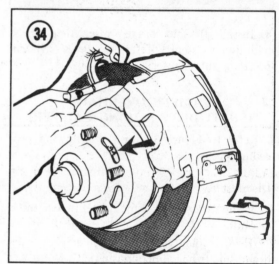

3. Remove caliper assembly as outlined previously.

4. Remove dust cap, cotter pin, nut, washer, and outer bearing.

5. Remove brake disc from the spindle.

6. Remove inner bearing cone and seal (discard the seal).

Installation

1. If a new hub and brake disc is to be installed, remove protective coating or any dirt or grease deposits with degreaser.

2. Pack the inner and outer bearings with wheel bearing grease.

3. Install inner bearing cone and seal, then install the hub and brake disc on the spindle.

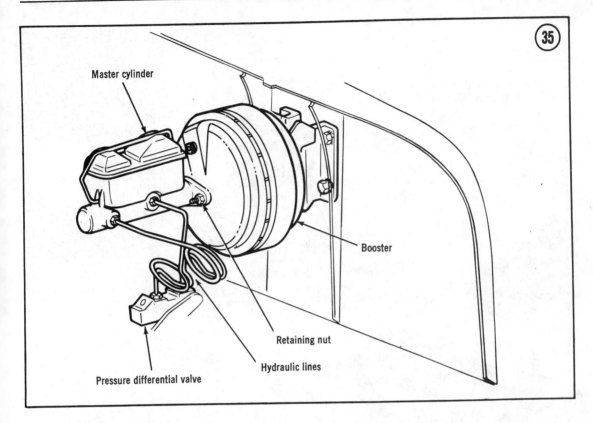

Master cylinder

(35)

Booster

Retaining nut

Hydraulic lines

Pressure differential valve

4. Install outer bearing cone, washer, and nut. Adjust bearing end play and install cotter pin and dust cap (refer to Chapter Eleven, *Wheel Bearing Adjustment* section).

5. Install caliper as outlined previously in this chapter.

6. Install wheel, remove jackstand, and lower vehicle.

MASTER CYLINDER

Removal

Refer to **Figure 35** for the following procedure.

1. With engine stopped, press down on brake pedal to expel vacuum from brake booster system.

2. Disconnect hydraulic lines from master cylinder, then remove brake booster-to-master cylinder nuts and lockwashers and remove master cylinder.

> NOTE: *It is best to install a reconditioned master cylinder, rather than to install a kit, as the reconditioned master*

cylinders have been overhauled under completely clean, controlled conditions. However, if you want to overhaul the kit yourself, refer to the following section.

Overhaul

Refer to **Figure 36** for the following procedure.

1. Clean outside of master cylinder, then remove reservoir cover and diaphragm. Drain all brake fluid.

2. Unscrew piston stop from bottom of cylinder body. Then remove O-ring seal from piston stop (discard seal).

3. On master cylinders so equipped, unscrew piston stop screw from bottom of secondary reservoir. (There is no O-ring seal on this piston stop screw.)

4. Remove snap ring (**Figure 37**) holding primary and secondary piston assemblies in the cylinder body.

5. Remove primary piston assembly from master cylinder (discard primary piston assembly).

9

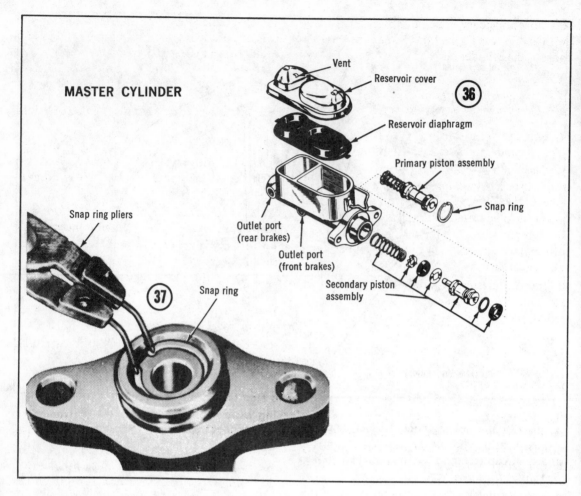

MASTER CYLINDER

Vent

Reservoir cover

Reservoir diaphragm

Primary piston assembly

Snap ring

Outlet port
(rear brakes)

Outlet port
(front brakes)

Secondary piston
assembly

Snap ring pliers

Snap ring

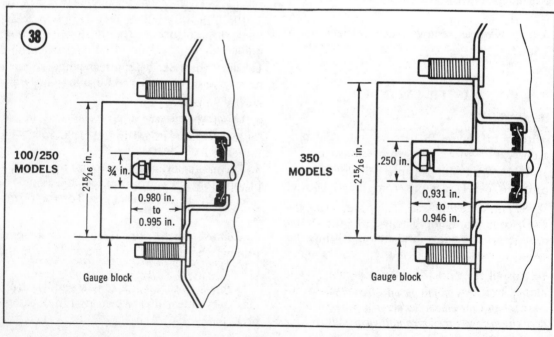

100/250
MODELS

2¹⁵/₁₆ in.

¾ in.

0.980 in.
to
0.995 in.

Gauge block

350
MODELS

2¹⁵/₁₆ in.

.250 in.

0.931 in.
to
0.946 in.

Gauge block

6. Blow secondary piston out of cylinder body with an air hose applied to the rear brake outlet port of the cylinder body.

CAUTION
Use only low air pressure to avoid personal injury or damage to the piston.

7. Remove return spring and cup protector from secondary piston (discard piston).

8. Clean all parts in clean isopropyl alcohol, then inspect for chipping, wear, or damage. Check all openings, recesses, and internal passages to be sure they are clean and free from foreign particles. Use the air hose to blow any dirt and cleaning solvent out. Lay all parts out on a clean surface.

9. Inspect master cylinder bore for pitting, rust, etc. If any damage or excessive wear is noted, replace the master cylinder.

10. Be sure that all parts are extremely clean. Dip all parts *except the cylinder body* in clean brake fluid. Coat the bare walls of the cylinder bore with clean brake fluid.

11. Assemble the secondary cup and O-ring in the grooves near the end of the secondary piston. Then assemble the cup protector, primary cup, spring retainer, and secondary piston return spring on the other end of the secondary piston. Install the secondary piston assembly in the master cylinder.

NOTE: *Wet the seals with clean brake fluid and use caution when inserting the piston assemblies into the bore to prevent seal damage.*

12. Install a new O-ring on the piston stop. Start the stop into the cylinder body.

NOTE: *Always follow the instructions that come with each master cylinder repair kit.*

13. On master cylinders so equipped, install the piston stop screw in the bottom of the secondary reservoir. There is no O-ring seal on the screw.

14. Install the primary piston assembly in the master cylinder. Push the primary piston inward, then tighten the secondary piston stop to hold the secondary piston in the bore.

15. Place the stop plate and snap ring on the primary piston. Depress the primary piston and install the snap ring in the cylinder body.

Master Cylinder Bleeding

Prior to installing the master cylinder, bleed it as follows.

1. Support the master cylinder body in a vise (protect it with soft pieces of wood placed on each side of the body). Fill the master cylinder with fresh brake fluid.

2. Loosely install the plugs in the front and rear brake outlet bores. Depress the primary piston a few times until no air bubbles appear in the brake fluid.

3. Tighten the plugs. Attempt to depress the piston. If there is still piston travel, air is still present in the master cylinder. Bleed again until piston travel is restricted.

4. Remove the plugs and install the cover and diaphragm assembly. Be sure that the cover retainer is tightened securely.

Installation

1. Check the distance from the outer end of the booster assembly pushrod to the front face of the brake booster assembly. Turn the pushrod adjusting screw in or out until you obtain the specified length as shown in **Figure 38**.

2. Place the master cylinder assembly over the booster pushrod and onto the mounting studs on the booster assembly. Install the attaching nuts and washers and tighten evenly.

3. Connect the hydraulic brake lines to the master cylinder.

4. Bleed the brake system (refer to *Brake System Bleeding* earlier in this chapter). Check for leaks.

5. Cautiously road test the car to be sure that the brakes are in proper working order.

NOTE
Some 1979 F-series light trucks may be equipped with improperly heat-treated pushrod-to-brake pedal retaining pins. Return the vehicle to a dealer for inspection and correction, if not already done.

9

NOTE: If you own a 1980 or later model, first check the Supplement at the back of the book for any new service information.

CHAPTER TEN

CLUTCH AND TRANSMISSION

This chapter covers practical maintenance procedures for the manual and automatic transmission and the clutch. Only minor adjustments are given for the automatic transmission, which is a complex component whose care should be entrusted to a Ford dealer or automatic transmission specialist.

> *NOTE*
> *Some 1977-1978 F-250 light trucks equipped with a C6 transmission may have mislocated park cam plate stops cast into the extension housing. Certain 1979 F-series trucks equipped with a C6 transmission may have improperly heat-treated parking pawls which will become deformed or prematurely worn. Return the vehicle to a dealer for inspection and correction, if not already done.*

AUTOMATIC TRANSMISSION

Adjustments for Ford's three-speed automatic transmission are given for the linkage and neutral start switch, as follows:

Linkage Adjustment

1. Place the transmission selector lever in D (DRIVE) with the engine off, and hold against the D stop by applying an 8-pound weight to the selector lever knob.

2. Loosen the shift rod adjusting nut at point A, **Figure 1**.

3. Shift the lever at the transmission into the D (DRIVE) position by pulling the lever all the way to the rear, then advancing it forward 2 detents.

4. With selector lever and transmission manual lever still in the D position, tighten the nut at point A to 12-18 ft.-lb. Avoid motion between the stud and rod.

5. Remove the 8-pound weight from the steering column selector lever knob. Operate the lever in all positions to be sure that the manual lever at the transmission is in full detent in all gear ranges. Readjust linkage if necessary.

6. Check neutral start switch adjustment. Error must not exceed ⅛ detent.

> NOTE: *Under no circumstances is it permissible to adjust linkage in any position other than the D position.*

Neutral Start Switch Adjustment

Refer to **Figure 2** for the following procedure:

1. Loosen the 2 neutral start switch attaching screws and hold the selector lever against the neutral stop.

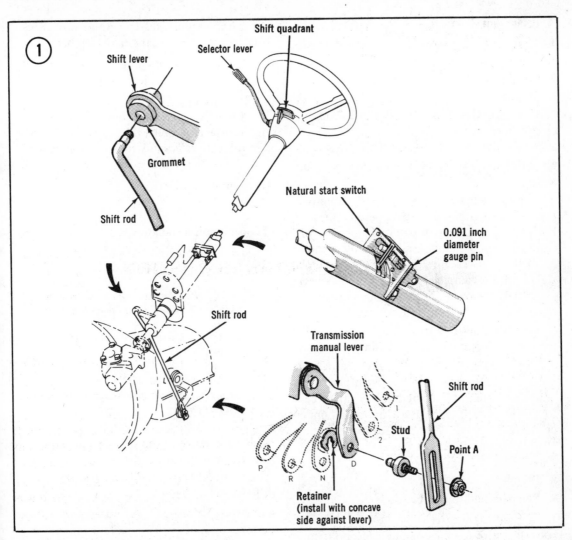

① Shift lever
Selector lever
Shift quadrant
Grommet
Shift rod

Natural start switch
0.091 inch diameter gauge pin

Shift rod

Transmission manual lever

Shift rod

Stud

Point A

P R N D

Retainer
(install with concave side against lever)

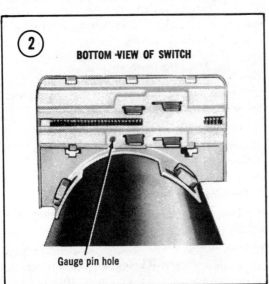

② **BOTTOM VIEW OF SWITCH**

Gauge pin hole

2. Move the sliding block on the neutral switch to the neutral position. Work from the rear of the switch and insert a 0.091 in. diameter gauge pin (No. 43 drill) into the gauge pin hole.

3. Slide the switch as necessary to permit the actuating lever to contact the sliding block.

4. Tighten the 2 switch attaching screws to 13-17 in.-lb. and remove the gauge pin.

5. Check the operation of the switch. The engine should start only with the transmission selector lever in NEUTRAL or PARK.

Transmission Fluid Check

Refer to Chapter Three, *Periodic Checks and Inspections* section under *Automatic Transmission Oil Level* for the proper fluid check procedure.

10

Transmission Removal

1. Remove engine compartment cover (work from inside the vehicle).

2. Disconnect neutral start switch wires at plug connector.

3. If V-8 equipped, remove flexhose from air cleaner heat tube.

4. Remove upper converter housing-to-engine bolts (3 bolts on 6-cylinder engine; 4 bolts on V-8).

5. Raise vehicle on hoist, then place drain pan under transmission fluid pan. Loosen attaching bolts, starting at rear of pan and working forward, and allow fluid to drain. Finally, remove all of the bolts except 2 in the front, to allow fluid to drain completely. After fluid has been completely removed, install 2 bolts on rear side of pan to temporarily hold it in place.

6. Remove converter drain plug access cover from lower end of converter housing.

7. Remove converter-to-flywheel attaching nuts. Turn converter with a wrench placed on crankshaft pulley attaching bolt, to gain access to converter drain plug. Place drain pan under converter to catch fluid, then remove the plug. Reinstall plug after fluid has been completely removed.

8. Disconnect drive shaft.

9. Remove fluid filler tube.

10. Disconnect starter cable at starter, then remove starter-to-converter housing bolts and remove starter.

11. Position engine support bar to the side rail and engine oil pan flanges.

12. Disconnect cooler lines from transmission, then disconnect vacuum lines from vacuum diaphragm unit. Remove vacuum line from retaining clip at transmission.

13. Remove speedometer driven gear from extension housing.

14. Disconnect manual and downshift linkage rods from transmission control levers.

15. Position transmission jack under the transmission, then install safety chain to hold transmission. Remove bolt and nut holding the rear mount to the crossmember, then remove 6 bolts holding crossmember to side rails, and remove 2 support gussets. Raise transmission with jack and remove the crossmember.

16. Remove bolt holding transmission filler tube to the cylinder block. Lift filler tube and dipstick from the transmission.

17. Remove remaining converter housing-to-engine attaching bolts, then lower the jack and remove converter and transmission assembly from under the vehicle.

18. Remove converters.

Transmission Installation

1. Tighten converter drain plug, then position converter on the transmission.

> NOTE: *Be sure that the converter drive flats are fully engaged in the pump gear.*

2. With converter installed, place transmission on the jack.

> CAUTION
> *Secure the transmission to the jack with a safety chain.*

3. Rotate converter until studs and drain plug are aligned with their holes in the flywheel. Move the converter and transmission assembly forward into position.

> CAUTION
> *Take care not to damage the flywheel and converter pilot.*

> NOTE: *The converter must rest squarely against the flywheel. This will ensure that the converter pilot is not binding in the engine crankshaft.*

4. Install lower converter housing-to-engine attaching bolts, then the converter-to-flywheel nuts.

5. Install crossmember and rear mount-to-crossmember bolt and nut.

6. Remove safety chain and remove jack from under the vehicle, then remove the engine support bar.

7. Install a new O-ring on lower end of transmission filler tube and insert tube in case.

8. Connect vacuum line to vacuum diaphragm (be sure that line is secured in the retaining clip).

9. Connect transmission cooler lines.

10. Install speedometer driven gear into extension housing.

11. Connect transmission linkage rods to control levers (be sure that you use new retaining ring and grommet).

12. Attach shift rod to steering column shift lever. Align the flats of the rod slot and insert stud through the rod. Assemble adjusting stud nut and washer to a loose fit, then adjust the linkage as outlined in the *Linkage Adjustment* procedure earlier in this chapter.

13. Install converter housing cover, then install starter.

14. Install drive shaft (refer to Chapter Eleven, *Drive Shaft Assembly* section), then lower vehicle to ground.

15. Install upper converter housing-to-engine attaching bolts.

16. On V-8 equipped vehicles, install flex hose to air cleaner heat tube.

17. Connect neutral start switch wires at plug connector.

18. Fill transmission with fluid (refer to Chapter Three, *Automatic Transmission Fluid Change* section).

19. Raise vehicle and check for leaks. Then lower vehicle and have your Ford dealer or automatic transmission specialist perform the final, critical throttle and linkage adjustments.

THREE-SPEED
MANUAL TRANSMISSION

This section covers removal/installation procedures, and adjustments for the three-speed manual transmission.

Linkage Adjustments

Refer to **Figure 3** for the following procedure:

1. Install a $\frac{3}{16}$ in. gauge pin through the steering column shift levers and the locating hole in the plastic spacer.

2. Loosen nuts A and B and place the transmission shift levers in the neutral detents.

3. Tighten nuts A and B to 12-18 ft.-lb. Be sure that there is no motion between the stud and rod.

4. Remove the gauge pin and check the linkage operation.

> NOTE: *Always use new retaining rings and insulators when making transmission control attachments. The concave side of the retaining ring must be toward the lever.*

Transmission Removal

Refer to **Figure 4** for the following procedure:

1. Raise the vehicle and support it with jackstands for safety. Place a jack and wood block under the engine oil pan.

2. Drain the transmission lubricant by removing lower extension housing-to-transmission bolt.

3. Place a jack under the transmission for support.

4. Disconnect gearshift linkage at transmission; disconnect the speedometer cable, and then the drive shaft from the transmission.

5. Raise the transmission as needed and remove the rear support.

6. Remove the transmission-to-clutch housing attaching bolts.

7. Move transmission rearward until input shaft clears clutch housing, then lower transmission to the floor.

> NOTE: *Do not depress the clutch pedal while removing the transmission.*

Transmission Installation

1. Apply a light film of lubricant to the release bearing inner hub surfaces, release lever fulcrum and fork, and transmission front bearing retainer. Be sure that the clutch disc does not become contaminated with grease.

10

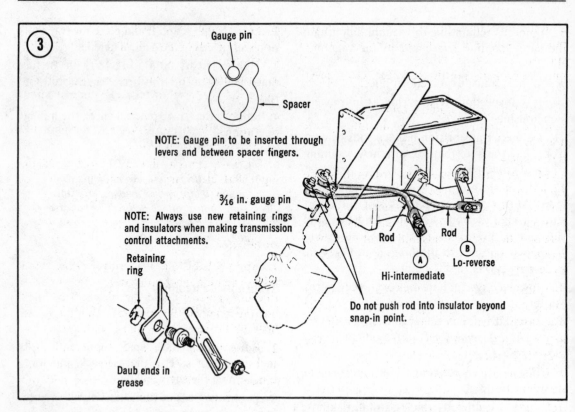

Gauge pin

Spacer

NOTE: Gauge pin to be inserted through levers and between spacer fingers.

$\frac{3}{16}$ in. gauge pin

NOTE: Always use new retaining rings and insulators when making transmission control attachments.

Retaining ring

Daub ends in grease

Rod

Rod

Ⓐ Hi-intermediate

Ⓑ Lo-reverse

Do not push rod into insulator beyond snap-in point.

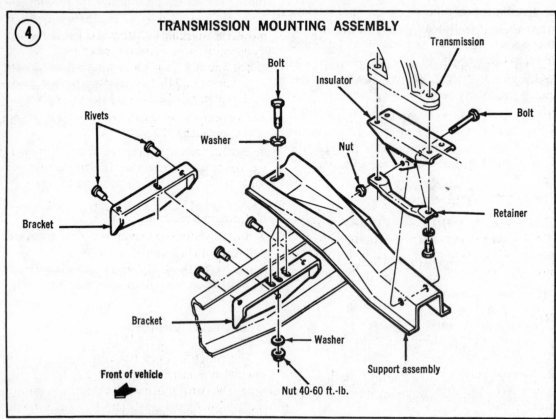

TRANSMISSION MOUNTING ASSEMBLY

Bolt

Transmission

Insulator

Bolt

Rivets

Washer

Nut

Bracket

Retainer

Bracket

Washer

Front of vehicle

Nut 40-60 ft.-lb.

Support assembly

2. Raise the transmission on a jack until the input shaft splines are in line with the clutch disc splines. The clutch release bearing and hub must be properly positioned in the release lever fork.

3. Install a guide stud in each lower clutch housing-to-transmission case mounting bolt and align the input shaft splines with the clutch disc splines.

4. Move the transmission forward on the guide studs until it makes contact with the clutch housing. Install the 2 transmission-to-flywheel housing upper mounting bolts and nuts. Remove the 2 guide studs and install the lower mounting bolts. Tighten the 4 mounting bolts to 42-50 ft.-lb.

5. Install the rear support and tighten attaching bolts and nuts to 42-50 ft.-lb. Remove the transmission jack and engine jack.

6. Connect the speedometer cable and driven gear, then install the drive shaft.

7. Connect each shift rod to its respective lever on the transmission and adjust if required (refer to *Linkage Adjustments*, earlier in this section).

8. Install the lower extension housing-to-transmission bolt, then fill the transmission to the proper level with an approved lubricant (refer to Chapter Three).

9. Connect the gearshift linkage and adjust the clutch pedal free travel and shift linkage as required (refer to *Clutch* section, later in this chapter, for procedure).

4-SPEED TRANSMISSION

The Warner T-18, T-19, and New Process 435 4-speed transmissions are equipped with a center, floor-mounted gear shift lever (**Figure 5**). Therefore, no linkage adjustment is necessary.

Removal

1. Disconnect the back-up light switch located at rear of gearshift housing cover.

2. Remove rubber boot, mat, and body floor pan cover, then remove gearshift lever and weather pad.

3. Raise vehicle and support with jackstands for safety. Place a jack under the transmission for support, and disconnect speedometer cable.

4. Disconnect drive shaft or coupling shaft and clutch linkage from the transmission and wire it to one side.

5. Remove the transmission rear support and transmission attaching bolts.

6. Slide the transmission to the rear until the input shaft clears the clutch housing.

7. Lower the transmission to the floor.

Installation

1. Apply a light film of lubricant to the clutch release bearing inner hub surfaces, release lever fulcrum and forks, and the transmission front bearing retainer. Be sure that the clutch disc does not become contaminated with grease.

2. Raise transmission on a jack until input shaft splines are aligned with clutch disc splines. The clutch release bearing and hub must be properly positioned in the release lever fork.

3. Install guide studs in clutch housing and move the transmission forward on the guide studs until it is properly positioned on the clutch housing. Install attaching bolts and nuts and tighten to 37-42 ft.-lb. Remove the guide studs and install the 2 lower attaching bolts.

4. Connect the speedometer cable and driven gear and clutch linkage.

5. Install bolts attaching the front U-joint of the coupling shaft to the transmission output shaft flange. Install the transmission rear support.

6. Connect back-up light switch.

7. Install shift lever and lubricate the spherical ball seat with lubricant.

8. Install weather pad, floor pan cover, floor mat, and boot.

CLUTCH

The clutch in Ford vehicles covered in this manual is a mechanically operated single disc type. The two adjustments to the clutch control mechanism (pedal travel and free play) should

10

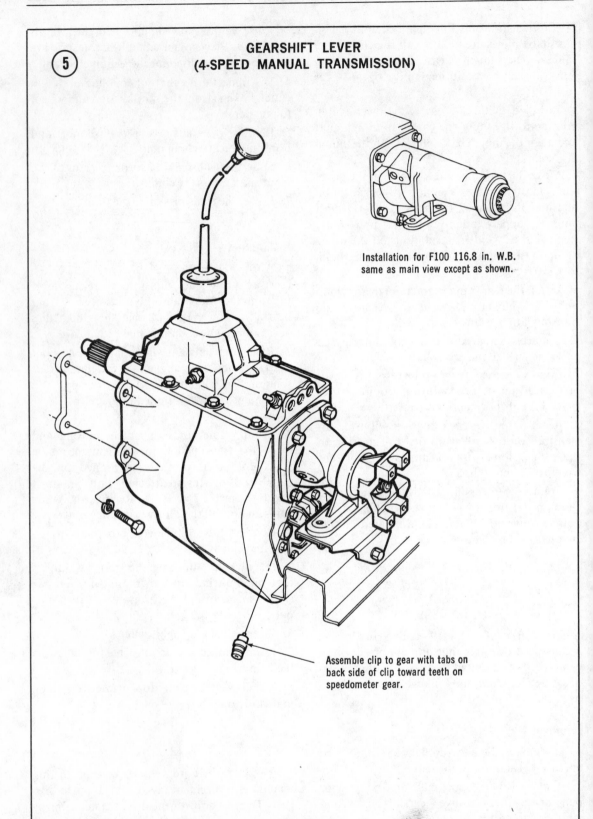

**GEARSHIFT LEVER
(4-SPEED MANUAL TRANSMISSION)**

⑤

Installation for F100 116.8 in. W.B.
same as main view except as shown.

Assemble clip to gear with tabs on
back side of clip toward teeth on
speedometer gear.

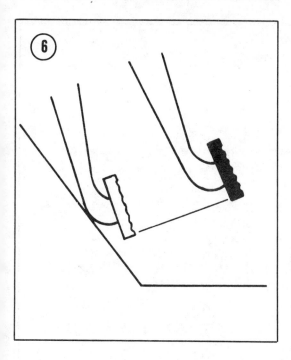

be checked and corrected if necessary when clutch slippage or shifting difficulties are experienced.

Adjustment

1. Measure the total travel of the clutch pedal, from fully extended to the floor (**Figure 6**). The correct travel is 7⅜-7¾ in. on models through 1972 (from 1973 on, there is no adjustment provided). If the actual travel is greater or less than indicated, move the clutch pedal bumper up or down as necessary to correct the travel (**Figure 7**).

2. Check the clutch pedal free play (or travel) by measuring the distance of the clutch pedal to the steering wheel when the pedal is fully extended (**Figure 8**). Slowly depress the clutch pedal until the clutch fingers can be felt to touch the clutch release bearing; measure this distance and compare it with the first. The

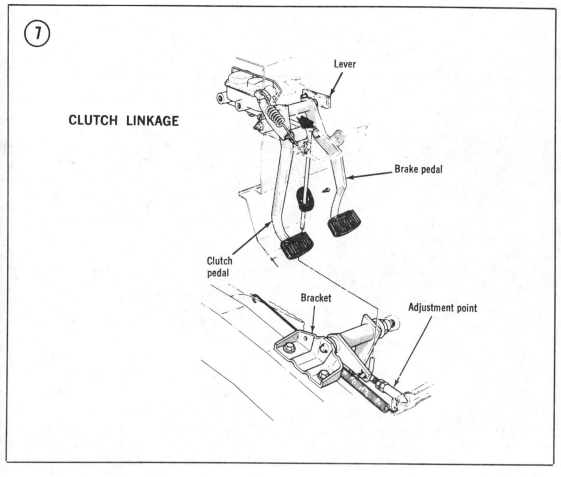

CLUTCH LINKAGE

Lever

Brake pedal

Clutch pedal

Bracket

Adjustment point

10

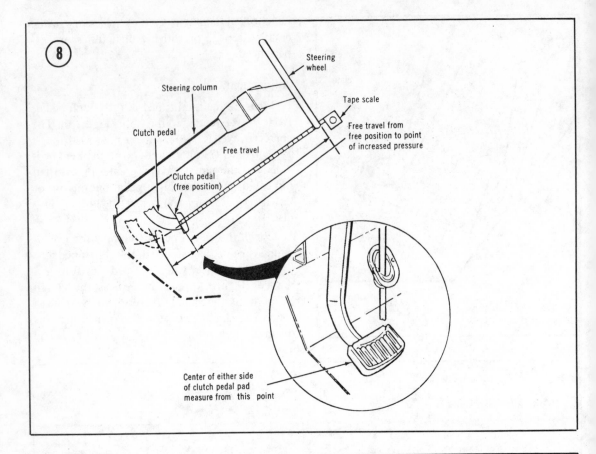

⑧

Steering wheel

Steering column

Tape scale

Clutch pedal

Free travel from free position to point of increased pressure

Free travel

Clutch pedal (free position)

Center of either side of clutch pedal pad measure from this point

distance (clutch free play) should be ¾-1½ in. If not, loosen the locknut on the clutch release rod and turn the adjusting nut as required to move the "bullet" until the free play is correct. Then, without further turning the adjusting nut, tighten the locknut securely against the adjusting nut.

> NOTE: *The free play can be accurately set by disconnecting the lever return spring and pressing the bullet firmly against the release lever; insert a 0.020 in. flat feeler gauge between the adjuster nut and the locknut (Figure 9); turn the locknut by hand as required until the gauge is held slightly; then remove the gauge, and without further turning the locknut, turn the adjuster nut until it contacts the locknut and then tighten it securely.*

3. When the adjustments are complete, double check them and then road test the vehicle to ensure that the clutch releases and engages satisfactorily.

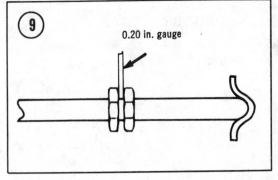

⑨

0.20 in. gauge

Removal

Refer to **Figure 10** for the following procedure:

1. Disconnect release lever retracting spring and pushrod assembly at the lever.

2. Remove transmission (refer to *Transmission* section earlier in this chapter).

3. If clutch housing is not provided with a dust cover, remove starting motor. Remove flywheel housing attaching bolts, then remove housing.

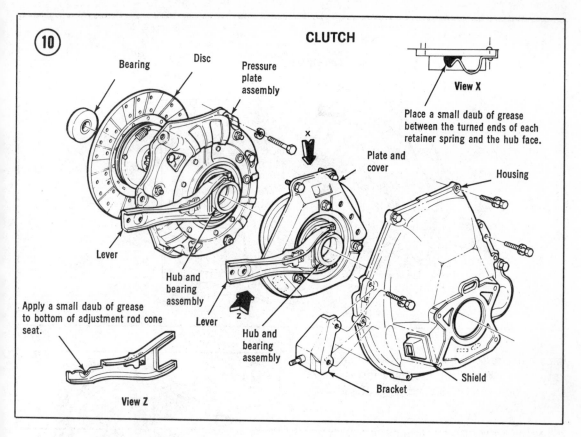

CLUTCH

10

Bearing · Disc · Pressure plate assembly

View X

Place a small daub of grease between the turned ends of each retainer spring and the hub face.

Plate and cover

Housing

Lever

Hub and bearing assembly

Apply a small daub of grease to bottom of adjustment rod cone seat.

Lever

Hub and bearing assembly

Shield

Bracket

View Z

4. If housing is provided with a dust cover, remove it. Remove release lever and bearing from clutch housing.

5. Scribe a mark on the pressure plate/cover assembly and flywheel, so that you can install them in the same relative position later.

6. Loosen all pressure plate/cover attaching bolts evenly until pressure plate springs expand, then remove bolts.

7. Remove the pressure plate/cover assembly and clutch disc from the flywheel or through the opening in the bottom of the clutch housing.

> NOTE: *Remove the pilot bearing only if it is obviously damaged. Refer to* **Clutch Pilot Bearing Removal/Installation** *procedure, later in this chapter.*

Inspection

Check the clutch disc for oil or grease, glazing, warping, loose or missing rivets, facings worn down to rivets, and broken springs (loose springs are normal).

Replace the disc if any of these conditions are present. The disc should also be replaced if the facings are worn and a new pressure plate is being installed.

Check the pressure plate for scoring, overheating (blue-tinted areas), or cracks.

Clean the flywheel friction surface with a non-petroleum base cleaner such as trichloroethylene or alcohol. Inspect the plate for cracking or scoring. If necessary, have the flywheel reconditioned by an automotive machine shop or your dealer. Replace the flywheel if damage is severe.

Installation

Refer to **Figure 10** for the following procedure:

1. Position the clutch disc on the flywheel. Using a pilot tool, align the disc.

2. If you are installing the original pressure plate/cover assembly, be sure that the scribe marks which you made during the removal procedure align properly. Position the pressure

10

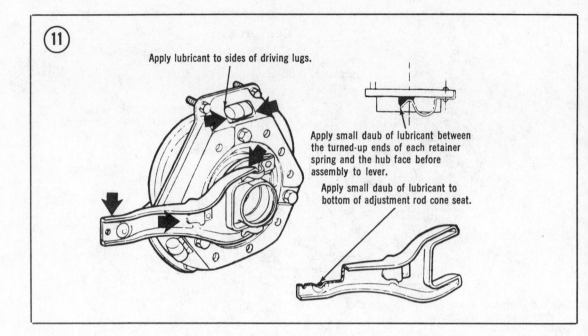

⑪

Apply lubricant to sides of driving lugs.

Apply small daub of lubricant between the turned-up ends of each retainer spring and the hub face before assembly to lever.

Apply small daub of lubricant to bottom of adjustment rod cone seat.

plate/cover assembly on the flywheel and align the pressure plate and disc, then install the retaining bolts and tighten evenly. Remove the clutch pilot tool.

3. Apply a light film of lithium-base grease to the sides of the driving lugs (**Figure 11**). Be sure that the clutch is fully released.

4. Position the clutch release bearing and hub on the release lever. Install the release lever on the trunnion in the flywheel housing. Apply a light film of lithium-base grease to the release lever fingers and to the lever trunnion or fulcrum.

5. If flywheel housing has been removed, install it against the engine rear cover plate and install the attaching bolts. Tighten bolts evenly.

6. Install starter motor, then install transmission assembly on the clutch housing and tighten all bolts evenly.

7. Install slave cylinder on vehicles so equipped and tighten bolts evenly.

8. Adjust release lever pushrod assembly. Connect release lever retracting spring.

9. If so equipped, install clutch housing dust cover.

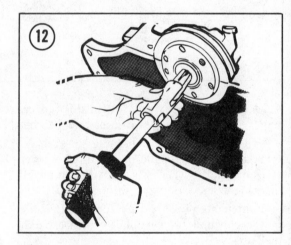

⑫

Clutch Pilot Bearing Removal/Installation

A needle roller bearing and adaptor assembly is used as a clutch pilot bearing, inserted directly into the engine crankshaft. The assembly cannot be serviced separately. The needle bearing clutch pilot can only be installed with the seal end of the bearing facing the transmission. The bearing and seal are pregreased and do not require extra lubrication. Be sure to install a new bearing whenever a bearing is removed.

1. Remove the transmission, clutch pressure plate, and disc, as outlined earlier in this chapter.

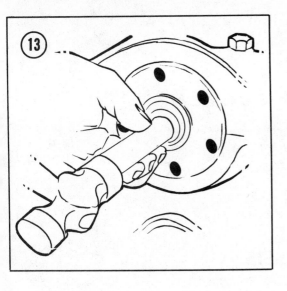

2. Remove the pilot bearing (Ford tools T59L-100B and T48L-101-A are shown in **Figure 12**. Equivalent tools can be used.

3. To install, use Ford tools T74P-7137-A and T74P-7137-H or equivalent, as shown in **Figure 13**. Install the pilot bearing with the seal facing the transmission so that the adaptor is not cocked.

4. Install the clutch pressure plate, disc, and transmission, as outlined earlier in this chapter.

CAUTION

Be careful that you do not damage the bearing during transmission installation while the transmission input shaft is being inserted into the bearing.

10

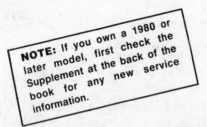

NOTE: If you own a 1980 or later model, first check the Supplement at the back of the book for any new service information.

CHAPTER ELEVEN

CHASSIS

This chapter covers major front and rear suspension components, with the exception of certain procedures which require the use of specialized tools which are not readily available to the average home mechanic.

Chassis work should be confined to the procedures described below. All other work should be entrusted to a Ford dealer or a qualified specialist.

SUSPENSION

All vehicles covered in this manual use two I-beam type front axles (one for each wheel). Each axle is connected at one end to the spindle and a radius arm, and to a frame pivot bracket on the opposite side of the vehicle at the other end (refer to **Figure 1**).

Each spindle is positioned on the axle by a spindle pin which pivots in bronze bushings pressed into the upper and lower ends of the spindle. A thrust bearing is installed between the lower end of the axle and the spindle to support the load on the axle. A steering arm is an integral part of the spindle (refer to **Figure 2**).

The rear suspension uses semi-elliptic, leaf-type springs with the forward end of each spring attached to a bracket on the frame side member. The rear end of the spring is shackled to a bracket on the frame side member (refer to **Figure 3**).

SHOCK ABSORBERS

The shock absorbers can be routinely checked while installed on the vehicle. However, this is only a general indication of their condition; if there is any doubt about their serviceability, they should be removed as described later and checked more accurately.

To check their general condition, first bounce the front, then the rear, of the vehicle up and down several times and release. The vehicle should not continue to bounce more than twice. Excessive bouncing is an indication of worn shock absorbers. Keep in mind, however, that this test is not conclusive; the spring stiffness of a pickup or van makes it difficult to detect shock absorbers in marginal condition. If there is doubt about the condition of the units, remove them and have them tested.

Removal/Installation (Front)

1. Jack up the front of the vehicle and support it on frame stands. Remove the front wheels.

2. Unscrew the nut and bolt from the lower mount.

3. Unscrew the self-locking nut from the upper mount (**Figure 4**), remove the washer and bushings, and pull the shock absorber off the mounting arm.

① **I-BEAM SUSPENSION**

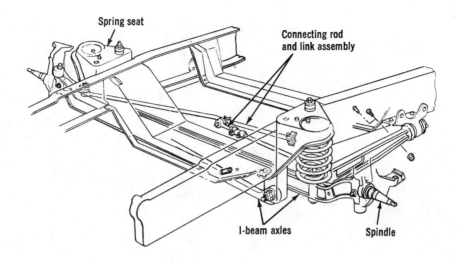

Spring seat

Connecting rod
and link assembly

I-beam axles

Spindle

F-250/F-350

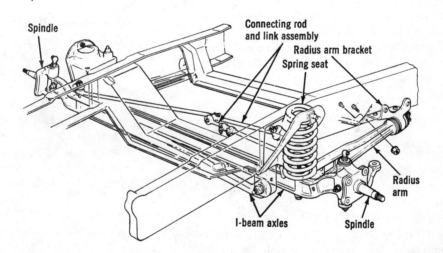

Spindle

Connecting rod
and link assembly

Radius arm bracket

Spring seat

I-beam axles

Spindle

Radius
arm

F-100/F-150

11

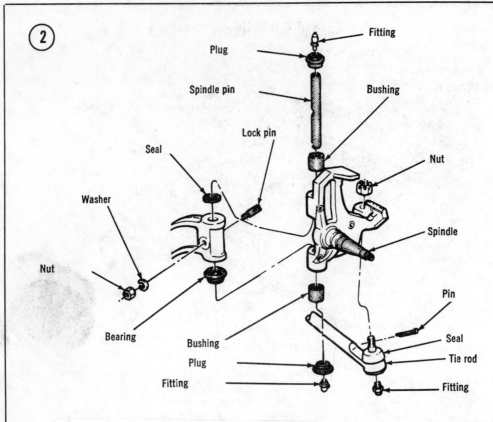

F250-350

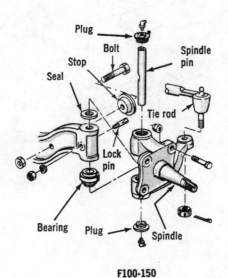

F100-150

SPINDLE

REAR SPRING

③

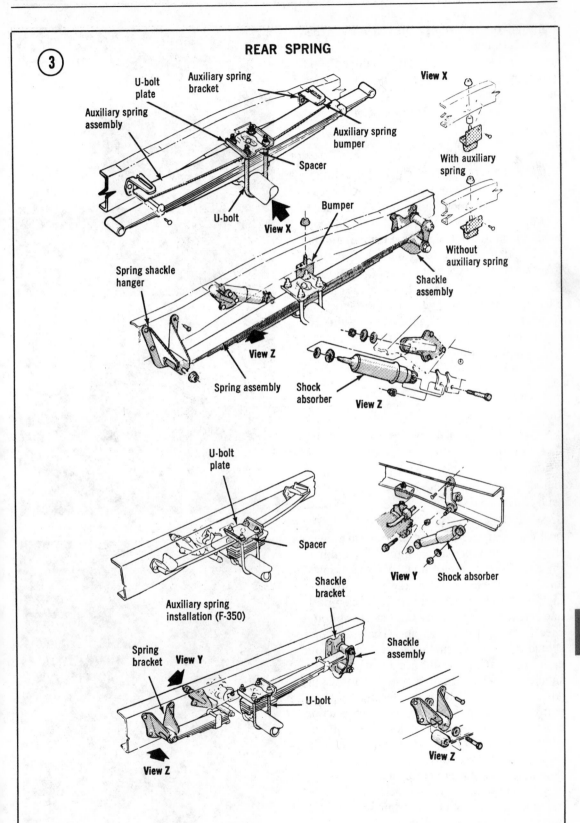

U-bolt plate

Auxiliary spring bracket

Auxiliary spring assembly

Auxiliary spring bumper

Spacer

U-bolt

View X

View X

With auxiliary spring

Without auxiliary spring

Bumper

Spring shackle hanger

Shackle assembly

View Z

Spring assembly

Shock absorber

View Z

U-bolt plate

Spacer

Auxiliary spring installation (F-350)

Shackle bracket

View Y

Shock absorber

Spring bracket

View Y

Shackle assembly

U-bolt

View Z

View Z

11

4. Install the new shock absorbers with new rubber bushings. Install the upper end of the shock absorber first, but do not tighten the nut until the bottom has been installed. Then tighten the upper nuts to 15-20 ft.-lb.; the lower nuts to 40-60 ft.-lb.

Removal/Installation (Rear)

1. Jack up the rear of the vehicle and support it on frame stands. Remove the rear wheels.

2. Unscrew the upper mounting nut (**Figure 5**) and remove the washer and bushing. Unscrew the nut from the bottom bolt (**Figure 6**) and tap the bolt out with a soft mallet. It may be necessary to drive the bolt out with a soft drift.

3. Install the new shock absorbers with new bushings. Install the upper end of the shock absorber first, but do not tighten the nut until the lower end has been lined up with the bracket and the bolt installed. Then tighten the upper nuts to 40-60 ft.-lb.; the lower nuts to 45-60 ft.-lb.

Inspection

1. Check the piston rod for bending, galling, and abrasion. If any are found, replace the rod.

2. Check for fluid leakage. A light film on the rod is normal, but severe leakage is reason for replacement.

3. With the shock absorber in the installed position, completely extend the rod, then invert the shock absorber and completely compress the rod. Do this several times to expel trapped air. Clamp the lower end of the shock absorber in a vise fitted with jaw protectors. Compress and extend the piston rod as fast as possible and check the damping action. The resistance should be smooth and uniform throughout each stroke, and the resistance during extension should be greater than during compression. Also, the action of both shock absorbers in a pair should feel the same. If the damping action is erratic, or resistance to quick extension and compression is very low, or if resistance is the same in both directions, the shock absorbers should be replaced, preferably as a set. The exception here would be for a shock absorber that has failed because of physical damage while the opposite unit performs satisfactorily.

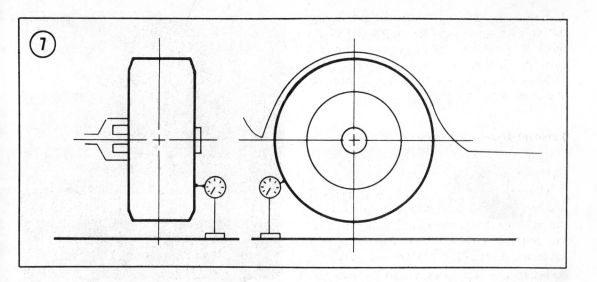

NOTE: *Comparing a used shock absorber that is believed to be good to a new shock absorber is not a valid comparison; the new shock absorber will seem to offer more resistance because of greater friction of the new rod seal.*

WHEEL ALIGNMENT

Wheel alignment should be checked periodically by a Ford dealer or an alignment specialist. Misalignment is usually indicated first by incorrect tire wear (see *Tire Wear Analysis*, in Chapter Two), or steering or handling difficulties.

NOTE: *Precision frame and wheel alignment equipment is required to accurately measure caster, camber, and toe-in. If steering, handling, and tire wear difficulties cannot be corrected by the checks and corrections presented below, the vehicle should be entrusted to a Ford dealer or an automotive alignment specialist.*

Inspection

Steering and handling problems which may appear to be caused by misalignment may very well be caused by other factors which are readily correctable without expensive equipment. The checks and inspections which follow should be carried out if steering, handling, or tire wear problems exist, and also before toe-in is adjusted.

1. Check all tire pressures and correct them if necessary, referring to **Table 1**, Chapter Three. It is essential that the pressures be checked when the tires are cold.

2. Raise the front of the vehicle and support it with frame stands. Check the end play of the wheel bearings by grasping the tire front and rear and attempting to move it in or out. If bearing end play can be felt, refer to the section on wheel bearing service in this chapter and inspect and adjust the bearings.

3. Refer to the section on steering service in this chapter and check the steering components for wear and all fasteners for looseness. Pay particular attention to the steering gear mounting bolts.

4. With the aid of a dial indicator (**Figure 7**), check radial and lateral runout of both front tires. Place the indicator against the tread first and slowly rotate the wheel. Then place the indicator against the outer sidewall of the tire and again rotate the wheel slowly. If either the radial or lateral runout is greater than 0.080 in., the tire should be deflated and rotated 90 degrees on the wheel.

NOTE: *It will probably be necessary to soap the wheel rim before the tire can be turned.*

Reinflate the tire to the correct pressure shown in **Table 1**, Chapter Three, and recheck the runout. If necessary, the tire should be rotated again if the runout is still excessive.

11

5. Examine the radius arms (**Figure 8**) for signs of damage that may have bent them. Check the condition of the bushings and the nuts and bolts at the radius arm connections (**Figure 9**). Replace any worn bushings as described later in this chapter and tighten the fasteners to the specified torques.

If steering, handling, and tire wear problems cannot be corrected by carrying out the above inspections and adjustments, the vehicle should be referred to a Ford dealer or alignment specialist for a precision inspection and for corrective work.

SPRINGS

Front Spring
Removal/Installation

Refer to **Figure 10** for the following procedure.

1. Raise front of vehicle and install jackstands for safety.

2. Disconnect shock absorber from lower bracket, then remove spring upper retainer attaching bolts from upper spring seat and remove retainer.

3. Remove nut holding spring lower retainer to lower seat and axle. Remove the retainer.

4. Carefully lower the axle and remove spring.

5. To install, position the spring and slowly raise the front axle.

6. Position the spring lower retainer over the stud and lower seat. Install the attaching nut and torque to 30-70 ft.-lb.

7. Position the upper retainer over the spring coil and against the spring upper seat. Install the attaching bolts and torque to 18-25 ft.-lb.

8. Connect lower shock absorber to lower bracket and torque the connecting nut to 40-60 ft.-lb. Install rebound jacket.

9. Remove jackstands and jack.

Rear Spring Removal/Installation

Refer to **Figure 3** for the following procedure.

1. Raise the rear of the vehicle until the weight is off the rear spring (tires still lightly touching the floor).

2. Remove all nuts from the spring U-bolts, then tap each U-bolt from its plate. (If so equipped, remove the auxiliary spring and spacer.)

3. Remove the spring retaining nut and bolt at the front of the spring; then remove the upper and lower shackle retaining nuts and bolts from the rear of the spring.

4. Remove the spring and shackle assembly from the rear shackle bracket.

5. If bushings are worn in the spring or shackle, replace them.

6. To install the spring, position it in the shackle, then install the upper shackle-to-spring bolt and nut (with bolt head facing outward).

7. Position the front end of the spring in the bracket and install the attaching nut and bolt.

8. Position the shackle in the rear bracket and install the attaching nut and bolt.

9. Position the spring on top of the axle (with the spring tie bolt centered in the hole provided in the seat). Install the auxiliary spring and spacer (if so equipped).

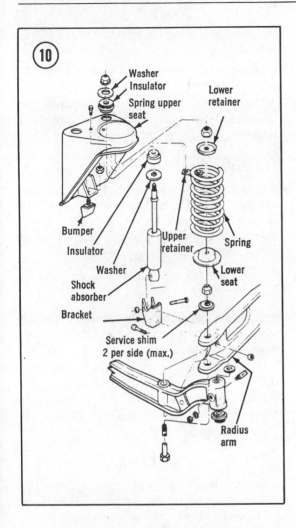

Washer
Insulator
Spring upper seat
Lower retainer
Bumper
Insulator
Upper retainer
Spring
Washer
Lower seat
Shock absorber
Bracket
Service shim 2 per side (max.)
Radius arm

10. Install the U-bolts, plate, and nuts.

11. Lower the vehicle to the floor. Tighten the U-bolt nuts to 85-115 ft.-lb. on F150 and F250 models, and to 110-160 ft.-lb. on F350 models.

12. Tighten the front hanger-to-spring bolt and nut to 75-105 ft.-lb. on F100-F150 models; and to 150-200 ft.-lb. on F250 and F350 models. Tighten the rear hanger-to-spring bolt and nut to 75-105 ft.-lb.

SPINDLE

Removal

Refer to **Figure 2** for the following procedure.

1. Raise the front end of the vehicle and install jackstands for safety.

2. Remove the wheel and tire.

3. Remove the caliper assembly from the rotor (support it out of the way with a piece of wire). Refer to Chapter Nine for procedure.

4. Remove dust cap, cotter pin, nut, retainer, washer, and outer bearing; then remove rotor from spindle.

5. Remove inner bearing cone and seal (discard old seal).

6. Remove the brake dust shield and the caliper anchor plate (if so equipped).

7. Disconnect steering linkage from integral spindle and spindle arm.

8. Remove nut and lockwasher from locking bolt, then remove locking bolt.

9. Remove upper and lower spindle pin plugs. Drive spindle pin out from top of axle and remove spindle and bearings. Drive out the spindle pin seal.

Installation

1. Clean up spindle pin bore in axle and inspect for nicks, burrs, etc. Coat the bore with grease.

2. Install a new spindle seal with metal backing facing the bushing. Carefully press into place (do not distort the casing).

3. Install a new thrust bearing with the lip flange facing down towards the lower bushing. Press until bearing is firmly seated against surface of the spindle.

4. Lightly coat the bushing surfaces with grease. Place spindle in position on the axle.

5. Install spindle pin with the "T" stamped on one end facing towards the top, and the notch in the pin aligned with the lock pin hole in the axle. Drive pin through the bushings and axle from the top until the spindle pin notch and axle lock pin hole are aligned.

6. Install lock pin with the threads pointing forward and the wedge groove facing the spindle pin notch. Drive the lock pin into place and mount the lockwasher and nut. Tighten the nut to 38-62 ft.-lb.

7. Install spindle pin plugs into threads at top and bottom of the spindle. Tighten plugs to 35-50 ft.-lb. Position the 45° zerk fittings to ensure access when the brake and wheel components are installed.

8. Lubricate the spindle pin and bushings through both fittings until grease seeps past up-

11

per seal at the top and from the thrust bearing slip joint at the bottom. (If grease does not appear, recheck the installation procedure to correct the problem. Lack of proper lubrication will result in rapid wear.)

9. Install the dust shield and caliper anchor plate (if so equipped).

10. Pack inner and outer bearing cone with bearing grease.

11. Install inner bearing cone and seal (refer to *Front Hub and Bearing Lubrication* section, this chapter). Install hub and rotor on spindle.

12. Install outer bearing cone, washer, and nut. Adjust bearing end play and install cotter pin and dust cap (refer to *Front Wheel Bearing Adjustment* section, this chapter).

13. Install caliper (refer to Chapter Nine for procedure).

14. Connect steering linkage to spindle. Torque the nut to 50-75 ft.-lb. and advance the nut as required for installation of the cotter pin.

15. Install wheel and tire, and remove jackstands.

16. Lower vehicle to ground.

17. Have front end alignment checked by a competent alignment shop or your Ford dealer.

RADIUS ARMS

Handling and steering problems can arise from worn or deteriorated bushings and insulator pads at the radius arm connections. If looseness is suspected, remove the cotter keys from the rear of the arms and tighten the nuts to 80-120 ft.-lb and install new cotter keys. If tightening does not correct the looseness, the bushings may require replacement. This work should be entrusted to a dealer or suspension specialist.

STABILIZER BAR

The optional front stabilizer bar is situated forward of the front axle and is attached to the I-beam through a link assembly that is dampened by an insulator sandwich where it attaches to the I-beam link assembly. Refer to **Figure 11**.

Removal

1. Disconnect each end of the stabilizer bar

from the link assembly attached to the I-beam bracket.

2. Disconnect frame side rail retaining bolts and remove the stabilizer bar.

3. Disconnect stabilizer link assembly by loosening right and left locknuts from the I-beam brackets.

Installation

1. Connect each stabilizer link to the I-beam brackets by sliding the bolt through the I-beam bracket hole toward the inside of the side rail. Install the lockwasher and nut, and torque the nut to 40-60 ft.-lb.

> NOTE: *The link must be installed with the bend facing forward.*

2. Connect stabilizer bar to the frame side rails with 2 retainers on the bottom of the side rails. Tighten the 4 through-bolts to 15-25 ft.-lb.

3. Connect stabilizer bar left and right ends to the left and right link assemblies, respectively. Be sure that the washers and 2 insulators are properly positioned (refer to **Figure 11**). Tighten the nuts to 15-25 ft.-lb.

STEERING

Service to the steering gear is limited to checking and correcting the lubricant level and correcting play in the steering wheel and column (refer to Chapter Three, *Steering* section).

WHEEL BEARING ADJUSTMENT

The front wheel bearings are adjustable and can be cleaned and repacked with grease relatively easily.

The rear wheel bearings are sealed and receive their lubrication from the oil carried in the rear differential. There is no adjustment required for the rear bearings and their expected service life is quite long. A hydraulic press is required in order to remove and install the bearings, and it is recommended that this be referred to a Ford dealer or an automotive machine shop.

Front Wheel Bearings

Check the front bearing adjustment with the front of the vehicle raised and supported by

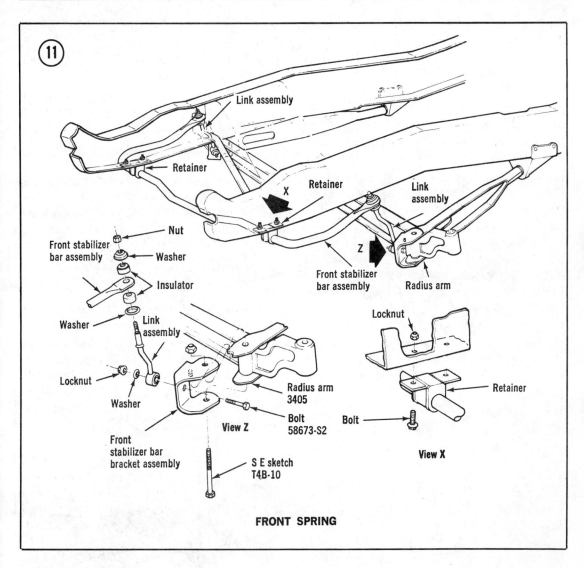

FRONT SPRING

jackstands. Grasp the wheel, front and rear, and try to move it in and out. If any movement is felt, the bearings should be adjusted.

1. Rotate the wheel to ensure that the brake is not dragging. If it is, adjust the brakes. Refer to Chapter Nine, and to **Figure 12** (for drum brakes).

2. Refer to **Figure 13** and remove the grease cap. Wipe the grease from the end of the axle. Remove the cotter pin and discard it. Remove the nut lock.

3. Tighten the adjusting nut to 17-25 ft.-lb. and, at the same time, rotate the wheel. This will force excess grease out from between the bearings and the cups so that the clearance can be accurately set.

4. Install the nut lock so that it is against the nut. Align the hole in the axle with the nearest notch in the nut lock. Then, back off the adjuster nut and the nut lock 2 notches and install a new cotter pin. *Do not bend the ends of the pin over just yet.*

5. Rotate the wheel to ensure that it turns smoothly. Also check to see that it has no appreciable end play. If the wheel is still loose, or if its rotation is rough or noisy, the bearings and cups should be checked for dirt, wear, and damage as described below. When the condition and adjustment of the hub is correct, bend the ends of the cotter pin over to lock it in place and install the grease cap.

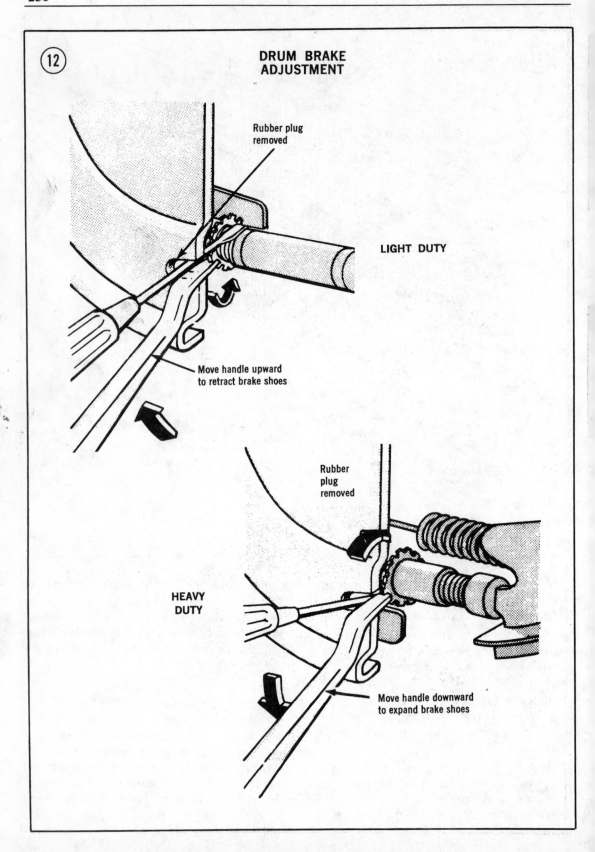

⑫ DRUM BRAKE
    ADJUSTMENT

Rubber plug
removed

LIGHT DUTY

Move handle upward
to retract brake shoes

Rubber
plug
removed

HEAVY
DUTY

Move handle downward
to expand brake shoes

(13)

FRONT HUB AND BEARINGS

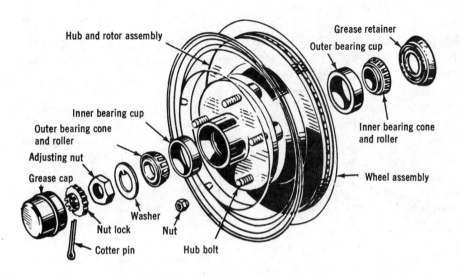

Hub and rotor assembly

Grease retainer

Outer bearing cup

Inner bearing cup

Outer bearing cone and roller

Adjusting nut

Inner bearing cone and roller

Grease cap

Wheel assembly

Washer

Nut lock

Nut

Cotter pin

Hub bolt

DISC BRAKE

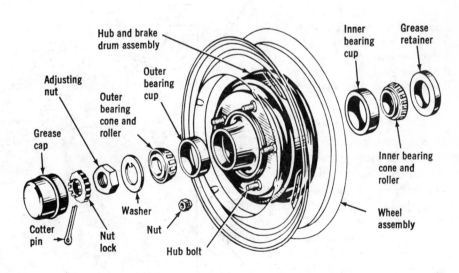

Hub and brake drum assembly

Inner bearing cup

Grease retainer

Adjusting nut

Outer bearing cup

Outer bearing cone and roller

Grease cap

Inner bearing cone and roller

Cotter pin

Nut lock

Washer

Nut

Wheel assembly

Hub bolt

DRUM BRAKE

11

FRONT HUB AND
BEARING LUBRICATION

The front hubs should be serviced at the intervals discussed earlier.

1. Raise the front of the vehicle and support it on jackstands.

2. Disassemble the hubs as described under bearing adjustment above. Continue disassembly by unscrewing the bearing adjusting nut.

3. Pull out on the wheel and remove the wheel, brake drum, and hub as an assembly. This will also remove the outer bearing assembly from the axle spindle.

> NOTE: *For trucks equipped with front disc brakes, refer to Chapter Nine and remove the caliper. Be sure that it is suspended and not allowed to hang by the brake line.*

4. Drive the inner bearing cup and the bearing out of the hub using either a bearing driver **(Figure 14)** or a soft drift, tapping progressively around the inner edge of the bearing assembly.

5. Thoroughly clean the bearings and the inside of the hub with solvent and blow them dry with compressed air.

WARNING
Do not spin the bearings with the air jet; it is capable of rotating the bearings at speeds far in excess of those for which they were designed. The bearing could disintegrate, causing damage and injury.

Check the bearing rollers and the cups for signs of wear and damage and replace them as a set if they are less than satisfactory. If the bearings are to be replaced, carefully drive the outer cups out of the hub using a soft drift and tapping evenly around the edges of the cups. Seat the new cups squarely in the hub and carefully tap them into place with the drift, evenly around the circumference of each cup.

6. Clean the brake assembly as much as possible, using a stiff, *dry* brush; do not use any solvents to clean any of the brake components. In particular, make sure no solvents come in contact with the brake lining material. Solvent will render the lining unserviceable, requiring replacement.

> NOTE: *This is a good opportunity to check the serviceability of the brake linings. Refer to Chapter Nine and inspect and measure the lining as described.*

7. When the brake has been cleaned and all dirt and foreign matter removed, carefully clean the spindle with solvent, taking care not to get any on the brake.

8. Pack the inside of the hub with a multipurpose grease until it is level with the inside diameter of the outer bearing cups **(Figure 15)**. Thoroughly pack the bearing assemblies with grease, working it in carefully by hand, and apply a film of grease to the inner cone. Install the inner bearing assembly into the outer cup. Set a new seal squarely into the hub and carefully tap it into place evenly around the circumference.

9. Install the wheel, keeping the hub centered around the spindle to prevent damage to the spindle threads and the seal. Install the outer bearing assembly and screw on the bearing adjusting nut. Refer to the procedure for bearing adjustment and adjust the end play of the hub and complete the reassembly. Repeat the above procedure for the opposite wheel.

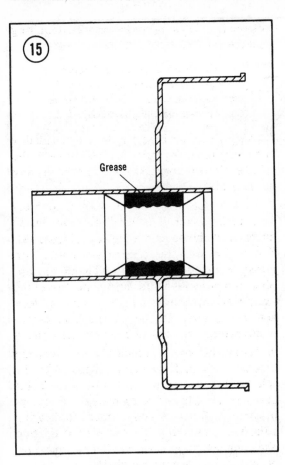

Grease

DRIVE SHAFT ASSEMBLY

The drive shaft assembly consists of universal joints (U-joints), connecting shaft(s), attaching flanges, and slip yokes. (The number of shafts and U-joints used depends on the vehicle type.) Refer to **Figure 16** for the one-piece drive shaft slip-yoke design, and to **Figure 17** for the two-piece design which attaches to the transmission with U-bolts.

Vehicles equipped with one-piece, slip-yoke drive shafts use a U-joint and splined slip yoke at the transmission end of the shaft. Alignment is maintained by a bushing in the transmission rear extension. Fore and aft movement of the drive shaft is permitted by the slip yoke. An oil seal prevents leakage and protects the slip yoke from foreign matter. An additional U-joint is located at the rear of the drive shaft where the shaft connects to a companion flange. It is held in place by U-bolts or straps.

Vehicles equipped with two-piece drive shaft assemblies incorporate a "necked down" coupling shaft stub with a "blindspline" feature which ensures positive phasing action. A U-joint assembly is incorporated on the fixed yoke system (refer to **Figure 17**) between the center bearing assembly and the slip yoke.

11

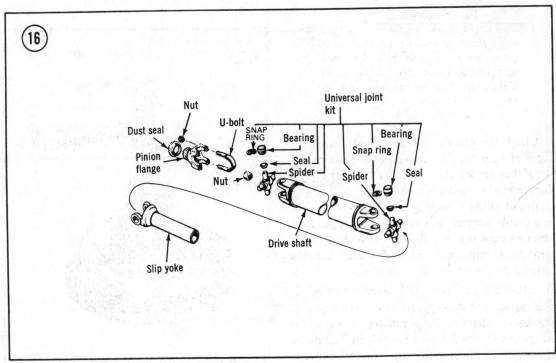

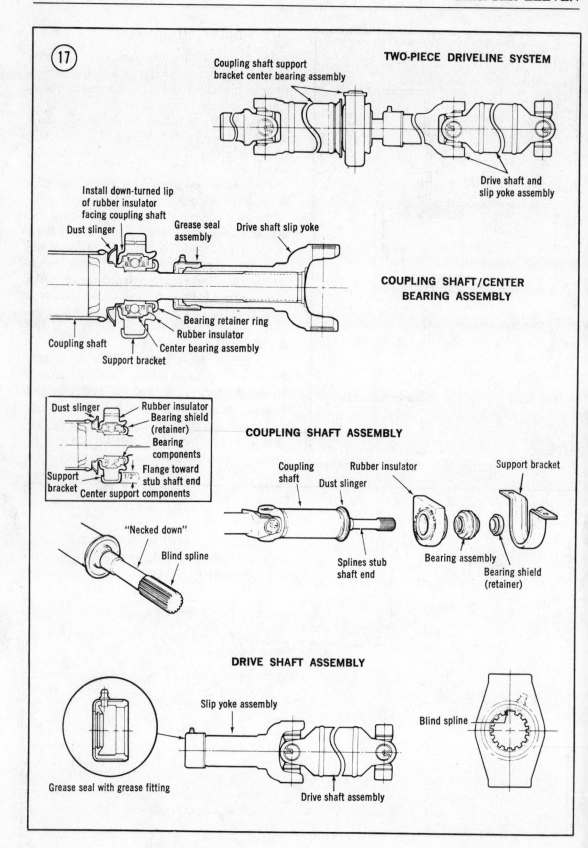

17

Coupling shaft support
bracket center bearing assembly

TWO-PIECE DRIVELINE SYSTEM

Drive shaft and
slip yoke assembly

Install down-turned lip
of rubber insulator
facing coupling shaft

Dust slinger

Grease seal
assembly

Drive shaft slip yoke

COUPLING SHAFT/CENTER
BEARING ASSEMBLY

Bearing retainer ring

Rubber insulator

Coupling shaft

Center bearing assembly

Support bracket

Dust slinger   Rubber insulator
                    Bearing shield
                    (retainer)
                    Bearing
                    components

Support   Flange toward
bracket   stub shaft end
        Center support components
        1/2"

COUPLING SHAFT ASSEMBLY

Coupling
shaft   Rubber insulator

Dust slinger

Support bracket

Splines stub
shaft end

Bearing assembly

Bearing shield
(retainer)

"Necked down"

Blind spline

DRIVE SHAFT ASSEMBLY

Slip yoke assembly

Blind spline

Grease seal with grease fitting

Drive shaft assembly

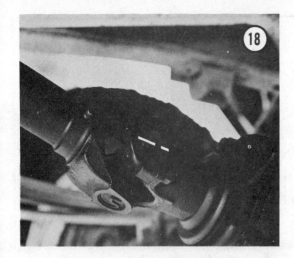

Vehicles equipped with two-piece drive shaft assemblies use center support bearings that are prelubricated and sealed for the life of the bearing.

All U-joints are equipped with lifetime-lubricated needle bearings, and are retained on the U-joint spiders with snap rings or U-bolts.

Drive Shaft Removal/Installation (One-Piece Models)

Refer to **Figure 16** for the following procedure.

1. If yellow alignment marks are not visible, mark both halves of the yoke at the axle with light-colored chalk or crayon so the phasing of the drive shaft and differential will be the same when the drive shaft is reconnected (**Figure 18**).

2. Unscrew the 4 U-bolt nuts at the axle end of the drive shaft (**Figure 19**) and carefully tap the U-bolts back and disconnect the end of the shaft. Tape the bearing caps in place so they will not fall off.

3. Pull the drive shaft toward the rear of the vehicle until the slip yoke clears the transmission extension housing and seal.

4. If the U-joint needs attention, perform this procedure at this time (refer to *U-Joint Replacement* section, following).

5. To install the drive shaft, clean the yoke, bearing caps, and U-bolts. Line up the end of the shaft with the differential yoke, making sure that the marks are on the same side.

6. Tap the U-bolts into place and screw on the nuts and tighten them in a crisscross pattern to 8-15 ft.-lb.

Drive Shaft Removal/Installation (Two-Piece Models)

Refer to **Figure 17** for the following procedure.

1. Disconnect the drive shaft from the rear axle flange.

2. Disconnect the drive shaft slip yoke from the coupling shaft yoke.

3. Tape the bearing caps in place so they will not fall off.

4. Remove the 2 center bearing support brackets (coupling shaft), then remove the coupling shaft assembly from the transmission extension.

5. Pull the slip yoke off the drive shaft.

6. Remove the dust cap, cork seal, and spacers from the slip yoke.

7. If the U-joint needs attention, perform this procedure at this time (refer to *U-Joint Replacement* section, following).

8. To install the drive shaft, clean the drive shaft splines with a wire brush and solvent; remove hardened grease deposits, dirt, or rust; clean all dirt from the slip yoke splines and slip yoke assembly; wash all parts except the sealed center bearing and rubber insulator in cleaning fluid.

11

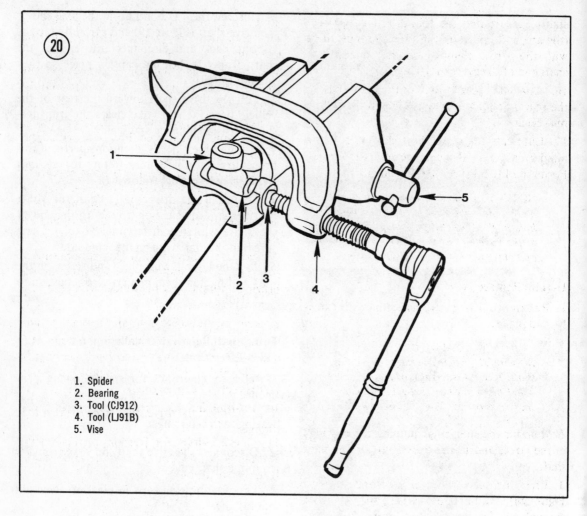

1. Spider
2. Bearing
3. Tool (CJ912)
4. Tool (LJ91B)
5. Vise

CAUTION
Do not immerse the sealed bearing in cleaning fluid. Simply wipe the bearing and rubber insulator with a cloth dampened with cleaning fluid.

NOTE: *Replace the slip yoke cork seal if necessary.*

9. Rotate the inner center support bearing race while holding the outer race. If any wear or roughness is evident, replace the bearing.

10. Inspect the rubber insulator for cracking, deterioration, or hardening. Replace if suspect.

11. To install the drive shaft assembly, lubricate the coupling shaft yoke splines, then install the front yoke of the coupling shaft assembly on the transmission output shaft.

CAUTION
Do not allow the slip yoke assembly to bottom on the output shaft with excessive force.

12. Attach the center bearing support bracket to the frame crossmember with the center supporting attaching bolts. Torque to 40-50 ft.-lb.

13. Slip the dust cap, cork seal, and spacers onto the splined shaft of the drive shaft. Coat the entire splined stub shaft end of the drive shaft with grease prior to assembling the drive shaft and slip yoke. Be sure to lubricate the female splines of the slip yoke with grease (use a clean, long-handle brush).

14. Assemble the drive shaft slip yoke to the coupling shaft. Tighten the U-bolt securely.

15. Slip the front (splined) end of the drive shaft into the rear slip yoke on the coupling

shaft. Be sure that the splines are in "phase" (the arrow stamped on the slip yoke must align with the arrow stamped on the splined stub shaft end of the drive shaft).

16. Attach the rear U-joint of the drive shaft to the rear axle pinion flange. Tighten the U-bolt nuts securely.

17. Lubricate the drive shaft slip yoke with a hand grease gun, through the zerk fitting with Ford long-life lubricant or equivalent.

> NOTE: *To ensure thorough lubrication of the slip yoke splines, plug the vent hole in the "welch" type plug situated at the yoke-end of the slip yoke, while applying grease through the zerk fitting.*

U-Joint Replacement

1. Remove the drive shaft as outlined previously, and place it in a vise.

> CAUTION
> *Be careful not to damage the drive shaft. Wrap it with rags, or place a soft wood block on both sides of the drive shaft to protect it from the vise jaws.*

2. Remove the snap rings holding the bearings in the yoke, and in the drive shaft or coupling shaft.

3. Press the bearing out of the yoke (refer to **Figure 20**) with Ford tools CJ912 and CJ91B or equivalent. If bearing cannot be pressed completely out of the flange, remove it with Vise Grips or channel lock pliers. Mark the yoke and drive shaft with a crayon or piece of chalk to be sure that they are aligned properly during reassembly.

4. Reposition the tool so it presses on the spider in order to remove the bearing from the opposite side of the flange.

5. Remove flange from spider, then remove bearings and spider from drive shaft or coupling in same manner.

6. To install, position a new bearing in place in the yoke at rear of drive shaft, then position the spider in the rear yoke and press the bearing ¼ in. below the surface. Remove the tool and install a new snap ring.

7. Start a new bearing into the opposite side of the yoke, then install the tool and press on the bearing until the opposite bearing comes in contact with the snap ring.

8. Remove the tool and install a new snap ring.

9. Reposition the drive shaft or coupling shaft and install the new spider and 2 new bearings in the front yoke (follow the same procedure used on the rear yoke, preceding).

10. Position the spider flange and install 2 new bearings and snap rings.

11. Check U-joint for freedom of movement. If it binds, tap the ears of the drive shaft sharply to relieve the bind.

> CAUTION
> *Do not install the drive shaft if the U-joints bind. Disassemble it to find out what is causing the binding.*

11

SUPPLEMENT

1980 AND LATER SERVICE INFORMATION

This supplement contains basic service and maintenance information for 1980 and later Ford F-series light trucks. This information supplements the procedures in the main body (Chapters One through Eleven) of the book, referred to in this supplement as the "basic book."

The chapter headings and titles in this supplement correspond to those in the basic book. If a chapter is not included in the supplement, there are no changes affecting 1980 and later models. Use the information given for 1979 models. If your vehicle is covered by this supplement, carefully read the supplement and then read the appropriate chapters in the basic book before beginning any work.

CHAPTER THREE

LUBRICATION AND MAINTENANCE

GASOLINE ENGINE

Engine Oil and Filter Change

Oil labeled SF should be used with 1980 and later trucks. It can also be used instead of SE oil with 1979 and earlier models.

The oil dipstick on all 1983 and later F-series engines has been recalibrated to eliminate the possibility of incorrectly reading the dipstick due to varying vehicle ride angles. An "O" mark has been added to the dipstick (**Figure 1**) to indicate the *maximum* oil fill limit. Any oil level between the "O" limit and the upper "SAFE" limit should be considered acceptable. If the oil level is above the "O" limit, drain the oil until the level is at or slightly below the "O" limit.

Axle Oil Level

A new integral-carrier rear axle with an 8.8 in. ring gear is used with 1983 and later F-100, 150 and 250 light trucks. The Traction-Lok differential used with this axle contains slip-limiting clutches with a new composition friction facing bonded to the steel plates. The use of this new material eliminates the need for a 7,500 mile lubrication change. The lubricant to be used with this differential is changed from EOAZ-19580-D to EOAZ-19580-A (Ford specification ESP-M2C154-A) plus 4 ounces of C8AZ-19B546-A (Ford specification EST-M2C118-A) friction modifier.

Hydraulic Clutch Fluid Level

Check the hydraulic clutch fluid level whenever the brake fluid level is check. Clean the clutch reservoir. The fluid level should be between the 2 marks embossed on the reservoir. If it is not, remove the reservoir cap and top up with DOT 3 brake fluid from an unopened container.

Power Steering Fluid

Power steering fluid specification has been changed to Type F automatic transmission fluid with 1981 and later models.

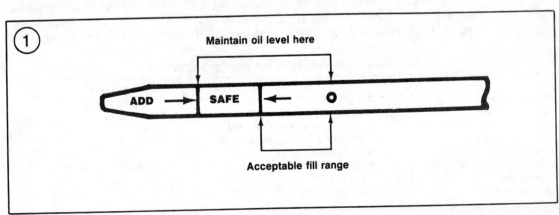

Maintain oil level here

Acceptable fill range

12

LUBRICATION, MAINTENANCE AND TUNE-UP

Power Steering Fluid Leaks (1982-1985)

A new center vent power steering pump dipstick/cap assembly (part No. E6DZ-3A006-A) with additional baffling is available to combat the problem of power steering fluid leakage caused by fluid spilling past the dipstick cap assembly on 1982-1985 models. When installing the new dipstick/cap, adjust the amount of Type F ATF in system so that the fluid level falls between the "COLD FULL" and "ADD" marks on the new dipstick.

Transmission Oil

Transmission oil grades and capacities for the new transmissions offered in 1980 and later models are listed in **Table 1**.

Ford now recommends the use of Type CJ or DEXRON II, Series D automatic transmission fluid in all C6 automatic transmissions. This supersedes the previous recommendations to use Type F fluid. If you are currently using Type F ATF in your C6 automatic transmission, replace it with Type CJ or DEXRON II, Series D at the next drain and fill interval.

Manifold Torque

Intake and exhaust manifold fastener torque specifications are in **Table 2**.

DIESEL ENGINE

A complete maintenance schedule for trucks with the 6.9 liter diesel engine is provided in **Table 3**. The schedule is intended only as a guide. If your vehicle is subjected to conditions of severe service such as heavy dust, extensive idling, continuous short trips or towing trailers, more frequent servicing will be required.

Many services shown in the schedule are identical to those performed on F-series trucks with gasoline engines. Refer to Chapter Three of the basic book. Services which differ because of the diesel engine are detailed in this supplement.

Engine Oil and Filter Change

Engine oil should be selected to meet the demands of the temperatures and driving conditions anticipated. Ford Motor Co. recommends the use of oil with the letter designation SF/CD or SF/CC for all F-series diesel engines. Engine oils labeled SE or CC only do not provide the necessary lubrication qualities required by a diesel engine.

Under normal driving conditions, diesel engine oil and oil filter should be changed every 5,000 miles or 6 months. If your F-series truck is driven under the severe service conditions listed in the introductory paragraphs, change the engine oil every 2,500 miles and the oil filter every 5,000 miles. For severe service operation, Ford specifies the use of SF/CD oil in either SAE 30 or SAE 15W-40 weight.

The procedure for changing the oil in a diesel engine is identical to that for gasoline engines. The oil filter is a disposable canister type (Motorcraft FL-784 or equivalent) and is located in a position similar to the gasoline engine oil filter. The diesel engine crankcase capacity is 10 quarts with a filter change.

Table 1 TRANSMISSION OIL AND CAPACITY

Transmission	Oil grade	Approximate refill capacity
SROD 4-speed manual	SAE 80W transmission lubricant	4.5 pt.
TOD 4-speed manual	SAE 80W transmission lubricant	4.5 pt.
T-19B 4-speed manual	SAE 50W engine oil	7.0 pt.
Automatic overdrive (AOD)	Dexron II ATF	24.0 pt.
C5 automatic	Type H ATF	24.0 pt.
C6 automatic	Dexron II ATF	23.5 pt.

Table 2 INTAKE AND EXHAUST MANIFOLD FASTENER TORQUE (1980-ON)

Engine	Fastener	Ft.-Ib.
232 cid	Exhaust manifold to cylinder head	15-22
232 cid	Intake manifold to cylinder head	18.4
300 cid	Exhaust manifold to cylinder head	28-33
300 cid	Intake manifold to cylinder head	22-32
255/302/351W	Exhaust manifold to cylinder head	18-24
255/302/351W	Intake manifold to cylinder head	23-25
351M/400	Exhaust manifold to cylinder head	18-24
351M/400	Intake manifold to cylinder head 3/8 in.	22-32
	Intake manifold to cylinder head 5/16 in.	19-25
460 cid	Exhaust manifold to cylinder head	28-33
460 cid	Intake manifold to cylinder head	22-32

Table 3 DIESEL MAINTENANCE SCHEDULE

At 5,000 miles or 6 months	• Change engine oil and filter[1] • Check/adjust idle speed • Check throttle operation/idle return • Drain fuel/water separator • Lubricate U-joints and slip yoke • Lubricate steering linkage • Lubricate front axle spindle • Check/adjust wheel lug nut torque
At 15,000 miles or 6 months	• Check/adjust drive belts • Replace fuel filter • Inspect fan/fan shroud[2]
Every 12 months	• Check cooling system components • Check coolant condition
At 30,000 miles or 6 months	• Replace air cleaner element • Inspect exhaust system • Check air induction system • Check clutch master cylinder reservoir fluid level • Inspect disc brakes • Inspect drum brakes • Repack/adjust front wheel bearings

1. **SEVERE SERVICE OPERATION**
   If the vehicle is used under any of the conditions listed below, change the engine oil and filter every 2,500 miles or 3 months and automatic transmission fluid at 20,000 mile intervals.
   a. Extended periods of high-speed operation (fully loaded vehicle, maximum GVWR).
   b. Operation under severe dust conditions.
   c. Trailer towing.
   d. Extensive idling.
2. F-350 over 10,000 lbs. GVWR only.

12

CHAPTER FOUR

TUNE-UP

SPARK PLUGS

All 1984 and later engines equipped with a TFI-IV ignition system (see Chapter Seven section of this supplement) use standard thread, tapered seat spark plugs. The 302 cid and 351 cid V8 engines use a 14 mm plug; the 300 cid inline-6 engine uses an 18 mm plug. See the VECI decal in the engine compartment for spark plug type and gap.

IGNITION COIL

A high voltage arc in the E-core ignition coil used with 1983 and later models can result in stumbles, stalls, poor performance, erratic electronic clock operation or ignition noise in the radio.

An open or high resistance in the coil secondary winding will cause the arc, which generates a high frequency noise in the electrical system and can disrupt the EEC-IV system operation.

To check for this problem:

1. Make sure the ignition switch is OFF.
2. Disconnect the primary and secondary leads at the E-core coil.
3. Measure the resistance between the coil primary + terminal (red lead) and the high voltage secondary terminal with an ohmmeter. Replace the coil if resistance exceeds 14,000 ohms.
4. Reconnect the secondary and primary leads at the coil.

DIESEL ENGINE TUNE-UP

Diesel engines do not require a tune-up in the same sense as gasoline engines, primarily because the diesel engine uses compression for ignition instead of an electrical ignition system. Fewer maintenance tasks are thus required on a diesel engine, but the required tasks are just as important, if not more so, as

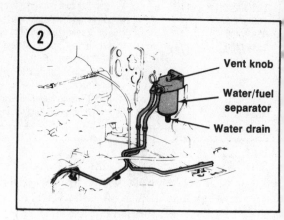

the more extensive gasoline engine maintenance. The required tasks and the intervals at which they should be performed are given in **Table 3**.

Owner maintenance on diesel engines should be limited to the tasks described in **Table 3**. Tampering by an unskilled mechanic, especially with the injection system, can lead to serious (and expensive) damage.

Fuel Filter Replacement

The canister-type fuel filter screws into an adapter unit bracket-mounted on the top front of the engine. The fuel filter element should be replaced every 15,000 miles (or more frequently if clogged) with a new Motorcraft FD-811 filter (or equivalent).

1. Disconnect the negative battery cable from both batteries.
2. Using a suitable filter wrench, turn the filter element counterclockwise and remove. Be careful not to spill fuel from the filter element.
3. Wipe the gasket sealing surface on the adapter clean with a paper towel.
4. Apply a thin film of clean diesel fuel to the sealing gasket on the new filter.

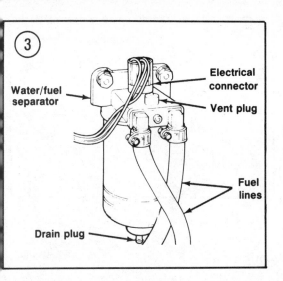

5. Thread the filter element into the main body and turn clockwise until the sealing gasket just contacts the main body sealing surface. Tighten the filter element another 1/2 to 3/4 turn *by hand.*

6. Clean any spilled fuel from the top of the engine.

7. Reconnect the negative battery cables to each battery.

8. Start the engine and check for leaks.

Water/Fuel Separator

A water/fuel separator is located inside the engine compartment at the left-hand side (**Figure 2**). When the water level in the separator reaches a specified point (1/3 full), an indicator lamp on the instrument panel lights to warn the driver that the separator should be drained. The water/fuel separator should be serviced every 5,000 miles or whenever the "WATER IN FUEL" lamp remains on with the engine running.

The 1983 water/fuel separator has vent and drain plugs (**Figure 3**). The 1984 unit uses a pull ring instead of the drain plug. The pull ring is located on top of the unit in place of the 1983 vent plug.

NOTE
The engine must be off before draining the separator to prevent air from entering the fuel system.

1. Place a suitable container under the drain plug hose at the bottom of the unit.

2A. 1983 models—Unscrew the vent plug 2 1/2-3 turns. Unscrew the drain plug 1 1/2-2 turns and let the water drain into the container. Close the drain plug finger-tight, then turn it an extra 1/4 turn.

2B. 1984 models—Grasp the pull ring and pull upwards as far as possible. Hold the pull ring in this position for 15 seconds or until the water has drained completely, then release the ring.

3. Remove the container of water from the engine compartment and discard the contents.

4. Start the engine. The "WATER IN FUEL" indicator lamp should not be lit. If it remains on, have a dealer check and repair the fuel system as appropriate.

Idle Speed Adjustment

NOTE
A special photoelectric tachometer must be used on the 6.9 liter diesel engine. Most tachometers for gasoline engines operate from the electrical ignition system impulses and will not work on diesel engines.

Idle speed should be adjusted at the first 5,000 miles or 12 months, then at every 10,000 miles thereafter. Adjust idle speed with the engine at normal operating temperature and the transmission in NEUTRAL (manual) or DRIVE (automatic).

1. Set the parking brake. Block the rear wheels.

2. Place the transmission selector lever in NEUTRAL or DRIVE as required.

3. Connect the tachometer according to the manufacturer's instructions.

4. Start the engine and let it warm to normal operating temperature (upper radiator hose hot).

NOTE
*The throttle lever (**Figure 4**) has 2 adjusting screws. The spring-loaded screw at the rear is the low idle speed screw; the front screw is a full throttle positioner and has a locknut to maintain its factory setting. **Do not** adjust the front screw.*

5. Turn the low idle speed adjusting screw on the injection pump at the rear of the throttle

lever (**Figure 4**) to obtain an engine speed of 750 rpm.

6. Open the throttle until the solenoid plunger is fully extended. The tachometer should read 950 rpm. If not, adjust the solenoid mounting bracket screw until an engine speed of 950 rpm is obtained with the plunger fully extended against the throttle lever.

7. Shut the engine off and disconnect the tachometer.

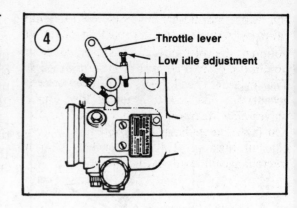

CHAPTER FIVE

ENGINE

ENGINE

The 255 cid and 351W cid V-8 engines available in some 1980 and later Ford F-series trucks are similar to the 302 cid V-8 engine described in the basic book and can be serviced using the procedures given for the 302. Engine specifications for the 255 cid and 351W cid engines appear in **Table 4** of this supplement. Torque specifications are the same as those given for the 302 cid engines with the exception of the 351W engine's connecting rods, which are tightened to 40-45 ft.-lb; its main bearings, which are tightened to 95-105 ft.-lb; and its cylinder head bolts, which are tightened in 3 stages: first to 85, then to 95, and finally to 105-112 ft.-lb.

The 460 cid V8 replaces the 400 cid as an engine option on 1983-on F-series trucks. All service procedures, specifications and most torque values are the same as those provided in Chapter Five of the basic book. Torque values which have changed for 1983-on usage are provided in **Table 5**.

300 CID INLINE-6 ENGINE

Rocker Arms

The rocker arms on 1985 and later 300 cid engines are a stamped steel design using powdered metal cylindrical fulcrums. Bolts are used instead of stud nuts to retain the rocker arms to the cylinder head and shold be tightened to 17-23 ft.-lb.

The cylinder head on such models has been modified to accept the new rocker arms. The coolant flow passage in the head has been enlarged to promote better heater performance. Cylinder heads are not interchangeable with earlier engines.

Front Crankshaft Seal

A slightly revised seal similar to that used on the 302 cid V8 is installed on 1986 engines. Use of this seal eliminates the need to remove the front cover when seal replacement is required.

Seal remover part No. T70P-68070-8 and installer part No. T70P-68070-A are required to properly replace the front seal.

1987 Engine Modifications

Several modifications have been made to the 1987 300 cid engine. A high-swirl combustion chamber uses shrouded intake valves to increase the swirling action of the air-fuel mixture as it enters the cylinder. Since the valve shrouding increased compression ratio by reducing the combustion chamber volume, the piston dish was deepened to obtain the desired compression ratio of 8.8:1. The cylinder head has been reworked to accept the fuel injection manifolds. Intake valves also incorporate a 30° chamfer on the rear face. These changes promote faster, more efficient burning. The cylinder head is not interchangeable with earlier models.

Intake/Exhaust Manifolds

A 2-piece aluminum intake manifold with tuned runners and dual plenums supports the EFI system added to the 300 cid engine for 1987. See Chapter Six of this supplement for details on the injection system.

Two cast iron exhaust manifolds are used. One services the front three cylinders; the other services the three rear cylinders.

Removal/Installation

1. Disconnect the negative battery cable.
2. Relieve fuel system pressure as described in Chapter Six of this supplement.
3. Label and disconnect the following vacuum lines:
   a. EGR valve.
   b. Thermactor air bypass valve.
   c. SHED evaporative emissions lines at the throttle body.
   d. Fuel pressure regulator.
   e. Upper intake manifold vacuum tree.
4. Unplug the electrical connectors at the:
   a. EVP sensor on the EGR valve.
   b. Throttle position sensor on throttle body.
   c. Air bypass valve.
5. Disconnect the PCV hose at the fitting on the underside of the upper intake manifold.
6. Remove the shield covering the throttle linkage. Disconnect the throttle cable (and speed control cable, if so equipped) at the throttle body. Remove the retracting spring and cable bracket from the cylinder head. Position cable and bracket assembly out of the way.
7. Disconnect the air inlet lines at the throttle body.

8. Remove the 2 nuts holding the Thermactor tube assembly at the lower intake manifold.
9. Remove the nut holding the bypass valve bracket to the lower intake manifold.
10. Remove the spring clips holding the injector heat shield to the lower intake and exhaust manifolds. Remove the shield.
11. Remove the seven studs holding the upper intake manifold and throttle body assembly to the lower intake manifold. Remove the upper intake manifold support bracket. Remove the upper intake manifold/throttle body. Remove and discard the gasket.
12. Reposition the vacuum harness away from the lower intake manifold and remove the injector cooling manifold from the lifting eye attachment.
13. Disconnect the fuel inlet and return line quick-disconnect fittings at the fuel rail. See Chapter Six of this supplement. Work carefully to prevent bending the fuel lines.
14. Remove the 16 bolts holding the lower intake manifold to the cylinder head (some of these bolts also retain the exhaust manifolds). Remove the lower intake manifold. Remove and discard the gasket.
15. If exhaust manifolds are to be removed, remove the remaining bolts holding them to the cylinder head. Remove the 2 exhaust manifolds.
16. Installation is the reverse of removal, plus the following:
    a. Tighten all manifold attaching bolts to 22-32 ft.-lb. (29.8-43.8 N•m) working from the center to the end.
    b. Tighten the upper intake manifold bolts to 12-18 ft.-lb. (16-24.4 N•m).
    c. Tighten the EGR tube fittings to 25-35 ft.-lb. (33-47 N•m).

232 CID V6 ENGINE

The 232 cid V6 engine available in some 1982-1983 Ford F-100 trucks is similar to the V8 engines in construction and components. It can be serviced using the procedures provided for V8 models with the exceptions noted below.

12

Engine specifications and tightening torques are provided in **Table 6** and **Table 7**. See **Figure 5** and **Figure 6** for internal and external engine construction. See **Figure 7** for ignition wire routing.

Cylinder Head

The 232 cid V6 engine uses aluminum cylinder heads and requires the use of a special coolant containing a corrosion inhibitor to avoid radiator damage. Prestone II is one of the recommended coolants which meets Ford specification ESE-M97B43-A.

Spark plugs must not be removed when the engine is hot or the plug hole threads in the cylinder head may be stripped by plug removal. If plug hole threads are damaged or stripped, they can be repaired by a Ford dealer using a Tapersert kit.

The procedure involves cutting new threads in the spark plug hole. After the hole is rethreaded, a sleeve with inside and outside threads is installed in the hole. The outside of the sleeve threads into the reworked hole in the cylinder head. The inside of the sleeve provides new threads to accept the spark plug. If this service is necessary, remove the cylinder head and take it to a Ford dealer.

Cylinder Head Torque

The 232 cid V6 uses stretch-type cylinder head bolts. Once these bolts have been torqued to specification, they cannot be reused. Torquing the bolts stretches them and they cannot hold the specified torque if reused.

NOTE
*Power or air-driven tools should **not** be used for removing or installing cylinder head bolts.*

Follow the pattern shown in **Figure 8** and tighten the cylinder head bolts as follows:
   a. First stage—47.9 ft.-lb. (65 N•m).
   b. Second stage—55.3 ft.-lb. (75 N•m).
   c. Third stage—62.6 ft.-lb. (85 N•m).
   d. Fourth stage—74.5 ft.-lb. (101 N•m).
   e. Final torque—Back off all bolts 2-3 turns and repeat the 4-stage sequence.

Aluminum Components

In addition to the use of aluminum cylinder heads, the 232 cid V6 engine makes extensive use of aluminum components. The accessory brackets, intake manifold, front cover, water pump, pistons and oil pump are all aluminum. Since aluminum is softer than cast iron, use care in removing and installing fasteners in these components to prevent possible thread damage.

NOTE
*Power or air-driven tools should **not** be used for removing or installing fasteners which thread into aluminum components. All such fasteners should be removed and installed with hand tools to avoid cross-theading or stripping of the aluminum threads.*

Silicone Rubber Sealant

This material is used extensively in place of gaskets during assembly at the factory and is specified for repair procedures.

When using silicone sealant, apply in the bead size indicated and run the bead around the *inside* of any bolt holes. Complete the assembly of the parts to be joined within 15 minutes of applying the sealant. After this time, the sealant begins to "set-up" and may lose its sealing qualities as a result.

The following surfaces should be sealed in this manner using the bead size indicated.
   a. Oil pan-to-engine block: Run a 1/8 in. bead along the sides of the oil pan rail on the engine block. Run a 1/4 in. bead on the front cover rail with extra material on the front cover-to-block joint (**Figure 9**). Run a 1/8 in. bead at each end of the rear seal where the rear main cap and engine block meet (**Figure 10**).
   b. Thermostat housing: Run a 1/16 in. bead.
   c. Rocker arm cover-to-cylinder head: Run a 3/16 in. bead.
   d. Intake manifold-to-engine block: Run a 1/8 in. bead at each corner where the head joins the block and at each end of the block where the intake manifold

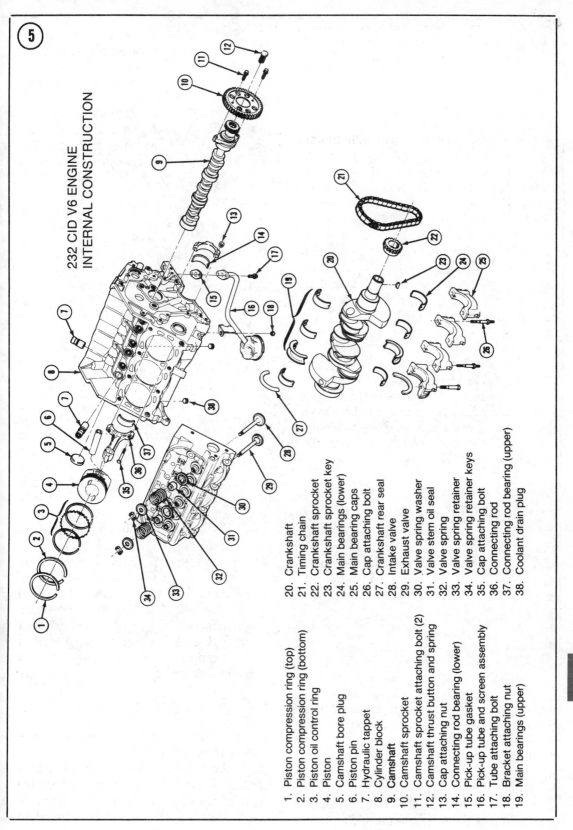

5

232 CID V6 ENGINE
INTERNAL CONSTRUCTION

1. Piston compression ring (top)
2. Piston compression ring (bottom)
3. Piston oil control ring
4. Piston
5. Camshaft bore plug
6. Piston pin
7. Hydraulic tappet
8. Cylinder block
9. Camshaft
10. Camshaft sprocket
11. Camshaft sprocket attaching bolt (2)
12. Camshaft thrust button and spring
13. Cap attaching nut
14. Connecting rod bearing (lower)
15. Pick-up tube gasket
16. Pick-up tube and screen assembly
17. Tube attaching bolt
18. Bracket attaching nut
19. Main bearings (upper)

20. Crankshaft
21. Timing chain
22. Crankshaft sprocket
23. Crankshaft sprocket key
24. Main bearings (lower)
25. Main bearing caps
26. Cap attaching bolt
27. Crankshaft rear seal
28. Intake valve
29. Exhaust valve
30. Valve spring washer
31. Valve stem oil seal
32. Valve spring
33. Valve spring retainer
34. Valve spring retainer keys
35. Cap attaching bolt
36. Connecting rod
37. Connecting rod bearing (upper)
38. Coolant drain plug

12

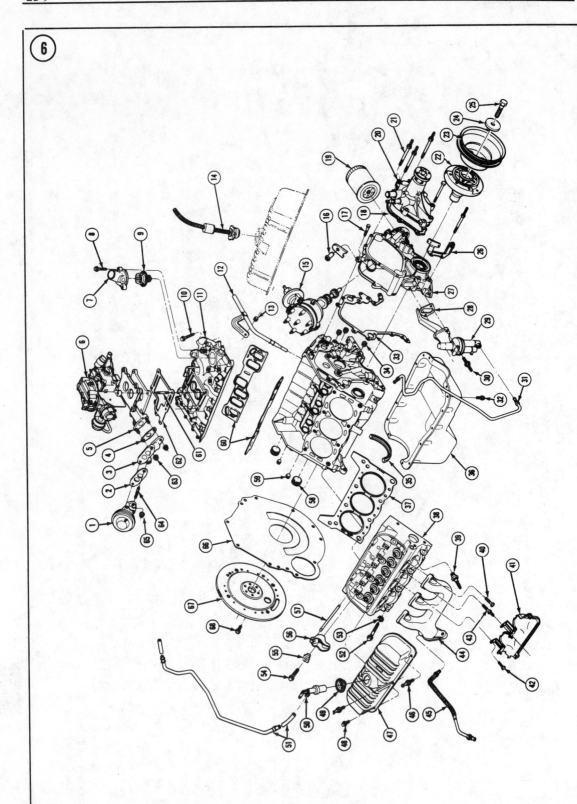

232 CID V6 ENGINE
EXTERNAL CONSTRUCTION

1. EGR valve
2. Valve gasket
3. EGR valve adapter
4. Adapter gasket
5. Carburetor spacer
6. Carburetor
7. Thermostat housing
8. Housing attaching bolt (3)
9. Thermostat
10. Manifold attaching bolt (14)
11. Intake manifold
12. Oil level indicator tube
13. Tube attaching nut (1)
14. Tube and filter assembly oil fill cap
15. Ignition distributor
16. Distributor hold-down clamp and bolt
17. Cover attaching bolt (7)
18. Pump gasket (water)
19. Oil filter
20. Water pump
21. Water pump attaching bolts (8)
22. Crankshaft damper
23. Crankshaft pulley
24. Damper bolt washer
25. Damper attaching bolt
26. Ignition timing indicator
27. Front cover
28. Pump gasket
29. Fuel pump
30. Pump attaching stud/bolt (2)
31. Fuel line-pump to carburetor
32. Pan attaching bolt (14)
33. Cover gasket
34. Oil gallery plug

35. Oil pan rear seal
36. Oil pan
37. Cylinder head gasket
38. Cylinder head
39. Spark plug
40. Manifold attaching bolts (6 each side)
41. Hot air intake shroud
42. Shroud and manifold attaching stud bolt
43. Manifold and shroud attaching bolt with stud
44. Exhaust manifold
45. EGR tube
46. Cover attaching bolt with stud (2 each side)
47. Valve cover
48. Cover attaching bolt (3 each side)
49. Valve grommet
50. PCV valve
51. PCV valve hose and tube
52. Cylinder head attaching bolt (8 each side)
53. Cylinder head bolt washer
54. Fulcrum attaching bolt (12 each side)
55. Rocker arm fulcrum
56. Rocker arm
57. Pushrod
58. Water jacket plug
59. Oil gallery plug
60. Manifold gasket
61. Carburetor attaching stud (4)
62. Carburetor gasket
63. Adapter attaching nut (2)
64. Valve attaching stud (2)
65. Valve attaching nut (2)
66. Rear cover plate
67. Drive plate
68. Plate attaching bolt (5)

12

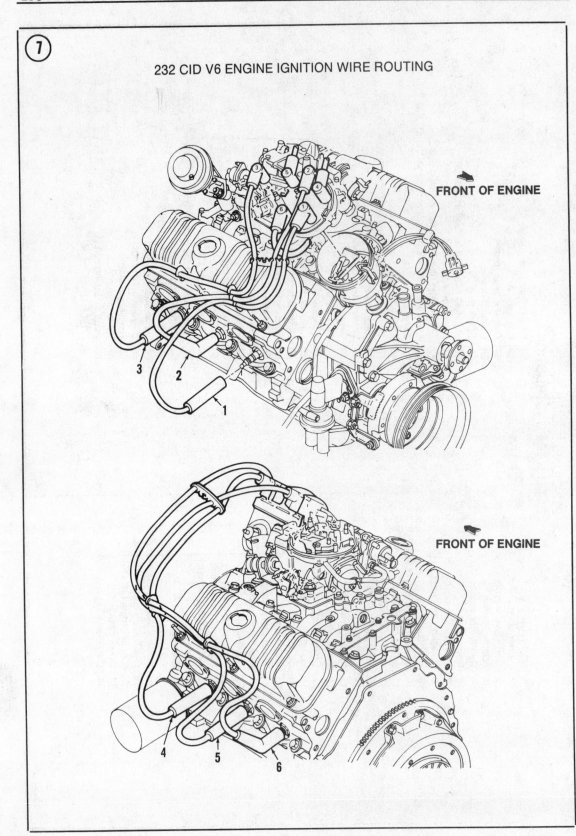

⑦ 232 CID V6 ENGINE IGNITION WIRE ROUTING

FRONT OF ENGINE

FRONT OF ENGINE

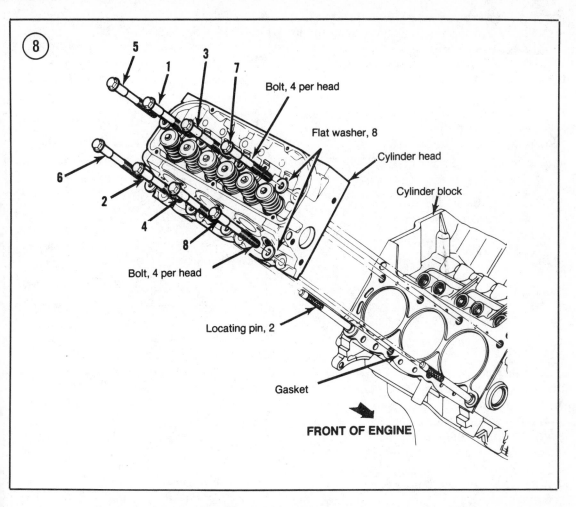

8

5 1 3 7

Bolt, 4 per head

Flat washer, 8

Cylinder head

6

2

Cylinder block

4

8

Bolt, 4 per head

Locating pin, 2

Gasket

FRONT OF ENGINE

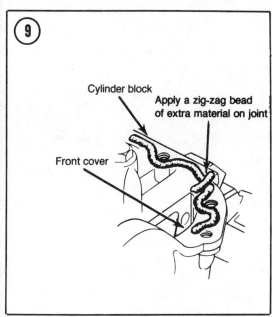

9

Cylinder block

Apply a zig-zag bead
of extra material on joint

Front cover

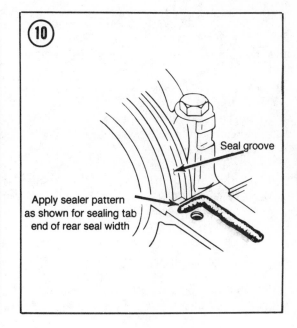

10

Seal groove

Apply sealer pattern
as shown for sealing tab
end of rear seal width

12

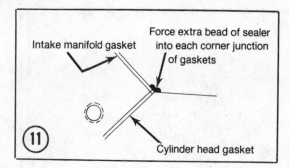

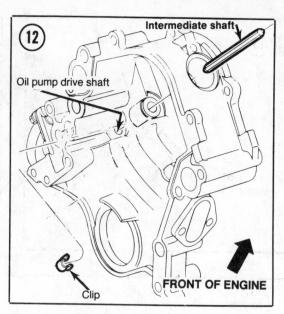

seats against it. Force an extra bead into each corner junction of the intake manifold and cylinder head gaskets (**Figure 11**).

e. Air injection secondary cover-to-intake manifold: Run a 1/16 in. bead.

Front Cover

A new front cover design houses the oil pump. The oil pump is driven by the distributor through an oil pump drive shaft and intermediate shaft (**Figure 12**). Since the distributor is mounted on the front cover instead of the block, it must be removed before the front cover is removed. The distributor hold-down bolt uses a Torx head and must be removed with an appropriate Torx head driver.

The intermediate shaft is held in place in the cover by a retaining clip. When the intermediate shaft is fully engaged in the oil pump drive shaft, the installed dimension to the top of the clip should be 1.18-1.29 in. (30-33 mm). See **Figure 13**.

A camshaft spring and button is used to maintain camshaft end play (**Figure 14**). This assembly is held in place by the front cover. Whenever the front cover is removed, the face of the camshaft button should be lubricated with Lubriplate or equivalent before reinstalling the cover.

Pistons and Connecting Rods

The aluminum pistons are connected to a forged steel connecting rod. Piston dome and

rod button identification should be on the same side and face the front of the engine when the assembly is installed. The rod and cap should be assembled with the cylinder bore number on the outside when installed in the cylinder bore.

Piston and rod assemblies should be installed in the block in the following order: No. 1 and No. 5, No. 2 and No. 6, No. 3 and No. 4. Torque the rod nuts to 31-36 ft.-lb. (41-49 N•m). Back off the nuts 2-3 turns and retorque to 31-36 ft.-lb. (41-49 N•m).

Serpentine Drive Belt

A single serpentine drive belt is routed around all accessory drive pulleys and is driven by the crankshaft pulley (**Figure 15**). A spring-loaded idler pulley holds the belt tight against the accessory pulleys. Drive belt tension is adjusted by a vertical screw in the idler adjustment bracket located above the idler pulley.

Thermostat

The thermostat housing contains a locking recess to prevent incorrect thermostat

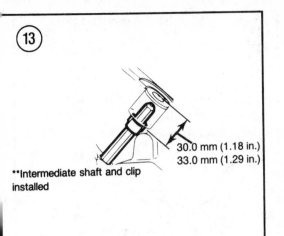

13

30.0 mm (1.18 in.)
33.0 mm (1.29 in.)

**Intermediate shaft and clip
installed

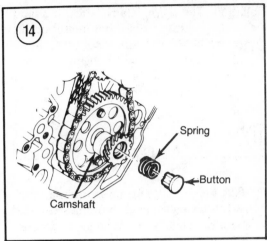

14

Spring

Button

Camshaft

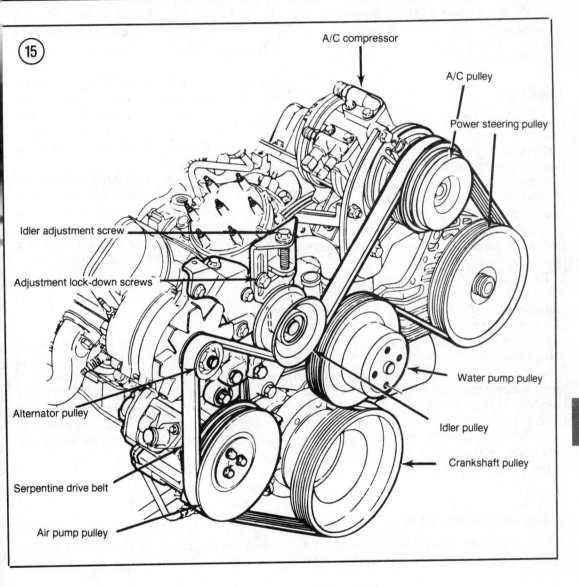

15

A/C compressor

A/C pulley

Power steering pulley

Idler adjustment screw

Adjustment lock-down screws

Water pump pulley

Alternator pulley

Idler pulley

Crankshaft pulley

Serpentine drive belt

Air pump pulley

12

installation. The thermostat has locking tabs which engage this recess. To remove the thermostat, rotate it counterclockwise until the tabs disengage the housing recess. Thermostat installation requires a clockwise turn to engage the tabs in the recess.

6.9 LITER
DIESEL ENGINE

A 6.9 liter (420 cid) V8 International Harvester diesel engine is optional in 1983 and later F-250 heavy-duty and F-350 trucks. Service by amateur mechanics, except for the maintenance procedures given in the Chapter Three and Chapter Four sections of this supplement, is not recommended.

460 CID V8 ENGINE

Intake Manifold

Ford has issued revised instructions for the use of RTV sealant with intake manifold gaskets on the 1986 and later 460 cid V8. Earlier models required application of the sealant bead to each corner of the block, parallel to the cylinder head along the parting line between the head and block.

The revised method involves a change in the direction of the sealant bead. It is now applied at a right angle to the cylinder head across the parting line between the block and head. Once the gasket is in place, a second bead of sealant should be applied across the bottom edge of the gasket where it rests on the parting line between the head and block.

Table 4 ENGINE SPECIFICATIONS (255/351W V8)

	255	351W
General		
Bore	3.68 in.	4.00 in.
Stroke	3.00 in.	3.50 in.
Firing order	1-5-4-2-6-3-7-8	1-3-7-2-6-5-4-8
Cylinder bore		
Diameter	3.6800-3.6835 in.	4.0000-4.0052 in.
Out-of-round (max.)	0.0015 in.	0.0015 in.
Piston		
Clearance bore	0.0018-0.0026 in.	0.0018-0.0026 in.
Piston rings		
Number per cylinder	5	5
Ring end gap		
Top	0.010-0.020 in.	0.010-0.020 in.
Bottom	0.010-0.020 in.	0.010-0.020 in.
Oil	0.010-0.035 in.	0.010-0.035 in.
Ring side clearance		
Top	0.0019-0.0036 in.	0.0019-0.0036 in.
Bottom	0.002-0.004 in.	0.002-0.004 in.
Oil	Snug	Snug
Piston pin		
Diameter	0.9119-0.9124 in.	0.9119-0.9124 in.
Clearance		
In rod	interference fit	interference fit
In piston	0.002-0.004 in.	0.003-0.005

(continued)

Table 4 ENGINE SPECIFICATIONS (255/351W V8) (continued)

Crankshaft

End play	0.004-0.008 in.	0.004-0.008 in.
Main bearing journal		
Diameter	2.2482-2.2490 in.	2.9994-3.0002 in.
Taper	0.0005 in.	0.0005 in.
Out-of-round	0.0006 in.	0.0006 in.
Main bearing clearance	0.0008-0.0015 in.	0.0008-0.0015 in.
Connecting rod journal		
Diameter	2.1228-2.1236 in.	2.3103-2.3111 in.
Taper	0.0006 in.	0.0006 in.
Out-of-round	0.0006 in.	0.0006 in.

Connecting rods

Side clearance	0.010-0.020 in.	0.010-0.020 in.
Bearing clearance	0.0008-0.0015 in.	0.0008-0.0015 in.

Camshaft

Journal diameter	No. 1 2.0805 in.	2.0815 in.
	No. 2 2.0655 in.	2.0665 in.
	No. 3 2.0505 in.	2.0515 in.
	No. 4 2.0355 in.	2.0365 in.
	No. 5 2.0205 in.	2.0215 in.
Runout	0.005 in.	0.005 in.

Valve system

Lifter type	Hydraulic	Hydraulic
Rocker arm ratio	1.61:1	1.61:1
Valve lash, intake and exhaust	0.123-0.173 in.	0.123-0.172 in.
Intake valve		
Face angle	44 degrees	44 degrees
Seat angle	45 degrees	45 degrees
Seat width	0.060-0.080 in.	0.060-0.080 in.
Stem-to-guide clearance	0.0010-0.0027 in.	0.0010-0.0027 in.
Seat run out	0.002 in.	0.002 in.
Exhaust valve		
Face angle	44 degrees	44 degrees
Seat angle	45 degrees	45 degrees
Seat width	0.060-0.080 in.	0.060-0.080 in.
Stem-to-guide clearance	0.0015-0.0032 in.	0.0015-0.0032 in.
Seat run-out	0.002 in.	0.002 in.
Valve springs		
Free length	2.04 (intake)	2.04 (intake)
	1.85 (exhaust)	1.85 (exhaust)
Load @ length (lb. @ in.)		
Closed	74-82 @ 1.78 (intake)	74-82 @ 1.78 (intake)
	76-84 @ 1.60 (exhaust)	76-84 @ 1.60 (exhaust)
Open	190-212 @ 1.36 (intake)	190-210 @ 1.36 (intake)
	190-210 @ 1.20 (exhaust)	190-210 @ 1.20 (exhaust)
Installed height		
Intake	$1\frac{43}{64}$-$1\frac{45}{64}$	$1\frac{49}{64}$-$1\frac{51}{64}$
Exhaust	$1\frac{37}{64}$-$\frac{39}{64}$	$1\frac{37}{64}$-$1\frac{39}{64}$

12

Table 5 460 CID TIGHTENING TORQUES (1983)

Fastener	ft.-lb.	N·m
Connecting rod nut	45-50	55-61
Main bearing cap bolt	95-105	129-142
Oil pump inlet tube	12-18	16-24
Water outlet	12-18	16-24
Water pump	12-18	16-24

Table 6 ENGINE SPECIFICATIONS (232 V6)

General
  Bore   3.8l in.
  Stroke   3.39 in.
  Firing order   1-4-2-5-3-6 (No. 1 right front)
Cylinder bore
  Diameter   3.81 in.
  Out-of-round service limit   0.0002 in.

Piston
  Bore clearance   0.0014-0.0022 in.
Piston rings
  Ring width
    Top   0.0772-0.0783 in.
    Bottom   0.0772-0.0783 in.
    Oil   0.0006 in. (0.15 mm) maximum
  Ring gap
    Top   0.001-0.002 in.
    Bottom   0.001-0.002 in.
    Oil   0.0015-0.0037 in.
  Ring side clearance
    1st   0.0016-0.0037 in.
    2nd   0.0016-0.0037 in.
Piston pin
  Diameter   0.9119-0.9124 in.
  Clearance
    In rod   Press fit
    In piston   0.0002-0.0005 in.
Crankshaft
  End play   0.004-0.008 in.
  Main bearing journal
    Diameter   2.5190-2.5l98 in.
    Taper   0.0003 in.
    Out-of-round service limit   0.0002 in.
  Main bearing clearance   0.0005-0.0023 in.
  Connecting rod journal
    Diameter   2.3103-2.3111 in.
    Taper   0.003 in.
    Out-of-round   0.0003 in.
Connecting rod
  Side clearance   0.0047-0.0114 in.
  Bearing clearance   0.0005-0.0023 in.
Camshaft
  Journal diameter (all)   2.0515-2.0505 in.
  Runout   0.02 in.

(continued)

Table 6 ENGINE SPECIFICATIONS (232 V6) (continued)

Valve system	
Lifter type	Hydraulic
Rocker arm ratio	1.73:1
Intake valve	
Face angle	44°
Seat angle	45°
Stem-to-guide clearance	0.001-0.0027 in.
Seat runout	0.003 in.
Exhaust valve	
Face angle	44°
Seat angle	45°
Stem-to-guide clearance	0.0015-0.0032 in.
Seat runout	0.003 in.
Valve springs	
Free length, intake and exhaust	1.70-1.78 in.
Load @ length (lb. @ in.)	
Closed (intake and exhaust)	75 @ 1.70
Open (intake and exhaust)	215 @ 1.79
Collapsed tappet gap	
Intake and exhaust	0.088-0.189 in.

Table 7 ENGINE TIGHTENING TORQUES (232 V6)

Fastener	Ft.-lb.	N•m
Main bearing cap bolt	65-81	88-110
Camshaft sprocket to cam bolt	15-22	20-30
Connecting rod nut	31-36	41-49
Front cover to block	15-22	20-30
Water pump to front cover	15-22	20-30
Oil inlet tube to main bearing cap	30-40	40-55
Oil pan to block	80-106 in.-lb.	9-12
Oil filter adaptor to front cover	18-22	25-30
Rocker arm fulcrum to head	18.4-25.8	25-35
Rocker arm cover to head	36-61 in.-lb.	4-7
Flywheel to crankshaft	54-64	73-87
Crankshaft pulley to damper	20-28	26-38
Crankshaft damper to crankshaft	93-121	125-165
Thermostat housing to intake manifold	15-22	20-30
Clutch plate to flywheel	15-19	20-27
Clutch housing to block	40-50	54-68
Exhaust manifold to block	15-22	20-30
Oil drain plug to pan	15-25	21-33
Flex plate to torque converter	20-34	27-45
Engine mount to crossmember	25-35	33-47

12

CHAPTER SIX

FUEL AND EXHAUST SYSTEMS

MOTORCRAFT
7200VV CARBURETOR

Some 1980-1983 F-series trucks are equipped with the Motorcraft model 7200VV (Variable Venturi) carburetor. This carburetor is able to vary the area of the venturi according to the load and speed demands placed upon it by the engine. The throttle position and engine vacuum control the dual venturi valves.

When the load on the engine changes, the position of the venturi valves automatically changes, determining the area of air flow to the 2 throats of the carburetor. The venturi valves are connected to 2 main fuel metering rods. These metering rods vary fuel flow by changing the area of the metering jets.

The model 7200VV has been built with tamper resistance in mind. Special tools and some machine shop operations are required for most service operations.

If any major problems should arise with the carburetor, it should be referred to a dealer or a qualified specialist.

MINOR CARBURETOR
ADJUSTMENT (7200VV)

Minor carburetor adjustment consists of the engine idle setting. This setting is maintained by a throttle positioner. Depending on the engine size and transmission type, vehicles have one of 3 different types of throttle positioners. Refer to **Figures 16-18** and identify the type of

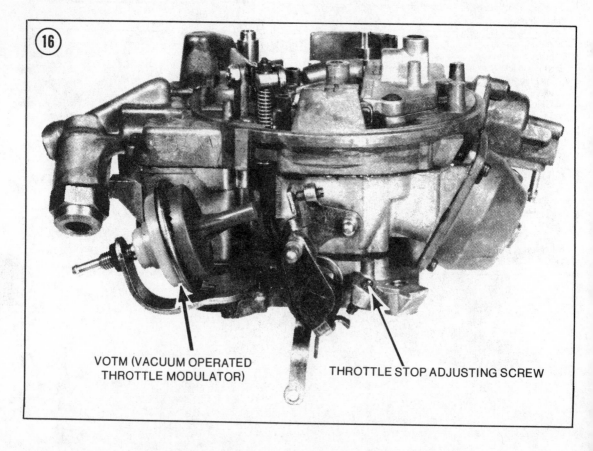

(16)

VOTM (VACUUM OPERATED
THROTTLE MODULATOR)

THROTTLE STOP ADJUSTING SCREW

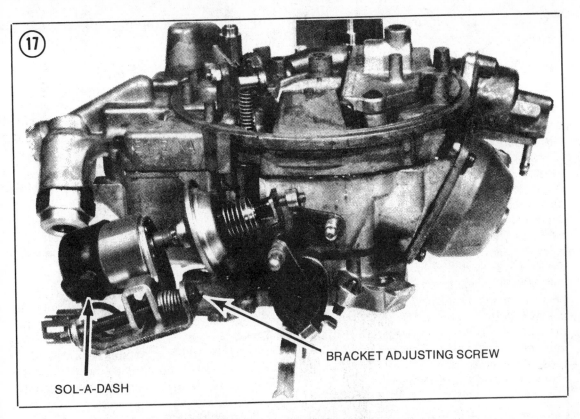

BRACKET ADJUSTING SCREW

SOL-A-DASH

SLOW IDLE ADJUSTING SCREW

KICKER DASHPOT

positioner used on the carburetor being serviced.

Idle air-fuel mixture settings affect the exhaust emission levels and cannot be accurately adjusted without the aid of an exhaust gas analyzer.

Slow Idle Speed Preadjustment Procedure (All Models)

1. Set the parking brake and block the drive wheels. Turn off all accessories (air conditioning, tape deck, etc.)
2. Disconnect the fuel evaporative purge valve hose at the vacuum tee connection, cap the open port, and plug the hose.
3. Disconnect and plug the EGR vacuum hose at the EGR valve. Warm the engine to normal operating temperature.

CAUTION
If your vehicle is equipped with a catalytic converter, do not allow the engine to idle for extended periods. The converter may overheat and cause extensive underbody damage.

4. Recheck the parking brake and the drive wheel blocks. Place automatic transmissions in DRIVE and manual transmissions in NEUTRAL.
5. Connect a tune-up tachometer to the engine. Refer to the basic book for hook-up points.

Adjustment With VOTM (Vacuum Operated Throttle Modulator)

Refer to **Figure 16** for the following procedure.
1. With the engine running, remove the air cleaner assembly and tap the throttle pedal to drop the engine into slow idle. See the Vehicle Emission Control Information (VECI) decal in the engine compartment for the specified idle speed.
2. If the idle speed is too high, turn the throttle stop adjusting screw counterclockwise until the engine reaches the specified idle.
3. If the idle speed is too low, shut the engine off, then turn the idle stop adjusting screw clockwise 2 full turns. Restart the engine and

recheck the idle rpm. Repeat Step 2 or 3 as necessary.

Adjustment With Sol-A-Dash (Solenoid Dashpot)

Refer to **Figure 17** for the following procedure.
1. With the engine running, remove the air cleaner assembly and tap the throttle pedal to drop the engine into slow idle. See the Vehicle Emission Control Information (VECI) decal in the engine compartment for the specified idle speed.
2. If the idle speed is incorrect, set it to specification by turning the bracket adjusting screw.

Adjustment With Kicker Dashpot

Refer to **Figure 18** for the following procedure.
1. Turn off the engine and remove the air cleaner assembly. Check the throttle linkages for freedom of movement and lubricate them with a lightweight oil if necessary.
2. Restart the engine. Recheck the parking brake and wheel blocks. Place automatic transmissions in DRIVE and manual transmissions in NEUTRAL.
3. Refer to the Vehicle Emission Control Information (VECI) decal in the engine compartment for the specified idle speed. If idle speed is too high, turn the curb idle adjusting screw counterclockwise. If the idle speed is too low, turn the adjusting screw clockwise.
4. Turn the engine off and wait a couple of minutes. Restart the engine and run it for 10 seconds at 2,000 rpm, then let it idle for at least 1 minute. Recheck the idle speed and readjust if necessary. Repeat Step 4 until the specified idle speed is obtained.

CARTER YFA 1V CARBURETOR

A feedback version of the Carter YFA-1V carburetor is used on 1983 49-state and high altitude F-series trucks and all 1984 F-series trucks (under 8,500 lb. GVW) equipped with the 300 cid inline 6-cylinder engine.

The carburetor differs from other YFA models in that it uses a feedback solenoid attached to the air horn near the bowl vent tube. This solenoid meters air into both the idle and main circuits on command from a microprocessor (MCU) in 49-state trucks or an altitude compensator switch in high altitude applications. Service and adjustment procedures are esentially the same as for other YFA carburetors.

MODEL 2150A CARBURETOR

The Model 2150A carburetor is a feedback version of the 2150 carburetor. It is used on 1983-1985 F-series trucks under 8,500 lb. GVW (Gross Vehicle Weight) equipped with the 302 cid V8 engine and 1984 F-series trucks (under 8,500) lb. GVW) equipped with the 351 cid V8 engine. A pulsing solenoid is used instead of a stepper motor to control the carburetor duty cycle. See **Figure 19**. The solenoid meters air into both the idle and main vacuum passages on command the EEC-III or EEC-IV module.

Model 2150 carburetors used on 1983 high altitude applications use the 2150A main altitude compensator mounted in place of the feedback solenoid (**Figure 20**). Altitude compensation on 1984 and later carburetors is a function of the EEC-IV microprocessor and no altitude compensator is used.

Service procedures are essentially the same as for other Model 2150 carburetors.

Fuel Filter

The Holley 4180C carburetor used on some 351 and all 460 cid V8 engines has an inlet fitting type fuel filter. To change the filter on this carburetor:
1. Remove the air cleaner.
2. Hold the filter inlet hex nut with an appropriate size open-end wrench. Unscrew the fuel line nut from the filter inlet with a second open-end wrench.
3. Remove and plug the fuel line to prevent leakage.
4. Unscrew and remove the fuel inlet fitting.
5. Remove the gasket, filter and spring (if used). Discard the gasket and filter.

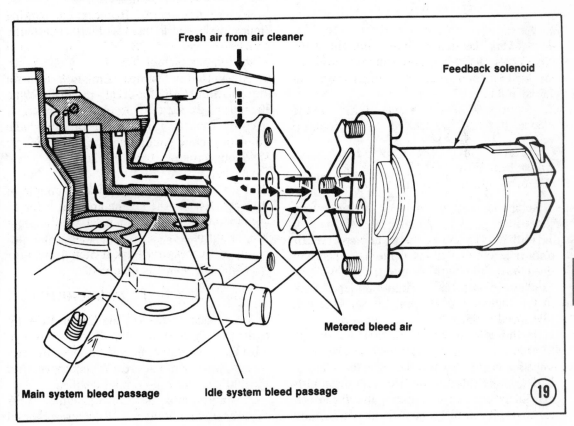

Fresh air from air cleaner

Feedback solenoid

Metered bleed air

Main system bleed passage   Idle system bleed passage   ⑲

12

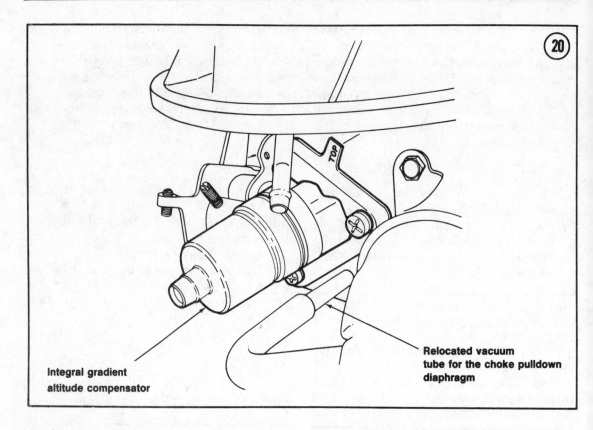

Integral gradient
altitude compensator

Relocated vacuum
tube for the choke pulldown
diaphragm

6. Installation is the reverse of removal. Use new gaskets. Tighten the fuel inlet fitting to 22-26 ft.-lb. (30-35 N•m). Tighten the fuel line nut to 15-18 ft.-lb (20-24 N•m). Start the engine and check for leaks.

ELECTRONIC FUEL INJECTION (EFI) SYSTEM

The Central Fuel Injection (CFI) system used on 1985 1/2 F-series 302 cid V8 engines is renamed the EFI system and its use extended to all 1986 and later 302 V8 engines and all 1987 300 cid I6 engines. This multipoint, pulse time, adaptive speed/density fuel injection system is installed in F-series pickups under 8,500 GVW. Fuel is injected through 8 (V8) or 6 (I6) injectors into the intake air stream on command from the electronic engine control (EEC-IV) microprocessor. The microprocessor contains adaptive logic that allows it to automatically sense and compensate for changes in altitude, as well as allow manual transmission vehicles to be push-started.

Figure 21 shows the major components of the V8 EFI system.

The fuel rails used on 1985 applications were connected by a crossover tube held to the rails with spring-lock connectors. On 1986 302 cid V8 engines:

a. The fuel rail is a single assembly which does not require the spring-lock connectors.

b. The pressure test fitting (Schrader valve) is moved from the fuel supply line to the fuel rail.

c. The throttle body has provisions for circulating engine coolant through its base to improve cold driveability during sub-zero temperatures.

On 1987 302 cid V8 engines:

a. Fuel injectors have been redesigned with a new flow rate to minimize the problem of clogging.

b. The 2 fuel rail banks are now connected at the front and rear to improve fuel flow.

c. The pressure test fitting remains in the same location as 1986 models.

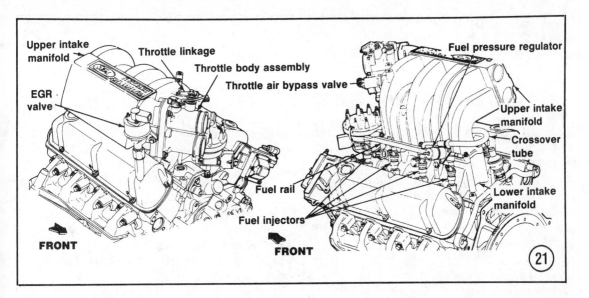

System Operation

Filtered fuel is supplied to the fuel rail assembly by a 2-stage delivery subsystem. Turning the ignition switch to START energizes the power relay in the microprocessor, which sends current to the fuel pump relay. If the engine does not start within 1-2 seconds, a timer in the microprocessor grounds the fuel pump relay, cutting off current to the fuel pump.

Once energized, a low-pressure electric pump mounted in the fuel tank sends fuel to a reservoir and filter assembly mounted on the left-hand frame rail in the middle of the vehicle. An inline electric fuel pump located on the left-hand side rail in the engine compartment picks up fuel from the reservoir and sends it to the injectors at approximately 39 psi.

Fuel flow through the injector located at each cylinder intake port is controlled by varying the duration of injection according to signals from the EEC-IV microprocessor. Each bank of injectors is energized at alternate crankshaft revolutions. Excess fuel passes through a pressure regulator on the fuel rail and is returned to the fuel tank.

A throttle position sensor (TPS) mounted on the throttle body informs the microprocessor of throttle valve position. An idle air screw in the throttle body assembly maintains a pre-programmed idle speed according to directions from the EEC-IV microprocessor. An inertia switch is designed to open on impact and shut down fuel flow.

Since the system is controlled by the EEC-IV microprocessor and the idle speed control device, engine idle speed is self-compensating and cannot be changed by the usual adjustment procedures. Attempts to change the system operating limits should not be made by the home mechanic. Owner service should be limited to component replacement only. If the EFI system is not working properly, take the vehicle to a Ford dealer for diagnosis and adjustment.

System Pressure Relief

Before opening any fuel line connection on an EFI-equipped engine, fuel pressure must be relieved to reduce the risk of fire and personal injury.
1. Place the transmission in PARK (automatic) or NEUTRAL (manual).
2. Set the parking brake and block the drive wheels.
3. Disconnect the electrical connection to one of the following:
    a. Fuel pump relay (engine compartment).
    b. Inertia switch (see owner's manual for location).
    c. Inline fuel pump (engine compartment).

12

4. Crank the engine for about 10 seconds. The engine will start and run until the fuel remaining in the lines is used up. When the engine stops, crank the engine again for 5 seconds. This will dissipate any remaining fuel pressure and permit safe disconnection of the fuel lines.

5. When fuel system service has been completed and all lines reconnected, reconnect the electrical connections which were disconnected in Step 3.

6. Turn the ignition switch ON, but do not start the engine. Inspect system connections for leaks and repair if necessary before starting the engine.

Fuel Charging Manifold Assembly Removal/Installation

Refer to **Figure 21** and **Figure 22** for this procedure.

1. Relieve system pressure as described in this chapter.

2. Remove the fuel tank cap to relieve any pressure in the tank.

3. Disconnect the negative battery cable.

4. Disconnect the electrical connectors at the air bypass valve, throttle position sensor (TPS) and EGR position sensor.

5. Disconnect the throttle linkage. If equipped with an automatic transmission, disconnect the transmission linkage at the throttle body.

6. Remove the 2 bolts holding the throttle cable bracket to the intake manifold. Move bracket and cables out of the way.

7. Disconnect all vacuum lines to the vacuum tree, EGR valve and fuel pressure regulator.

8. Disconnect the PCV hose from the rear of the upper manifold.

9. Disconnect the 2 canister purge lines (and water heater lines, if so equipped) from the throttle body.

10. Unscrew the flange nut at the EGR valve and disconnect the EGR tube.

11. Remove the upper intake support bracket to upper manifold bolt.

12. Remove the 6 upper intake maifold bolts. Remove the upper intake manifold and throttle body from the lower intake manifold

as an assembly. Remove and discard the gasket.

NOTE
*Push-connect fittings are used on all fuel injection connections and must be separated using the tools specified in Step 13. Two different types of retaining clips are used on some of these fittings. See **Figure 23**. These clips should be replaced whenever a connection is opened. Other connectors use a garter spring.*

13. Disconnect the crossover fuel hose, fuel supply and return lines at the fuel supply rail. See **Figure 24**. Use Ford tool part No. T81P-19623-G or part No. T81P-19623-G1 as shown in **Figure 25**.

14. Remove the 2 fuel supply rail bolts (**Figure 26**) on each side of the engine.

15. Disconnect the fuel supply rail at each injector. See **Figure 27**. Carefully remove fuel supply rail.

16. To remove the injectors, grasp each by the body and rock it from side to side while pulling upward.

17. Remove and discard the 2 injector O-rings. Install a clean injector cap on the injector end to protect it from contamination.

CAUTION
Do not use silicone grease or other substitutes in Step 18. These can clog the injectors.

18. To reinstall, lubricate 2 new O-rings with a light grade of oil (Ford part No. ESF-M6C2-A or equivalent) and install on each injector removed.

19. Install each injector with a downward rocking motion, twisting as required to seat the injector and align the electrical connector horizontally.

20. Reverse Steps 1-15 to complete installation. Tighten upper intake manifold fasteners to 12-18 ft.-lb. (17-24 N•m). Before connecting any fuel lines, check the connection for a damaged or missing garter spring, if used. If necessary, remove the old spring with a hooked wire and install a new one. If a retaining clip is used, be sure to install a new one. Connect the fitting by

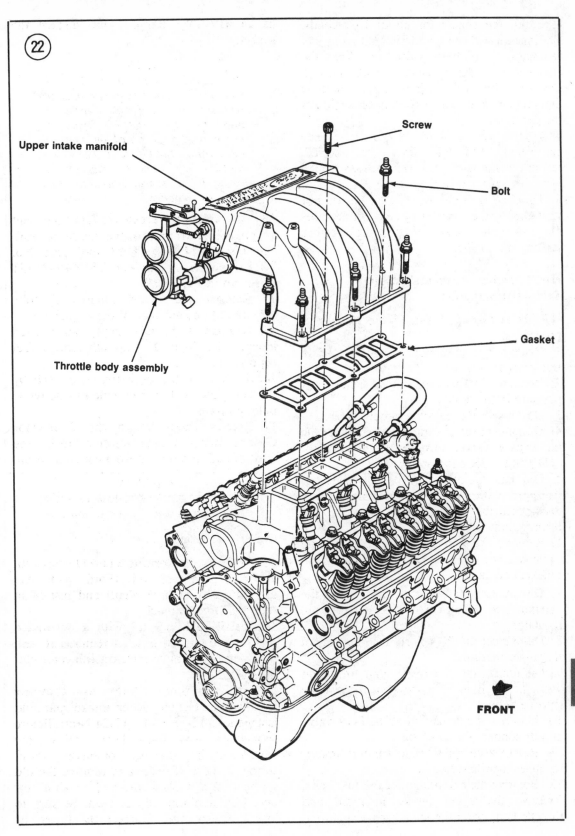

㉒

Screw

Upper intake manifold

Bolt

Gasket

Throttle body assembly

FRONT

12

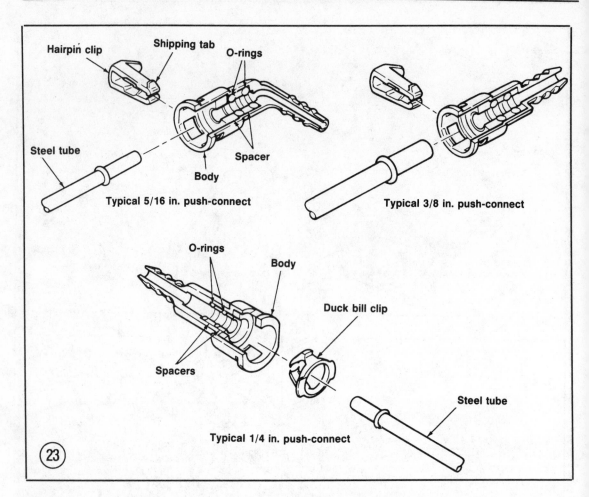

Hairpin clip Shipping tab O-rings

Steel tube

Spacer

Body

Typical 5/16 in. push-connect

Typical 3/8 in. push-connect

O-rings

Body

Duck bill clip

Spacers

Steel tube

Typical 1/4 in. push-connect

(23)

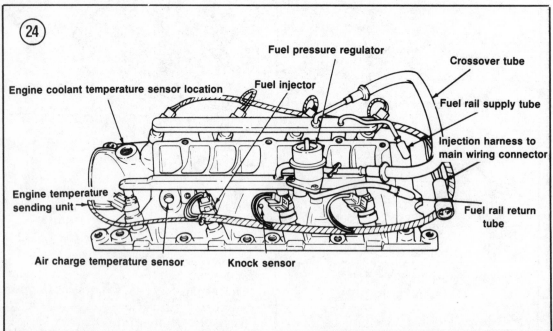

(24)

Fuel pressure regulator

Crossover tube

Engine coolant temperature sensor location Fuel injector

Fuel rail supply tube

Injection harness to main wiring connector

Engine temperature sending unit

Fuel rail return tube

Air charge temperature sensor Knock sensor

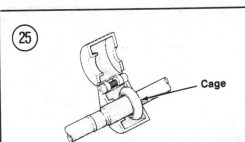

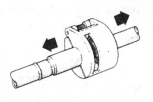

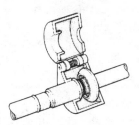

25

Cage

1. Tool must enter cage to release garter spring.

2. Push tool into cage to release female fitting from spring.

3. Pull male and female couplings apart.

4. Remove tool.

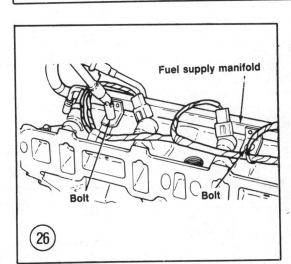

Fuel supply manifold

Bolt   Bolt

26

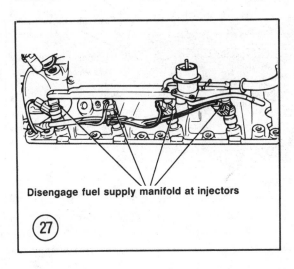

Disengage fuel supply manifold at injectors

27

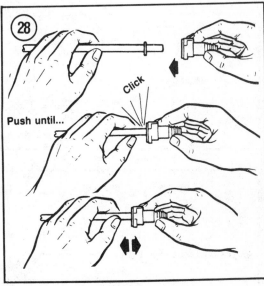

28

Push until...

Click

pushing the 2 lines together with a slight twisting motion, then pull outward to make sure the connection is secure. See **Figure 28**.

Intake Manifold
Removal/Installation

The intake manifold on an EFI engine is a 2-piece assembly, with the fuel rail sandwiched in between. The upper intake or fuel charging manifold removal/installation is described under *Fuel Charging Manifold Assembly Removal/Installation* in this

12

supplement chapter. The following procedure is used to remove the lower intake manifold.

1. Drain the cooling system. See Chapter Eight of the basic book.

2. Perform Steps 1-15 of *Fuel Charging Assembly Removal/Installation* as described in this supplement chapter.

3. Disconnect the spark plug wires. Remove the distributor cap and wires as an assembly. Remove the distributor. See Chapter Seven of the basic book.

4. Disconnect all sensor electrical connectors. See **Figure 24**.

5. Disconnect the injector wiring harness at the main harness assembly.

6. Note position of the exhaust gas oxygen sensor ground lead for reinstallation reference and disconnect it from the intake manifold stud.

7. Disconnect the upper radiator hose at the thermostat housing and the heater hose at the intake manifold. Loosen the water pump bypass hose clamp and disconnect hose at thermostat housing.

8. Remove the 2 intake manifold and 1 exhaust manifold nuts holding the air cleaner bracket in position.

9. Remove the coil bracket nut. Move the coil and bracket out of the way.

10. Note location of intake manifold studs. Remove manifold studs and bolts. See **Figure 29**. Remove the manifold from the engine.

11. Clean all gasket and RTV sealant residue from the block and manifold mating surfaces.

12. Apply a 1/8 in. bead of RTV sealant (Ford part No. D6AZ-19562-B or equivalent) at the points shown in **Figure 30**.

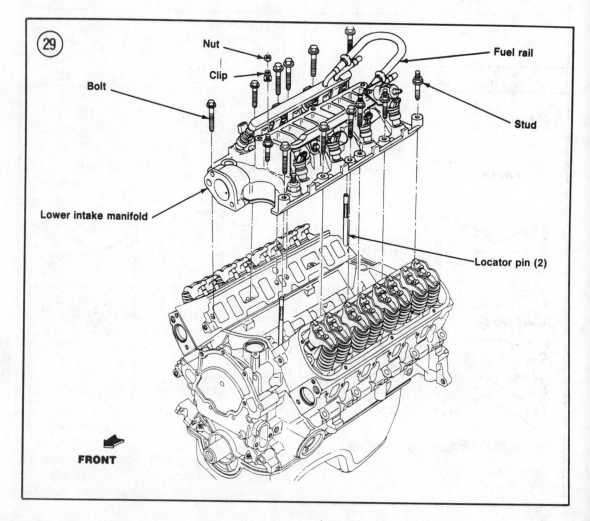

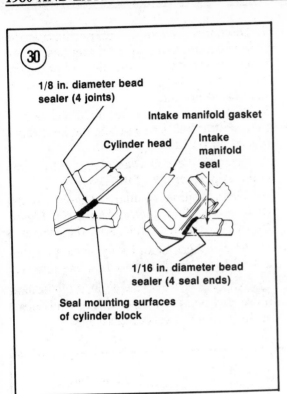

1/8 in. diameter bead sealer (4 joints)

Intake manifold gasket

Cylinder head

Intake manifold seal

1/16 in. diameter bead sealer (4 seal ends)

Seal mounting surfaces of cylinder block

13. Apply a 1/16 in. bead of RTV sealant to the outer end of each intake manifold seal for the full width of the seal. See **Figure 30**.

14. Install new seals on the block. Install new gaskets on the heads with the gasket trademark facing the heads. The gaskets should interlock with the seal tabs and their holes should align with those in the cylinder heads.

15. Install locator pins at the points shown in **Figure 29**. Lower the intake manifold into place on the cylinder block and heads. Once in position, run a finger around the seal area. If seals are not in place, remove the manifold and reposition the seals.

16. Remove the locator pins and install the manifold studs and bolts finger-tight. Torque all fasteners to 23-25 ft.-lb. (32-43 N•m) in the sequence shown in **Figure 31**. Wait 10 minutes and retorque the fasteners to specifications in the same sequence.

17. Reverse Steps 1-9 to complete installation.

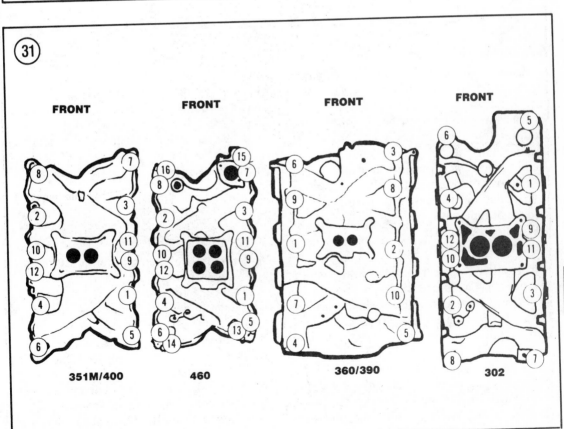

351M/400   460   360/390   302

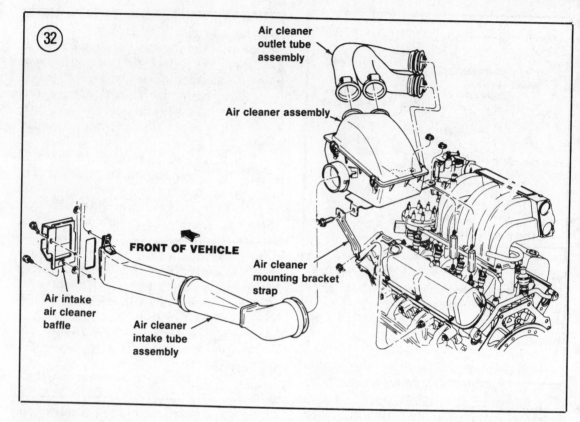

(32)

Air cleaner
outlet tube
assembly

Air cleaner assembly

FRONT OF VEHICLE

Air cleaner
mounting bracket
strap

Air intake
air cleaner
baffle

Air cleaner
intake tube
assembly

EFI Engine Air Cleaner

Figure 32 shows the 302 cid V8 EFI engine air cleaner assembly components. To replace the filter:

1. Unclamp and remove the air supply tubes from the throttle body.
2. Unclamp the air cleaner housing cover. Remove the cover from the housing.
3. Remove and discard the filter element.
4. Installation of a new filter element is the reverse of removal.

EFI Inline Fuel Filter
Removal/Installation

The filter element used in the inline reservoir has a surface of approximately 200 sq. in. and Ford states that it should last the life of the vehicle under *normal* conditions. Should the filter become clogged, the high pressure fuel pump will become excessively noisy and a loss of power above idle will be noted. Refer to **Figure 33** for this procedure.

1. Remove the fuel tank filler cap.
2. Relieve the system pressure as described in this chapter.

3. Raise the vehicle with a jack and place it on jackstands.
4. Remove the bolts holding the protective shield around the reservoir. Remove the shield.
5. Place a suitable container under the reservoir, as the filter canister will be full of fuel when removed.

NOTE
A flexible strap-type oil filter wrench can be safely used to remove the filter canister in Step 6, if necessary.

6. Unscrew the filter canister and slide it out from the frame rail.
7. Drain the contents of the canister into the container under the pump. Dispose of this fuel in a safe manner.
8. Remove the filter element from the canister. Remove the O-ring from the canister groove and discard it.
9. Wash the canister with solvent and blow dry with compressed air, if available.
10. Insert a new filter element in the canister housing.

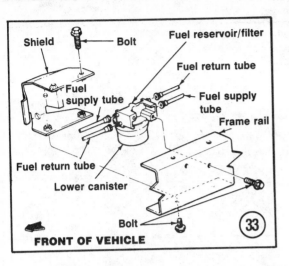

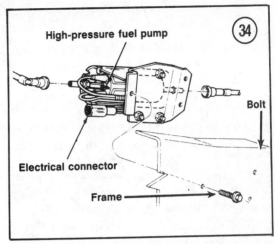

11. Install the new O-ring provided with the filter element in the canister groove.

12. Hold the canister level to avoid dislodging the O-ring and reposition it on the bottom of the reservoir housing.

13. Screw the canister housing onto the reservoir *by hand* until the O-ring just touches the housing. At this point, there will be a very slight resistance when turning the canister as the rubber grommet on the filter seats on the housing pilot stud.

14. Tighten the canister another 1/6 turn with a flexible strap-type oil filter wrench.

15. Install the protective shield around the reservoir.

16. Remove the jackstands and lower the vehicle to the ground.

17. Install the fuel tank filler cap.

18. Start the engine and check for leaks.

EFI Engine Electric Fuel Pump Testing

Fuel pump testing on EFI engines requires the use of special test equipment that has been modified. Have a Ford dealer test the fuel pumps on EFI engines.

The electric fuel pump used on 1985-1986 fuel injected engines may be the cause of a failure to start or a miss during acceleration. If the spade terminal connections at the fuel pump are loose or otherwise make a poor connection, the resulting low voltage will cause improper pump operation and fuel starvation.

Before replacing the fuel pump, check the connections as follows:

1. Disconnect the negative battery cable.

2. Raise the vehicle with a jack and place it on jackstands.

3. Disconnect the wiring harness connectors at the fuel pump.

4. Connect an ohmmeter or self-powered test lamp between the terminals in the pump motor wiring harness connector.

5. Lightly push/pull on the connectors under the rubber boots while watching the meter or test lamp for signs of an open or intermittent condition.

    a. If the connections are good, the problem is in the fuel pump.

    b. If open or intermittent continuity is noted, roll the boots back and retest to make sure that proper contact was made. If proper contact was made and the meter or test lamp still indicates an open or intermittent continuity condition, repair the wiring harness/connector as required.

Removal/Installation (High-pressure Pump)

Refer to **Figure 34** for this procedure.

1. Relieve fuel system pressure as described in this supplement chapter.

2. Disconnect the negative battery cable.

3. Raise the vehicle with a jack and place it on jackstands.

12

4. Disconnect the fuel pump electrical connector.

5. Disconnect the fuel inlet and outlet lines:

a. If lines use push-connect fittings with duck bill clips (**Figure 23**), use Ford tool part No. T82L-9500-AH or equivalent.

b. If lines use push-connect fittings with hairpin clips (**Figure 23**), depress clip by hand and work it out of the connection.

c. Plug the lines to prevent fuel leakage.

6. Remove the 3 bolts holding the pump assembly to the frame. Remove the pump assembly with bracket.

7. Remove the 3 bolts holding the pump to the bracket.

8. Installation is the reverse of removal. Install new retaining clips. Start the engine and check for leaks.

Removal/Installation (Low-pressure Pump)

To replace the in-tank fuel pump, remove the fuel tank and rotate the locking ring in a counterclockwise direction with Ford tool part No. T74P-9275-A or equivalent to remove the fuel pump and sending unit from the tank. See **Figure 35**. Installation is the reverse of removal.

300 CID I6 EFI SYSTEM

The EFI system installed on all 1987 300 cid I6 engines operates in essentially the same way as the 302 cid V8 system described in this supplement, with 3 injectors energized at a time (1-3-5 and 2-4-6).

In addition, an auxiliary blower and distribution tube is used to provide extra cooling to the injectors. The blower is mounted on the right front wheelwell.

The electronically controlled blower uses a temperature switch on the fuel rail which activates the blower whenever fuel rail surface temperature exceeds a calibrated value. The blower will run until the temperature falls below the switch calibration, or for a maximum of 15 minutes.

The inertia switch is located on the toeboard just to the right of the transmission hump.

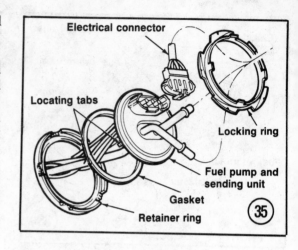

Fuel Supply Manifold Assembly Removal/Installation

A single tubular fuel rail assembly provides the injectors with high-pressure fuel. A Schrader valve pressure test connection is provided on the fuel rail.

1. Perform Steps 1-14 of *Intake/Exhaust Manifold Removal/Installation* as described in Chapter Five of this supplement.

2. Remove the nut holding the injector cooling manifold to the fuel rail stud. Remove the cooling manifold.

3. Unplug the electrical connector at the fuel manifold temperature switch.

4. Disconnect the vacuum line at the fuel pressure regulator.

5. Remove the strap holding the fuel manifold, injector electrical harness and main vacuum harness.

6. Remove the 3 fuel supply manifold retaining studs.

7. Carefully disconnect the fuel supply manifold from the injectors. Remove the manifold assembly.

8. To remove the injectors, grasp each by the body and rock it from side to side while pulling upward.

9. Remove and discard the 2 injector O-rings. Install a clean injector cap on the injector end to protect it from contamination.

> *CAUTION*
> *Do not use silicone grease or other substitutes in Step 10. These can clog the injectors.*

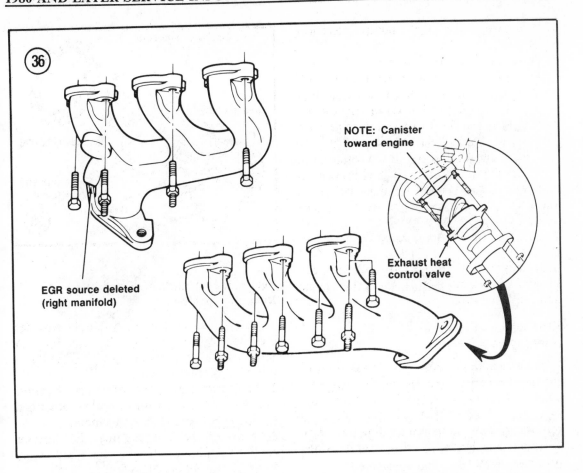

NOTE: Canister toward engine

Exhaust heat control valve

EGR source deleted (right manifold)

10. To reinstall, lubricate 2 new O-rings with Ford ESE-M2C96-G oil and install on each injector removed.

11. Install each injector with a downward rocking motion, twisting as required to seat the injector and align the electrical connector horizontally.

12. Installation is the reverse of removal. Tighten retaining studs and cooling manifold nuts to 15-22 ft.-lb. (20-30 N•m). Before connecting any fuel lines, check the connection for a damaged or missing garter spring. If necessary, remove the old spring with a hooked wire and install a new one.

Fuel Filter

The 300 cid I6 engine is fitted with an inline fuel filter mounted underneath the vehicle on a frame rail, similar to that used with the 302 cid V8. Replacement procedure is essentially the same as described earlier in this supplement chapter.

EMISSION CONTROL SYSTEM COMPONENTS

Exhaust Heat Control Valve

A vacuum-operated exhaust heat control valve (**Figure 36**) is installed on late 1982 and all 1983 232 cid V6 engines.

Intake Manifold Heat Control Valve

A new heat control valve has been added to the manifold of 1983 and later 302 cid V8 F-series engines (**Figure 37**). This new valve works in conjunction with the exhaust heat control valve used on previous models. Both valves are operated by intake manifold vacuum managed by a 3-port PVS valve with a 128 degree F temperature calibration.

During a cold start, the exhaust heat control valve is closed by vacuum to warm the engine and the intake manifold heat valve is opened by vacuum to warm the exhaust

12

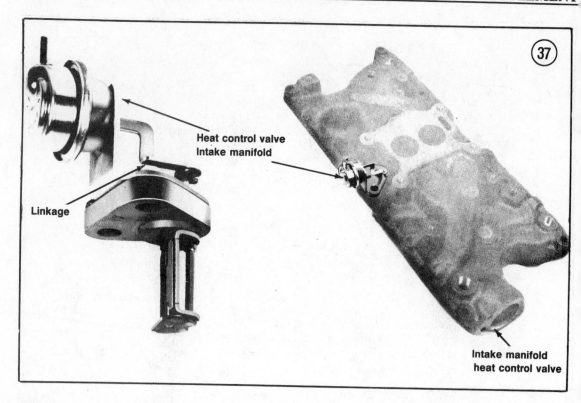

Heat control valve
Intake manifold

Linkage

Intake manifold
heat control valve

crossover in the manifold for better fuel vaporization. At 128° F, vacuum to both valves is vented and the exhaust heat valve opens while the manifold heat valve closes.

Both valves are tested with the same procedure. Vacuum applied to the valve port shroud with a hand vacuum pump should close the exhaust heat valve and open the manifold heat valve. If one or both valves do not follow this sequence when vacuum is applied, either the diaphragm(s) is leaking or the linkage(s) is binding.

PCV SYSTEM
(V8 EFI ENGINE)

Figure 38 shows the location of the EFI engine PCV system components.

PCV SYSTEM
(I6 EFI ENGINE)

The PCV hose on 1987 300 cid I6 EFI engines is routed under the upper intake manifold runners and connects to a vacuum fitting on the intake air plenum.

EGR SYSTEM
(EFI ENGINE)

Figure 39 shows the location of the EFI engine EGR system components. The EGR tube assembly connects the exhaust manifold to the EGR valve mounted on the upper intake or fuel charging manifold.

A stainless steel EGR valve is used on 1987 302 cid V8 engines. This minimizes the possibility of clogging. The EGR solenoids have been replaced by an electronic vacuum regulator (EVR).

The 1987 300 cid I6 engine EGR system consists of an EGR valve, EGR valve position sensor (EVP) and electronic vacuum regulator (EVR). The system is controlled by the electronic control assembly (ECA).

EMISSION CONTROL SYSTEM
MAINTENANCE

Fuel Filter

The 7200-VV and Holley 4180C carburetors use an inlet fitting type fuel filter. See **Figure 40**. To change the filter on these carburetors:

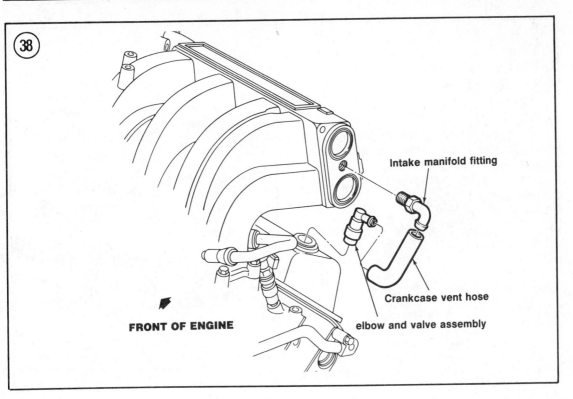

Intake manifold fitting

Crankcase vent hose

FRONT OF ENGINE

elbow and valve assembly

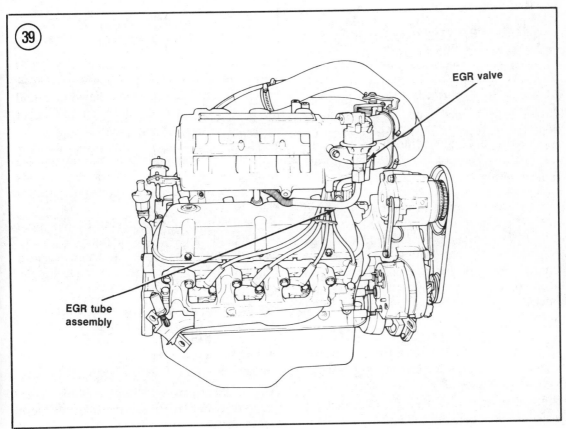

EGR valve

EGR tube
assembly

12

1. Remove the air cleaner.

2. Hold the filter inlet hex nut with an appropriate size open-end wrench. Unscrew the fuel line nut from the filter inlet with a second open-end wrench.

3. Remove and plug the fuel line to prevent leakage.

4. Unscrew and remove the fuel inlet fitting.

5. Remove the gasket, filter and spring.

6. Discard the gasket and filter.

7. Installation is the reverse of removal. Tighten the fuel inlet fitting to 22-26 ft.-lb. (30-35 N•m). Tighten the fuel line nut to 15-18 ft.-lb. (20-24 N•m). Start the engine and check for leaks.

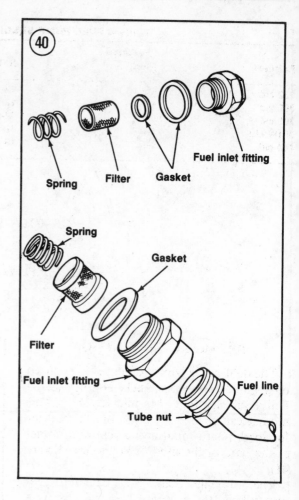

Fuel Pump

Fuel pump specifications for 1982 and later engines are provided in **Table 8**.

Emission Maintenance Warning Lamp

All 1985-on F-series trucks have an amber emission maintenance warning (EMW) lamp on the instrument panel, with a sensor module installed under the panel. Each time the ignition key is turned to the On position, the EMW lamp lights for 2-10 seconds to indicate that the system is working properly. If the lamp does not come on during this time, or if it comes on and does not turn off, have the vehicle checked by a Ford dealer.

The sensor module acts as an inferred mileage sensor by measuring the accumulated time the ignition key is turned On. At 2,000 miles of key-on time, the module considers the vehicle has traveled 60,000 miles and activates the EMW lamp to alert the driver to the need for emission system maintenance. When emission maintainance has been completed, the dealer will either reset or replace the module as required.

The module is an electronic inferred mileage sensor that measures key-on time. After 2,000 hours of vehicle operation (the duration of time required to approximate 60,000 miles of operation), the sensor turns on the amber lamp. The sensor must be reset to turn the lamp off. To reset the sensor:

1. Locate the module under the instrument panel.

2. Insert a phillips-head screwdriver through the sticker marked RESET on the module.

3. With the screwdriver depressed and held down, turn the ignition key to ON. Count to 10 and release the pressure on the screwdriver. The lamp should turn off within 2-3 seconds, indicating that the module has been properly reset.

4. Check reset operation by turning the ignition key to ON. The lamp should light briefly and then go off. If it does not, the reset operation was not performed properly and must be repeated. If the lamp will not turn off despite repeated efforts at resetting the module, replace it with one carrying part No. E5TZ-12B514-A.

Table 8 FUEL PUMP SPECIFICATIONS

Engine	Pressure (psi)	Mounting bolts	
		ft.-lb.	N•m
232 cid	6-8	12-18	16-24
300 cid	5-7	12-18	16-24
302 cid	6-8	19-27	26-37
351W cid	6-8	19-27	26-37
460 cid	6-8	19-27	26-37

CHAPTER SEVEN

ELECTRICAL SYSTEM

BREAKERLESS IGNITION

The dual-mode ignition module introduced on some 1978 F-series trucks is now called a Universal Ignition Module (UIM). This module can be identified by a third connector for spark retard input and a yellow grommet at the base of the module connector (**Figure 41**).

The module has the capability of responding to a control signal from a barometric pressure switch, ignition timing vacuum switch or microprocessor control unit (MCU) according to engine calibration. When it responds to such a signal, the module allows additional spark timing control by shutting off the ignition coil current flow at a different time than it would according to the distributor signal.

Although both are used with a Duraspark II distributor, the UIM and standard Duraspark modules are not interchangeable.

The module used with 1983 300 cid 6-cylinder engines has a new knock/spark retard function.

ELECTRONIC ENGINE CONTROLS (EEC-IV)

All 1984-on 50 state 300 cid inline-6 and 351W cid V8 engines and the 1984 California and 1985-on 50 state 302 cid V8 (under 8,500

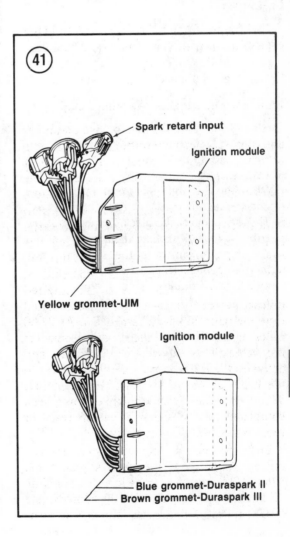

(41)

Spark retard input

Ignition module

Yellow grommet-UIM

Ignition module

Blue grommet-Duraspark II
Brown grommet-Duraspark III

12

lbs. GVW) are equipped with EEC-IV and an ignition system with Universal distributor and E-core coil.

EEC-IV is an engine control system in which an electronic control module (ECA) monitors various engine functions through a series of sensors and controls air-fuel mixture, idle speed, ignition timing, EGR and Thermactor air flow. An idle speed control device maintains the correct carburetor idle speed for cold and warm engine operation according to the computer program. No carburetor or distributor adjustments should be attempted. If the vehicle is not running right, return it to a dealer or qualified specialist for a comprehensive test of the EEC-IV system.

DISTRIBUTOR

The cam gear-driven Universal distributor uses a TFI-IV (Thick Film Integrated) module, a Hall-effect vane switch stator assembly and contains no centrifugal or vacuum advance mechanisms. Both advance functions are controlled by the EEC-IV computer. Distributor calibration is not required and initial timing is not a normal adjustment.

When the distributor is removed from the engine, it must be reset to a base timing of 10° BTDC. Disconnect the black connector at the distributor to lock timing at no advance and adjust the distributor to the specified base timing. Reconnect the black connector and the EEC-IV module resumes control over timing.

The multi-point rotor used in 1983-1985 distributors has been replaced by the earlier blade-type design. Multi-point rotors do not require the use of silicone dielectric compound (part No. D7AZ-19A331-A) when replaced. All blade-type rotors, however, require the application of a 1/32 in. coating on the electrode surfaces which protrude from the plastic rotor housing.

DIELECTRIC SHIELDS

Dielectric shields are used on 1986-on EFI engines. These shields are installed on the water outlet fitting and the ends of the fuel rail to prevent arcing between the components and the ignition wires. Make sure the shields are properly installed and in good condition.

LIGHTS

Aero headlamps replace the sealed beam headlamps on 1987 models. Aero headlamps consist of a replaceable halogen bulb mounted in a composite headlamp assembly that is designed as a part of the vehicle's overall styling. A replacement halogen bulb should *not* be plugged into the headlamp connector to see if it is good unless the bulb has been properly installed in the headlamp assembly. Bulb replacement does not alter headlamp alignment, thus it should not be necessary to re-aim the headlamp. To replace the bulb:

1. Make sure the headlamp switch is off or disconnect the negative battery cable.
2. Reach inside the engine compartment and unplug the electrical connector at the bulb.
3. Rotate the plastic retaining ring on the bulb assembly about 1/8 turn counterclockwise. Slide ring off the plastic base.
4. Carefully pull the bulb assembly straight back and remove it from the reflector socket. Do not rotate the bulb during removal.

WARNING
A halogen bulb contains gas under pressure and can shatter if scratched or dropped. Handle new bulbs only by their plastic base, as skin oils contacting the bulb envelope can cause staining and premature failure.

5. Hold the new bulb with the flat on its base facing up and align the grooves in the bulb base with the socket locating tabs. Insert the bulb straight into the reflector socket until its mounting flanges mate with the socket face.
6. Slide the plastic retaining ring removed in Step 3 into position against the mounting flange and rotate it clockwise until it stops.
7. Reconnect the bulb connector. Turn on the headlamp switch or reconnect the negative battery cable and check the lamp operation.

CHAPTER EIGHT

COOLING, HEATING AND AIR CONDITIONING

FAN

Two types of viscous fan clutch assemblies are used on 1983 and later engines. A screw-on type (**Figure 42**) is installed on the 300 cid 6-cylinder engine. The fan clutch assembly and water pump shaft have *left-hand* threads. A special pulley holder (Ford part No. T83T-6312-A) and nut wrench (Ford part No. T83T-6312-B) are necessary to torque the screw-on clutch to 37-46 ft.-lb. (50-62 N•m). The fan-to-clutch screws are torqued to 15-20 ft.-lb. (20-27 N•m).

A standard foot-mounted fan clutch assembly is used on 302 and 351 cid V8 engines (**Figure 43**). The fan-to-clutch screws are tightened to 15-20 ft.-lb. (20-27 N•m) and the clutch-to-pulley screws to 12-18 ft.-lb. (16-24 N•m).

RADIATOR

A vacuum brazed aluminum design with nylon end tanks is used on 1985 and later F-series gasoline engines. Diesel models use a copper/brass core radiator with metal header tanks. Work carefully when removing or installing hoses to a nylon end tank. If excessive pressure is applied, the fitting may crack or break. If this happens, the radiator must be removed and the end tank replaced.

HEATER

The heater supply tube for 1983 F-100 trucks equipped with the 232 cid V6 engine uses 2 PVS valves.

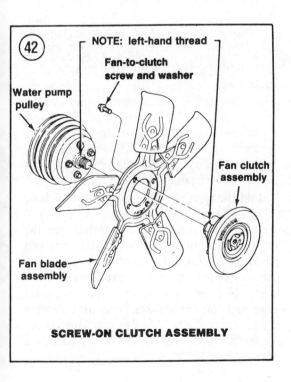

SCREW-ON CLUTCH ASSEMBLY

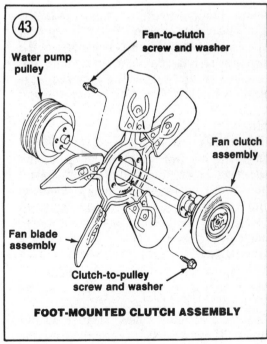

FOOT-MOUNTED CLUTCH ASSEMBLY

12

WATER PUMP

An aluminum water pump is used on 1987 302 cid V8 engines. This pump (and the cast iron pump used on 1987 300 cid I6 engines) rotates in the opposite direction from previous pumps due to the use of the new (I6) or revised (V8) serpentine belt system. The pump hub has right-hand threads. Cooling system flow and bolt torques remain unchanged.

DRIVE BELTS

A serpentine (V-ribbed) drive belt is used on 1987 300 cid I6 engines. The serpentine drive belt arrangement used on 302 cid V8 engines is revised for 1987. Both systems use an automatic belt tensioner and do not require periodic tension adjustment. If the tension is not correct when checked with a belt tension gauge (part No. T63L08620-A or equivalent), the tensioner assembly is replaced.

CHAPTER NINE

BRAKES

Master Cylinder

An aluminum master cylinder with translucent plastic reservoir is used on all 1987 models. The master cylinder contains a fluid level indicator and integral proportioning valve. This changes the function of the brake warning light on the instrument panel to a low fluid level indicator light.

Rear Anti-Lock
Brake System (RABS)

Electronic control has been added to the rear brake system on all 1987 F-series pickups. The RABS system prevents light-load lockup on wet or slippery surfaces by constantly monitoring rear wheel speed and regulating hydraulic pressure to the rear brake system.

The system consists of a magnetic speed sensor mounted in the rear axle, a dual mode (hold/dump) valve to the rear brakes and a microprocessor (module). An amber instrument panel warning lamp alerts the driver to an abnormal condition or system failure.

The microprocessor receives signals from the magnetic sensor. Pedal application is interpreted by the module as a drop in vehicle speed. If the deceleration rate indicates that lockup will occur, the microprocessor activates a dual solenoid control valve which closes an internal isolation valve. This shuts off fluid pressure to the rear wheel cylinders. If the axle sensor continues to indicate wheel lockup, the control module then energizes a dump valve solenoid which bleeds off wheel cylinder pressure into a spring-loaded accumulator piston. When the lockup condition no longer exists, the module de-energizes the solenoids and normal braking operation is resumed.

Diagnosis of this system should be performed by a Ford dealer, since its failure to operate properly constitutes an extreme safety hazard. Components are non-serviceable and must be replaced if defective.

CHAPTER TEN

CLUTCH AND TRANSMISSION

Some 1980 and later F-series trucks are equipped with an automatic overdrive (AOD) transmission. The C5 automatic transmission with lock-up converter replaced the C4 application for 1982 and later models and is serviced in the same manner.

CAUTION
Be sure to use only DEXRON II fluid in the C6 and automatic overdrive transmissions. Use only Type H fluid in the C5 transmission.

This supplement covers adjustment procedures for the automatic overdrive (AOD) transmission only. Adjustment procedures for the C5 automatic transmission are essentially the same as the C4 covered in the basic book.

Some 1980-1983 F-series trucks are equipped with a single-rail overdrive (SROD) manual 4-speed transmission. A top-shift overdrive (TOD) 4-speed transmission replaced the SROD in 1984 models. The Warner T-19B 4-speed manual transmission is used with 1983 and later F-250 and F-350 trucks equipped with the 6.9 liter diesel engine.

The SROD, TOD and T-19B transmissions have no external shift rods or levers, thus no adjustment is possible. Removal and installation instructions for the manual transmission are given in this supplement. See the basic book for automatic transmission removal and installation. If a major problem should arise with either unit, see a dealer or transmission specialist.

AUTOMATIC OVERDRIVE TRANSMISSION

Shift Linkage Adjustment

The procedure for shift linkage adjustment with the automatic overdrive transmission is

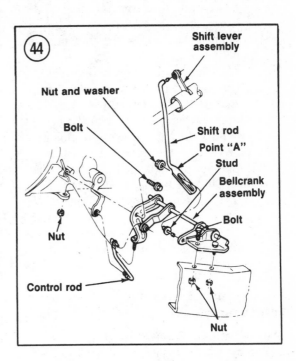

the same as that given in Chapter Ten of the basic book. **Figure 44** shows the linkage design and adjustment point.

Throttle Valve Control Adjustment (1982-1985 Carburetted 302 V8)

All 1982-1985 carburetted 302 V8 applications use a linkage rod system for throttle valve (TV) control. This system requires an adjustment at the carburetor and one at the transmission.

Carburetor linkage adjustment

1. Check the engine slow idle speed and set to specifications, if necessary. See the basic book and this supplement.
2. Set the parking brake and place the transmission selector in NEUTRAL.
3. With the engine at normal operating temperature, tap the throttle pedal to drop the

12

engine into slow idle speed. Shut the engine off, leaving the transmission selector in NEUTRAL. Remove the air cleaner.

4. Turn the linkage lever adjusting screw counterclockwise until the end of the screw is flush with the face of the linkage lever (**Figure 45**). If no gap exists between the linkage lever adjusting screw and throttle lever, refer to the *Transmission Linkage Adjustment* section of this supplement and adjust the transmission linkage before continuing.

5. Insert a 0.005 in. feeler gauge between the linkage lever adjusting screw and the throttle lever (**Figure 46**). Without putting any load on the linkage lever, turn the adjusting screw clockwise until the feeler gauge is a snug fit in the gap. Withdraw the feeler gauge.

6. Without putting any load on the linkage lever, turn the adjusting screw clockwise 3 full turns (1982) or 4 full turns (1983-on). If the travel is limited, one turn (1982) or 2 turns (1983-on) is the minimum permissible. If the minimum permissible number of turns is not possible, refer to the *Transmission Linkage Adjustment* section of this supplement and adjust the transmission linkage, then repeat this carburetor linkage adjustment procedure.

Transmission linkage adjustment

> *NOTE*
> *Engine slow idle speed must be set to specification before you attempt any transmission linkage adjustments.*

Refer to **Figure 47** for the following procedure.

1. Set the parking brake and put the transmission selector in NEUTRAL, then start the engine and allow it to warm up to operating temperature. When the engine has warmed, tap the throttle pedal to drop the engine into slow idle, then shut the engine off. Keep the transmission in NEUTRAL.

2. Place the linkage lever adjustment screw approximately at its mid-point.

> *WARNING*
> *The remaining steps involve working close to the exhaust system. Let the exhaust system cool before continuing.*

3. Raise the front of the vehicle with a jack and place it on jackstands.

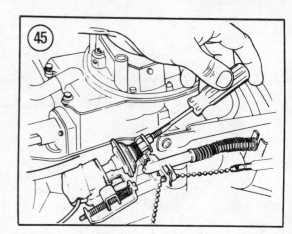

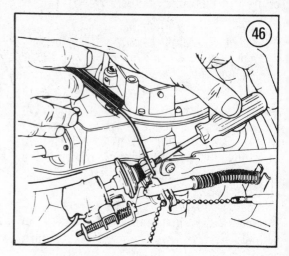

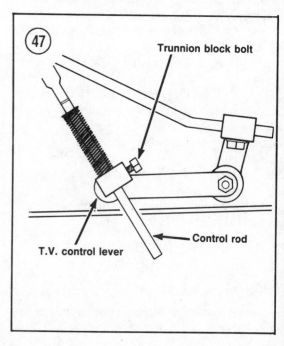

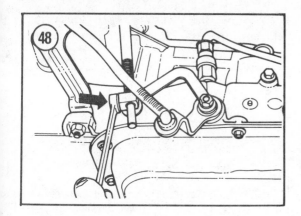

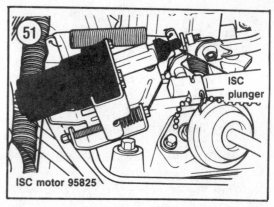

ISC
plunger

ISC motor 95825

7. Release pressure on the control rod. It should stay in place.

8. Firmly push up on the TV (throttle valve) control lever until it stops. The control rod should not bind in the trunnion block. Hold pressure on lever and tighten trunnion block bolt (**Figure 50**).

9. Remove the jackstands and lower the vehicle to the ground. Make sure the throttle lever is still positioned against the idle stop. If it is not, repeat this transmission linkage adjustment procedure.

**Throttle Valve Control Adjustment
(1983-on Inline 6-cylinder
and 1985-on EFI 302 V8)**

The 1983-on inline 6-cylinder and 1985-on EFI 302 V8 engines use a cable system for throttle valve (TV) control. TV cable adjustments are preset during assembly at the factory. Readjustment is necessary only when the carburetor (I6), throttle body (V8), transmission or TV cable is replaced, or if an idle speed adjustment (I6) of more than 150 rpm is made.

Carburetors on 1984 and later I6 engines use an idle speed control motor operated by the ECA to maintain the proper idle speed. See **Figure 51**. When the engine is shut off, the motor plunger automatically extends to preset the throttle lever at the fast idle position for the next restart. Since idle speed adjustment is automatic, a throttle valve linkage adjustment should not normally be required on these engines. If it is, retract the idle speed control plunger as follows *before* making an adjustment.

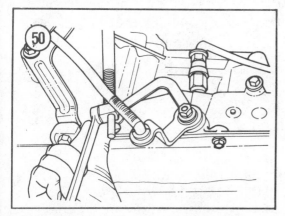

4. Loosen the bolt on the trunnion block located on the TV control rod (**Figure 48**) with a 13 mm box wrench.

5. Remove any dirt or corrosion from the control rod to allow the trunnion block to slide freely.

6. Push up on the lower end of the control rod to ensure that the carburetor linkage lever is held firmly against the throttle lever (**Figure 49**).

12

a. Locate the self-test and self-test input connectors in the engine compartment. See **Figure 52**.

b. Connect a jumper lead between the self-test input connector and the signal return pin on the self-test connector (**Figure 52**).

c. Turn the ignition key ON but do not start the engine.

d. Wait 10-12 seconds to allow the plunger to fully retract.

e. Turn the ignition key OFF, remove the jumper lead and manually move the carburetor linkage off the fast idle cam.

f. Start the adjustment procedure with Step 2.

1. 1983 I6 engine—Check engine idle speed. Adjust if necessary to specifications with and without the throttle solenoid positioner activated. See the Vehicle Emission Control Information (VECI) decal in the engine compartment for specifications and procedure. Shut the engine off.

2. Remove the air cleaner.

3. Set the parking brake and place transmission selector lever in NEUTRAL.

4. Push up the cable locking tab, then pry the tab from the bracket to free the cable. See **Figure 53**.

5. Raise the vehicle with a jack and place it on jackstands.

6. Install a retaining spring on the TV control lever at the transmission (**Figure 54**). The spring used must have about 10 lb. pull in order to hold the lever as far to the rear as it will go. If a single spring is not available with this amount of pull, use a pair of passenger car V8 engine TV return springs.

7. I6 engine—Make sure the carburetor throttle lever is off the fast idle cam and in the anti-diesel idle position. Check to see that the take-up spring at the carburetor end of the cable tensions the cable properly. If the spring is loose or bottomed out, inspect the cable brackets for bending.

8. Depress the locking key until it is flush with the cable housing (**Figure 55**).

9. Remove the retaining spring(s) from the transmission TV lever.

10. Remove the jackstands and lower the vehicle to the ground. Install the air cleaner.

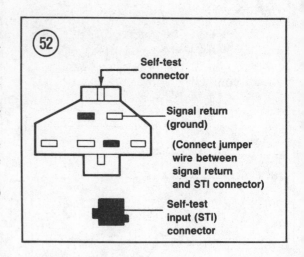

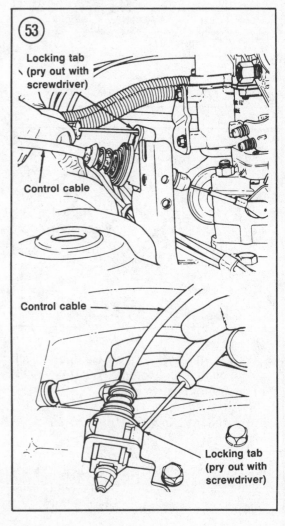

C5 AND C6 TRANSMISSIONS

Neutral Start Switch Adjustment

Refer to **Figure 56** for this procedure.
1. Set the parking brake.
2. Make sure the transmission linkage is properly adjusted.

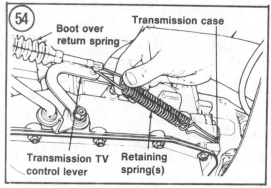

Transmission case
Boot over return spring
Transmission TV control lever
Retaining spring(s)

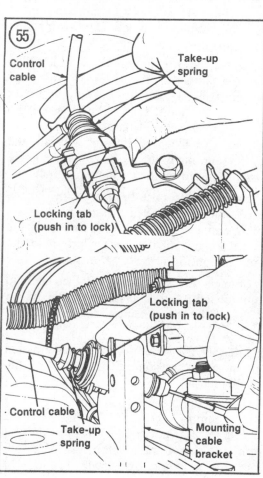

Control cable
Take-up spring
Locking tab (push in to lock)
Locking tab (push in to lock)
Control cable
Take-up spring
Mounting cable bracket

3. Raise the front of the vehicle with a jack and place it on jackstands.
4. Loosen the 2 switch attaching bolts.
5. Place the transmission selector in NEUTRAL. Rotate the switch and insert the shank end of a No. 43 drill in the switch gauge pin holes. The drill must be inserted a full 31/64 in. into the 3 holes in the switch.
6. Tighten the 2 attaching bolts to 55-75 in.-lb. (6.8-8.0 N•m). Remove the drill from the switch.
7. Remove the jackstands and lower the vehicle to the ground.
8. Check switch operation. The engine should start only with the transmission selector in PARK or NEUTRAL and the back-up light should come on only when the transmission selector is moved into REVERSE.

MANUAL TRANSMISSIONS (SROD, TOD and T-19B)

ROD Shift Lever

Removal/Installation

1. Set the parking brake.
2. Remove the floor mat and loosen the 3 bolts holding the shift lever retaining plate.
3. Lift the retaining plate, dust boot and shift lever as an assembly away from the transmission.
4. Installation is the reverse of removal.

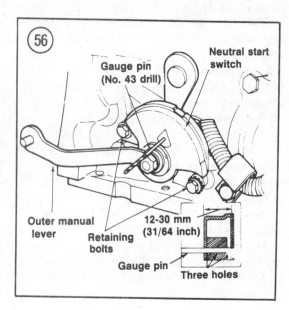

Neutral start switch
Gauge pin (No. 43 drill)
Outer manual lever
Retaining bolts
Gauge pin
12-30 mm (31/64 inch)
Three holes

12

TOD Shift Lever
Removal/Installation

1. Set the parking brake.
2. Remove the screws holding the boot and pad to the floor plate.
3. Place the transmission in NEUTRAL.
4. Remove the boot and twist off the gearshift housing cap with a suitable oil filter wrench.
5. Remove the shift lever.
6. Installation is the reverse of removal. Align lever slots with housing pins before pressing shift lever into gearshift housing.

Warner T-19B Shift Lever
Removal/Installation

1. Remove the screws holding the boot and pad to the floor pan cover.
2. Place the transmission in 2nd gear.
3. Remove the lock pin from the shift lever.
4. Remove the shift lever from the gearshift housing.
5. Installation is the reverse of removal.

Transmission Removal
(SROD, TOD and T-19B)

This procedure is essentially the same for all 3 transmission models. Refer to **Figure 57** (typical).
1. Remove the shift lever assembly.
2. Raise the vehicle and support it with jackstands.
3. Disconnect the drive shaft from the differential, then slide the drive shaft off the transmission output shaft.
4. Disconnect the speedometer cable, back-up lamp switch and high-gear switch (if so equipped) from the transmission or extension housing.
5. Drain the transmission fluid.
6. Support the rear of the engine with a jack, then remove the bolts from the transmission crossmember support.
7. Raise the rear of the engine high enough to remove the transmission's weight from the crossmember. Remove the bolts holding the transmission to the crossmember, then remove the crossmember from the frame.
8. Support the transmission on a jack and remove the bolts holding the transmission to the flywheel housing.

9. Move the transmission and the jack rearward until the input shaft of the transmission clears the flywheel housing, then lower the transmission and remove it from the vehicle.

CAUTION
On models equipped with a hydraulic clutch, do not depress the clutch pedal while the transmission is out of the vehicle.

Transmission Installation
(SROD, TOD and T-19B)

This procedure is essentially the same for all 3 transmission models. Refer to **Figure 57** (typical).

1. Make sure that the mating surfaces of the transmission and flywheel housing are free of dirt and burrs. Saw the heads off of 2 extra flywheel housing lower mounting bolts. Install the sawed-off bolts by hand into the 2 lower mounting bolt holes. These will act as guide pins for the next step.

2. Put the transmission on a jack and raise it into the frame of the vehicle. Move the transmission and jack forward onto the guide pins until the input shaft splines engage the clutch hub splines and the transmission case touches the flywheel housing. Install the upper mounting bolts, then remove the guide pins and install the lower mounting bolts.

3. Use a jack to raise the rear of the engine and then install the transmission crossmember to the vehicle frame. Lower the engine and install the bolts which hold the transmission to the crossmember.

4. Connect the speedometer cable, back-up lamp switch and high-gear switch (if so equipped) to the transmission or extension housing.

5. Slide the drive shaft onto the transmission output shaft, then connect the rear U-joint to the differential.

6. Lower the vehicle and install the shift lever assembly.

7. Fill the transmission to the proper level with the appropriate lubricant. Carefully check your work by slowly driving the

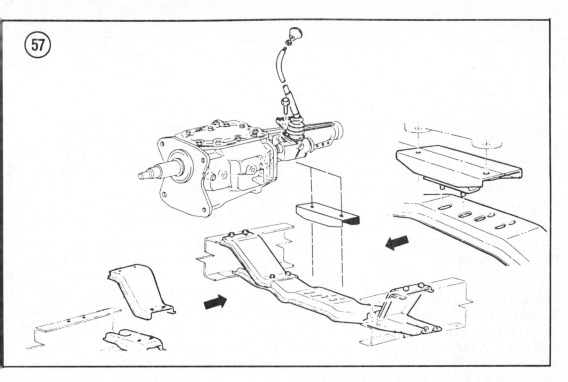

(57)

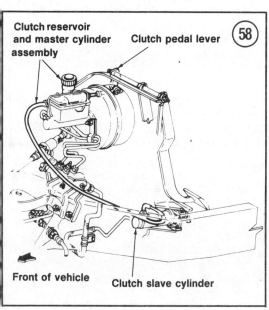

Clutch reservoir and master cylinder assembly

Clutch pedal lever (58)

Front of vehicle

Clutch slave cylinder

and manual transmission to help provide greater fuel economy. The system consists of a control unit located to the right of the steering column under the instrument panel, a vacuum switch at the rear of the rocker arm cover and a top gear switch installed in the top right side of the transmission case. When engine speed exceeds 1,900 rpm and engine vacuum is greater than 5 in. Hg, the shift indicator lamp on the instrument panel lights. This tells the driver the best shift points for optimum fuel economy.

HYDRAULIC CLUTCH SYSTEM

All 1983 and later F-250 and F-350 trucks equipped with the 6.9 liter diesel or 460 cid V8 engine and manual transmission use a hydraulic clutch. The system consists of a clutch master cylinder and reservoir, a slave cylinder and nylon connecting hose. The combination clutch master cylinder and reservoir is attached to the firewall at the right side of the brake vacuum booster. The slave cylinder is attached on the bell housing. **Figure 58** shows the system components.

vehicle. Check the shift lever for smooth crossover operation and full gear engagement.

SHIFT INDICATOR LIGHT

A shift indicator light system is incorporated on 1983 F-100 and F-350 trucks equipped with the 300 cid 6-cylinder engine

12

The hydraulic clutch system is serviced as a complete assembly. If the clutch does not operate properly, the entire system should be removed and replaced as a unit. Individual parts are not available. Bleeding the system is not recommended and should not be attempted. The new assembly is furnished pre-filled with fluid and bled at the factory.

Hydraulic Clutch Adjustment

The hydraulic clutch system automatically keeps the clutch adjusted. No clutch linkage or pedal position adjustment is required.

Slave Cylinder Travel

If the hydraulic clutch system is suspected of a malfunction, measure the slave cylinder travel before removing the system.
1. Raise the front of the truck with a jack and place it on jackstands.
2. Remove the screw holding the dust shield to the clutch housing (**Figure 59**).
3. Have an assistant fully depress and hold the clutch pedal while you measure the pushrod travel. The pushrod should extend at least 0.53 in. (13.5 mm) against the release lever. The hydraulic system should not be removed if pushrod travel is greater than the specified distance.

System Removal

CAUTION
Before performing any service which requires removal of the slave cylinder pushrod from the release lever, the master cylinder pushrod must be disconnected from the clutch pedal. Depressing the clutch pedal with the slave cylinder removed will cause permanent damage to the slave cylinder.

1. Working inside the cab, remove the cotter pin holding the clutch master cylinder pushrod to the clutch pedal. Disconnect the pushrod from the pedal and remove the bushing. See **Figure 60**.
2. Raise the front of the truck with a jack and place it on jackstands.
3. Remove the dust shield at the clutch housing.

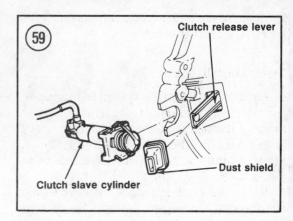

Clutch release lever

Dust shield

Clutch slave cylinder

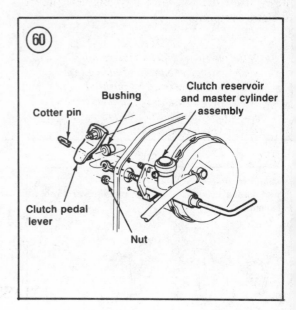

Cotter pin

Bushing

Clutch reservoir and master cylinder assembly

Clutch pedal lever

Nut

4. Push the slave cylinder to the rear and disengage it from the recess in the housing lugs. Slide the cylinder outward, disengaging the pushrod at the release lever.

NOTE
If there are plastic inserts installed between the pushrod end and the release lever, save for reuse if the old slave cylinder is to be reinstalled. Discard if a new hydraulic system is to be installed.

5. Working inside the cab, remove the 2 nuts holding the clutch master cylinder to the firewall.
6. Note the clutch hose routing through the engine compartment and remove the master cylinder assembly from the firewall.

7. Remove the entire hydraulic system from the engine compartment.

System Installation

1. Position the hydraulic system in the engine compartment and insert the clutch master cylinder through the firewall opening.
2. Working in the cab, install the clutch master cylinder attaching bolts and tighten to 15-20 ft.-lb. (21-27 N•m).
3. Route the hose and slave cylinder to the bell housing. The nylon hose should be kept away from contact with any engine exhaust system components.

NOTE
If the old slave cylinder is reinstalled, be sure to install the plastic bearing insert (if any) between the pushrod and release lever. New slave cylinders have a shipping strap attached to pre-position the pushrod for installation. This strap also contains a plastic bearing insert. Install a new cylinder with the strap attached. Operating the clutch pedal when the system is installed will break the strap and provide normal system operation.

4. Insert the slave cylinder pushrod into the clutch release lever and slide the cylinder into the lugs on the clutch housing. Make sure the cylinder is fully seated in the recess in the lugs.
5. Install the dust shield to the clutch housing.
6. Lightly lubricate the master cylinder pushrod bushing with clean engine oil. Attach the bushing and pushrod to the clutch pedal and install a new cotter pin.
7. Depress the clutch pedal a minimum of 10 times to check for smooth operation and release. Check the clutch master cylinder reservoir and top up with clean DOT 3 brake fluid, if necessary.

CHAPTER ELEVEN

CHASSIS

All 1982 and later F-100 and F-150 trucks use a new stamped I-beam type front axle design (**Figure 61**) with upper and lower ball-joints instead of spindle pins.

Camber adjustment is provided by the use of adjustment sleeves (**Figure 62**).

Ball Joint Inspection

Refer to **Figure 63** for this procedure
1. Raise the front of the truck with a jack. Place jackstands under the I-beam below the coil spring.
2. Have an assistant grasp the lower edge of the wheel/tire assembly and move it in and out.
3. Observe the amount of movement between the lower spindle arm and lower part of the axle jaw. If the movement exceeds 1/32 in., replace the lower ball-joint.
4 Have an assistant grasp the upper edge of the wheel/tire assembly and move it in and out.
5 Observe the upper part of the axle jaw. If the movement exceeds 1/32 in., replace the upper ball-joint.

Ball-joint Replacement

Ball-joints can be replaced using a C-clamp and ball-joint receiver cup (Ford part No. D81T-3010-A).

12

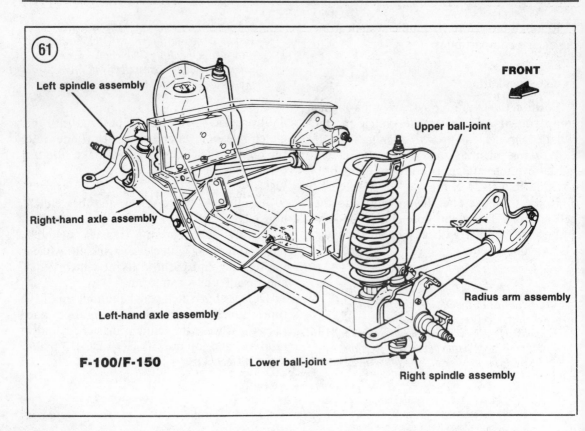

61

Left spindle assembly

FRONT

Upper ball-joint

Right-hand axle assembly

Radius arm assembly

Left-hand axle assembly

F-100/F-150

Lower ball-joint

Right spindle assembly

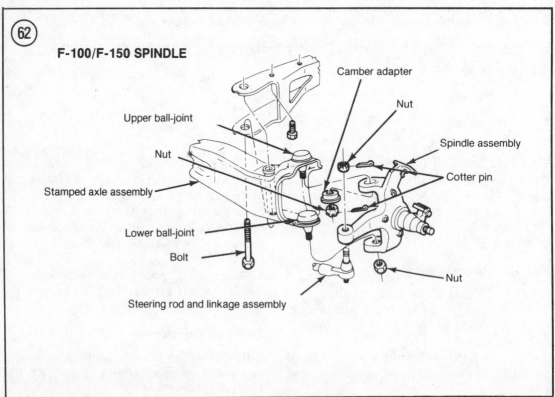

62

F-100/F-150 SPINDLE

Camber adapter

Nut

Upper ball-joint

Spindle assembly

Nut

Cotter pin

Stamped axle assembly

Lower ball-joint

Bolt

Nut

Steering rod and linkage assembly

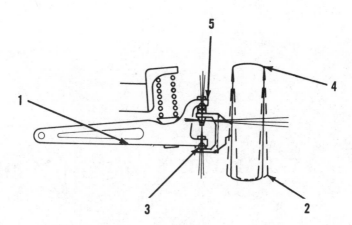

1. Raise the vehicle on a hoist and position safety stands under the I-beam below the coil spring.

2. Grasp the lower edge of the tire and move the wheel in and out.

3. Observe the lower spindle arm and the lower part of the axle jaw. A 0.794 mm (1.32 in.) or greater movement indicates the lower ball-joint must be replaced.

4. To check the upper ball-joint, grasp the upper edge of the tire and move the wheel in and out.

5. A 0.794 mm (1/32 in.) or greater movement between the upper part of the axle jaw indicates the upper ball-joint must be replaced.

12

SKILL LEVEL AND TIME ESTIMATING GUIDE

The time estimates and skill level data that follow were prepared in conjunction with Mitchell International, Inc., the leader in providing this material to professional mechanics, garages and fleet operators.

This section will tell you 2 vital things about 128 different jobs on the Ford F-Series Pickups and Econoline vans 1974-1986:

How long the job takes.

How complicated the job is.

1. How long the job takes: This is the same time figure used by dealers and independent shops to estimate labor charges. Times are shown in tenths of an hour (6-minute intervals). For example, a labor time of 0.3 is 3 tenths of an hour or 18 minutes.

These times are estimates which generally reflect the needs of an average trained auto mechanic using factory recommended tools and following factory recommended procedures. They include allowances for repair preparation, normal cleanup associated with repair, road testing, mechanic personal needs, preventive measures and any other service that would normally accompany an individual operation.

Times do not include allowances for diagnosis, machine operations or obtaining substitutes for factory recommended special tools.

Estimated labor time can be used in 2 ways:

a. If you decide to have a job done professionally, you can compare the time specified in this chart with the shop's labor estimate for the same work.

b. If you decide to do a job yourself, you can use the estimated time, together with the job's skill level, to estimate how long it will take you.

WARNING

Unless you are a professional mechanic with a fully equipped shop, you should expect a job to take you longer than the estimated time. Since the skills and equipment possessed by home mechanics vary widely, it is impossible to estimate how long a job should take a home mechanic. Use the estimated labor times as a rough guide only. Never hurry a job, trying to finish within the estimated time. You may damage the vehicle or injure yourself.

2. How complicated the job is: Each job is placed in one of 4 skill levels:

A. HIGHLY SKILLED—Requires the use of precision measuring tools and highly specialized measuring equipment. Also requires thorough knowledge of complicated systems and strong diagnostic ability. Some jobs in this category can be done by home mechanics. Often, money can be saved by removing and installing a part yourself and having a shop do only the part of a job which requires special training and equipment. The manual will tell which of these jobs can be done by home mechanics.

B. SKILLED—Requires the use of basic tools and simple measuring devices. Accurate diagnosis is required using special test equipment. Must have basic knowledge of complex systems. Many skilled jobs can be done by a beginner using the Clymer manual. Often it is faster and more economical to have the job done by a shop, and the manual will point out such instances.

C. SEMI-SKILLED—Diagnosis is limited to a single possible cause of a problem. Must have basic knowledge of component or system operation. Can be done by a beginner using the Clymer manual.

D. LOW SKILLED—Repair consists of part replacement only. Can be done by a beginner using the Clymer manual.

The letter indicating skill level follows each job description.

Model Identification

Vehicles in this list are identified by model year, model code and date of manufacture. To identify your vehicle's model year and model code, refer to the vehicle identification plate in the engine compartment. Date of manufacture is usually listed on a plate on the driver's doorjamb.

Abbreviations

Several abbreviations are used in this guide. They are:

a. R&R: Remove and replace. Includes removal of part or assembly from vehicle, transfer of attached parts to new part or assembly and installation of new part or assembly on vehicle. Includes any alignment necessary to reposition new part or assembly.

b. R&I: Remove and install. Includes removal of part or assembly from vehicle and installation of same part or assembly on vehicle. Includes any alignment necessary to reposition part or assembly.

c. O/H: Overhaul. Overhaul times include removal of assembly (R&I) from the vehicle, disassembly, cleaning and inspection, replacing necessary parts, reassembly, reinstalling and making any necessary adjustments.

13

SKILL LEVEL AND TIME ESTIMATING GUIDE

1. Accelerator cable R&R (C)
Labor time
F100/350 .... 0.5

2. Air conditioner belt replacement (D)
Labor time 0.5

3. Air filter element R&R (D)
Labor time
Dry type 0.5
Oil type 0.6

4. Air pump belt replacement (C)
Labor time
Inline 0.7
V6 .... 0.9
V8
Exc 351M,400 engines 0.8
351M,400 engines 1.1

5. Alternator belt replacement (D)
Labor time
1974-1977
Exc 460 engine 0.5
460 engine 0.9
1978-1985
Inline
1978-1984 .... 0.8
1985
F100/350 .... 0.6
V6 .... Not available.
V8
Exc 460 engine 0.6
460 engine 1.0

6. Alternator R&R (D)
Labor time
F100/350
1974-1976 .... 0.8
1977-1986
Six 0.6
V8 .... 0.7
Additional time:
Where necessary to transfer pulley, add 0.1

7. Automatic choke overhaul
Not applicable.

8. Automatic transmission overhaul (A)
C4 & C5 Trans
Includes: Inspect and replace necessary parts, clean and check converter, flush converter and cooler lines, adjust and road test.
Labor time
F100/250
1974-1979 C4 Trans 9.1
1980-1983
C4 Trans 8.8
C5 Trans 8.6
1984-1986 C5 Trans 8.6
FMX (1974-1977) 7.2
Includes: Clean and check converter, inspect and replace necessary parts, adjust and road test.
Labor time 10.9

8. Automatic transmission overhaul (A) (cont.)
A.O.D. Trans
Includes: Inspect and replace necessary parts, clean and check converter, flush converter and cooler lines, adjust and road test.
Labor time
1981-1983 .... 10.9
1984-1985
F100/350 .... 10.4
C6 Trans
Includes: Inspect and replace necessary parts, clean and check converter, flush converter and cooler lines, adjust and road test.
Labor time
F100/350
1974-1982 exc 460 eng 8.9
460 engine 10.6
1983-1984 .... 8.3
1985
Exc 460 engine 9.9
460 engine 9.5

9. Automatic transmission throttle linkage adjustment (B)
Labor time
C4 & C5 .... 0.5
FMX 0.8
C6 .... 0.6
A.O.D.
At carb
F100/350 .... 0.5
At carb and trans
F100/350 .... 0.6

10. Automatic transmission neutral safety switch R&R (C)
Labor time 0.5

11. Battery test (C)
Includes: Hydrometer and load test.
Labor time 0.3

12. Battery R&R (C)
Includes: Test.
Labor time 0.5

13. Brake booster R&R (C)
Labor time
F100/350 .... 0.7

14. Breaker point R&R (C)
Includes: Adjust ignition timing. Does not include distributor R&I.
Labor time
1974-1979
Six
F100/350 .... 0.6
V8 .... 0.7

15. Camshaft R&R (B)
Includes: R&I oil pan and barrel type lifters and remove carbon with cylinder head removed. Does not require oil pan removal on 232, 255, 302, 351W, 360 and 390 engines.
Labor time
Six inline
F100/350
1974-1984 .... 6.9
1985 .... 7.3
V6 .... 8.3
V8
302
w/ fuel injection 8.1
w/o fuel injection 8.3
351M 8.1
351W 8.0
460
1974-1983 .... 7.9
1984-1986 .... 12.1
F100/F350
255, 351W 6.3
302
w/ fuel injection 8.1
w/o fuel injection 6.3
351M 7.5
360, 390 .... 6.1
460
1974-1983 .... 7.0
1984-1986 .... 8.9
Additional time:
Where air conditioning interferes, add:
1974-1980
F100/350
360, 390, 460 .... 2.0
Where pwr steering interferes, add:
1974-1982
F100/350
360, 390, 460 .... 0.3
1983-1984 .... 0.3

16. Carburetor overhaul (B)
Includes: Install carburetor kit, adjust idle speed and fuel mixture.

SKILL LEVEL AND TIME ESTIMATING GUIDE (continued)

16. Carburetor overhaul
  (B) (cont.)
  Labor time
  Six
    F100/350
      1 Bbl 2.1
      2 Bbl 2.3
    V8
    1974-1983
      2 Bbl
        Exc 2150-2V AFB,7200vv
          carbs 2.4
        2150-2V AFB,7200vv
          carbs 3.4
      4 Bbl
        FoMoCo 2.6
        Holley 3.4
    1984-1986
      2 Bbl
        2150-2V carb 2.6
        2150-2V AFB carb 3.6
      4 Bbl (Holley) 3.6

17. Carburetor R&R (B)
  Includes: adjust idle speed and
  fuel mixture.
  Labor time
  Six
    F100/350 .... 1.1
  V8
    1974-1983 .... 1.3
    1984-1985 .... 1.6

18. Charging system test (B)
  Includes: Check battery, regulator
  and alternator output.
  Labor time 0.6

19. Clutch plate or
  disc R&R (C)
  Labor time
  3 speed
    F100/350
    1974-1976
      w/ access cover 2.2
      w/o access cover 2.5
    1977-1986
      300, 302, 460
        w/ access cover 2.0
        w/o access cover 2.5
      351, 400 .... 2.8
  4 speed
    F100/350
    1974-1976
      w/ access cover 3.2
      w/o access cover 3.5
    1977-1979
      300,302,460 engines
      Ford Trans
        w/ access cover 2.0
        w/o access cover 2.3
      New Process, Warner Trans
        w/ access cover 3.2
        w/o access cover 3.5
      351,400 engines
      Ford Trans 2.9
      New Process, Warner
        Trans 4.1

ABBREVIATIONS
For full explanation of
abbreviations, see the
first page of this section.
Skill levels:
  A. Highly skilled
  B. Skilled
  C. Semi-skilled
  D. Low skilled
R&R: Remove and replace
R&I: Remove and install
O/H: Overhaul

---

19. Clutch plate or
  disc R&R (C) (cont.)
  Labor time (cont.)
  4 speed (cont.)
    F100/350 (cont.)
    1977-1979 (cont.)
    1980-1986
    Ford Trans
      Code RTS 3.1
      Code RUG 2.2
      New Process trans 3.4
  Additional time:
    With multi-piece driveline,
    add 0.2
    Where necessary to R&I carpet,
    add 0.7

20. Clutch pedal adjustment (C)
  Labor time 0.5

21. Clutch bleeding (C)
  Labor time 0.6

22. Clutch release
  bearing R&R (C)
  Labor time
  3 speed
    F100/350
    1974-1976 .... 1.9
    1977-1985 .... 1.6
  4 speed
    F100/350
    Ford 2.9
    New Process, Warner
      Code RTS 2.6
      Code RUG 1.7
  Additional time:
    With multi-piece driveline, add
    0.2
    Where necessary to R&I carpet
    add 0.7

23. Clutch master
  cylinder R&R (C)
  Labor time 0.8
  1974-1984 .... 0.8
  1985-1986 .... 0.9

24. Clutch slave cylinder R&R (C)
  Labor time 0.8

---

25. Compression test (C)
  Labor time
  F100/350
    Six inline 0.8
    V6 .... 1.0
    V8 .... 1.0

26. Connecting rod R&I (A)
  Includes: Remove carbon and
  cylinder ridge, burnish
  cylinders, replace rod bearings,
  adjust idle speed. and timing.
  Labor time
  Six
    F100/350
    Inline
      One 7.0
      All 10.3
    V6
    One
      Right side 8.4
      Left 8.2
      All 13.3
  V8
  F100/350
    255, 351W engines
      One 7.8
      One each side 9.5
      All 14.1
    302
      w/ fuel injection
        One 9.6
        One each side 10.6
        All 17.2
      w/o fuel injection
        One 7.9
        One each side 9.7
        All 13.9
    351M,400, engines
      One 7.3
      One each side 9.1
      All 13.8
    360,390 engines
      One 7.4
      One each side 8.7
      All 13.1
    460 engine
    1974-1979
      One 8.7
      One each side 10.6
      All 16.7
    1983-1984
      One 7.7
      One each side 9.7
      All 13.5
  Additional time:
    Where air conditioning
    interferes, add:
    1974-1980
      F100/300 w/ 360, 390 ..... 2.1
    Where pwr steering interferes,
    add:
    1974-1980
      F100-350
      w/ 360, 390, 460 .... 0.3

13

SKILL LEVEL AND TIME ESTIMATING GUIDE (continued)

26. Connecting rod R&I (A) (cont.)
Additional time (cont.)
Where pwr steering interferes,
  add: (cont.)
  1981-1984
    F100/350
      255, 302 .... 0.3
      351M, 400 .... 0.2
      351W 0.3

27. Connecting rod bearing R&R (B)
Labor time
  Six
    F100/350
      Inline
        One 3.3
        All 4.8
      V6
        One 2.6
        All 3.6

28. Cooling system flushing (D)
Labor time 0.7

29. Crankshaft R&R (A)
Includes: R&I engine, replace
bearings and oil seals, adjust
idle speed and ignition timing.
Labor time
  Six
    F100/350
      Inline
        Standard trans 8.6
        Auto trans
          1974-1980 .... 8.8
          1981-1983 .... 8.3
          1984 .... 9.9
          1985-1986 .... 10.3
      V6 .... 9.3
  V8
    F100/350
      255,302,351W engines
      1974-1983
        Standard trans 8.1
        Auto trans 9.2
      1984
        Standard trans 8.4
        Auto trans 9.3
      1985-1986
        Standard trans 8.8
        Auto trans 10.0
      351M,360,390,400 engines
        Standard trans 8.2
        Auto trans 8.7
      460 engine
      1974-1979 .... 9.8
      1983-1986
        Standard trans 9.9
        Auto trans 10.2
Additional time:
Where air cond interferes, add:
  F100/350
    Six 0.5
    V8
      255,302,351,400 .... 0.5
      360, 390, 460, ... 2.0

ABBREVIATIONS
For full explanation of
abbreviations, see the first page of
this section.
Skill levels:
  A. Highly skilled
  B. Skilled
  C. Semi-skilled
  D. Low skilled
R&R: Remove and replace
R&I: Remove and install
O/H: Overhaul

---

29. Crankshaft R&R (A) (cont.)
Additional time (cont.)
Where air cond interferes,
  add: (cont.)
  1981-1986
    Six 0.4
    V8
      F100/350 .... 0.2
Where pwr steering interferes,
  add:
  1974-1980
    F100/350
      Six inline, V8 .... 0.3
  1981-1986
    F100/350
      Six inline 0.3
      V8 .... 0.2

30. Crankshaft pulley R&R (C)
Labor time
  Six inline
    F100/350 .... 0.9
  V6 1982-1983 .... 1.0
  V8
    F100/350
      255,302 engines 0.9
      351M,400 engines 1.0
      351W engine 0.9
      360,390 engines
        .... Not available.
      460 engine 0.9

31. Crankshaft rear seal R&R (B)
Upper rope type seal includes
  pack and add only.
Split lip type seals include
  replacing top and bottom
  halves. If it is necessary
  to replace upper rope seal,
  use job No. 29.
Labor time
  Six
    F100/350
      1974-1983
      Inline
      Standard trans
        3 speed 2.9
        4 speed 3.5
        Auto trans 3.4
      V6 .... 3.8

---

31. Crankshaft rear seal R&R (B) (cont.)
Labor time (cont.)
  Six (cont.)
    1984-1986
      Standard trans
        3 speed 2.7
        4 speed 3.7
      Auto trans
        A.O.D. 4.2
        C5,C6 .... 3.4
  V8
    F100/350
      255,302,351W engines
      1974-1979 .... 2.8
      1980-1985
        Exc one piece de-
        sign, circular
        Standard trans 3.9
        Auto trans 3.5
        One piece design (circular)
        Standard trans 3.5
        Auto trans 3.6
      351M,400 engines
      1977-1979
        Standard trans 3.9
        Auto trans 3.5
      360,390 engines 3.0
      460 engines
      1974-1979 .... 4.5
      1980-1985 .... 3.9
Additional time:
Where necessary to R&I carpet,
  add 0.7

32. Cylinder head gasket R&I (C)
Includes: Remove carbon, adjust
valves, clean spark plugs and
adjust ignition timing where
necessary.
Labor time
  Six
    F100/350
      Inline
        1974-1984 .... 4.3
        1985 .... 5.0
      V6
        Right side 6.8
        Left 6.4
        Both 8.9
  V8
    255,302,351W engines
    F100/350
      Right side 4.9
      Left 4.7
      Both 6.9
    351M,400 engines
      One side 5.1
      Both 7.2
    360,390 engines
      One side 5.6
      Both 7.1
    460 engine
    F100/350
      One side 6.4
      Both 8.8

SKILL LEVEL AND TIME ESTIMATING GUIDE (continued)

33. Differential overhaul (A)
Labor time
1974-1977
F100/150 .... 6.5
1978-1986
100-150
Non-locking axle 6.3
Locking axle 7.3
34. Differential R&R (B)
Labor time
1974-1985 .... 2.3
35. Distributor cap R&R (C)
Labor time
F100/350 .... 0.5
36. Distributor R&R (C)
Includes: Adjust ignition timing.
Labor time 0.7
37. Drag link R&R (4WD)
Not applicable.
38. Drive plate R&I
See Flywheel, Auto trans.
39. Drive shaft R&I (C)
Labor time
To front axle 0.7
To rear axle
One piece driveline 0.5
Two piece driveline
Front shaft or both 0.8
Rear 0.5
40. Drive shaft center bearing R&R (C)
Labor time 1.0
41. EGR valve R&R
Includes: R&I carburetor and separator plate.
Labor time
1974-1983
Six exc. 300 .... 0.5
300 .... 0.6
V8 .... 0.5
1984
Six 0.4
1985-1986 .... 0.8
42. Engine mount R&R (D)
Labor time
Six
F100/350
Inline
One side 0.6
Both 0.7
V6
Right side 0.9
Left 0.7
Both 1.1
V8
F100/350
255,302,351W engines
One side 0.6
Both 0.8
351M,400 engines
One side 0.9
Both 1.2
360,390 engines
One side 0.7
Both 0.9

ABBREVIATIONS
For full explanation of abbreviations, see the first page of this section.
Skill levels:
A. Highly skilled
B. Skilled
C. Semi-skilled
D. Low skilled
R&R: Remove and replace
R&I: Remove and install
O/H: Overhaul

42. Engine mount R&R (D) (cont.)
Labor time (cont.)
V8 (cont.)
F100/350 (cont.)
460 engine
One side 0.8
Both 1.0
43. Engine oil and filter change (gas) (D)
Labor time 0.3
44. Engine oil and filter change (diesel) (D)
Labor time 0.3
45. Engine R&I and overhaul (A)
Includes: Replace rings, main and rod bearings, crankshaft and camshaft. Remove cylinder ridge, burnish cylinders, grind valves, clean and test hydraulic lifters, adjust idle speed and timing.
Does not include rebore or pin fit and align.
Labor time
Six
F100/350
Inline
Standard trans 22.6
Auto trans
1974-1980 .... 23.0
1981-1983 .... 22.5
1984 .... 24.3
1985-1986 .... 25.3
V6 .... 24.5
V8
F100/350
255,302,351W engines
1974-1983
Standard trans 26.9
Auto trans 27.4
1984
Standard trans 27.3
Auto trans 28.2
1985
Standard trans 28.7
Auto trans 29.9

45. Engine R&I and overhaul (A) (cont.)
Labor time (cont.)
V8 (cont.)
F100/350 (cont.)
351M, 360, 390, 400 engines
Standard trans 27.0
Auto trans 27.5
460 engine
1974-1979 .... 29.4
1983-1986
Additional time:
Where air conditioning interferes, add:
F100/350 V8
255, 302, 351W 0.3
351M, 400 .... 0.5
360, 390 .... 0.6
460
1974-1979 .... 0.5
1983-1986 .... 0.3
Where pwr strg interferes, add:
F100/350
255, 351M, 400 .... 0.2
302, 351W 0.3
360, 390 .... 0.4
460
1974-1979 .... 0.2
1983-1984 .... 0.3
46. Engine R&I (C)
Includes: R&I only those components necessary for the removal of the complete engine assembly.
Does not include transfer parts or tune engine.
Labor time
Six
F100/350
Inline
Standard trans 3.2
Auto trans
1974-1980 .... 3.8
1981-1983 .... 3.1
1984 .... 4.9
1985-1986 .... 5.2
V6 .... 5.5
V8
F100/350
Diesel
1983-1984
Standard trans 6.8
Auto trans 7.4
1985-1986
Standard trans 7.7
Auto trans 8.3
Gas
255,302,351W engines
1974-1983
Standard trans 4.0
Auto trans 4.4

13

SKILL LEVEL AND TIME ESTIMATING GUIDE (continued)

46. Engine R&I (C) (cont.)
Labor time (cont.)
 V8 (cont.)
  F100/350 (cont.)
   Gas (cont.)
    255,302,351W engines (cont.)
    1984
     Standard trans 4.3
     Auto trans 5.2
    1985-1986
     Standard trans 4.6
     Auto trans 5.8
    351M,360,390,400 engines
     Standard trans 3.5
     Auto trans 4.2
    460 engine
     1974-1979 .... 5.0
     1983-1986 .... 5.9

47. Engine short block R&R (A)
Consists of cylinder block fitted
with pistons, rings, connecting
rods, camshaft, crankshaft and
bearings, timing chain and
sprockets or gears.
Includes: Grind valves, clean and
transfer cylinder heads, fuel and
electrical assemblies, engine
mounts, manifolds, valve
covers, oil pan and pump,
timing cover, water pump,
clutch assembly and flywheel.
Adjust idle speed, timing and
valves where applicable.
Labor time
 Six
  F100/350
   Inline
    Standard trans 13.6
   Auto trans
    1974-1980 .... 14.1
    1981-1983 .... 13.5
    1984 .... 15.3
    1985-1986 .... 15.6
  V6 .... 16.9
 V8
  F100/350
   Diesel
   1983-1984
    Standard trans 23.6
    Auto trans 24.3
   1985-1986
    Standard trans 24.0
    Auto trans 24.7
  Gas
   255,302,351W engines
   1974-1983
    Standard trans 19.4
    Auto trans 19.9
   1984
    Standard trans 19.8
    Auto trans 20.8
   1985-1986
    Standard trans 19.8
    Auto trans 21.0

ABBREVIATIONS
For full explanation of
abbreviations, see the first page of
this section.
Skill levels:
 A. Highly skilled
 B. Skilled
 C. Semi-skilled
 D. Low skilled
R&R: Remove and replace
R&I: Remove and install
O/H: Overhaul

---

47. Engine short block
R&R (A) (cont.)
Labor time (cont.)
 V8 (cont.)
  F100/350 (cont.)
   Gas (cont.)
   351M,360,390,400 engines
    Standard trans 16.7
    Auto trans 17.6
   460 engine
    1974-1979 .... 19.1
    1983-1986 .... 19.8

48. Evaporative emission
canister R&R (C)
Labor time 0.5

49. Flywheel R&R (C)
Labor time
 Add 0.3 to job No. 19.

50. Float R&R (B)
Includes: Adjust float level, idle
speed and fuel mixture.
Labor time
 1974-1979
  Six 0.8
  V8
   F100/350
    2 Bbl 0.7
    4 Bbl
     Exc 460 engine 1.8
     460 engine 0.9
 1980-1985
  F100/350
   Six
    w/ limiter caps 1.3
    w/o limiter caps 1.1
   V8
    w/ limiter caps 1.6
    w/o limiter caps 1.1

51. Fuel filter R&R (C)
Labor time 0.6

52. Fuel pump R&R (B)
Labor time
 Mechanical (engine type)
  Six inline 0.6
  V6 .... 0.6

---

52. Fuel pump R&R (B) (cont.)
Labor time (cont.)
 Mechanical (engine type) (cont.)
  V8
   F100/350
    1974-1983 .... 0.6
    1984-1986
     Exc 460 engine 0.6
     460 engine 0.7
 Electric (low pressure tank type)
  1974-1983
   Drum tank 0.8
   Frame tank 0.7
   Saddle tank (one) 0.8
   Step tank (one) 1.6
  1984-1986 (each) 0.8

53. Front shock absorber R&R (C)
Labor time
 F100/350
  One side 0.5
  Both 0.7

54. Front spring R&R (B)
Does not include alignment.
Labor time
 F100/350
  One side 0.7
  Both 1.1

55. Front hub R&R
Included in job No. 56.

56. Front wheel bearing R&R (C)
Includes: Replace inner and/or
outer bearings and cups
repack.
Labor time
 100/150 Ser
  One side 1.0
  Both 1.6
 250/350 Ser
  One side 1.0
  Both 1.8

57. Front axle R&R (4WD)
Not applicable.

58. Free wheel hub R&R (4WD)
Not applicable.

59. Free wheel hub overhaul
(4WD)
Not applicable.

60. Front brake pad or
shoe R&R (C)
Includes: Bleed system and adjust
brakes and parking brake where
necessary.
Labor time *
 100/150 Ser
  1974-1977
   Drum brakes 1.5
   Disc brakes 1.0
  1978-1986 .... 1.0

SKILL LEVEL AND TIME ESTIMATING GUIDE (continued)

60. Front brake pad or shoe R&R (C) (cont.)
Labor time (cont.)
  200/350 Ser
  F250/350
   1974-1984
    Semi-floating axle 1.1
    Full floating axle
     Drum brakes 1.5
     Disc brakes 1.0
   1985-1986 .... 1.1

61. Front brake caliper R&R (C)
Includes: Bleed system and replace pads if necessary.
Labor time
 1974-1977
  100/150 Ser
   One side 1.1
   Both 1.7
  250/350 Ser
   One side 1.5
   Both 2.5
 1978-1985
  5 stud wheel
   One side 0.8
   Both 1.2
  8 stud wheel
   One side 0.9
   Both 1.3

62. Front caliper R&I and overhaul (C)
Includes: Bleed system and replace pads if necessary.
Labor time
 1974-1977
  100/150 Ser
   One side 1.5
   Both 2.5
  250/350 Ser
   One side 1.9
   Both 3.3
 1978-1985
  5 stud wheel
   One side 1.2
   Both 2.0
  8 stud wheel
   Single piston type
    One side 1.3
    Both 2.1
   Dual piston type
    One side 1.4
    Both 2.3

63. Fuel pump pressure test (B)
Includes: Check capacity.
Labor time
 1974-1979
  Six 0.7
  V8
   F100/350 .... 0.8
 1980-1983 .... 0.5
 1984-1985
  Mechanical pump 0.5
  Electrical pump 0.7

ABBREVIATIONS
For full explanation of abbreviations, see the first page of this section.
Skill levels:
  A. Highly skilled
  B. Skilled
  C. Semi-skilled
  D. Low skilled
R&R: Remove and replace
R&I: Remove and install
O/H: Overhaul

---

64. Headlight R&R (D)
Does not include adjust headlamps.
Labor time
  One side 0.3
  Both 0.4

65. Headlight switch R&R (B)
Labor time
  F100/350 .... 0.6

66. Heater hose replacement (D)
Labor time
  F100/350 .... 0.8

67. Heater core R&R (A)
Does not include evacuate or charge system.
Labor time
 F100/350
  1974-1977
   w/ a/c 1.9
   w/o a/c 1.6
  1978-1979
   w/ a/c 2.0
   w/o a/c 1.5
  1980-1986
   w/ a/c 1.1
   w/o a/c 1.5

68. Horn R&R (D)
  Labor time 0.5

69. Idle mixture adjustment
Not available.

70. Idle speed adjustment
Included in job No. 121.

71. Igniter R&R
Not applicable.

72. Ignition coil R&R (C)
Includes: Test.
Labor time
 1974-1983
  F100/350 .... 0.6
 1984-1985
  Not available.

73. Ignition switch R&R (B)
Labor time
 F100/350
  (74-77) 0.5
  (78-86) 0.7

---

74. Ignition timing adjust (C)
Includes: Adjust dwell angle.
Labor time
  F100/350 .... 0.5

75. Load sensing valve R&R
Not applicable.

76. Lower ball-joint R&R
Labor time ....
  add 0.2 per side to job No. 110.

77. Lower suspension arm (I-beam axle) R&R
Does not include alignment.
Labor time
 1974-1975
  One side 1.7
  Both 3.0
 1976-1979
  One side 1.6
  Both 2.7
 1980-1981
  One side 1.8
  Both 3.0
 1982-1986
  Forged axle
   One side 1.8
   Both 3.0
  Stamped axle
   One side 2.5
   Both 4.4

78. Lower suspension arm shaft R&R
Labor time
 Included in job No. 77.

79. Manifold R&I (C)
Labor time
 Intake (carburetted)
 Six
  F100/350
   Inline
    1974-1982 .... 1.5
    1983-1986 .... 4.2
   V6 .... 3.1
 V8
  F100/350
   1974-1979
    302 engine 2.3
    351M,400 engines 2.2
    360,390 engines 3.4
    460 engine 2.7
   1980-1986
    255,302 engines 2.0
    351M,400 engines 2.6
    460 engine 2.7
 Six
  Upper 1.5
  Lower 2.8
 V8
  F100/250
   Upper 1.5
   Lower 4.0

13

SKILL LEVEL AND TIME ESTIMATING GUIDE (continued)

79. Manifold R&I (C) (cont.)
Exhaust
Labor time
Six
  F100/350
    Inline
      1974-1977
        Exc FMX Trans 3.1
        FMX Trans 3.4
      1978-1982 .... 3.1
      1983-1986 .... 4.2
    V6
      Right side 1.9
      Left 1.6
      Both 3.2
V8
  302,351W engines
  F100/350
    1974-1979
      One side 0.7
      Both 1.1
    1980-1986
      One side 0.9
      Both 1.5
  351M,400 engines
    One side 1.0
    Both 1.6
  360,390,460 engines
    1974-1979
    F100/350
      One side 0.9
      Both 1.3
    1980-1986
      One side 1.1
      Both 1.8
Additional time:
  Where air conditioning
  interferes:
    1984-1986 V6 add 0.3

80. Master cylinder R&R (C)
Includes: Bleed system.
Labor time
  1974-1977 .... 0.7
  1978-1986
    Man brakes 0.8
    Pwr brakes 0.7

81. Master cylinder R&I and overhaul (B)
Includes: Bleed system.
Labor time
  1974-1977 .... 1.1
  1978-1986
    Man brakes 1.2
    Pwr Brakes 1.1

82. Oil pan R&R (C)
Labor time
Six
  F100/350
    Inline
      1974-1983 .... 2.8
      1984-1986 .... 3.1
    V6 .... 2.4

ABBREVIATIONS
For full explanation of abbreviations, see the first page of this section.
Skill levels:
  A. Highly skilled
  B. Skilled
  C. Semi-skilled
  D. Low skilled
R&R: Remove and replace
R&I: Remove and install
O/H: Overhaul

---

82. Oil pan R&R (C) (cont.)
Labor time (cont.)
V8
  F100/350
    255, 351W
      1974-1979 .... 1.9
      1980-1983
        Standard trans 3.0
        Auto trans 2.6
      1984-1986
        Standard trans 2.8
        Auto trans 3.2
    302
      1974-1979 .... 1.9
      1980-1984
        Standard trans 3.0
        Auto trans 2.6
      1985-1986 .... 4.2
    351M, 400
      1977-1979
        Standard trans 2.7
        Auto trans 2.3
      1980-1982 .... 3.1
    360, 390 .... 1.8
    460
      1974-1979 .... 3.1
      1983-1986
        Standard trans 2.8
        Auto trans 3.1
  351M,400 engines
    1977-1979
      Standard trans 2.7
      Auto trans 2.3
    1980-1982 .... 3.1
  360,390 engines 1.8
  460 engine
    1974-1979 .... 3.1
    1980-1986
      Standard trans 2.8
      Auto trans 3.1

Additional time:
  Where air conditioning
  interferes, add:
    Six 0.4
    V8 Except 460 .... 0.3
    V8 460 .... 0.7
  Where power steering interferes,
  add 0.3

---

83. Oil pump R&R (C)
Labor time
  V6 .... 0.9
  All others
    Add 0.2 to job No. 82.

84. Power steering belt replacement (D)
Labor time
  F100/350
    Six
      1974-1979 .... 0.3
      1980-1984 .... 0.7
      1985-1986 .... 0.5
    V8
      Diesel 0.6
      Gas
        Exc 460 engine 0.6
        460 engine 1.0

85. Piston R&R (A)
Includes: Remove carbon and cylinder ridge, burnish cylinders, replace rod bearings, adjust idle speed and timing.
Labor time
  Add 0.3 to job No. 26.

86. PCV valve R&R (C)
Labor time 0.3

87. Pitman arm R&R (B)
Does not include alignment.
Labor time 0.7

88. Power steering pump R&R (B)
Labor time
  F100/350
    1974-1977 .... 0.9
    1978-1986
      Six
        Inline 0.8
        V6 .... 0.9
      V8
        Exc 460 engine
          1978-1984 .... 0.8
          1985-1986 .... 0.9
        460 engine 0.7

89. Power steering pump R&I and overhaul (A)
Labor time
  F100/350
    1974-1977 .... 1.7
    1978-1985
      Six
        Inline 1.5
        V6 .... 1.6
      V8
        Exc 460 engine
          1978-1984 .... 1.5
          1985-1986 .... 1.6
        460 engine 1.4

90. Radiator R&R (D)
Includes: Replace hoses.
Labor time
  F100/350
    Six 1.1

SKILL LEVEL AND TIME ESTIMATING GUIDE (continued)

90. Radiator R&R (D) (cont.)
Labor time (cont.)
F100/350 (cont.)
V8
1974-1979 .... 1.2
1980-1986 .... 1.0

91. Radiator hose R&R (D)
Labor time
Upper or lower 0.7
Both 1.0

92. Rear axle housing R&R (A)
Does not include overhaul.
Labor time
1974-1977
F100/150
Removable carrier 4.6
Integral carrier 7.1
F250/350 .... 9.3
1978-1986
F100/150
Removable carrier 4.7
Integral carrier 7.1
F250/350
Spicer 60,61 .... 8.3
Spicer 70
1978-1979 .... 9.3
1980-1986 .... 7.7

93. Rear axle shaft R&R (C)
Includes: R&R bearing, oil seal
and flange studs on
semi-floating axles.
Labor time
Semi-floating axle
100/150 Ser
Ball Brgs
One side 0.9
Both 1.2
Tapered roller Brgs
One side 1.0
Both 1.8
250 Ser
One side 1.4
Both 2.2
Full floating axle
250/350 Ser
One side 0.5
Both 0.8

94. Rear wheel bearing R&R (C)
On full floating axle, labor time
includes: Replace inner and
outer wheel bearings and
repack.
Labor time
Semi-floating axle
100/150 Ser
Ball bearings
One side 0.8
Both 1.1
Tapered roller bearings
One side 0.9
Both 1.6
250 Ser
One side 1.3
Both 2.0

ABBREVIATIONS
For full explanation of
abbreviations, see the first page of
this section.
Skill levels:
A. Highly skilled
B. Skilled
C. Semi-skilled
D. Low skilled
R&R: Remove and replace
R&I: Remove and install   N
O/H: Overhaul

**94. Rear wheel bearing
R&R (C)** (cont.)
Labor time (cont.)
Full floating axle
250/350 Ser
One side 1.1
Both 2.0

95. Rear brake drum R&R (C)
Does not include adjust brakes.
Labor time
Semi-floating axle
One side 0.6
Both 1.0
Full floating axle
1974
One side 1.3
Both 2.4
1975-1986
One side 1.0
Both 1.8

96. Rear brake shoe R&R (C)
Includes: Bleed system and adjust
brakes and parking brake where
necessary.
Labor time
F100/150
1974-1984 .... 1.8
1985-1986 .... 1.6
F250/350
1974-1984
Semi-floating axle 1.9
Full floating axle 2.4
1985-1986
Semi-floating axle 1.7
Full-floating axle 2.2

**97. Rear wheel cylinder
R&R (B)**
Includes: Bleed system and
replace shoes if necessary.
Labor time
1974-1984
100/200 Ser
One side 1.6
Both 2.8
250/350 Ser
One side 1.7
Both 3.0

**97. Rear wheel cylinder
R&R (B)** (cont.)
Labor time (cont.)
1985-1986
150 Ser
One side 1.5
Both 2.6
250/350 Ser
One side 1.5
Both 2.6
Additional time:
w/ full floating axles 250/350 Ser
add 0.3 to each side.

**98. Rear wheel cylinder
overhaul (B)**
Includes: Bleed system and
replace shoes if necessary.
Labor time
1974-1984
100/200 Ser
One side 1.7
Both 3.0
250/350 Ser
One side 1.8
Both 3.2
1985-1986
100/200 Ser
One side 1.6
Both 3.2
250/350 Ser
One side 1.7
Both 2.9
Additional time:
With full floating axles
(250/350 Ser), add 0.3 to
each side.

99. Regulator R&R (B)
Includes: Test regulator.
Labor time
1974-1982 .... 0.5
1983-1986 .... 0.3

100. Rings, piston R&R
Labor time add 0.3 to job No. 26

101. Rocker assembly R&I
Not available.

**102. Shock absorber R&R,
rear (D)**
Labor time
F100/350
One side 0.5
Both 0.8

103. Spark plugs R&R (C)
Labor time
F100/350
Six inline 0.6
V6,V8 .... 0.8

104. Spring R&R, rear (C)
Labor time
F100/150
1974-1977
One side 1.6
Both 3.0

13

SKILL LEVEL AND TIME ESTIMATING GUIDE (continued)

104. Spring R&R, rear (C) (cont.)
Labor time (cont.)
F100/150 (cont.)
1978-1986
One side 1.3
Both 2.4
F250/350
1974-1977
One side 1.9
Both 3.6
1978-1986
5 lug wheel
One side 1.3
Both 2.4
8 lug wheel
One side 1.5
Both 2.8

105. Stabilizer bar R&R
Labor time .... Not available.
106. Starter R&R (D)
Labor time 0.5
107. Starter test (B)
Labor time 0.5
108. Steering damper R&R
Not applicable.

109. Steering gear R&R (C)
Labor time
1974-1983
F100/350
1974-1979
Man Strg 1.0
Power steering 1.8
1980-1983 .... 1.0
1984-1986
Man Strg 1.0
Power steering
1984 .... 1.1
1985-1986 .... 1.2

110. Steering knuckle R&R (B)
Does not include alignment.
Labor time
1974-1975
F100/350
One side 1.9
Both 3.1
1976-1979
One side 2.0
Both 3.1
1980-1984
Ball joint design (F100/150)
One side 1.8
Both 2.7
King pin design
F100/150 (80-82)
One side 1.6
Both 2.4
F250/350
One side 1.9
Both 2.6
1985
Ball joint design (F100/150)
One side 2.2
Both 3.1

110. Steering knuckle R&R
(B) (cont.)
Labor time (cont.)
1985 (cont.)
King pin design (F250/350)
One side 2.0
Both 2.7
111. Tension strut R&R
Not applicable.
112. Thermostat R&R (D)
Labor time
Six
F100/350
Inline 0.6
V6 .... 0.8
V8
F100/350
1974-1982
302,360,390,
460 engines 0.8
351,400 engines
1977-1979 .... 0.6
1980-1982 .... 0.7
1983-1986 .... 0.8
113. Tie rod end R&R (B)
Includes: Adjust toe-in only.
Labor time
1974-1979
Inner (rod) 1.1
Outer (end) 1.0
Both 1.3
1980-1985
F100/350
Inner (rod) 1.1
Outer (end)
One side 1.0
Both 1.4
Inner & outer
left side 1.3
Inner & both outers 1.6
114. Timing chain R&I (B)
Includes: R&I camshaft sprocket and adjust ignition timing.
Does not include oil pan removal on 232, 255, 302, 360 and 390 engines.
Labor time
F100/350
V6 .... 5.1

114. Timing chain R&I (B) (cont.)
Labor time (cont.)
F100/350 (cont.)
V8
255,302,351W engines
1974-1983 .... 3.1
1984 .... 3.1
1985 .... 3.6
351M,400 engines 4.9
360,390 engines 2.9
460 engine
1974-1979 .... 3.6
1983 .... 3.1
1984-1986 .... 4.2

115. Toe-in adjustment
Includes: Adjust to steering gear high point and center steering wheel.
Labor time 0.7
116. Torsion bar R&R
Not applicable.
117. Transfer case overhaul (B)
Not applicable.
118. Transfer case R&I (C)
Not applicable.
119. Transmission mount R&R (D)
Labor time
Six
F100/350
Inline 0.8
V6 .... 0.6
V8
F100/350 .... 0.8
120. Transmission R&I and overhaul (B)
Labor time
(Manual transmission)
3 speed 4.5
4 speed
F100/350
Ford
Code RTS 4.8
Code RUG 4.2
New Process 5.4
Warner 5.1
121. Tune-up (B)
Labor time
Breaker-point ignition
Includes: Check compression, clean and adjust or replace air filter spark plugs, points and condenser. Inspect distributor cap, rotor and ignition wires. Adjust ignition timing and carburetor idle speed.
1974-1979
F100/350
Six 1.8
V8 .... 2.2
Electronic ignition
Includes: Check compression. Clean or replace spark plugs and air filter. Inspect distributor cap, rotor and

SKILL LEVEL AND TIME ESTIMATING GUIDE (continued)

121. Tune-up (B) (cont.)
Labor time (cont.)
 Electronic ignition (cont.)
  ignition cables. Adjust ignition
  timing and idle speed.
 Six inline
  F100/350 .... 1.3
  F100/350 .... 1.6

122. Universal joint R&R (C)
Labor time
 One piece driveline
  Front joint 0.9
  Rear joint 0.8
  Both 1.3
 Two piece driveline
  Front joint 1.3
  Intermediate joint 1.3
  Rear joint 1.1
  All 2.2

123. Upper ball-joint R&R
Add 0.2 per side to job No. 110.

124. Upper suspension arm R&R
Not applicable.

**125. Upper suspension arm
shaft R&R**
Not applicable.

126. Valve grind complete (A)
Includes: Remove carbon, clean
 valve guides, compression check
 and tune engine minor.
Labor time
 Six
  F100/350
  Inline
   1974-1984 .... 7.6
   1985-1986 .... 8.3
  V6
   Right side 8.6
   Left 8.3
   Both 12.7

ABBREVIATIONS
For full explanation of
abbreviations, see the first page of
this section.
Skill levels:
 A. Highly skilled
 B. Skilled
 C. Semi-skilled
 D. Low skilled
R&R: Remove and replace
R&I: Remove and install
O/H: Overhaul

**126. Valve grind complete
 (A) (cont.)**
Labor time (cont.)
 V8
  255,302,351W engines
  F100/350
   Right side 7.5
   Left 7.3
   Both 11.3

  351M,400 engines
   One side 7.7
   Both 11.7

  360,390 engines
   One side 8.2
   Both 11.6

  460 engine
  F100/350
   One side 7.8
   Both 13.5

Additional time:
 Refer to additional times
 following job No. 32.

---

127. Water pump R&R (C)
Labor time
 F100/350
 Six
  Inline
   1974-1979 .... 1.3
   1980-1986
    w/ a/c 1.3
    w/o a/c 1.1
  V6 .... 1.6
 V8
  255,302,351W engines
   w/ a/c 1.7
   w/o a/c 1.5
  351M,400 engines
  1977-1979
   w/ a/c 1.8
   w/o a/c 1.6
  1980-1982
   w/ a/c 2.2
   w/o a/c 1.9
  360,390 engines
  w/ Air Cond
   Man Strg 1.8
   power steering 2.2
  w/o Air Cond
   Man Strg 1.3
   power steering 1.8
  460 engine
   1974-1979 .... 2.0
  1984-1986
   w/ a/c 2.7
   w/o a/c 2.6

128. Wiper motor R&R (C)
Labor time
 F100/350
 1974-1979
  w/ air cond 1.3
  w/o air cond 0.9
 1980-1986 .... 1.1

13

INDEX

14

14

14